43

Social History of Canada

H.V. Nelles, general editor

Vulcan: The Making of a Prairie Community

In 1904 thousands of pioneers, mostly from Ontario and the American mid-west, swarmed into the Vulcan area of southern Alberta seeking their fortunes through speculation in frontier land and the production of wheat. Agrarian capitalists, they intended to establish 'progressive' settlements that would incorporate the best features of both the metropolis and the communities they had come from while avoiding the disadvantages of each.

Paul Voisey describes the complex manner in which these settlers forged a distinctive way of life over three decades. He shows how frontier conditions and a dryland environment advanced the goals of the settlers in some ways and frustrated them in others, but always exerted a powerful influence. He challenges accepted models of frontier society, demonstrating that no single historical theory can do justice to the complex interaction of the forces of frontier setting, local environment, transplanted heritage, and metropolitan influences.

Grounding his interpretation in extensive statistical evidence as well as traditional literary sources, Voisey traces the history of Vulcan through a series of thematically ordered chapters, focusing in turn on the settlement process, especially the characteristics and attitudes of the pioneers and the process of acquiring and using land for both agriculture and town-building; agricultural production, concentrating on crop selection, cultivation techniques, farm size and expansion; social activities and institutions, notably schools and churches; and the structure and nature of local society. His study of the communities around Vulcan substantially expands and refines our understanding of economic and social development on the Canadian prairies.

PAUL VOISEY is Assistant Professor of History at the University of Alberta.

PAUL VOISEY

VULCAN
The Making of a Prairie
Community

UNIVERSITY OF TORONTO PRESS
Toronto Buffalo London

© University of Toronto Press 1988
Toronto Buffalo London
Printed in Canada

ISBN 0-8020-2642-7 (cloth)
ISBN 0-8020-6676-3 (paper)

♾

Printed on acid-free paper

Canadian Cataloguing in Publication Data

Voisey, Paul Leonard
    Vulcan : the making of a prairie community

(The Social history of Canada ; 43)
Includes bibliographical references and index.
ISBN 0-8020-2642-7 (bound) ISBN 0-8020-6676-3 (pbk.)

1. Frontier and pioneer life – Alberta – Vulcan
Region. 2. Land settlement – Alberta – Vulcan Region.
3. Agriculture – Alberta – Vulcan Region. 4. Vulcan
Region (Alta.) – History. I. Title. II. Series.

FC3699.V8V64 1988   971.23′4   C87-094773-7
F1079.5.V8V64 1988

Social History of Canada 43

This book has been published with the help of a grant from the Social Science
Federation of Canada, using funds provided by the Social Sciences and
Humanities Research Council of Canada.

For D. and G.

Contents

Illustrations

x Illustrations

FIGURES

Acknowledgments

Many people provided me with valuable assistance in the preparation of this book. I owe a special debt to the people of the Vulcan area who consented to interviews and often lent me their privately owned manuscripts, scrapbooks, and photographs. In particular I thank M.D. Keenan for allowing me access to his huge personal collection. While many archivists and librarians helped me to track down material, Doug Cass of the Glenbow-Alberta Institute was especially diligent.

The following people have all read portions of the manuscript and offered useful advice or assistance on points both minor and major: Carl Berger, Donald Kerr, and J.M.S. Careless of the University of Toronto; Gilbert Stelter of the University of Guelph; R.C. Macleod, Doug Owram, David Hall, and David Mills of the University of Alberta; David Jones of the University of Calgary; Barry Ferguson of the University of Manitoba; and Gerald Hallowell and Susan Kent of University of Toronto Press. I especially thank R.C. Brown of the University of Toronto, who supervised the portions of this book originally submitted as my doctoral dissertation.

The Canada Council and the Social Sciences and Humanities Research Council of Canada provided research funding for those portions of the manuscript submitted for my doctoral dissertation. The latter institution also provided separate funding in the form of a private scholar's grant to revise the manuscript and add new chapters. The University of Alberta's Endowment for the Future provided funds for the graphs and maps prepared by T.G. Fisher.

A contract breaking outfit, 1908. Some pioneers turned to contractors in order to break large tracts of land quickly. Note the water wagon needed to feed the huge steam engine.

E.E. Thompson's General Store at Old Brant, 1904–10. General stores were the earliest, most decentralized, and among the most profitable frontier businesses.

Main Street, Carmangay, 1912. Like many prairie towns, Carmangay aspired to metropolitan grandeur. Note the false fronts on some stores.

Town boosting, Vulcan, 1922. Slim Moorehouse delivered eight wagons of wheat pulled by thirty horses in a promotional campaign to put Vulcan 'on the map.'

The Vulcan tornado, 1927. In spite of the destructive subject of this photo, Vulcan could not resist using it to advertise the town.

The bumper crop of 1915. Huge yields and high prices during the Great War brought prosperity to the Vulcan area and confirmed the decision to specialize in wheat.

Stooked wheat, 1928. The flat, treeless terrain of the Vulcan area encouraged mechanized wheat production on a mammoth scale.

Feeding poultry, 1905–6. The care of farm animals usually fell to women. Note the contrast between this homestead shack and the grounds of the Dyment Farms.

Manager's house, Dyment Farms, 1915. The architecture and landscaping suggest an attempt to recreate a farmstead in southern Ontario or the American midwest.

Dust storm at Vulcan, 1920. Dust storms brought discredit on the dry-farming system and encouraged the search for better tillage techniques.

Binding wheat, 1910s. Farmers experimented with tractor and horse power. Here a giant steamer pulls five binders, while four horses pull only one.

A contract thresher working near Carmangay, 1913. Harvesting with a threshing machine called for a grand assembly of men, machines, and horses.

A combine thresher, 1920s. The combine promised substantial reductions in harvest labour costs.

Vulcan's Elevator Row, 1928. Vulcan emerged as one of the greatest wheat-producing and -shipping points on the prairies. Note the reliance on horses for hauling grain well after the development of gasoline trucks.

Chautauqua tent at Vulcan, late 1910s. The pioneers flocked to any event that presented an opportunity for socializing.

The one-room school at Reid Hill, 1921. Tiny enrolments and multiple grades presented rural teachers with formidable challenges, suggested here by the sour expressions on the children's faces.

VULCAN: THE MAKING OF A PRAIRIE COMMUNITY

The Problem of New Communities

In southern Alberta, midway between Calgary and Lethbridge, lie a thousand square miles of high plain referred to in this study as the Vulcan area (see Maps 1 and 2). Semi-arid and treeless, its mixture of short grasses bent to the high winds for centuries before man ploughed them under. The Blackfoot pitched only temporary hunting camps. Around 1890 the mammoth Circle Ranch of Montana invaded the plain, but it too only established camps at round-up time. In 1892 the Calgary and Edmonton Railway stretched south from Calgary to Fort Macleod, but during the subsequent depression it lured few settlers. Further east a few small ranchers squatted along the Little Bow River and the Snake Valley – the Circle considered them intruders and tried to drive them away – but settlers did not storm the area until 1904.[1] Over the next ten years modern, prosperous agricultural communities sprang to life. Wheat bound for world markets poured from mechanized farms and bustling rail towns. A battery of economic, social, and political institutions appeared. A complex society developed. Its sudden emergence and the influences that shaped it is the subject of this study.

It is an old theme, and familiar tools stand ready to work it. The oldest and most familiar approach argues that pioneers reconstructed former ways of life in the wilderness. The frontier thesis counters that the wilderness itself moulded the new society, while geographic determinism insists that physical environment, be it wilderness or not, forged distinctive features. The powerful and more recent metropolitan thesis insists that great cities directed and controlled frontier development.

Although scholars for decades have pondered and argued about the shape of civilization as it spread across the continent, ample reason remains to pursue the theme, especially in western Canada, where application of the various approaches has been fragmentary and unsatisfying. The earliest English Cana-

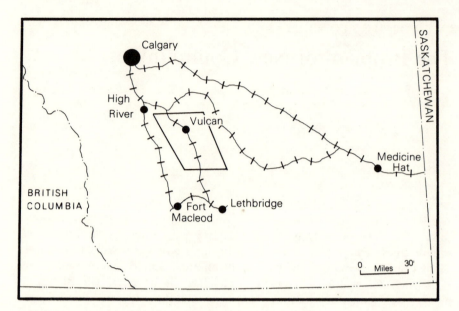

MAP 1
Southern Alberta: Location of study area and some railways

MAP 2
Study area

dian historians believed that old-world traditions shaped new societies; by emphasizing Canada's British character, they drew a favourable contrast with the rebellious republic. After flirting with continentalism, most shunned the application of Frederick Jackson Turner's frontier thesis to Canada, partly because it implied great similarities based on common experiences, but they admitted that the theory might explain the American character. Thus in many accounts tradition guided one nation, frontier experience the other. Indeed, long after American scholars declared war on the Turner thesis, Canadians sometimes wrote as though it remained acceptable and applicable to Americans. Their comparisons of the American and Canadian wests often ignored many important topics and lingered fondly on such favoured themes as law and order where differences seemed striking.[2]

If few scholars explained Canadian society in terms of pioneering experiences, many favoured environmental interpretations to account for regional differences, or, when they emphasized water routes, to establish a geographic basis for national development. They welcomed the metropolitan approach, for it reinforced the idea of an east-west economy and highlighted a distinctive Canadian experience of continental expansion. Although historians often combined certain approaches, some pursued an adversary zealously; they provided evidence for favoured interpretations and sought to discredit others. Debates flared occasionally in suggestive essays and brief passages in books, but most lacked the intensive research necessary to sustain their conclusions, and few drew their ammunition from the experiences of actual communities. The refusal of both friends and foes to define the frontier or its relationship to the physical environment clearly also marred the argument, although advocates of metroplitanism took greater care to define their concept. Often, too, the pioneers emerged from these debates as inanimate objects battered by forces they could not understand or control.[3]

Here it is argued that none of the familiar theories alone adequately explains the formation of new communities in the Canadian west. Tradition, frontier, environment, and metropolis interacted in extremely complex ways to exert uneven pressure on various aspects of community life. The pioneers themselves consciously sought to influence the outcome. In some respects they struggled to recreate the life they had left; in others, to copy a new metropolitan style; and in still others, they confidently expected the new setting to mould them in some desirable way, for they also nurtured preconceived notions about the frontier, the new environment, and the west in general. Yet sometimes, without much thought or concern, they also allowed old habits or new circumstances to sway them.

Exploring new communities requires clear conceptual maps. Here metropolitanism incorporates the thesis of its most prominent Canadian advocate,

J.M.S. Careless, who calls it a 'feudal chain of vassalage,' whereby large cities not only dominate their own countrysides but smaller cities and their countrysides, economically, socially, politically, and culturally.[4] Thus rural southern Alberta might be shaped by its larger towns, and they in turn by Calgary, Calgary by Toronto and Montreal (and perhaps Winnipeg), and those cities by London and New York. And all would simultaneously exert some influence on rural southern Alberta. But if Lethbridge and Calgary qualify as metropolitan places shaping the early twentieth-century frontier, can they not just as easily qualify as frontier places themselves? For purposes at hand, metropolitanism has been expanded to describe any outside influence directed at the local community, although it can be noted that such a force might itself be informed and influenced by frontier conditions.

Frontier remains a vague, troublesome notion with no universally accepted definition. None the less, a pragmatic one may be improvised for a specific purpose, even though it may not adequately describe new settlements for all times and places. Here it simply means the process of building communities in areas where none existed. Such a definition may not serve to describe settlements that experienced frequent contacts with native populations, where the problem of adjusting to a 'host culture' may arise, but the government banished the tribes that had roamed the Vulcan area to reserves long before settlers arrived. And although the Indians occasionally passed through the area, startling the settlers with requests for tea and tobacco, these brief encounters exerted no influence on the new society. The definition also has dubious application to vast regions visited by explorers, hunters, and traders and where tiny settlements might anchor in a sea of wilderness for decades. For the settlement of a limited, uninhabited locale, however, it seems appropriate.

In spite of its simplicity, the definition implies much. Some argue that many traits attributed to the frontier should be credited instead to the peculiar demography of newly settled places.[5] But since frontiers characteristically lure certain kinds of people, such a distinction does not seem reasonable. Hence the definition here incorporates the traditional low man-to-land ratio, which may be more precisely described as a sparse population relative to resources, a population that depends more on migration than natural increase for its growth and includes a preponderance of single young men. Thus a frontier study need not confine itself to those traits identified by Turner and his disciples, who concentrated on egalitarianism, democracy, innovation, and stages of economic development.[6] Nor is one of their major concerns, the impact of the frontier on settled places, appropriate for the study of the new community itself. Historians traditionally mark the passing of the frontier era when an area matures in some sense – when vacant land disappears, or population stabilizes, or perhaps when certain institutions appear. But since places experience continuous change, maturity is a slippery idea that should be ignored, for some frontier traits may linger long after the death of the conditions that gave rise to them. As defined here, frontier is quite distinct from the physical environment. Although the frontier process must occur in the wilderness, wilderness implies only the absence of man and has nothing to do with any specific climate or geography. Frontiers (or wilderness) may disappear, but physical environments never do.[7] The physical environment is subject to severe modification, however, and human structures may become part of it, but here the term encompasses only nature and excludes anything man-made.

The idea that pioneers reconstructed former ways of life on the frontier seems so straightforward that few historians have theorized about it, yet it imposes onerous demands on the researcher.[8] It insists on a broad knowledge of life in the old society and calls for repeated references to it, but most frontier communities, including this one, drew settlers from diverse cultural, social, and geographical backgrounds not easily characterized by single generalizations. Pioneers acquired their habits and attitudes from scattered experiences in many places, including other frontiers. Such distinctions must always be duly noted and explained.

Although an infinite variety of forces continually bombard human society, here it is assumed that everything about a new community in an area lacking a native host culture can ultimately be traced to environment, tradition, frontier, and metropolis. To expand this list invites chaos. Consider technology, increasingly studied as the focal point of social change. Sometimes it might properly be considered an extension of the metropolis. Great cities controlled both railroads and motion pictures, for example, and both influenced life in the hinterland. Agricultural machinery, by contrast, defies such simple classification. Even though most innovations sprang from settled places rather than frontiers, from towns instead of farms, and from the imagination of blacksmiths and engineers rather than farmers, exceptions abounded, especially in southern Alberta, where unique circumstances inspired much local ingenuity. Furthermore, many eastern and urban manufacturers designed implements specifically for use in distant hinterlands, and frontiersmen often modified imported technology or put it to new uses.[9] From another perspective all technology might just as logically be regarded as part of the physical environment – in the case of cities, an environment more forceful in impact than nature. Hence, rather than considering technology as a primary influence, this study will regard it as the product of more basic ones.

To overcome the complaint that most judgments on the nature of the western Canadian frontier rest on a few carefully selected subjects, this study examines a wide variety of topics grouped around three broad themes: settlement, agriculture, and social life. The study thus canvasses a broad range of local activities, but it still omits many subjects a reader might wish for. The point bears repeating. The study does not attempt to investigate everything about, or even everything of importance to the life of the community. Elsewhere I have argued that writing general surveys about local communities frequently results in diluted, bland, and largely pointless textbooks.[10] This investigation is therefore better regarded as a case-study that employs various aspects of the local community's history to explore a particular thesis.

Intensive investigation also demanded that spatial restrictions be placed on the study. Both theoretical and practical considerations led to the selection of the Vulcan area for a case-study approach. On the practical side, it yielded a cornucopia of research material. Because of western Canada's ethnic diversity and its many economic and geographical subregions, the typical prairie community may not exist, but the Vulcan area shared major traits with hundreds of settlements. First homesteaded heavily in 1904, it typified the circumstances of the great Laurier settlement boom. Railway, homestead, Hudson's Bay Company, and school lands chequered the area in the precise pattern of the classic prairie township, unblemished by bloc settlements or other special land grants. As in most prairie communities born of new railways, settlement proceeded rapidly, but the pioneers arrived independently at various times from various places for various reasons. The majority represented the most numerous of all prairie cultural groups, the English-speaking Protestants of Ontario and the United States.

Their chosen destination nestled in the great prairie subregion of treeless plain and semi-arid climate. Like most such environments, it blossomed quickly as a wheat-growing district. Although entrepreneurs carved an irrigation reservoir along the area's eastern border in 1910, its water flowed far to the southeast, and Vulcan remained a typical dryland farming area. Nothing altered the monolithic nature of the economy. As in most prairie communities, ranching virtually disappeared once the homesteaders invaded. Although pioneers used local coal for fuel, they did not export it beyond the area. Mining employed few men and exerted little impact on the economic and social structure. Natural gas deposits rested undisturbed until after the Second World War. The towns bound themselves solely to the service of King Wheat. They failed to lure large government institutions, and manufacturing in any meaningful sense failed to germinate. While the area experienced the violent economic fluctuations that shook the wheat belt, it enjoyed more prosperity than most communities. While Vulcan is less typical in this respect, its wealth expanded the choices open to the settlers and thus furnishes important clues about their attitudes and preferred way of life. None the less, other features of the area atypical of most prairie communities stemmed from this relative wealth and greater reliance on wheat: the pioneers arrived with more capital; they began with larger farms that expanded more rapidly, and they employed new technology earlier and more extensively.

Several considerations determined the size of the study area. Although small enough to invite intensive scrutiny, the Vulcan area none the less provided numerous examples of agrarian communities of differing scale: several rail-towns and their hinterlands, a dozen or so off-railway hamlets, and a great many rural neighbourhoods centred only on a country store, school, or church. The area also proved large enough to compensate for gaps in documentation: what one locality would not reveal in the way of information, another usually did. The time-span of the study also requires some explanation. While the initial arrival of large numbers of settlers in 1904 provides an obvious starting-point, the study ranges to the mid-1930s to see how various activities and institutions weathered over time, particularly through periods of boom and bust. The depression of the 1930s provided an especially important benchmark, for it severely tested institutional durability, leaving some intact and substantially altering others. None the less, the emphasis throughout is on the frontier period, the first decade or so when pioneers established the area's basic traditions and institutions.

Much statistical information is presented in this study. Properly documenting it presents a particular problem, for much of it derives from counting, sorting, and linking data provided by many disparate sources. Citing the sources and method of compilation for each such statistic would involve lengthy, tedious, and often repetitious explanations. Similarly, although the published census provided the basis for many aggregate statistics, many were modified by a variety of other sources. For these reasons I have eschewed documenting statistics unless they were taken unaltered from a single source. Readers should refer to the appendix, A Note on Statistics, for a fuller explanation of how data were compiled.

PART I: SETTLEMENT

1

Pioneers

High rates of geographic mobility have prevailed among rural North Americans, and the pioneers who settled the Vulcan area shared this restlessness. Map 3 shows where 1,200 heads of families who arrived between 1904 and 1920 spent most of their childhoods. Map 4 shows where they lived in the two years prior to arrival. The maps indicate an extensive westward shift but do not reveal the full extent of mobility. Both show large numbers living in southern Ontario, but in most cases they were not the same people. Many who grew up there migrated to the American midwest or Manitoba before coming to the Vulcan area, while many who arrived directly from Ontario had grown up further east or in Britain. Vulcan's American settlers not only came from the same states as did American settlers to western Canada generally, but followed the same paths to get there. Midwesterners typically headed for North Dakota or the Inland Empire (the upper Columbia River basin that encompasses eastern Washington, northeastern Oregon, and northern Idaho) before settling in Vulcan. One settler wandered progressively westward, living in Wisconsin, South Dakota, North Dakota, Montana, Idaho, and then Washington before landing in the Vulcan area.[1]

Some, especially bachelors, had moved with startling frequency considering their youth upon arrival in the Vulcan area. Frank Racher first left Ontario for Winnipeg, then Calgary. After labouring throughout British Columbia, he panned for Klondike gold and soldiered in South Africa before returning to Ontario. Still only thirty-three, he homesteaded in the Vulcan area in 1905. But even whole families moved regularly. One woman remembered packing five times in her first five years of marriage. 'My childhood was one of many moves, different homes,' recalled another pioneer. Ezra Thompson's father dragged his family from farm to farm, from New Jersey to Pennsylvania to Ohio. After Ezra's birth they pioneered in Iowa. As a young man Ezra left the

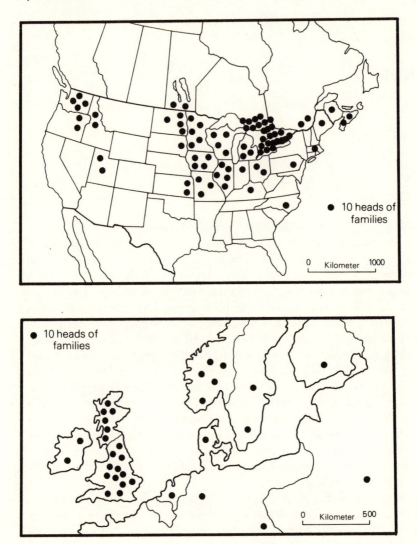

MAP 3
Childhood homes of 1,200 heads of families entering Vulcan area, 1904–20

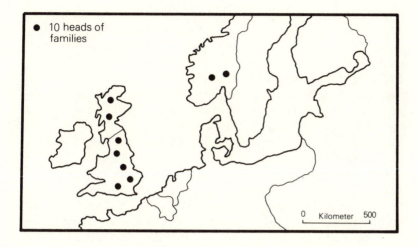

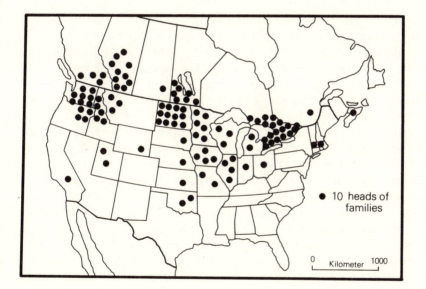

MAP 4
Last permanent homes of 1,200 heads of families entering Vulcan area, 1904–20

family for frontier Nebraska. Following unsuccessful attempts to secure land grants in Mexico and Brazil, he ranched at Spring Coulee, Alberta, before coming to the Vulcan district. Later he wandered across various parts of California and Texas.[2]

Some studies now concede that the European-born, once believed more stable, moved just as readily as native North Americans, as the migration maps for the Vulcan area suggest. Hugo Geschwendt, for example, moved with his family from Germany to Michigan. He worked throughout the state and, following an extended visit to Europe, lived in Oregon and then California before settling in the Vulcan area in 1908 at age thirty-two. Many Vulcan-area settlers believed that the English-born especially came only to prove up a homestead, sell out, and leave.[3] One well-known study considers the Americans who settled in western Canada particularly restless,[4] but Canadians in the Vulcan area had packed their bags just as often. The two nationalities are practically indistinguishable anyway, since many settlers from the American midwest had been born in Ontario and others had crossed the border several times.

How did such a scattered group converge on the Vulcan area? Besides listing reasons for leaving particular regions and nations, many studies credit government and railroad promotional activities for luring settlers to western Canada. The Canadian government immigration agent in eastern Washington, for example, distributed twelve thousand pamphlets and received fifteen to twenty-five visitors and thirty inquiries daily in 1904, the very year that many Washington farmers headed for the Vulcan frontier.[5] Yet few claimed to have moved because of the literature. As with most frontier migrations, they came on the recommendation of friends and relatives who had stumbled into the Vulcan area largely by accident. Visitors, itinerant harvesters, and other travellers along the Calgary and Edmonton Railway south of Calgary learned of the vast unclaimed lands to the east, and many, like George Crane, 'wrote fabulous yarns to the folks back in Michigan, telling of the country's great potential for producing wealth.' Others, like J.L. Base from North Dakota, received many inquiries about the new area from former neighbours. 'I had a good job and good prospects [in Ontario],' remembered D.O. Jantzie, 'but left at the urging of a sister and her husband who were going out.' Sometimes Vulcan settlers enclosed a locally published promotional pamphlet along with their personal recommendation. 'When Martin sent us a brochure showing fields of gold grain, we were ready to move,' recalled a frustrated Colorado farmer.[6]

The earliest Vulcan settlers often filed homesteads or bought land for friends back home. Thus the area acquired pockets of settlers from Monmouth and Galesburg, Illinois; from the Palouse country and Walla Walla, Washington;

from Galt and Bruce County, Ontario; from Pomme DeTerre, Minnesota; Finns from Astoria, Oregon; and French Canadians from western Massachusetts. Ten families of Matlocks arrived at various times before 1920. A clan of twenty-two Johnstons from Carman, Manitoba, selected eight homesteads in 1905.[7] By 1920 almost everyone in the Vulcan area found a hometown friend or relative living nearby. Typical of many frontier areas, these personal contacts eased the social and economic adjustment of newcomers, undermining the argument that frontier communities suffered anomie because migration severed intimate relationships.[8]

Although the foreign-born constituted more than two-thirds of Vulcan-area adults by 1921, those of British stock accounted for more than 60 per cent of the population. Nearly all the rest were German, Scandinavian, and Dutch, but some French, Russian, Finnish, and Chinese settlers also appeared. Most of the non-English population consisted of Anglicized second-generation immigrants, and by 1931, 96 per cent of the population could speak English only. Protestantism claimed more than 85 per cent of the settlers; most belonged to the Anglican, Methodist, and Presbyterian churches.

Self-employed farmers, merchants, and tradesmen swelled the ranks of the new arrivals, confirming the old dictum about the selective process of frontier migration: the very poor could not afford to come; the very rich had no reason to. The Canadian government sought only farmers for its homesteads and generally succeeded in finding them. Most Vulcan homesteaders could claim prior farming experience, yet nearly all had also worked at something unrelated to agriculture. Some had even acquired other vocations, which they would pursue part-time while farming in the Vulcan area. Others would subsequently return to them full-time. Most homesteaders sought winter jobs to finance their first years – as miners or loggers in British Columbia, tradesmen or labourers locally or in the city, as teamsters, store clerks, or construction workers building new railways, towns, and irrigation systems. By 1935 half of Vulcan's farmers had averaged 5.3 years at other occupations. Similarly, although most town pioneers would launch businesses familiar to them, they too had changed occupations often, and most even had some farming experience.[9]

Changes in address frequently meant changes in occupation. LeRoy Haney, for example, farmed in Iowa, homesteaded in Kansas, then roamed several states, where he taught school, served as a justice of the peace, and worked for a railway. In Oregon he returned to farming before homesteading in the Vulcan district.[10] Because of their chequered occupational histories, many had moved back and forth between small cities, towns, and farms. Many had lived temporarily in large cities, but of the 1,200 heads of families portrayed on the migration maps, perhaps no more than 50 to 70 had ever spent two years in a city of 100,000. Although most pioneers came from the middle class, the variety of their occupational experiences would prove useful, perhaps even crucial, to building the frontier economy.

In other ways Vulcan's settlers resembled not only frontier populations generally but mobile people everywhere. With the fewest ties to their home communities, young adults, especially single men or those with small young families, most readily moved, whether to the frontier or elsewhere.[11] But since everyone arriving in a frontier society is by definition mobile, such characteristics dominated the new society. The frontier assumed the demographic traits of settled places only gradually, as those who stayed grew older and as the marriage of their children and the birth of grandchildren balanced the sex ratio.

Figure 1 demonstrates the aging of Alberta's population, and similar curves appear if the entire population under 45 is considered. Settlers in Vulcan's township 17-25-4 averaged only 31.7 years of age at the time of homestead entry, and those under 40 constituted 79 per cent. But by 1935 a survey revealed that less than one quarter of Vulcan's farmers were under 40, and the average age had risen to 50.[12] The predominance of adults in the prime of life, and less than normal proportions of the old, the sickly, the mentally and physically handicapped, and others who might require financial support, help to explain the often spectacular economic growth of frontier regions.

Extreme imbalances in the sex ratio especially marked the earliest years (see Figure 2), for even married men often arrived in advance of their families. 'At first there are nothing but men,' observed the Carmangay *Sun* on 12 November 1914 as settlers swarmed into each new township; 'gradually the women and children increase.' Many of these first women claimed they could count no neighbours for miles save bachelors, and some even complained that they did not see another woman during the first year or two of homesteading.[13]

Although studies agree that a preponderance of males characterizes frontiers, some now maintain that such claims exaggerate the imbalance and overlook a surprisingly high number of families.[14] Yet men dominated the adult population of the Vulcan area and overwhelmed the unmarried population. Township 17-25-4, for example, attracted 149 males for every 100 females between 1904 and 1910. If children under 18, who naturally appeared in roughly equal numbers of girls and boys, are eliminated, the figure climbs to 204. Among unmarried adults, it soars astronomically; 31 single men and only 1 single woman lived in the township. Similarly, 123 men lived in Alberta for every 100 women in 1921, the earliest year for which a statistical breakdown exists, but the number of unmarried rural males per 100 unmarried rural females between the marriageable years of 20 to 44 ranged from 358 to 894, depending on the 5-

19 Pioneers

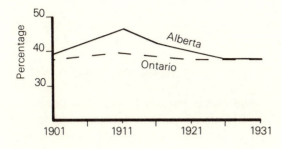

FIGURE 1
Percentage of population between 20 and 44 years of
age

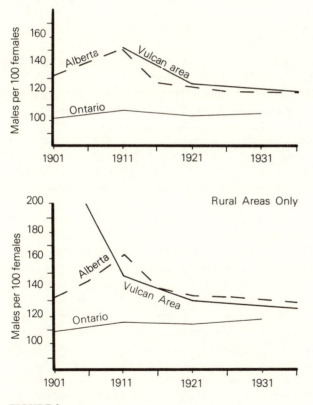

FIGURE 2
Males per 100 females

year age group considered, compared to a range of 175 to 222 in Ontario. Greater imbalance undoubtedly prevailed in Alberta before 1921, less thereafter.

The search for brides outside the community, and the coming of age of pioneer daughters, soon began to balance the sex ratio, but it never balanced completely, not in new rural communities like Vulcan, not even in the century-old ones of Ontario (see Figure 2). Farming attracted single men, but neither rural frontiers nor settled rural areas anywhere offered single women many opportunities to earn a living. More often than men, single women fled to cities, where a variety of options abounded. Thus females constituted more than half of those leaving the Vulcan area between 1931 and 1936, while males accounted for over half of those entering it. Even small towns, however, cried out for teachers, secretaries, store clerks, hotel waitresses, and telephone operators. Thus by 1921 the number of males per 100 females had fallen to 107 in Carmangay, while it remained 139 in the surrounding municipal district of Little Bow.

Thus young men, most single, some married, some with small young families, invaded the Vulcan area. Self-employed men of modest means, they had experienced many kinds of work in various places, but mostly in the English-speaking Protestant heartland of rural North America. Although these characteristics suggest much about the shape of the new communities, they merely hint at pioneer social attitudes. The independent, innovative frontiersman of Turner once strode boldly through the wilderness, but more recently historians have exposed his conservative and imitative nature. Some even argue that he ran to the wilderness to recapture the past, to escape an unwelcome future in his home community.[15]

Unfortunately, frontier historians have usually debated innovation and imitation in absolute terms, but if we accept the argument that all societies are basically conservative and attempt to resist change, frontier conservatism can only be assessed by comparison with settled places. Although recognizing changes, rural observers in the early twentieth century insisted that farmers were still more conservative in all respects that urban dwellers.[16] It follows that conservatism should reign supreme on the frontier, devoid as it was of large cities. But if cities bred innovation because heterogeneity, complexity, and turbulent growth constantly challenged traditional ideas, then ironically the frontier shared more of those traits than the rural east. It threw strangers together, challenged them to organize communities (often in unfamiliar environments), and subjected them to rapid growth and change. Before acquiring a stake in the established order, young people commonly reject the conservative views of their elders, and frontiers typically attracted the young. The Vulcan area attracted the youth of the North American midwest, one of the least conservative rural areas on the continent. In most respects their behaviour does not seem conservative when compared to that of settled rural populations. Sometimes it suggests a curious blend of conservatism and innovation. But is it appropriate to measure pioneer attitudes along a single continuum from imitative to innovative? Closer probing reveals that Vulcan-area pioneers nurtured many ideas about frontier community-building that defy this simple classification.

Historians commonly refer to the years from 1900 to 1914 as the 'Progressive Era.' Often used to describe reform movements of the period, progressivism also embodied several popular notions that permeated North American society generally. The rise of the giant corporation, which ironically many progressives sought to destroy or regulate, inspired many of these ideas, for it promised a better society through technology, science, business efficiency, and administrative expertise. Emerging from a booming economy, these new articles of business faith stressed the most effective ways to make money, but many progressives believe they could be applied to other aspects of society; even government, education, and religion could be approached rationally and administered in an efficient, businesslike manner.[17]

Although these ideas sprang from urban-industrial society, the countryside soon felt their impact. Led by a new breed of specialists like farm economists and rural sociologists, religious bodies, school boards, government agencies, and universities undertook to make rural life more industrial, modern, progressive, scientific, efficient, and businesslike. The American Country Life Commission of 1908 epitomized this desire, and such efforts justly qualify as progressive-era reform movements.[18] Although one study argues that urban leaders imposed the concepts of modernization on a reluctant rural population to serve such urban purposes as ensuring a cheap food supply, strengthening the foreign trade balance, and creating a strong hinterland market for urban goods and services, many rural people in the relatively well-educated and prosperous midwest welcomed the new gospel.[19]

Their enthusiasm often sprang from a fascination with the technology that began to revolutionize rural life – electric lights, telephones, automobiles, motion pictures, steam and gasoline tractors, and later, radios. These spectacular wonders instilled respect for the scientific discipline that supposedly created them. Progressive ideas also promised to help the farmer financially. Making as much money as possible has seldom embarrassed North Americans, but when the economy surged out of the depression of the 1890s, this ambition gained new respectability. During agriculture's 'golden age,' farmers suddenly began making more money than they had for decades. What better promise to make even more than with the help of technology, science, and efficiency? One might despise the giant corporation, but who could deny that its utilization of these principles helped make it successful?

Progressive ideas also appealed to farmers psychologically. With the emergence of a sizeable generation of North American city dwellers who had never lived in the countryside, myths about rural people became increasingly fashionable. Travelling salesmen and entertainers, people of suspect status in the city, bolstered their self-esteem with fantastic tales of the gullibility, crudeness, and even the sexual laxity of the hicks they encountered in the countryside. Although still generally praised in public as the backbone of society, country folk increasingly sensed private ridicule and would soon burn under the acid tongues of critics like William Allen White, Sinclair Lewis, and Henry Mencken.[20] For those who found no comfort in Jeffersonian clichés, progressive ideals offered a natural defence. Rural dwellers could show the city that they were as modern and sophisticated as anyone.

Young people of the rural continental midwest readily absorbed these notions and carried them to the Dakotas and the Inland Empire, and then to the Vulcan frontier. The words progressive, scientific, efficient, and businesslike peppered their vocabulary and that of the pioneer press. Without a word about traditional agrarian ideals, the president of a local agricultural society announced that 'the scope for intellect in raising stock and grain' constituted the major advantage of rural life. The provincially sponsored Women's Institutes vowed to make the rural home more efficient through scientific applications, and young ladies of the Vulcan area who attended the new agricultural school in the neighbouring town of Claresholm enrolled not in housekeeping but in 'home economics' and 'domestic science.' Organizers of local cultural institutions fancied themselves amateur social scientists and sponsored lectures with such grand titles as 'The Socialization of the Rural Community.'[21]

The economic promise of progressive ideas especially captivated Vulcan pioneers. The passion for making money burned brightly on the frontier, and it fired every issue of the pioneer press. The settlers' infatuation with new technology also explains, and simultaneously illustrates, the popularity of progressive concepts. Next to people, the settlers photographed automobiles and farm implements more than anything else. Long after their memory of many events had faded, they could still recall precise details about machinery they had owned half a century before. One minister's memoirs largely chronicle his adventures with his first automobile and other gadgets.[22] Nor did the social and psychological appeal of progressivism escape the Vulcan frontier. An enthusiastic response rewarded the speaker who told local pioneers that the day they could be considered 'hayseeds and clodhoppers' had passed, thanks to the birth of 'scientific agriculture.'[23]

The pioneers did not absorb progressive ideas as completely and consistently as suggested here, of course, for the idea of agriculture as a science and a business emerged only hesitantly from the social philosophy of agriculture as a way of life. It paralleled a century-long shift towards commercial farming, and a complete transition of values never occurred. Thus some Vulcan settlers still defended an agrarian code that emphasized the naturalness, independence, moral superiority, and social and family-rearing benefits of rural life, and many more believed that by strengthening the rural economy, progressivism might help to preserve those traditional virtues. Furthermore, progressive ideas wilted somewhat after the First World War, when environmental problems increasingly demonstrated that the pioneers had preached scientific farming and business efficiency more readily than they had practised it. By the 1930s a second generation of farmers, more cynical than their predecessors, had begun to emerge. None the less, the progressive outlook flowered brightly under the sunny optimism of the booming settlement years, and although generally ignored by historians, it represents an important aspect of the Anglo-American approach to pioneering.

With their faith in science, technology, and efficiency, and a desire to shake the image of hicks, Vulcan-area pioneers eagerly kept abreast of developments in the city and the outside world generally. The impact of the metropolis on frontier regions has always depended on the level of communications technology in society and on how quickly and fully it penetrated new areas. As a relatively modern, prosperous frontier, the Vulcan area soon acquired the most advanced communications technology of the day.

When settlers first arrived in 1904, the nearest towns – High River, Nanton, and Claresholm – squatted on the Calgary and Edmonton Railway fifteen to forty miles to the west. These tiny nerve-endings received news of the outside world through the railway, telegraph, mail service, and travellers. Because of the distance, the slowness of horse travel, winter weather, and poor roads, Vulcan-area pioneers visited these towns only occasionally, but within two years rural post offices in most districts brought the news through letters, newspapers, and magazines much more frequently. The construction of the Kipp-Aldersyde line created new towns after 1910, bringing all information services much closer. Although some memoirs complain about how seldom the family went to town, most rural settlers went at least once a week.

Two technological developments brought the city and small town still closer to the farm family. The first automobile clattered into the area in 1909, and by the First World War hundreds of them rumbled along newly constructed roads. 'The farmer who has not got his car yet considers himself without one of the essentials of one who lives in the country,' reported the local press, which predicted 'that in another year or two buggies will be scarce at gatherings in the district.'[24] As in other rural areas the press praised the automobile for the freedom it gave farmers to travel far afield, broadening their horizons and sharpening their knowledge of the world outside their own communities.

The telephone exerted a similar if less dramatic impact. In 1904 Dan Richmond linked his neighbours together by running signals through barbed-wire fences. In 1907 they ran a line to the general store in nearby Brant and from there to a hardware store in Nanton, eighteen miles away. Many others built barbed-wire networks, and when new towns appeared on the Kipp-Alder-syde railway, telephone lines quickly radiated in every direction.

The pioneers craved outside news so much that the new town of Carmangay fought for daily mail service in order to 'get the Calgary morning papers every day.'[25] Local newspapers soon appeared: the Carmangay *Sun* in 1910, the Vulcan *Review* in 1912 (which later became the *Advocate*), and the Champion *Spokesman* in 1914 (later the *Chronicle*). The local editors regularly received many metropolitan newspapers and magazines, and they reprinted stories in their own weeklies. Some settlers read an astonishing variety of periodicals. One family subscribed to one local newspaper, two Calgary papers, two Winnipeg papers, a family magazine, a farm journal, two women's magazines, and occasionally bought and kept back issues of British and New York magazines. Although these were unusually voracious readers, many settlers must have shared their interest, for a Carmangay merchant boasted to friends back in Michigan, 'in our store we have ... the lastest and best periodicals and magazines and have a wonderful sale on them.'[26]

Newspapers and magazines, especially the advertisements and mail-order catalogues, bombarded frontiersmen with urban attitudes and life-styles. One woman remembered that magazines gave her 'a glimpse of the world of shops and fashions and coloured illustrations of the Gibson Girls with high pompadours and shirtwaist dresses. The Munsey Magazines introduced me to the sophisticated world of New York at the turn of the century. I steeped myself in it till Tifanny's, Fifth Avenue, Delmonico's, the brown-stone mansions of the Vanderbilts and their ilk, seemed as real to me as Nanton.'[27] Urban sophistication appealed so strongly to the pioneers that local merchants took care to advertise the metropolitan inspiration of their wares, especially women's fashions.

The railroad also carried some newly developed communications technology to the country: the motion picture, the phonograph, and later the radio. As early as 1910 an occasional movie entertained residents of the rising town of Carmangay. By the First World War farmers flocked to Carmangay, Champion, and Vulcan movie houses in such numbers that on 16 April 1919 the Vulcan *Advocate* claimed that films had quickly 'become part of the amusement tradition of everybody.' Even local organizations like the United Farmers of Alberta chapters showed films to their members. Few innovations brought the city to the countryside with the dramatic impact of the motion picture, which portrayed urban styles, attitudes, and ideas, as well as urban goods.

Sound, of course, did not enhance the movies until 1928, but radio arrived earlier and caused great excitement. 'This is truly a wireless town,' reported the *Advocate* on 8 November 1922. 'Poles are sticking up all over the place, and we get all that is going.' Merchants with receiving sets installed loudspeakers to attract customers, and the first farmers to buy sets were invaded by curious neighbours. By the 1920s, when Calgary's CFCN began broadcasting, radio listening occupied farm families for hours each day, especially in the winter. Even during the busy harvest season, the World Series of baseball lured many from their work. Because few signals as yet cluttered the air, listeners could easily tune in American stations hundreds of miles away, and although CFCN called itself 'the Voice of the Prairies,' and presented Calgary news, religious shows, and market reports, it also functioned as 'the Voice of New York,' for it relayed many American network shows. Thus Amos and Andy became as well known in the Vulcan area as anywhere in North America.[28]

The train also brought the city to the area in the form of travelling entertainers of every description. With its concerts, sermons, lectures, and plays, the chautauqua always attracted huge crowds. The train also whisked pioneers to the city. Each winter dozens of them migrated to winter homes in Vancouver, Portland, and especially Los Angeles, but even a special event in summer, like the 1905 Lewis and Clark Exposition in Portland, could draw huge numbers.[29] Special events in Calgary and Lethbridge lured settlers much more frequently, if only for a day or two at a time.

The high exposure of Vulcan settlers to voices from the outside world and their eagerness to listen to them does not imply that they agreed with or accepted every urban attitude or idea that came along. Indeed, they wanted automobiles, telephones, and motion pictures because they believed that the new communications technology, which combated isolation and loneliness, served the countryside better than the city.[30] But they also wished to know what happened in the city, and they anxiously copied its outward style. The tremendous enthusiasm for civic improvements suggests a desire to lack nothing the city could offer. Almost immediately the new towns sought to build sidewalks, pave streets, erect streetlights, and construct public buildings of every description. Local promotional literature always compared the area favourably with the metropolis. In its first year of existence Carmangay advertised itself as 'a beautiful flourishing little city with the modern conveniences of its larger metropolitan sisters.'[31]

Conversely, the pioneers scorned the image of a wild-west frontier. A lavish promotional spread in the Lethbridge *Herald* on 2 April 1910 emphasized the orderly character of Carmangay social life, the safety of its streets, and the sobriety of its citizens: 'there is a licensed bar, but the people are not drunkards.' The pioneers hoped to avoid those recreational excesses common to frontiers dominated by single young men: drunkenness, gambling, prostitution, and brawling. Such hopes largely explain their support for prohibition and other moral reforms.[32] The new towns quickly passed by-laws to curb disreputable activities and whatever else failed to meet their expectations of civilized behaviour: spitting and swearing in public, creating a disturbance, racing horses on the streets, vagrancy, begging, allowing children to run unsupervised at night, and riding bicycles on the sidewalks. And many local organizations, like the Sunny Glen United Farmers of Alberta, introduced by-laws to reprimand, fine, suspend, or expel members 'guilty of improper conduct at or away from meetings.'[33] The new town councils immediately hired constables to battle hell-raisers who threatened the moral tone of the new communities. The pioneers condemned rowdy behaviour, for only a respectable population could build progressive, civilized communities. Thus a Vulcan newspaper stringer described one of the town's most aggressive boosters as a 'gentleman as well as a hustler,' and an advertising campaign boasted that 'the people of Vulcan are energetic and a splendid type of townspeople generally, and the men at the head of it are men of ability and shrewd in business.'[34]

But the pioneer image of civilization, nurtured with such ease in promotional literature yet so difficult to create in reality, rested not only on social order and the frontier's ability to emulate the sophistication of the city but also on the faithful reproduction of those aspects of life back east most closely associated with civilization. While pioneers often reconstructed familiar institutions simply because no other method of organization occurred to them, sometimes they did so with deliberate determination. 'We wished to establish our environments – for home, school, and church as we had in our home lands,' said one woman.[35] This effort can be demonstrated in many specific ways, but perhaps best by the eager pursuit of high culture, for no other activity concerns itself more with the preservation of tradition.

While newspapers and magazines informed pioneers of outside events and urban styles, novels and history books bound them closely to their Anglo-American heritage. Many settlers brought large numbers of such books with them, and they borrowed from each other freely. When the new railtowns appeared, residents organized a circulating library of seven hundred volumes in a Carmangay drugstore and another in a Vulcan hardware store. In 1922 Vulcan constructed its own library building. Settlers could also borrow from the travelling libraries sponsored by the University of Alberta and the Alberta Department of Agriculture, which sent collections to rural areas, allowed them to circulate for a time, and then replaced them with new collections.[36]

Literary societies cropped up in most rural neighbourhoods within a few years of settlement, promoting book borrowing and discussion, public readings, and sometimes local drama. 'If the crowds attending the meetings of the [Little Bow Literary] Society keep on increasing,' noted the Carmangay *Sun* on 18 March 1910, 'they will have to enlarge the school.' Many societies also encouraged writing. The Berrywater Literary and Social Club produced novels by entrusting to each member the writing of one chapter, and both men and women wrote poems in great quantity.[37]

Other cultural pursuits quickly followed. A drama club in the tiny Brant settlement staged its first play in 1908; by the First World War the Vulcan area featured one or two locally produced plays a week throughout the winter. From the beginning of settlement, phonographs brought music to the frontier, and instructors in voice, dance, and piano soon invaded the area. With a shortage of musicians at the Saturday-night dances that livened dozens of rural schoolhouses, many settlers taught themselves to play musical instruments. The Brant settlers entertained the area with a large brass band in 1910, and other towns quickly followed their example.

Anxious to pass cultural traditions on to the next generation, the pioneers became obsessed with building schools and providing education. 'Nearly every man and woman I met mentioned the subject,' noted a traveller through the Vulcan area in 1906. Together with post offices, schools rose on the frontier long before other public institutions; dozens appeared before the area could boast a single church, railway, or even roads. Some pioneers even refused to bring their families into the area until schools were built.[38]

In spite of the early appearance of schools and the popularity of cultural organizations, the frontier did not blossom into a cultural mecca. Most organizations failed miserably to reach their professed goals, and many survived only for social and recreational reasons. Apathy subverted many plans, and some pioneers even regarded book-learning and culture as hogwash. Men more often expressed this hostile view, for both sexes assumed that women should bring culture, civilization, and refinement to the frontier, and the little promotional literature designed to lure women west stressed this role.[39] The women who came accepted the challenge willingly. Those institutions in which their views and decisions counted most heavily – home, school, church, cultural organizations – represented the most deliberate attempts to transplant tradition.

But neither did culture on the rural frontier evaporate as completely as many novelists suggested. Since these writers often came from rural communities, they virtually denied their own artistic existence and that of many others.[40] It seems true of the Vulcan area, as of frontiers generally, that a solid core of settlers, including men as well as women, nurtured culture as best they could: people like James Lindsay, who freely set aside part of his hardware store for Vulcan's first library, who would drop his work any time to help a child select a book and who often bought books for the more interested children; or Mrs Hugh Parker, an English schoolteacher who contributed articles to newspapers and magazines for thirty years; or families like the Wardens, who provided their children with new books every Christmas, maintained a library from 'floor to ceiling,' and purchased a variety of musical instruments and encouraged their children to sing and play. Such people seemed to fear that the frontier might strip them of every remnant of civilized society unless they exerted Herculean efforts to prevent it.[41]

This portrait of the Vulcan pioneers as progressive-minded people bent on emulating the city, fostering civilized behaviour, and recreating former ways of life might suggest that they would deny the influence of the frontier on their lives. But popular culture had always supplied easterners with romantic ideas about the frontier west, and the settlers brought these notions with them. Thus the daughter of one Carmangay pioneer wrote home in 1913:

Out West usually calls to mind great stretches of land, open air and cowboys, with a hint of recklesness about the very words that lend enchantment. This abundance of space gives every man a chance to become a property owner and to be his own master. The spirit of the West ... is very contagious. The air is full of freedom and the people live natural, carefree lives without much regard to the strict conventions of the East. Many a man has gone there just to have a fresh start in life because he is welcomed without any questions being asked concerning his past life, and he is valued for what he is, not for what his family were before him, or for what he has. It is, therefore, a purely democratic place where everyone is as good as his neighbor, but no better.[42]

This young lady might well have brought the essays of Frederick Jackson Turner west with her, but if few pioneers spoke so forcefully or articulately, they none the less expressed similar views.

They believed that special qualities distinguished them from other people: courage, enterprise, optimism, determination, independence, neighbourliness, generosity, straightforwardness, and honesty. Although vague about whether the frontier attracted people with such qualities or moulded them, the pioneers found these beliefs irresistible. The local press prattled incessantly about the 'courageous and enterprising spirit, unfailing good fellowship, and unselfish hospitality' of the pioneers. 'It didn't take me long to shake off the reserve of the East and assume the friendly western approach,' bragged a young clergy-man, who obviously came in hopeful anticipation of a new social climate. The settlers repeatedly assured themselves that a man's past was never held against him and that convention and conformity need not trouble him. 'Style or fash-ion nor the opinions of others seem to enter into the lives of these sturdy westerners,' boasted a settler to friends back home. Such views might be expressed in any connection or circumstance. Thus one southern Alberta min-ister argued that 'Presbyterianism specially suits this West. There is in it a virility, a strength, a democratic spirit, a practicalness, a straightforwardness, an aggressiveness, a genuine honesty and manliness in life that appeals to the ordinary Westerner.'[43]

Such beliefs elevated the pioneer to special status. Vulcan society soon divided itself into newcomers and old-timers. Old-timer, of course, did not refer to the elderly; a newspaper obituary described a thirty-two-year-old man as 'an old-timer in this district, having come here with his parents in the year 1904.' Inspired by earlier pioneer reunions, the most impressive celebration of the old-timer occurred in 1920, when residents of the Champion district launched the Cleverville Pioneer Club. Intended to preserve the early history of the community, it restricted membership to those present in the district before 31 December 1910. The inaugural meeting, hailed by the local press as 'one of the greatest events ever pulled off in Champion,' attracted over three hundred people, including many former residents, who listened to pioneer reminis-cences and danced until 5 a.m. The status of pioneer became so popular that the club later relaxed its membership requirements to admit anyone who had arrived in the district before 1 January 1913, their spouses, and their descend-ents.[44]

This cult-like worship of the pioneer suggests a Genesis motif: before 1904 history did not exist, and like Adam and Eve, the first settlers were responsible for its origin. As one Vulcan pioneer explained, 'We ... are the Makers of History of this great Western Canada; what will be the traditions of the future are being established today.'[45] Thus pioneers felt compelled to write memoirs, memoirs in which beginnings prevailed, for they typically recalled the trip west and the first year's pioneering efforts in great detail, while subsequent years received scant treatment.

Curiously, the cult of pioneering sprang not only from the reality of the pioneers' experience and from notions culled from popular culture but from the traditions of the North American midwest as well. The settlers' and old-timers' associations still common in that region taught youngsters to revere the communities' founders. In the very year that many farmers left Bruce County,

Ontario, for the Vulcan area, a new book appeared that praised the creative achievements of the county's settlers. The migrants now had the chance to duplicate such feats for themselves.[46]

The new physical environment also affected their thinking. The treeless grasslands of the Vulcan area rolled under a vast sky with striking visual effect, and the pioneers responded with more than mistaken notions about the climate, weather, and soil. As one settler observed of his fellows, 'there were vague premonitions, difficult to interpret ... no telling what could happen, they were so far from the world, cut off from the haunts of their fellow beings, and yet it seemed so spacious and beautiful to stand on the prairie and look around, especially when the shades of evening were falling.'[47] Long after they had understood that this environment had deceived them, its curious beauty and the raw sensations it evoked still found expression in pioneer poems and memoirs.

But the landscape stimulated more than an aesthetic response. It inspired the idea of large mechanized farms: no bush to clear, no stumps to pull, no rocks to pick, no hills, boulders, streams, or ponds to negotiate. This contrast in agricultural landscapes came to symbolize more general differences between east and west. The geographical interruptions that often delineated the small farms of the east suggested a place cramped not only physically, but socially. Crowded with too many people, its opportunities might be limited; cramped by too much tradition, new ideas might die. The new landscape did not suggest restraint or moderation but boldness and aggression, a place where one's vision need not be restricted either literally or figuratively. 'The Vulcan District sure looked good to our family,' recalled one woman, 'with its large wheat fields and close-up views.' The image of the east as small, cramped, and crowded became a popular motif in pioneer speech and writings, an image captured in the lines of one pioneer poem:

But the West seemed so large and the East so small
We couldn't stay there for good and for all.[48]

This conception of the prairie landscape seems to contradict much of what has been written about pioneer attitudes. It is well known that most pioneers also feared and disliked the wide open spaces, and abundant evidence demonstrates that they missed the forests, orchards, and flower gardens of eastern farm communities. But the pioneers resolved this conflict rather neatly by responding to the new environment in two distinct ways. In designing their farmyards they tried to plant the trees and gardens and build the barns and farmhouses of home. This attempt to reproduce the east in miniature provided them with the emotional security that comes from familiar surroundings, but as for the vast stretches of open landscape beyond the farmyard, they intended to preserve it for the important business of launching a progressive, mechanized wheat empire.

Collectively, pioneer notions about the frontier and the prairie environment contributed almost instantly to a western identity. Pioneers soon spoke of 'life in the west,' and compared it favourably with that in the east. Settlers no sooner arrived from the east than easterners became a strange breed to them. During a debate about the hiring of an American schoolteacher, one woman remarked, 'I think there are already too many foreigners here from Ontario.' Or consider the comments of Vulcan's first doctor, W.W. Upton, about the newly arrived student minister: 'We had to civilize him when he hit town . . . he thinks he has a crude bunch. I always try to shock him for he does not savvy Western conditions.' Doc Upton himself had left Toronto only two years earlier.[49]

Shocking the newcomer became a popular sport. Because acquaintances back home sometimes doubted true stories about the booming economy, the vast distances, the size of farms, and the extremes of climate and weather (especially those caused by the Chinook), the pioneers soon exaggerated them all deliberately, confusing newcomers until they could distinguish fact from fiction only through experience. Vulcan-area pioneers recalled hundreds of tall tales and pranks in their memoirs; they invited newcomers on snipe hunts, sent them to borrow farm machinery that did not exist, or painted their horses like zebras – 'so many really funny stunts were always in swing,' remembered one woman. But these pranks were seldom intended maliciously, and the victims who survived with humour intact gained admission into the club of western pioneers and joined them in new escapades. Thus tall tales and practical jokes not only relieved boredom and helped pioneers to cope with difficulties; they also contributed to a sense of western identity.[50]

The challenge of pioneering in a prairie environment did not excite everyone. In many frontier novels women in particular abhor the drudgery and hardship and the isolation and loneliness of the frontier; despondent, frightened, and homesick, some even go insane. In reality disenchanted men soon left the frontier, but many women felt trapped by determined husbands. One Vulcan woman actually escaped back to England, but when her husband refused to follow, she reluctantly returned seven months later. 'Both my mother, Mrs. Beaubier, and Mrs. Long refused to unpack their trunks for years believing they might be unable to endure the hardships of homesteading,' recalled one daughter. The new environment particularly depressed some of them. 'Mother was just sick when she saw it,' remembers a daughter. 'When I put my foot on that railway depot at Carmangay,' testified another woman, 'I said boy . . . don't you take my trunk off there . . . I'm not staying in this dried up old place.' Still another recalled: 'Having lived in big cities, the wide open spaces with Ainslie's Texas Longhorns roaming around didn't appeal to me and the first night I heard the coyotes' chorus I was just about petrified and ready to return east.'[51] Thus a degree of sexual specialization characterized the forging of new communities; men often entrusted women with the faithful transplantation of eastern ways, while they concentrated more on the unique opportunities of the frontier and the prairie environment.

Surprisingly, the pioneer vision of those opportunities often complemented the desire to imitate the city and the east, and the faith in progressive ideals. Where but on a frontier could the best features of the city be nurtured and the worst pruned away? The frontier could acquire many of its modern conveniences but need not take its saloons and brothels or its grimy factories and slums as part of the bargain. Within a decade of settlement, heroic stories of how pioneering days had transformed the wilderness into 'smart little cities' echoed from the podiums of local gatherings and the pages of local newspapers.[52] Where better than on the frontier to transplant the best institutions of the old home community? Shorn of the rot of entrenched interests, nepotism, family status, and antiquated notions, they would surely take healthier root in virgin soil. And where but on a frontier could the Anglo-American ideals of democracy, freedom, and social mobility best be realized? The frontier represented a clean slate, where any and all things might be possible. Thus the pioneers replaced the nineteenth-century vision of the west as potential garden to be cultivated by happy yeomen and their families with one more suitable to the progressive era; the frontier now emerged as the most logical place to launch a modern civilization committed to scientific principles, business efficiency, and progress.

The pioneers entertained grand ideas about the kind of communities they wanted. Inspired by their home communities, the metropolis, the frontier, and the new environment itself, these complex notions sometimes explain pioneer behaviour, but just as often they clashed with the realities of experience. The remaining chapters will examine the relationship between those attitudes and reality in considerable detail, beginning with the most important pioneer idea about the frontier, the one that encouraged them more than any other to leave their homes and strike into the unknown: the desire for wealth.

2

Farms

Population growth in the Vulcan area followed a familiar western pattern (see Figure 3). From nothing it soared rapidly, then increased slowly, peaked, and finally declined. A traditional interpretation explains this curve: pioneers quickly settled all the land, but with the birth of children and the appearance of towns, the population still grew slowly. Soon, however, the settlers discovered that a quarter-section farm could not support a family; land shortages, farm mechanization, economic problems, and other familiar agents of rural depopulation forced many off the land while more efficient farmers expanded. But however accurately this scenario explains net changes in population, it obscures the process by which they occurred and suggests erroneous notions.

Surprisingly, the greatest number of people left the Vulcan area while the net population still climbed. Wanderers before they arrived, many settlers did not linger on the new frontier. 'We grow so fast and change so much it really is hard to keep track of anybody,' complained a newspaper stringer in charge of local gossip.[1] Figure 4 explains his frustration. It shows the number of heads of farm families in Township 17-25-4 at regular intervals and estimates the number still present five years later. Generally, fewer than half the farmers remained in the township for as long as five years before 1920; thereafter about three-quarters stayed for at least that long. Figure 4 reveals mobility over five-year periods, but a yearly count discovers those who resided in the township for even shorter periods; thus twenty-one more farmers entered and left the township between 1910 and 1920 than the graph indicates. If disappearances due to death are eliminated from the count, then even higher mobility rates emerge for the pioneering era; over twice as many heads of families died in the twenty years after 1920 than in the sixteen years before. Farm tenants moved more often than owners, particularly within the Vulcan area, but they were

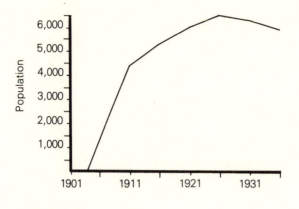

FIGURE 3
Population growth, Vulcan area

never numerous enough to affect the overall mobility rate substantially, for it declined after 1920, when tenancy began to rise.

Businessmen moved more readily still. Fewer than a quarter of the railway towns' founders remained in the area for five years, but as with farmers, subsequent arrivals stayed longer and in greater numbers; over half the businessman of 1925 remained in the area for at least five years (see Figure 4). Merchants probably moved more often than farmers because their smaller investments could be liquidated more easily. Although a large consistent sample is not available for analysis, non-property owners who flocked to the new townsites moved even more frequently than businessmen. Of 24 institutional managers listed in directories in 1914 (elevator agents, bank managers, clergymen, and the like), apparently only 3 remained in the Vulcan area by 1920; of 38 listed in 1922, only 8 remained in 1928.[2] Although virtually impossible to trace, labourers probably moved at a greater rate than any other group, decidedly so if the hordes of itinerant harvesters that entered and left the area each fall are included.

These findings agree with many studies that high mobility rates prevailed on rural frontiers and that they fell with maturity, particularly between 1920 and 1940.[3] Demographic changes partly explain this pattern. As chapter 1 demonstrated, the most mobile people in North America – young, healthy, single men – dominated early frontier populations, but as they married, acquired families, and sunk economic and social roots into communities, mobility rates naturally fell.

The transient frontiersman challenges the popular image of the prairie settler seeking a permanent new life. Such people existed, of course; Figure 5 reveals that some families remained in Township 17-25-4 for decades. Their

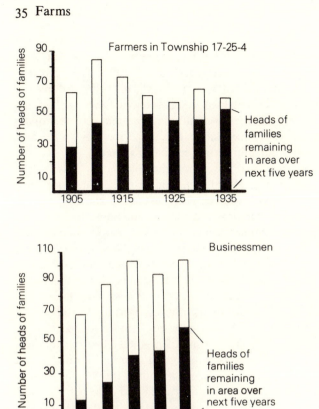

Farmers in Township 17-25-4

FIGURE 4
Geographic mobility of heads of families, Vulcan area

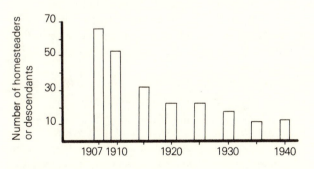

FIGURE 5
Successful homesteaders of 1907, or their descendants, still
present in Township 17-25-4 at various years

natural emergence as local historical authorities suggests a stability that never existed, for mobile families clearly outnumbered them.[4] Over half the pioneers who successfully proved up a homestead by 1907 fled the township within eight years, and by 1930 only a quarter remained – and even they considered leaving at one time or another.[5] As in other communities, original settlers rapidly became an endangered species. Homesteaders accounted for only 15 per cent of 441 Vulcan-area farmers studied in a 1938 economic survey.[6]

Most recent studies have measured geographic mobility more precisely than they have interpreted it. Technological and economic changes, population pressures, government policies, natural catastrophes, and social conflicts are frequently offered in explanation,[7] but why did some people move readily when similar people in the same circumstances did not? Many settlers soon abandoned the Vulcan area for no clear reasons that friends and neighbours, or even their own children, could discover, although some expressed vague concerns about their health.[8] Perhaps, as a Wallace Stegner novel suggests, they wandered in search of the *Big Rock Candy Mountain* (1938) because they lacked the patience and confidence to build one for themselves. When asked about his plans after leaving the Vulcan area in 1910, Frank Troxler replied that he would first visit his home town in Tennessee and then would either remain there permanently or return to Alberta unless he bought a farm in Florida.[9] But if unable to analyse their own restlessness, many assaulted the Vulcan frontier with a definite plan; they intended to turn a fast profit and clear out.

They arrived convinced that frontiers offered quick wealth; they spoke continually about 'grand opportunities,' 'great possibilities,' and about 'bettering one's condition.' 'Would I advise anyone to come here to live?' asked a settler in 1913. 'No, not the man of means, but the young man who has his fortune to make and is willing to work and keep his head – come . . . westerners are quick to act, take long chances and abide by the results . . . but the opportunities are great.'[10] After they arrived, money lost none of its initial importance, for in such a fluid new society, other means of acquiring social status appeared limited. Without embarrassment or apology, the local press wallowed in the details of the settlers' financial affairs.

The passion for making money embraced all kinds of schemes. Although one study claims that few prairie farmers invested in non-farm activities,[11] many residents of the prosperous Vulcan area plunged into the stock-market. Farmers even bought stock in the CPR and other giant corporations they reputedly despised, but they preferred speculative issues, and the Turner Valley oil strike of 1914 ignited a buying spree. 'Business is very quiet all over the District and money is scarce,' reported the Mounted Police, 'but it is astonishing how much money has been put into oil shares one way and another.'

Following insignificant gas strikes in the Vulcan area, locally owned oil companies mushroomed: 'The oil craze has got hold of some of the good people in the Loma district,' reported the Vulcan *Advocate* on 1 July 1914, 'many of them having either invested or going to invest in the near future.' Most failed miserably, but Vulcan Oils Ltd, launched by local merchants and farmers, drilled at Turner Valley and actually developed into a profitable company.[12]

Traditional forms of gambling also enjoyed wide popularity. The pioneers wagered on many sporting events, especially semi-professional baseball, which soon flourished throughout southern Alberta. In scathing editorials the local press blamed the 'gambling element' for the bribing of umpires and players, and the fistfights that occasionally marred the sport. The settlers also spent plenty of time at the poker table, for even the smallest hamlets of the Vulcan area boasted gambling establishments in back of livery stables and Chinese cafés. Local governments waged a long and losing battle against them; in 1935 the mayor of Vulcan still complained that they had 'troubled the council for many years.'[13]

Although gambling eased isolation and loneliness on bachelor–dominated frontiers, settlers in the Vulcan area wagered sums that transcended mere entertainment. When armed bandits raided the regular poker game above the City Café in the hamlet of Brant, they ran off with eight hundred dollars. Sometimes entire crops or even quarter-sections of land depended on the turn of a card or the outcome of a ball game.[14] Ironically, at the very time that Vulcan farmers heartily supported the wheat-pool ideal of eliminating evil speculators from the grain business, they were eagerly gambling themselves – on wheat futures, oil stocks, baseball, and poker. They did not oppose gambling so much as large competitors; mostly they only opposed losing.

Yet when pioneers spoke of the golden opportunities of the frontier, they referred to none of those activities, nor even to the profitable raising of crops, but to an enterprise that dwarfed them all: land speculation. More than any other money-making scheme it lured them to the Vulcan frontier, and later lured many away. When the economic fog that enveloped agriculture in the late nineteenth century finally lifted, rural land values in Ontario, the midwest, and the Inland Empire sky-rocketed. Many investors suddenly considered rural land a safe, stable investment. One Vulcan settler explained in the Nanton *News*, 13 February 1908, how the change affected young farmers in his native Washington: 'Land has reached such a price in that country [Washington State] that . . . as an investment the percentage of return is small, though safe and sure. The result is that the land is gradually being acquired by men of ample means wishing to retire from active life, and looking for a safe investment, even at low interest, while men of moderate wealth looking for wider opportunities are coming to new countries, like this one, where land is cheap and opportunities for development still appear unlimited.' With land fetching $65 to $150 an acre in the midwest between 1900 and 1914, a farmer could sell out, retire his debts, and still have enough capital to develop a larger farm on the frontier. Vulcan settlers reasoned that the new land would soon soar in value to continental levels, which explains their belief that frontiers offered 'opportunities for the energetic man not to be found in older settled countries.'[15]

Some studies argue that established farmers responded to this opportunity for social reasons: they wanted to keep their families on the land. But since they could not afford to establish their maturing sons in agriculture in their home communities, they migrated to the frontier, where inexpensive land permitted all of them to acquire farms.[16] While this consideration undoubtedly motivated some, the promise of huge capital gains lured many more, for Vulcan-area homesteads also attracted seal hunters, sailors, soldiers, policemen, tailors, shoemakers, and many others with tenuous psychological attachments to the land and farming. The conviction that land prices would rise substantially even swayed an occupational group professedly uninterested in material gain: clergymen. 'You did not come here to stay,' admitted one of them, 'you came to get rich.' At least six ministers dispatched to the Vulcan frontier abandoned the cloth for the plough. Rev. J.J. Kidder acquired four and a half sections and fled to Iowa triumphantly. Of 254 Vulcan farm pioneers whose occupational histories can be traced, slightly over half had not worked primarily in agriculture before, although most of them had grown up on farms or had some farming experience. Perhaps they now seized the opportunity to fulfil some dream of owning a farm, but as one homesteader's daughter recalled, 'Dad didn't care much more for farming than anything else.' Few pioneers in the Vulcan area developed an emotional attachment to their land. 'Only real dedicated farmers stayed,' recalled one man.[17] Most came intending to sell out later, and did so.

'Property continues to change hands like hot cakes,' cried the press in 1906, only two years after settlement began, and the chant still echoed in 1918: 'Land is changing hands around here in pretty lively fashion.'[18] Figure 6 charts land transactions in one Vulcan township, and if the initial acquisitions of raw land by original pioneers are eliminated, along with all subsequent transfers of land to direct descendants, including those resulting from death, then land speculation, like mobility, especially characterizes the 1906–20 period.

Most studies agree that dominion land policy efficiently populated the west and rapidly brought it under cultivation, but many argue that it failed in human terms, for free homesteads encouraged many without the resources or

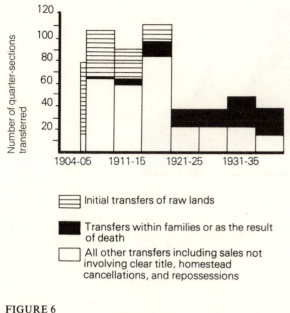

Initial transfers of raw lands

Transfers within families or as the result of death

All other transfers including sales not involving clear title, homestead cancellations, and repossessions

FIGURE 6
Changes in land ownership in Township 17-25-4 by five-year periods

ability to succeed. Furthermore, the quarter-section homestead proved too small for a viable farm, and although adjacent railway lands permitted some expansion without displacing other farmers, the need for even larger farms eventually forced many off the land.[19] But the displaced settlers can hardly be considered tragic victims. Intending to sell out anyway, most Vulcan pioneers did so for a handsome profit. Because they settled in a productive area that yielded good crops during a period of favourable weather conditions and grain prices, and because they improved their property and acquired such public facilities as roads, towns, schools, and a railway, the value of land rose substantially in the Vulcan area until the end of the First World War (see Figure 7). Figure 8, which traces the average values of farms rather than acres, charts a more dramatic rise, largely because farms increased in size and hence in value but also because it includes the value of implements, buildings, and livestock. Thus any landowner selling before 1920 might realize a capital gain of $1,000 to $10,000 per quarter-section. Robert and Sarah Robbie agreed between themselves to return to Ontario once their net worth topped $5,000, but their holdings jumped so rapidly in value that they revised the figure to $10,000,

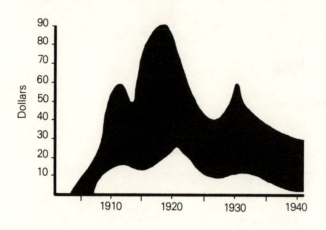

FIGURE 7
General range of land prices per acre, Vulcan area

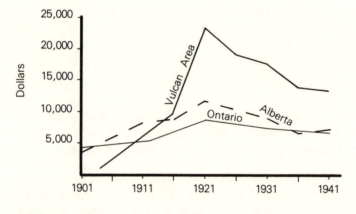

FIGURE 8
Average value* of farms

*Includes land, buildings, implements, livestock

then $25,000. Even small landowners who sold early left with a good stake. Cyrus Robinson arrived in 1907, proved up a homestead, sold out in 1910 for $3,000, and returned to Maine.[20]

Certainly the displaced settlers did not consider themselves victims of an inhuman settlement policy. 'Mr. Hall said he felt great regret in leaving

Alberta,' reported a newspaper stringer of a pioneer who sold out in 1910, 'for since coming here he had prospered as never before.' Another claimed that he 'made more money in Southern Alberta land in four years than in the clothing business in a good Iowa town in thirty years.' Many former residents confessed that they had failed to prosper as much after settling elsewhere: 'I sort of get a sick lost feeling when I look back on the time I left there,' lamented one man.[21] The real victims were those efficient, expanding farmers who failed to sell out before 1920 when the falling grain prices and environmental difficulties that foreshadowed the catastrophe of the 1930s sparked a long-term fall in land values. If not completely crushed by subsequent events, those Vulcan farmers who bought land during the First World War waited twenty-five years or more before their land returned to the prices they had paid for it.

Changing land values explain much about mobility rates. Population movements generally, and to frontiers especially, accelerate in times of prosperity. The massive influx of settlers into western Canada between 1896 and 1914 occurred during agriculture's 'Golden Age.' Because property values rose in a vigorous market, many could achieve their goal of moving in, acquiring land, selling out, and leaving. Conversely, property values usually tumble following a general decline in farm prosperity, and land speculation subsides. Mobility rates also slacken, even though a community might experience a net drop in population for the first time.[22] The explanation is simple. People most often move in expectation of economic advancement, and fewer opportunities appeared between the world wars. Unable to sell their property for what they paid for it, most farmers hesitated to suffer a loss, and many willing to leave could no longer afford it at all. Thus James and Margaret Minty cancelled their return to Scotland when a hailstorm levelled their bumper crop, and in the midst of the great depression N. Flebotte unsuccessfully appealed to his municipal district for financial assistance to move back to Massachusetts.[23]

How did so many manage to speculate on a frontier where government policy professed to discourage speculation? Although western Canadian land studies have recognized large-scale speculation by great railway, land, and colonization companies, they have not investigated the small speculator in much detail. Other studies, however, offer ample evidence that small speculators have always been active on the American frontier and as successful as large ones in circumventing American land policy.[24] Many settlers, Canadians and Americans alike, learned these techniques in the United States, brought them to the Vulcan frontier, practised them, and taught them to others.

Although one student has justifiably questioned the prevalence of the 'typical prairie township,' which so many studies offer as a description of dominion lands policy,[25] settlers arriving in the Vulcan area in 1904 encountered it in its classical, unblemished form (see Map 5). Surveyors had carved the land into square townships, divided them into thirty-six numbered sections, and subdivided them into quarter-sections of 160 acres. Road allowances ran every mile north and south and every two miles east and west. Each township embodied the various elements of dominion land policy. To satisfy the Hudson's Bay Company's claim to one-twentieth of all prairie lands when Canada acquired the west in 1870, the company retained section 8 and three-quarters of 26 in most townships, all of 26 in every fifth township. The government reserved the remaining even-numbered sections for homesteads, to be given away in quarter-section parcels to settlers willing to meet certain conditions. From the odd-numbered sections the government designated numbers 11 and 29 as school lands. It did not reserve them as sites for schools but intended to sell them and finance prairie education with the interest earned from investing the proceeds. The government granted the remaining odd-numbered sections to companies willing to build railways through the empty west; presumably their value would climb quickly once settlers swarmed to the homesteads that surrounded most railway sections, and their subsequent sale would offset the cost of constructing the lines.

Given the choice between buying frontier land or obtaining it free, settlers naturally took advantage of the homestead system first. In one local improvement district in the Vulcan area, homesteads disappeared by 1905, while sellers had disposed of only half their lands by 1909. Pre-empted and purchased homesteads, which the government had scrapped in 1890 and revived for certain areas after 1908, accounted for few land acquisitions. Pre-emptions applied only to eastern portions of the Vulcan area, and by 1908 few even-numbered sections remained unclaimed anyway. After its implementation in 1872, the homestead system underwent many minor changes designed to encourage settlement and discourage speculation. When pioneers arrived in the Vulcan area, the main obstacles to speculation included six months' residence on the homestead in each of three consecutive years, the construction of a house, and the cultivation of a certain acreage each year, depending on the quality of the land.

Almost every study agrees that the homestead system offered pioneers too little land, for the arid plains promised only light crops and demanded the practice of summerfallowing. Yet surprisingly, the average homesteader in Township 17-25-4 broke less than half his land throughout the three-year proving-up period. The need for pasture does not explain this apparent lethargy, since pioneers typically grazed work-horses on unoccupied odd-numbered sections during the homesteading years. A high proportion of waste land does not explain it, for by 1921 farmers were cultivating 82 per cent of the land

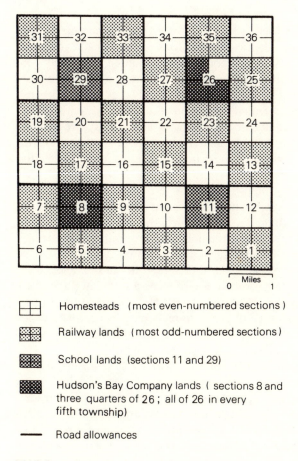

31	32	33	34	35	36
30	29	28	27	26	25
19	20	21	22	23	24
18	17	16	15	14	13
7	8	9	10	11	12
6	5	4	3	2	1

Miles
0   1

  Homesteads (most even-numbered sections)

Railway lands (most odd-numbered sections)

School lands (sections 11 and 29)

Hudson's Bay Company lands (sections 8 and
three quarters of 26 ; all of 26 in every
fifth township)

—— Road allowances

MAP 5
A typical township

in that district.[26] A Nebraska study argues that most homesteaders simply did
not command the financial, technological, and labour resources to farm even a
quarter-section,[27] but in the Vulcan area speculation undoubtedly accounted
for most of the unbroken land. Although not designed to do so, the homestead
system , like the railway land-grant system, appealed to many with little interest in agriculture.

Consider first those pioneers who failed to prove up their homesteads.
Numerous studies have discovered a high fatality rate among homesteaders; in
Nebraska, Kansas, and Minnesota two failed for every one that succeeded. In

four townships in the Vulcan area, 41 per cent of all homestead entries were cancelled, a failure rate almost identical to that for western Canada generally. Thus, while the three-year residency requirement promised to inhibit geographical mobility on the frontier, the homestead system as a whole probably encouraged it; by offering free land, it lured many who would fail and leave.[28] Historians have traditionally treated failed homesteaders sympathetically, often portraying them as casualties of government and railway propaganda seduced into attempting something beyond their capabilities. Such victims surely existed; the popular belief that most failed homesteaders fell into that category is at least questionable.

It has proved difficult to distinguish the characteristics of successful homesteaders from those of unsuccessful ones. Studies have found little correlation between birthplace, ethnic origin, age, family size, the quality of land, or its distance from railways and towns, and the ability to prove up a homestead.[29] But one critical quality cannot be quantified: determination. Many abandoned their homesteads not because of particular difficulties but out of choice, often for purely personal reasons. 'My brother Elmer came a little later and got a homestead,' recalled one pioneer. 'He didn't like the life or the country. I had a time to get him to stay long enough to prove up on it.' Another settler recalled a man who gave up his homestead because 'it was too far to walk into town and drink beer all afternoon and make it home again that night.'[30]

Many abandoned their homesteads because other pursuits absorbed their time and efforts. The creation of a new agricultural society required many skills besides farming. Excellent opportunities for merchants, skilled tradesmen, and labourers quickly appeared in the Vulcan area. Such men often applied for a homestead as well, for if it did not prove too troublesome or costly to earn title, it might be sold for a nice profit. If given up later, or cancelled by the homestead inspector, the loss would be small. They thought only of a capital gain; busy elsewhere, they did not expect to earn any income off the land.

Arguments have arisen about the cost of proving up a homestead. Some believe that pioneers needed only a few hundred dollars; others have suggested $975 to $1,425 as a minimum requirement. But the debate assumes that pioneers wanted to build a viable farm and that they complied with both the letter and the spirit of the regulations.[31] Those unwilling to invest the necessary money and effort resorted to cheating. Most often they simply lied about the number and quality of improvements on their homesteads. Nearly everyone lied about his residency, for even legitimate settlers often found it necessary to leave for more than six months a year in order to earn enough to establish working farms. Neighbours commonly swapped testimonials confirming each others' statements when applying for homestead patents.[32]

Still, the problem of unexpected visits from homestead inspectors remained. To circumvent residency and house-building obligations, pioneers in the Vulcan area did not construct portable houses, as many did in the United States and some parts of western Canada, but they perpetrated other elaborate frauds. Four brothers who all filed for homesteads on the same section built a single house in the middle with the corners resting on each quarter-section. Three of them returned to Ontario while the fourth created the impression that they all lived there. Another man with no intention of living on his homestead only constructed the three walls of a shack visible from the road. Those who lived and worked in towns regularly hauled ashes and garbage out to their homestead shacks to maintain a lived-in appearance.[33]

Speculators refused to invest much in farmhouses, not only because they would live in them only briefly, if at all, but because buildings often added little to the value of the property. An expanding farmer willing to buy out the speculator would already have a house of his own and would hesitate to pay extra for land because of improvements he neither needed nor wanted. This consideration sometimes explains the poor housing conditions often described in frontier travellers' accounts.

If the speculator grew weary of the homestead process (or the struggle to avoid it) before the end of the proving-up period, he might realize a profit anyway. Technically, he could not sell the homestead until he secured title, but he could sell it in effect by agreeing to abandon it officially in return for a sum paid by a prospective homesteader who wished to settle in a developed neighbourhood. Successful transactions required good timing – and subtlety. When Frank Nelson abandoned his homestead 'on account of other business,' he urged the land office to give the new entry to one Dudley Ellis, but it foiled his plan by awarding it to someone else.[34]

Conversely, the speculator who successfully evaded the homestead regulations and acquired title often found himself in possession of such a poorly developed farm that its value scarcely exceeded that of raw land. Instead of selling it, he could sometimes profit more by borrowing as much as possible on the land and absconding with the loans, leaving the creditors fighting over the homestead. Since financial agents combed the Vulcan frontier, and western Canada generally, begging farmers to take out mortgages, sums exceeding a farm's market value could sometimes be raised.[35]

For speculators engaged in other occupations but willing to make all the improvements specified in the homestead regulations, the work could be let out to contractors. Nearly all homesteaders relied on contractors to some extent. Although it is widely known that most pioneers escaped the enormous costs of harvest machinery by employing custom threshers, in the Vulcan area they also commonly hired steam-tractor contractors with heavy ploughs to break sod. Plenty of contractors also specialized in seeding, cultivating, haying, well-drilling, grist milling, grain hauling, fencing, or farm-building construction, and most of them accepted crop shares in payment, avoiding the need for cash. Even the CPR functioned as a contractor, for it built and sold a complete range of farm buildings: houses, barns, poultry houses, piggeries, and fences – it even offered a five- by four-foot prefabricated outhouses for thirty dollars. Settlers could also avoid wandering the prairie in search of a homestead. For five dollars a 'locator' promised to select a quality homestead on a good site and organize the paperwork. Indeed, a pioneer could prove up a homestead without doing any work himself. The idea so intrigued E.E. Thompson, one of the Vulcan area's most prominent merchant-farmers and land speculators, that he considered forming a company that would make all the necessary homestead improvements. Settlers would pay for the service entirely out of the crop, and would realize their profits on capital gains.[36]

Many speculators, of course, spent their time, finances, and skills not only to meet the homestead requirements but to exceed them. Many purchased additional land and developed fully improved farms to sell as complete units. J.H. Rosenberger, for example, arrived in the Carmangay district in 1905, selected a quarter-section homestead, and promptly bought five railway quarters at $5 an acre. Five years later he received title to the homestead and sold the entire farm for $33,640, or $35 an acre. Although pioneers could apply for title to their homesteads after three years, most, like Rosenberger, waited the permissible five years (or at least until they found a buyer) in order to escape property taxes. Of the sixty-seven homesteaders who successfully proved up homesteads in Township 17-25-4, twenty-one sold out within a year of obtaining title, but those who held on to their farms until the war boom reaped the greatest rewards. David Rice, for example, filed a homestead claim, then worked hard as a custom breaker and thresherman to earn enough for improvements and expansion. When he sold his farm in 1917, he netted $33,000.[37]

Such men might be considered professional pioneers, especially the older bachelors who had repeated the process of developing frontier farms many times. The McIntyre brothers, for example, left Scotland in 1852 to pioneer the backwoods of Grey County, Ontario. Some of them subsequently pioneered in the Dakota Territory, Oregon, and Oklahoma, before arriving in Vulcan in 1905. Another Vulcan settler had previously pioneered in Minnesota, Idaho, and Alberta. Another had homesteaded in every western province. Professional pioneers could often be identified by the advertisements they placed in newspapers. 'Wanted – well located raw land in exchange for a well improved and clean three-quarter section nicely located.' For them Vulcan simply represented another stop in a lifelong succession of frontier communities. And if they failed to get their price, they sometimes moved on anyway, renting the farm until the right offer appeared.[38]

Because the homestead system burdened the settler with obligations and allotted him only one quarter-section, or two in the rare case of pre-emption, those with money, or the ability to raise it, preferred to speculate in Hudson's Bay Company, school, or railway lands. But because those agencies asked a price for land at a time when it remained unmarketable, few purchasers came knocking until after free homesteads disappeared. Thus, settlers claimed all the homesteads in one Vulcan local-improvement district by 1905, but purchasers did not acquire over 90 per cent of the remaining land until 1914.

Of the three sellers, two asked exceptionally high prices. Unlike the CPR, which expected the sale and subsequent development of its lands to generate freight traffic, the Hudson's Bay Company could not hope to gain anything more once it sold its lands, so it waited until their value rose substantially. Between 1906 and 1927 the sale of Company land in western Canada averaged $12.10 an acre, compared to $8.55 for CPR lands.[39] The dominion government adopted a similar policy for school lands. Committed to raising as much as possible for education, it deliberately kept them off the market until surrounding sections filled up. In Local Improvement District 9-T-4 the CPR disposed of nearly three-quarters of its land before the first school lands appeared on the market in 1912. To boost returns further, the government sold them by auction. Buyers attempted to thwart this policy. As the Carmangay *Sun* noted on 14 July 1916, following the auction of 140 quarter-sections, 'bidding was stifled by an understanding among the farmers as to who wanted each piece and how much he was likely to bid for it.' Generally, however, school lands remained the last sold and most expensive raw lands in the west.

But the number of school and Hudson's Bay Company lands for sale shrank to insignificance compared to the vast quantity of railway sections. The Vulcan area constituted a small portion of the huge land grant awarded to the Calgary and Edmonton Railway in 1890. Compensation for ranchers who already held leases on those lands, the famous 'fairly fit for settlement' agreement, the withholding of some lands in exchange for loans, and the close association of the company with the CPR, all complicated the grant enormously. By the time land buyers arrived in the Vulcan district, however, the CPR effectively controlled all railway land sales in the area.[40]

Historians have accepted the CPR's claim that it sold land cheaply and quickly in order to increase freight traffic, and the discrepancy between the price of CPR land and Hudson's Bay Company land seems to support the argument. Yet perhaps the case has been overstated. The fact that the CPR had only sold one-third of its lands in Local Improvement District 9-T-4 five years after settlers had claimed all the homesteads suggests that the asking price often exceeded the market value. Even when sales picked up after 1910, Arthur Mitchell and Company, agent for the CPR in the Vulcan area, frequently urged the land department to lower prices. It usually refused, but sometimes complied reluctantly after much coaxing. While Mitchell and Company naturally sought quick sales to generate commissions, their complaint had validity, for some properties did not sell until the CPR cut prices.[41]

Although presumably interested in populating the land and bringing it into production, the company introduced few measures to prevent speculations before 1912. It even advertised its willingness to sell to absentee speculators, although it charged them higher interest rates than it did intending settlers, and demanded payment within five years instead of the usual ten if they bought more than one section. By 1913 the CPR decided to end sales to speculators, and it invited more purchases from settlers by spreading land payments over twenty years.[42] But the company discovered that it could distinguish real settlers from speculators no better than could the homestead administrators, and like them it merely complicated the problem without eliminating it.

A surprisingly high number of small speculators acquired CPR lands. Of sixty-six buyers in the Vulcan area whose transactions can be traced, over half bought no more than one quarter-section; over 80 per cent bought two or less, a finding that closely parallels another local land study. For the small speculator, buying a CPR quarter often required less cash than accepting a free homestead. With a down payment of two hundred to three hundred dollars, an amount less than that required to meet the homestead requirements, they could resell the land for a profit before the next annual payment fell due. Buyers resold one-fifth of the CPR quarter-sections in Township 17-24-4 within a year of acquiring them; in all they resold about half of the quarters before they had paid for them in full. Hoping for quick appreciation, some placed down payments on several quarters, but those who spread their capital thin risked losing the land altogether. Thus the CPR suffered the equivalent of the homestead cancellation. Between 1885 and 1930 it repossessed 22 per cent of its total land grant in western Canada, representing one-third of the value of all sales.[43]

Attempts to defraud the company, or subsequent buyers, seem as common as those to defraud the homestead system. In the Vulcan area speculators sometimes resold the land at inflated prices to those who failed to check the equity carefully. By the time the CPR began investigating late payments, the original buyer had disappeared, and the company, whose own sloppy records often complicated matters, became embroiled in angry correspondence with subsequent buyers, tenants, financial institutions, lawyers, and local tax collectors.[44]

For the wealthy investor the great advantage of CPR lands over the homestead system lay in the opportunity to acquire a huge parcel of land. Although only ten in a sample of sixty-six buyers in the Vulcan district bought a section or more, their purchases represented over 40 per cent of the acreage involved. A single acquisition could dominate an entire district. C.W. Carman, for example, bought 23 sections, almost 15,000 acres, at $3.50 an acre in the district that would bear his name. He improved much of the land and sold it off in small parcels. Lister Synder recalled that his father bought three Carman sections in 1908 at $26 an acre, which yielded Carman a gross return of over 600 per cent in three years.[45]

Escaping the homestead obligations provided another incentive for choosing CPR land. The purchaser could leave it raw, hire a breaking contractor, improve and farm it himself, or rent it to others. Indeed, if he bought through C.S. Noble and T.C. Milnes, who also sold land on behalf of the CPR, he need not trouble himself with the petty details. For a fee they would also break the land and then rent or sell it on behalf of the speculator. Absentee speculators appreciated the convenience of this all-inclusive service; at one point before 1909 Noble and Milnes employed sixty-five breaking outfits on railway lands stretching from Vulcan to Monarch. Dealing directly with the CPR, one could also buy land in various states of improvement. Besides selling partially improved repossessed properties, it built and marketed nineteen 'ready-made' farms in the Vulcan area, complete with full sets of farm buildings and fencing, as well as several sections on which it constructed only houses.[46]

Many speculators bought railway lands to free themselves from the most irksome homestead regulation of all: residency. No sharp distinction between local and absentee ownership can be drawn, however, for many Vulcan residents abandoned the area each winter. Of fifty-six homesteaders in Township 17-25-4 whose movements can be traced, only ten never moved off their homesteads in winter during the proving-up period. The bachelors all left, many to search for a bride. Many stayed away longer than the permissible six months to take advantage of temporary employment opportunities, but even after Vulcan farmers had married, established their farms, and no longer required supplementary incomes, many still evacuated the area in winter. Some moved only to the nearest town or city, others to their old home towns, some to the southwestern United States. Some even maintained permanent winter homes. One settler fled annually to Portland, Oregon, and another returned to Eng-

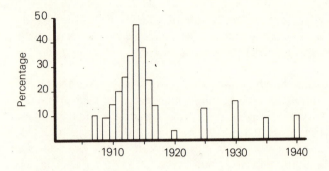

FIGURE 9
Percentage of land owned by non-residents* in four Vulcan-area
townships in various years

*The CPR, Hudson's Bay Company, and dominion government
owned all the land prior to settlement and much of it up to 1911,
but they are not considered non-residents here.

land nearly every winter for forty years. Many ultimately retired to these
retreats. Even a poor crop year like 1910 failed to halt the winter evacuation;
the *Sun* reported the sale of over fifty railway tickets at the Carmangay station
on a single day before Christmas. During the prosperous First World War
years so many farmers wintered outside the area, especially in California, that
municipal councils and school-boards often failed to establish quorums at their
meetings.[47]

None the less, railway lands permitted many to participate in frontier land
speculation without bothering to move there at all. Figure 9 demonstrates that
absentee landlords steadily increased their holdings in four Vulcan townships
until 1914, when they owned 47 per cent of the land. Two types of absentee
owners appeared. Almost weekly the local press announced the arrival of
touring investors in search of land: 'a Chicago capitalist [arrived last week]
looking for a location to speculate, and seemed favourably impressed with
town and surrounding country,' ran a typical story. Such men commonly
acquired huge tracts and resold them quickly. Stone and Wilmer of Rosalia,
Washington, for example, bought nineteen railway sections in 1905 and sold
them to O.W. Kerr and Company of Minneapolis two years later for a
reported profit of sixty thousand dollars. Kerr and Company immediately
launched excursions to bring in prospective settlers, a tactic also used by much
small speculators.[48]

But like resident speculators, most absentee landlords grabbed less than one section. Although the addresses of absentee owners in four Vulcan townships stretched across twenty-three states and seven provinces, most lived in those districts of the Inland Empire, the American midwest, and southern Ontario that had supplied Vulcan with its settlers. Usually friends or relatives of the departed adventurers, they bought railway land on their advice, often during a social visit to the area. Absentee speculators also bought homesteads from pioneers who had acquired title, and a homesteader might prefer to find an absentee buyer who would not be acquainted with the property's shortcomings. Many Vulcan settlers returned home in winter specifically to sell their farms or those of their neighbours. When S.Y. Evans visited his home town of Albany, Oregon, in 1909, he provided the local newspaper with a glowing account of the Vulcan frontier and added: 'If you want to know how you can own one of these sections, clear of expense in from one to three years . . . come and have a talk with me at the Willamette Valley Land Company as they have been kind enough to let me use their office for the next week.'[49] Since most absentee speculators hoped for quick resale, and since many active farmers embarked on vigorous expansion programs during the First World War, the percentage of land owned outside the Vulcan area soon fell dramatically (see Figure 9), and after 1920 the remainder consisted increasingly of retired farmers and widows who had moved away and rented their farms to sons or neighbours.

The same circumstances that attracted many settlers to the Vulcan area often accounted for their sudden departure. The value of Vulcan land had jumped quickly and substantially, sometimes to the point where the income from farming represented an insignificant return on capital. Encouraged by their experience, many young pioneers emulated the older professionals by moving to another frontier where they could repeat the process, but after 1910 only the most northerly or the most arid stretches of the Great Plains remained open. Many poured into the drylands of southeastern Alberta. Others headed south. A myth has persisted that the agricultural frontier disappeared in the United States before the twentieth century, but farmers broke fifteen million acres of new land in western Kansas, Nebraska, and the Dakotas in the decade after 1909, and millions more on the high plains of Montana, Wyoming, and Colorado. 'The exodus to Montana continues,' cried the Nanton *News* on 24 March 1910, while the Vulcan area's net population still soared. 'Settlers are being drawn to Montana,' reported the Mounted Police; 'they are selling out here and are getting good prices for their land.'[50]

Because of the aridity of the new frontiers, many failed to reap the windfall from rising land prices a second time. Often they simply moved once more. Of 126 men who abandoned farms in the arid community east of the Vulcan area,

72 per cent tried farming elsewhere within three years. One man who left the Vulcan area failed to establish a successful farm elsewhere in three attempts between 1910 and 1943. When the agricultural problems of the 1920s deteriorated into the disaster of the 1930s, the land game collapsed altogether. Discouraged, but not completely broken, many flocked to the ultimate symbol of western opportunity, California. 'Vulcan now has quite a colony down in California,' reported the *Advocate* as early as 7 November 1923, and by the 1930s so many former Carmangay residents lived there that reunions at Long Beach often attracted over seventy-five people.[51]

The game of musical farms, as played by Vulcan-area pioneers, suggests a number of revisions to traditional notions about prairie settlement. Our image of rural communities as sleepy, stable places seems mistaken. Their development depended on restless people constantly on the move; a number of them in succession might be responsible for transforming a stretch of raw prairie into a substantial farm. In addition, their rate of mobility ebbed and flowed with changing land values. The nature of that relationship should also challenge our concept of success and failure on the prairie frontier. The departure of a settler after a brief sojourn in the area did not always indicate failure. Financial catastrophe could strike the unpatented homesteader, the expanding farmer, or the huge land baron alike, but financial gain also accrued to members of all those groups. Speculation gripped them powerfully, and success depended far less on the scale or duration of their activities than on their timing.

3

Towns

Dabbling in farms represented only one aspect of land speculation, and not always the most important one. If the profits that pioneers harvested in the Vulcan area and subsequently attempted to harvest elsewhere do not seem sufficient wholly to explain their restless behaviour or the extent of speculation, it must be emphasized that some hoped to resell their land for far more than its agricultural worth warranted. With careful selection, crafty scheming, hard promotion, and lots of luck, farmland could be sold as urban real estate.[1]

Pioneers arrived in the Vulcan area conscious of how rapid frontier settlement had given rise to such metropolitan centres as Chicago, Minneapolis, Kansas City, and Winnipeg. They read about the fantastic rise of real estate prices when small towns like Calgary, Edmonton, Saskatoon, and Regina exploded into cities of tens of thousands within a decade. But they also knew that the sudden growth of even smaller places rewarded the speculator handsomely. Most of the home towns of the midwesterners had developed that way, and some settlers from the Inland Empire had themselves profited from the emergence of such frontier agricultural centres as Yakima, Walla Walla, and Spokane.[2] They sensed a great opportunity on the Vulcan frontier, for land acquired freely or cheaply would spiral in value if they could found a successful town.

A frontier with no pretence of self-sufficiency, the Vulcan area needed towns and railways to survive. When settlers arrived in 1904, the nearest towns nestled against the Calgary and Edmonton Railway, fifteen to forty miles to the west. High River, Nanton, and Claresholm shipped wheat, supplied goods and services for its production, and even provided the necessities of daily life. But the uncomfortable wagon trip over rough, muddy, or snow-drifted prairie involved time and money, and usually necessitated an overnight stay in a hotel. Travellers to town soon began purchasing supplies for their neighbours as well as themselves.[3]

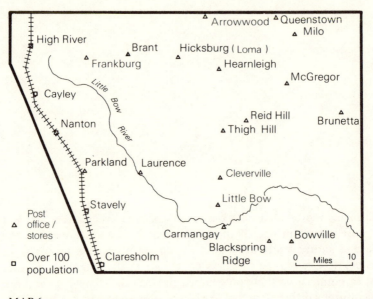

MAP 6
Central places, 1909

Appreciating the need for supply centres closer to home, some settlers opened general stores on their homesteads. Country hamlets sometimes evolved, offering specialized if limited services (see Map 6). E.E. Thompson, an experienced frontier land developer who began farming on a massive scale in the Vulcan area, surveyed a townsite in 1905 and built the Brant Store. He hired six men and added an implement agency, seed-grain business, and a warehouse. Thompson demonstrated that a country store could make money; he reportedly earned $150,000 in ten years.[4]

One pioneer described Brant as a 'hustling little burg,' and such hamlets aspired to greatness. 'Our future is before us,' thundered a man from the Thigh Hill settlement, 'watch our smoke.' To lure customers, country storekeepers applied for positions as postmasters, but real growth depended on attracting steel rails. Hamlet dwellers soon pestered railway companies with inquiries and petitions. 'The people of Brant are working like Trojans for a railway,' reported the press in 1907. The companies responded with premature announcements and surveys; in 1909 even Premier Rutherford confirmed that four lines would traverse the Vulcan area. New hamlets rose solely in anticipation of railways: 'It was rumoured that the Grand Trunk was to run through the Bowville district,' recalled one pioneer; 'consequently a village sprang up.'[5]

Few pioneers realized that most plans for frontier railways never materialized, or that railway companies did not intend to share townsite real-estate profits with anyone. But C.W. Carman of Chicago understood. Although scarcely a stream, the Little Bow River had cut a deep, wide ravine in the prairie skin. At one point it narrowed sharply. As a civil engineer, Carman reasoned that if a railway came to the area, that point provided the ideal location for a high-level bridge. His extensive land purchases from the CPR in 1904 surrounded the area. He quickly launched the bonanza Carmangay Farm Company and laid out the hamlet of Carmangay. Carman toyed with the idea of building an electric railway to Lethbridge but settled instead on a more modest plan. The Carmangay Transit Company used enormous steam tractors to haul wagon trains of freight between the hamlet and Claresholm on a regular basis.[6]

As Carman hoped, when the CPR decided to build the Kipp-Aldersyde line in 1909, the only railway that would ever serve the Vulcan area, it wished to cross the valley at his settlement. Carman agreed, however, to a new townsite one-half mile from the existing hamlet, where both parties could participate in the sale of lots by auction. Although they set a July date for the sale, by May merchants at the hamlet had already hoisted their buildings on skids and piled lumber near the new townsite. They discovered that outsiders planned to buy lots: businessmen from the Calgary and Edmonton Railway towns; national corporations, including grain companies and three banks; and speculators galore. One thousand buyers swarmed to the auction and paid $79,125 for 435 lots in less than three hours. Many bought six or more; scarcely a soul bought only one.[7]

Even though the CPR had sold much of its land in the Vulcan area and now had to buy it back for roadbeds and townsites, other speculators did not fare as well as Carman. At the new Champion townsite, one and one-half miles from the hamlet of Cleverville, the CPR attempted to buy farmland from Martin Clever through a third party, but when he guessed the real buyer and demanded a high price, the company simply bought from someone else. 'Although we knew where the townsite would be,' a pioneer recalled, 'we could not locate or build until lots were sold, with the result that everyone who expected to go into the different lines of business squatted near the Cleverville Post Office.' With fixed prices established for the town lots, everyone wanted to head the line on sale day, especially when rumours warned that Carmangay speculators planned to buy all the lots and resell them to the Cleverville merchants. The merchants commissioned two men to purchase property for everyone in the hamlet. 'To head off the speculators,' remembered one agent, 'my brother and I were delegated to hold down first place at the door of the office where lots were to be sold, which we did from Sunday night to Tuesday morning.' Even so, some lots resold at 100 per cent profit within an hour. Immediately after the sale, steam engines and draft horses lugged the entire hamlet of Cleverville on to the new townsite.[8]

Further north, speculators began buying farmland in anticipation of the next townsite, but the CPR sidestepped them and laid out Vulcan in an unexpected location. Speculators and merchants shivered in line the night before the town-lot sale, and the next morning 'business lots sold as fast as the purchasers could get their money down.' Even intending residents bought adjacent lots on speculation. Because speculators bought property that they knew certain businessmen wanted, lot swapping continued for a week, and the merchants soon clamoured for a new subdivision.[9]

Manoeuvring to outfox speculators, the CPR gave little thought to the practical spacing of towns. Ten miles separated some; only three and one-half separated others (see Map 7). The company ensured Kirkcaldy's stillbirth by planting it on Vulcan's doorstep and temporarily withholding its lots from sale. While the sale of the new Brant townsite, two miles from the old Brant settlement, triggered a three-day line-up, the close spacing of three new townsites split the merchants in several directions. Of 216 lots surveyed at new Brant, only 49 sold; at nearby Ensign, only 9 of 90. Blackie, the third townsite, lured most of the buyers. Farmers later argued before the Board of Railway Commissioners that building Ensign too close to Brant but too far from Vulcan had resulted in chaotic railway service. And the CPR's decision to connect the new line with the Calgary and Edmonton Railway at a company-owned site infuriated the town of High River. The CPR also selected poor locations. It planted both Champion and Vulcan in soft, low-lying areas, perhaps as a precaution against runaway boxcars, but the soft ground plagued road construction for decades, especially on Vulcan's elevator row. Both sites afforded poor water in short supply, occasionally forcing Champion to haul in its drinking water.[10]

In spite of these problems merchants abandoned their hamlets and swarmed to the new townsites because their businesses would not survive without rail service, and the CPR alone dictated its distribution. Although the townsites were small and situated on a mere branch line, the merchants anticipated a boom, for railway construction often initiated stampedes into new districts. Just as the flood of pioneers into the Vulcan area after 1904 ignited a boom in the Calgary and Edmonton Railway towns, so now did the Kipp-Aldersyde line promise to launch a new land rush to the partially unsettled east. Although incoming pioneers arrived with carloads of 'settlers' effects,' they still needed lumber, new machinery, and other supplies. In addition, the new line would spark many construction projects: a high-level bridge at Carmangay, the new

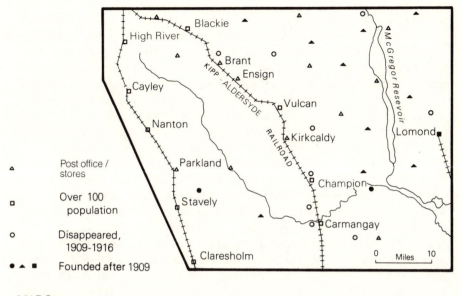

MAP 7
Central places, 1916

railbed itself, the giant grain elevators and other town buildings, and a huge reservoir fifteen miles east of the line that would irrigate lands far to the southeast. These immense undertakings all promised great rewards to those who could quickly supply the necessary goods and services. The CPR townsites typically featured two wide streets for commercial purposes: one parallel to the tracks for grain elevators, warehouses, and station, and another for retail businesses. Merchants competed with speculators for possession of these limited properties, especially the corner lots, and they scrambled to build their stores immediately because those first in business stood to reap the most profit. The Elves brothers' general store rested on skids near Vulcan, and after the townsite sale they hauled it on to their lot and immediately opened. 'They sure did quite a business,' recalled one settler, 'as it was the only store for miles around.'[11]

The townsites attracted many newcomers. James Lindsay arrived at the Vulcan town-lot sale armed with ten thousand dollars to start a hardware store, and A.B. Hogg fled a promising career at Arthur Meighen's Portage la Prairie law office to practise in Carmangay. Years later, he recalled the decision: 'At that time it was a big wheat growing area and showed real promise of becoming the wheat capital of the south. We all thought Carmangay was going to be another New York.' Just as many farmers speculated in town lots, the newly arrived townsmen often bought farmland or applied for homesteads, and they shared the same restless aspirations of the rural settler. They too hoped to 'make their harvest,' and clear out.[12] The false-front store suited the merchant perfectly; an imposing façade of stability masked his transient nature. And like the rural settlers, many merchants later fled to other frontiers – to wherever new railway construction promised to ignite a new town boom.

But merchants at the new townsites would not wait placidly for the boom to erupt; they intended to ignite it, and, if possible, sustain it. Anxious for any developments that might further raise rural land values, farmers eagerly joined them. 'The evident intention of the people of Carmangay is to found a Permanent, Large, and Prosperous City,' crowed the boosters. They predicted that Vulcan would advance 'with the strides of a young Chicago,' and that Champion would 'rank among the chief cities of the West.'[13]

Familiar with the organizational techniques of town promotion in the midwest and the Inland Empire, the merchants immediately established committees to run the campaign; the Carmangay Board of Trade actually convened before the sale of the townsite. Municipal incorporation became their first goal. At Carmangay residents voted for it unanimously, and at Vulcan 'almost unanimously.' Carmangay became a village in 1910 and pressed on to town status a year later. Vulcan attempted to bypass village status altogether but lacked the requisite population of four hundred. The province soon raised the requirements to seven hundred, forcing Vulcan to wait until 1921. Champion also settled reluctantly for village status, but old Brant had been so splintered by the arrival of steel that new Brant could not attain even that lowly title. Lacking the basic device of town promotion, it faded into obscurity.[14]

Town boosters tackled their work with robust enthusiasm, but limited manpower and financial impotency forced them to modify the promotional techniques used by cities. Town and village councils, for example, combined municipal functions with those normally performed by boards of trade. Like other urban places in the west, they lobbied corporations and governments for facilities and tempted them with free sites and tax incentives. Because the lure of large cash subsidies lay beyond their means, councils bargained coyly with developers. When a brick manufacturer asked Carmangay what inducements it offered, council asked him what kind of inducements he would like. Carmangay's victory over private ownership to establish a municipality owned electrical and waterworks system represented the only attempt to offer developers costly bait. As in many cities, council hoped to set 'rock bottom prices [that] ... will surely attract large manufacturing interests.'[15]

A serious but less expensive problem was that the towns were new and small and unknown, so advertising soon dominated booster activity, a preoccupation symbolized by one board-of-trade slogan 'You'll Hear From Champion.' Like many cities, the towns and rural municipalities published promotional literature, mailed it across the continent, and deposited it in hotels and train stations. Sometimes they distributed it more aggressively. Vulcan merchants once sent an automobile driver on a two-month round trip to Chicago to hand out brochures, give lectures, and answer questions. 'Vulcan was not a new name to any of them,' he triumphantly reported, with undoubtedly more enthusiasm than accuracy.[16]

Distributing literature proved costly enough, however, and towns often preferred advertising in city newspapers, particularly in special promotional editions intended for wide circulation. But local newspapers soon became the most common form of printed propaganda. From inception, advertisers moulded them into instruments of town promotion, inflicting terrible injury on journalistic ideals. Indeed, special editions scarcely resembled newspapers at all. It might be supposed that such efforts fizzled – that no one read the local press save local residents – but the absentee speculators who purchased farmland and later town lots in the area followed land prices by subscribing to local newspapers. The three main weeklies in the Vulcan area together printed about twelve thousand to fifteen thousand copies a week throughout the 1910s; perhaps hundreds reached readers beyond the area. Inquiries about investment opportunities reached local editors from readers in many parts of the continent.[17]

The boosters also relied on distant landowners to provide free advertising. They applauded the CPR for including Carmangay in its promotional literature and cheered the Toronto-based Western Canada Real Estate Company and the Equity Trust and Loan Company for advertising Carmangay, Champion, and Kirkcaldy real estate. Fraudulent claims often coloured these publications. Visiting Ontario in 1918, Harvey Beaubier of Champion found his cousins eager to buy Carmangay real estate after a salesman had supplied them with literature depicting the town's future streetcar system and other fictional wonders. The towns even hoped to achieve fame with the motion picture; in 1916 merchants convinced a crew to film a documentary about harvest operations in the Vulcan district.[18]

The boosters also expected individual efforts by residents to advertise the area. Large landowners like C.W. Carman, with business connections in Chicago and Grand Rapids, Michigan, could always be counted on to spread Carmangay's fame, but as the local press relentlessly repeated, boosterism was everyone's responsibility, and it reminded settlers also to recommend town lots when they wrote home urging friends to buy farmland. W.J. Morton, a Vulcan photographer, designed postcards specifically for the purpose. The newspapers back home actually published many of these letters. Rev. J.S. Ainslie, for example, promoted Carmangay real estate in articles about the Canadian west published by his old church newspaper, the *Congregationalist and Christian World* of Chicago.[19] To impress visitors, town and village councils sponsored campaigns encouraging all to clean, paint, repair, and landscape their property, and local newspapers always urged residents to 'talk up the town' to strangers.

Local events like sports days and fairs also served the boosters' purpose. Organizers of the 1915 Vulcan Stampede hoped to draw attention to the district by offering contestants large cash prizes, arranging for excursion trains to the event, and advertising heavily. Similarly, the Carmangay Fair sought to convince agricultural editors of the 'truly wonderfully rich and teeming ... possibilities' of the district. Circuses, chautauquas, and other spectacles could also draw visitors to the towns, and councils eagerly solicited all travelling entertainments. They also organized promotional exhibits at special events in other towns. Carmangay considered its agricultural society's participation at dry-farming congresses, held in various cities of the North American west in the 1910s, a model of effective boosting. And if a band could accompany such exhibits, it was 'one of the best advertisements a town can have.' Small towns often subsidized their bands for travelling in the cause of boosterism.[20]

Semi-professional baseball also excited the boosters. Imported by American settlers, baseball became a major social activity and a popular device for gambling, but everyone recognized its potential for town promotion as well. Would Vulcan 'stay on the map as a real live baseball town or sink into oblivion?' fretted the *Advocate* on 7 April 1920. To generate publicity, the teams had to be good enough to win tournaments throughout the province, if not beyond. Since many western towns hoped to spread fame this way, the task proved onerous. None the less, Carmangay, Vulcan, and especially Champion all assembled teams of sufficient quality to attract major-league scouts and to win many provincial tournaments. The teams consisted of talented local residents, some with semi-professional experience, and a core of recruited professionals. Even before Cleverville moved to the railway and became Champion, it actively recruited imports. Good players could always be pirated from opposing teams, but managers searched widely. Vulcan's first loss of 1919 prompted a mission to Portland, Oregon, to acquire three new players. Although a pitcher might be paid $175 a month, most imports received about $75. Teams offered other compensations, perhaps a part-time job or free room and board. Thus in 1914 the Vulcan club canvassed local merchants to see if any 'would give an opening to a catcher.' Lesser stars received jobs but no baseball salary. Teams paid players out of gate receipts and donations, which for a three-game series might total $1,000. Many players supplemented their income by gambling on the outcome of games (which led to endless trouble), by playing for more than one team, and by playing in the United States during the winter. Clubs hired some players by the season, others by the game, but the expense became so staggering that teams soon recruited only pitchers.[21]

The boosters searched endlessly for any gimmick to distinguish their town from countless others. Ralph 'Slim' Moorehouse, a grain hauler well known for linking horses and wagons in long caravans, arrived at the Vulcan grain elevators one day driving a thirty-head team pulling eight wagons of wheat. A reporter met him. 'We record an event,' announced the *Advocate* on 29 November 1922, 'that in type and pictures will give us publicity all over America and even to the Old Country.' The newspaper printed and mailed thousands of postcards, and requests for the story poured in from magazines and calendar makers. 'If you can accommodate me in this connection,' wrote Robert Stead, popular novelist and publicity director for the CPR, 'I think we can put over some good publicity for the Vulcan district.' When he arranged the publication of photographs in twenty-six British newspapers, the *Advocate* boasted that he had 'made Vulcan as well known almost as New York.' Although never openly admitted, the Moorehouse stunt was surely pre-arranged. The *Advocate* seemed suspiciously well prepared for the event, and several months later one Frank Kiever appeared before town council and applied 'for a grant towards expenses in connection with the wheat hauling record established by R. Moorehouse.' Moorehouse later drove even larger rigs to the Calgary Stampede, and Vulcan enjoyed free publicity courtesy of the Calgary Board of Trade.[22]

Desperate for recognition, boosters even publicized an incident that could only tarnish Vulcan's image. A tornado struck. It uprooted telephone poles and drove them into the sides of homes. It tore buildings apart, demolished threshing machines, and embedded blades of grass in fenceposts. D.C. Jones, a local druggist, photographed the tornado and gave the negative to a newspaper friend. When it received wide publication, residents forgot the destruction and basked in the fame it brought them – so much so that a local MLA, D.H. Galbraith, mailed out Christmas cards illustrating the twister. The crowning triumph came when an encyclopedia company decided to publish Jones' photograph under its tornado entry.[23] Ironically, tornadoes are not common in the area, and a worse advertisement would be hard to imagine, yet no one suggested suppressing the picture and for decades residents spoke of 'our tornado' with evident pride.

If the tactics of small-town boosterism sometimes displayed originality, its messages did not. Typically, they emphasized agricultural opportunities. Magnified claims about rich soil producing huge yields and a balmy climate blessed with abundant rainfall and 'practically immune from hail and frost' appeared with monotonous regularity. Of an area of the prairies most prone to violent fluctuations in climate and weather, one promotional tract boldly stated that visitors 'are agreeably surprised to find that the extremes of climate to which they have been accustomed are not known here.' Even an admittedly disastrous drought year like 1910 could be twisted to advantage, for as the boosters pointed out, it was a tribute to the district that Carmangay grew and prospered anyway. But while the town council polished the image of an agricultural Eden in public, it fretted in private about the problem of soil drifting and the embarrassing image it might present.[24]

Promoting agriculture might generate land resales, but it could not stimulate much new settlement. Most land west of the tracks had been settled before the birth of the towns, while land to the east filled in quickly. Not only was settlement almost wholly complete by the time the towns began promoting it, but the trend towards fewer and larger farms had already begun. This disturbing fact turned town boosters into fanatical advocates of mixed farming. The intensive development of small farms promised to support a larger population, and a wider variety of agricultural products might stabilize town incomes, which fluctuated with the yield and price of wheat. Mixed farming would also create new opportunities for food-processing industries. The towns all struggled to secure irrigation systems, meat-packing plants, flax mills, flour mills, and dairies.

Unhappily aware of the limitations of local agriculture, boosters exaggerated the importance of other resources. Small coal deposits scattered throughout the area and mined for fuel by homesteaders became in their minds the foundation for great transportation and industrial centres. 'This coal will have to come through Carmangay, supplying a demand from Oregon to Manitoba,' cried the press. Small natural-gas strikes fired local imagination more effectively than they would ever fire local industry: 'There is sufficient natural gas at Champion,' bragged the board of trade, 'to drive the wheels of a hundred factories.' With access to cheap fuel, Carmangay expected manufacturers to flock to town to exploit 'some of the finest and most valuable fire-clay, iron, stone, and alluvial deposits found anywhere in Canada.'[25]

Railways remained crucial to all resource and industrial development, and newspapers predicted that new lines would magically benefit their town alone. The completion of the Kipp and Aldersyde whetted the thirst for more lines, and railway companies continually announced new plans and commissioned surveys. Some even secured charters and purchased right-of-way for lines that would never materialize. Each town relentlessly petitioned railways for the prize of divisional point.[26]

Increasingly, roads also commanded attention, for improvements would speed farmers to town quickly and conveniently. Purchased in great numbers during the profitable war years, automobiles promised to destroy the tyranny of time and distance that horse and wagon imposed on farmers. The car inspired plans in 1919 for a provincial highway between Calgary and Lethbridge, and the towns mustered as much lobbying energy as they had for railway construction. 'Vulcan wants and must have this highway,' protested the *Advocate* when the route first proposed meant to bypass the town. Council successfully solicited the support of the rural municipal district of Royal and secured the road.[27]

When a rebuilding proposal ten years later raised the spectre of a route change, O.L. (Tony) McPherson, a Vulcan farmer and Alberta's minister of Public Works, called a meeting of the various municipalities involved. Most, including Royal, insisted that the road follow the railway through Vulcan, Ensign, and Brant. McPherson explained that since the municipalities would bear half the construction costs (a requirement later dropped by the province), they could save money by running the highway along municipal borders, thereby reducing the cost to each jurisdiction still further. The municipal district of Harmony nevertheless insisted that the road plunge through the middle of its territory connecting Carmangay with Champion. Royal then agreed to let the highway swing west through Vulcan, conveniently passing the doorstep of McPherson's farmhouse, but the municipality sacrificed the interests of Brant and Ensign by suggesting that the route turn due north and then west along the municipal border to secure cost-sharing with the adjacent municipality.[28]

As with roads and railways, boosters expected telephone lines to reinforce commercial ties with the countryside, and the towns raced to link the most farmers to their local exchanges. Even lines to rival towns would somehow benefit each booster's town but not that of the connecting rival, and towns begged provincial aid to establish long-distance.[29] In summary, town boosters pinned their hopes on a three-pronged policy of resource exploitation, transportation links, and industrial development. It is ironic that they joined western opposition to the National Policy while striving desperately to secure it in miniature.

For a brief period the boom at the new townsites confirmed local expectations. Huge crews soon tackled the major construction projects. The railway gang arrived, 150 to 250 strong. Teamsters and labourers began digging the Lake McGregor reservoir. Carpenters descended on the townsites. At Carmangay forty buildings rose within two weeks of the townsite sale. 'Carmangay is one month old today and a census ... shows that there are already 190 people here,' reported a new resident. By 1912 such a tide of people surged in

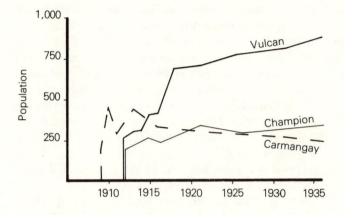

FIGURE 10
Town population growth

and out of town that the *Sun* warned against 'fly-by-night speculators ... here for a day and gone again,' and urged newcomers to seek advice only from 'long standing citizens of two years.' When building commenced at the Champion and Vulcan townsites, they too instantly acquired hundreds of new residents (see Figure 10). Still there remained a shortage of workers and an even greater shortage of accommodations. Labourers and merchants huddled in tents and shacks and packed the new hotels and boarding-houses. The Carmangay hotel reported fat profits, and the first houses completed rented at fantastic prices.[30]

Settlers poured into the east country. 'When we arrived in 1910,' wrote one eyewitness, 'Carmangay was a thriving little town ... newcomers arriving all the time. A common sight it was to see settler effects piled along the R.R. track waiting to be hauled out 10 or 20 miles to a homestead or purchased piece of land.' Since farmers also shopped at those places where they mailed correspondence and shipped grain, postal and freight records suggest their impact on the town boom. Between 1908 and 1917 gross postal revenues soared from less than five hundred dollars in the old hamlet post offices to more than eighteen thousand in the new towns, and with few elevators completed during its first year of operation, the Kipp-Aldersyde line shipped over three million bushels of grain from the Vulcan area.[31]

To serve the farmers, construction labourers, and other townspeople, over one hundred new businesses opened before 1914. Many prospered immediately; one merchant sold forty thousand dollars' worth of goods at the McGregor reservoir construction site in one month. Only random reports are available on sales, but of those locally owned businesses investigated by the

R.G. Dun Company, the proportion with credit ratings listed from good to high soared from 10 per cent in 1912 to 50 per cent by 1918; and those with 'estimated pecuniary strengths' of five thousand dollars or more rose from 15 per cent to 38 per cent over the same period.[32] Following the same pattern as farms, businesses of all sizes rose substantially in value until the end of the First World War.

Fired by a real boom, real-estate speculation accelerated. Whereas lots averaged $138 each at the Vulcan townsite sale in 1910, by 1912 they fetched $400 to $700.[33] Denied participation in the sale of the Champion townsite, Martin Clever laid out a subdivision of forty-six lots and sold them by auction in 1912. By 1914, one-fifth of the assessed lots in Champion and Vulcan traded outside the area, some as far away as Oregon and New England.[34]

But Carmangay became the darling of the Kipp-Aldersyde line. Like many prairie towns, it temporarily enjoyed the status of 'head of steel' and so commanded a huge trade area.[35] The CPR's decision to build subdivisions and the purchase of town lots by insiders like R.B. Bennett aroused suspicions that Carmangay awaited some secret destiny. The CPR, C.W. Carman, and Toronto speculators all built subdivisions larger in area collectively than the original townsites, and nearby farmers parcelled land into small acreages. Purchased on the advice of friends and relatives in the area, or through Chicago or Toronto agents, the town lots of Carmangay soon traded sight unseen in four nations, across nine provinces, and in fourteen American states. In one year E.W. Horne of Toronto marketed 119 lots throughout England, Quebec, and Ontario. By 1914 Carmangay residents owned less than 8 per cent of the town lots, and the CPR less than 5 per cent. Seventy-three property titles found their way to England and Scotland. Ontario investors owned 840 lots, about 61 per cent of all town land.[36]

But the boom soon faltered. Financial recession struck in 1913 and town-lot speculation collapsed across western Canada. 'Very few dealings have been made in real estate,' reported the local Mounted Police, 'and the value of property has been lowered.' Although the war rescued agriculture from the recession, permitting speculators to profit from a near-continuous rise in rural land values between 1904 and 1920, it could not revive town-lot speculation, and so the most vigorous booster campaign of all flourished for only four short years. The war boom did sustain the rising value of existing businesses, but their success did not spark further development. Few new businesses opened in the Vulcan area after 1913, and town populations no longer climbed by spectacular leaps (see Figure 10).[37]

The booster campaign failed to sustain growth because its ambitions clashed with reality. Government institutions in search of a home could safely ignore small, politically unimportant towns. The province scarcely acknowledged Carmangay's bid for the southern agricultural school. Coal added almost nothing to economic or population growth because of its low quantity and poor quality. It remained a convenient source of cheap home fuel locally, but served no industrial purpose. By 1936 the eight mines in the municipal district of Harmony employed only forty-five men, a figure inflated by the winter employment of local farmers. Of 52 mines opened up to 1967, only 17 surrendered coal for more than ten years; 8 had closed by 1915.[38] Natural-gas development awaited post–Second World War advances in technology and market price, and the value of other minerals remained a flight of booster fancy. Lacking raw materials, markets, sufficient water, and a cheap labour pool, manufacturers avoided the Vulcan area.

Soil remained the only natural resource feasible to exploit, and the towns remained inextricably bound to agriculture. Inevitably urban growth stabilized once merchants supplied the goods necessary for pioneering, and contractors completed building facilities for agricultural storage and transportation. The overdue closing of the Vulcan land office in 1918 symbolized the end of this settlement phase. Instead of irrigated mixed farms supporting a densely populated countryside, farms specialized in wheat, grew larger in size and fewer in number. This trend doomed most plans for food-processing industries. Carmangay's determination to have a creamery in spite of a lack of dairy cows in the area resulted in an anaemic business that operated at a loss under the ownership of private interests, then the board of trade, and finally the United Farmers of Alberta local, before closing forever.[39] No other processing plant appeared until a small flour mill opened in Vulcan in 1925.

For an agricultural town with no resources save land, there remained the hope of becoming an important distributing centre, but wholesalers required major transportation advantages. In southern Alberta the triangular skeleton of the railway network had already hardened prior to 1900, with primary joints at Calgary, Lethbridge, and Medicine Hat. Though scarcely more than small towns themselves in 1900, without competitors they mushroomed instantly under the impact of twentieth-century settlement. Filling in the network further benefited those centres, and new towns found it impossible to acquire the rail facilities and preferential freight rates necessary to overtake them. Indeed, new lines actually carved away small-town hinterlands instead of expanding them. Just as the building of the Kipp and Aldersyde in 1910 robbed the older Calgary and Edmonton Railway towns of trade territory, so too did its extension north strip Carmangay of its head-of-steel advantage, creating the new rivals of Vulcan and Champion. In 1914 the extension of a line from Suffield gave birth to the railhead of Lomond twenty-five miles to the

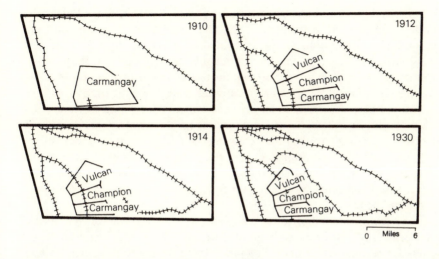

MAP 8
Idealized view of changes in town trade hinterlands

east, another competitor much feared by Carmangay merchants. Further extensions of this line in 1925 and 1930 created a string of new towns that stole even more trade from the Kipp and Aldersyde line (see Map 8). Instead of clamouring for more railway lines, the towns soon waged a losing battle to retain all their own rail services.[40] The scarcity of transportation routes, rather than their abundance, often briefly rewarded frontier towns with a metropolitan influence far exceeding that of similar-sized places in settled regions.

Although topography and transportation routes distorted somewhat the idealized pattern of towns predicted by central-place theory, the density of the rural population, the number of services it required, the frequency of its needs, and the time it required to travel various distances all largely determined the size, spacing, and number of urban places in the area. Within this hierarchy Vulcan, Carmangay, and Champion still commanded important if shrinking hinterlands, and all three retained the status among prairie centres described by some sociologists as 'independent towns' rather than 'dependent villages.'[41] At first they primarily supplied goods, but service businesses rapidly appeared, and by the First World War the economic functions of the towns had emerged more clearly. Except for the rise of automotive businesses, the number and type of services in many prairie communities changed little between the wars, and each townsman who moved away left a particular shop or trade that a newcomer might fill.[42]

While it is difficult to categorize some business – C.B. Shimp of Vulcan, for example, sold musical instruments, toys, and real estate – between 1915 and 1935 those primarily selling goods accounted for about 34 to 39 per cent of all businesses in the Vulcan area, divided roughly equally between those selling consumer goods (mostly food, clothing, furniture, and drugs) and those selling goods for agricultural production (mostly farm implements, hardwares, harness, and lumber). About 52 to 62 per cent primarily provided services, again divided roughly equally between farm services (grain elevators, blacksmithing, and other specialized trades) and consumer services (most of them professional, personal, or recreational in nature). A special category, automotive businesses, which sold both goods and services to both consumers and farmers, rose from nowhere to account for about 6 to 9 per cent of all businesses after 1917.[43]

But the towns could not settle complacently into the role of agricultural service centres following the collapse of their lofty ambitions. Increasingly, the boosters found themselves struggling just as hard simply to retain the trade of the immediate hinterland. The building of the Kipp and Aldersyde eliminated all country stores close to the line, but by stimulating new settlement farther east, it ensured the viability of distant hamlets and even gave rise to new ones (see Map 7). All across the prairies an expanding railway network perpetually rearranged, but failed to destroy, the constellation of country hamlets. By 1936 places with fewer than ten businesses still constituted 70 per cent of all central places in the prairie provinces, a proportion they had held since 1910. Farmers seemed reluctant to venture beyond five miles for everyday items, and as late as 1913 only about one-third of Vulcan-area farmers lived within five miles of a railway town; another third actually resided more than ten miles away. The general store remained by far the most decentralized business on the prairies.[44]

As for the goods and services available only at railways, farmers hardly became the captive customers of the closest town that observers of midwestern America once claimed they were. Although geographers often describe 'a zone of indifference' where farmers equidistant from towns might patronize one as readily as another, studies of the American midwest and the prairie provinces have shown that farmers often shopped at places far distant from the closest town. Vulcan-area farmers behaved no differently. Like other towns throughout North America, those on the Kipp and Aldersyde learned that automobiles and improved roads not only lured farmers from farther afield but also whisked those formerly bound to the town away to other centres. The highway that brought Carmangay within less than an hour of downtown Lethbridge hastened the decline of that town, while Vulcan's position halfway between Calgary and Lethbridge ensured at least slow growth. After the Second World

War Vulcan's location in terms of automobile driving time would allow it to benefit simultaneously from the centralization of local government functions and the decentralization of provincial ones. Overlapping and shifting trade zones help to explain the bitter rivalry between adjacent towns. When High River published literature boasting of huge wheat yields, Vulcan accused its competitor of using 'our farmers' to bolster 'their claims.'[45]

Farmers not only sought lower prices and greater selection by shopping in different towns; they also looked for liberal credit and convenient business hours. These issues sparked conflict between towns, and sometimes within them. Cheating repeatedly undermined agreements between merchants to restrict credit to thirty days, even in 1922, when all the merchants on the Kipp-Aldersyde line agreed to co-operate. Cash-only policies announced by Vulcan and Carmangay merchants collapsed in 1913, and again in 1916. Since the first country merchants usually opened stores in their homes, they willingly conducted business at all hours. During the building boom everyone remained open until nine or ten o'clock each night. The weary merchants soon pleaded for rest. During the war, merchants in most towns agreed to close at half past six except on Saturday, and at noon on Wednesdays in the summer. But whenever a special event brought farmers to town, many ignored the rules. One night when the Chautauqua at Vulcan let out at ten o'clock, the stores reopened with 'a good business done up to a late hour,' reported the *Advocate* on 20 August 1919. The towns apparently failed to enforce by-laws in accordance with the provincial Early Closing Act until 1930, and even then they granted exceptions at harvest time.[46]

When the drudgery of winter grain hauling began, farmers more readily yielded to the tyranny of distance and almost always shipped through the closest railway town. Indeed, farmers believed that there should be more towns, and in 1927 the municipal district of Harmony alarmed Champion and Carmangay by petitioning the CPR for grain-loading facilities between the two towns. Carmangay suffered a greater shock the next year when one of its own merchants convinced the CPR and four elevator companies to establish the siding of Peacock only four miles south of town.[47]

In the battle for trade, topographical problems easily overcome by cities profoundly affected the small town. Carmangay bragged that the water supply of the Little Bow River gave her an advantage over rivals, but worried that grain haulers north of the valley would not risk its steep grades when they could travel to Champion on level ground. The town could not afford a high-level bridge. The CPR and the elevator companies ignored pleas for facilities on the north side so that farmers might unload before crossing the ravine to shop. Vulcan rejoiced that the building of the McGregor reservoir brought money to town, but feared that the lake 'would shut the Brunetta district off from Vulcan.' Similarly, a great fire would scarcely slow the growth of a Chicago, but the flames that periodically enveloped the small town often resulted in rebuilding on a smaller scale.[48]

Besides competition from country stores and neighbouring towns, places as distant as Toronto invaded Main Street. No sooner did the new towns arise than the railway that created them began delivering a wide range of mail-order goods: clothing, furniture, hardware, even non-perishable foodstuffs. In harmony with small towns across the continent, local merchants cried out in protest.[49] During the 'Be Loyal to Your Own Community' campaign of 1914 and the 'Trade at Home' campaign of 1922, Vulcan merchants chronicled the sins of the mail-order houses: they demanded cash in advance and sold inferior goods that could not be inspected beforehand; delivery took weeks and exchanges even longer, and the goods actually cost more after the expense of postage and handling was added on. By contrast, local merchants offered credit and prompt service. The press depicted 'Bob Simpson' and 'Tim Eaton' as community wreckers who drained money out of the small town without returning a penny in local taxes or charitable contributions, thereby threatening local prosperity and even land values. 'Loyalty is the foundation upon which the whole structure of civilization rests [and] a moral obligation,' the merchants piously declared in the Vulcan *Advocate*, 12 June 1922.

Pedlars also invaded the small town, from door-to-door salesmen to itinerant wholesalers who sold boxcars of goods at cut-rate prices. Champion councillors protested in 1913 that resident merchants who built the community, extended credit, and paid taxes could not survive such unfair competitors. Merchants sternly warned the public against them, and town councils begged the province for power to tax them out of existence. Automobiles and improved roads soon gave the travelling salesman even greater mobility. In 1929 the new highway brought a tremendous increase in mobile services from Calgary and Lethbridge. When city trucking and bus companies forced local draymen out of business, the towns appealed again to the province for protection.[50]

Direct competition from chain stores also worried the merchants. From the towns' origins, distant corporations had owned all the banks and grain elevators, and most lumber yards, but a few grocery and hardware chain stores also appeared. Merchants soon began losing their purchasing independence and found it increasingly necessary to stock nationally advertised goods. This practice foreshadowed the franchise system, which first absorbed farm-machinery and automobile dealers.

The collapse of the boom not only disappointed speculators and merchants who failed to sell their town lots and businesses in time but burdened local governments with formidable problems. Streets hurriedly gridded at right angles across poor sites reflected concern only for low survey costs and fast real-estate sales. Builders had erected many substandard structures, and temporary shacks often became permanent. Only six years after Carmangay's birth, it was no longer safe to enter some buildings.[51]

Townspeople applauded far-flung property sales, hoping that development would follow, but speculators simply wanted quick resales. Hence farmland carved into small tracts often lay idle. 'Around Carmangay for four miles there is little but grass growing,' complained one farmer to the *Sun* on 31 December 1913. 'Who owns all this land? Why don't they do something with it? We are all tired of driving over this stretch of desert to reach town, and town people must be tired of seeing it.' Although Carmangay's principal business streets developed in a relatively compact manner, homes and minor commercial buildings sprawled across the townsite, interspaced by hundreds of weed-infested vacant lots. By 1921 Carmangay's incorporated area of 640 acres housed only 300 people. This dispersed pattern strained the ability of towns to provide public utilities and services.[52] If many financial difficulties of the rural west can be attributed to low population density, so too can those of many prairie towns.

Vacant lands created other problems. Until 1916 Alberta towns employed the single tax system – taxes could be levied on land but not improvements. Hence, if speculators did not pay land taxes, towns could not pay off debts acquired to finance civic improvements. These debts especially burdened frontier towns, where everything had to be built from scratch. The mill rate in Carmangay spiralled from 20 in 1910 to 50 in 1917, largely to pay off debentures issued for the municipally owned electrical and waterworks system. In the game of musical town lots, everyone tried to resell property before taxes came due, with the result that by 1913, 61 per cent of Carmangay's assessments had not been paid in full.[53] When recession struck that year and real-estate values collapsed, speculators refused to pay back taxes because many lots were suddenly worth less than the taxes owing on them.

Financial disaster followed. The debenture market dried up for western local governments and remained generally dry until the 1940s. Even short-term financing became unavailable. In 1914 the province learned that 'the affairs of [Carmangay] are in bad condition financially. The Bank has refused to advance money and the only remedy appears to be action on the part of the Town to collect some of the unpaid taxes.' Carmangay soon realized that seizing lots for back taxes eliminated forever any chance of collecting funds when the lots could not be resold at public auction. Council delayed action until the real-estate market should revive. When it failed to do so, Carmangay defaulted on its debenture payments in 1915. The longer speculators held the lots, the less chance they had to sell for a profit, for back taxes continued to mount. Consequently, they neither sold them nor paid the taxes. Still the towns hesitated to seize the lots. No one bid on any land seized by Carmangay in 1920. Although the town refused to approve applications for new subdivisions after 1913, it had eliminated fewer than 400 of 1,400 assessed lots by 1923.[54]

Residents resented paying taxes when absentee speculators did not, and they no longer paid on time or in full. The CPR, banks, and grain companies accused the towns of assessing them unfairly to make up the difference. In protest Vulcan grain companies refused to pay taxes for three years. In the mid-1920s the towns finally took action. With 'little taxes paid so far and the prospect not very encouraging,' Carmangay removed another 400 lots from the tax rolls, largely by transforming half of the CPR's subdivided properties into acreage. By 1925 Carmangay had seized two-thirds of all the town lots for back taxes. Champion took similar, if less extensive steps, and the municipal district of Royal eliminated many subdivided lands in the unincorporated villages of Brant and Kirkcaldy.[55]

Still the financial crisis deepened, and by the 1930s many residents could not even pay taxes on improved lots. 'If we lose our home, what are we to do?' pleaded one Vulcan woman. 'We have eight children ... My husband ... has not earned anything for six months.' The towns circumvented outdated tax regulations by refusing to seize improved properties, by continually postponing sales or refusing to advertise them, or by placing reserve bids on homes so high that no one would buy them. Hence massive financial readjustments, further seizures of vacant lots, and the release of incorporated land to rural municipalities did not resume until the late 1930s and the 1940s.[56]

Given the enormous problem of providing public services, enthusiasm for local politics steadily eroded. Attendance at ratepayer meetings fell, and fewer residents voted. The election of entire councils by acclamation became common. Increasingly, towns postponed nomination meetings because not enough candidates came forward to fill council vacancies. 'We have very few residents eligible on account of unpaid taxes and other causes,' reported the secretary-treasurer of Carmangay in 1928. The municipal inspector advised Carmangay to revert to village status, thereby reducing the required number of councillors from seven to three. But since the province had already started reorganizing the town's finances, many wished to eliminate elections altogether by hiring an administrator to run the town. Only thirteen ratepayers attended the meeting to decide the issue. Eight voted for village status; five opposed it.[57]

In towns suffering from apathetic despair, incompetent and unethical practices flourished undetected for long periods of time. At Vulcan these problems surfaced dramatically between 1929 and 1931. An Alberta Wheat Pool investigator claimed that the town's financial statements were inaccurate, misleading, and audited illegally by an unqualified individual. The town made no effort to collect taxes, and assessments contained irregularities. The mayor and secretary-treasurer no longer consulted with council, and residents had only 'the vaguest idea as to the position of the town's affairs.' The Alberta municipal inspector confirmed these allegations and added that the mayor had 'no idea of finance or administration,' that budgets had not been prepared for years, and that the 'existing state of the books and records was ... nothing short of disgraceful.' Complaints about the laziness and carelessness of the secretary-treasurer revealed corruption in both the town and the municipal district of Royal, including the elimination from the tax rolls of considerable sums owed by the mayor, among others. The banks cut off the town's credit, and a general tax strike ensued.[58]

Civic affairs seem to have operated according to some inverse law; the more boosterism inflated enthusiasm during the boom, the greater the collapse that followed. Citizens did not wholly abandon public affairs; they eagerly administered other local organizations, but as for tackling the crisis of local government, no one seemed interested. By the 1930s many believed that the towns might die anyway, but although Carmangay and Champion would ultimately lose most of their businesses, they would not disappear. The bulkiness of grain and the difficulty and expense of moving it ensured the decentralization of rail shipping centres, and some businesses associated with them could always survive.

Like the farmland around them, the country stores, hamlets, and railtowns of the Vulcan area had promised the urban pioneer a substantial capital gain, and good returns while he awaited it, for the commercial nature of prairie agriculture ensured towns a vital role in the settlement process. Because towns offered potentially greater rewards that rural land, pioneers concentrated their efforts on urban development, but no clear distinction between those who engaged in each type of speculation can be drawn. As we have seen, the owners of rural property hoped to transform their holdings into towns, just as townsmen actively participated in the farm real-estate market. An essential unity of purpose emerged in this respect, and the towns served as convenient rallying points for the promotion of both kinds of property. But since the pioneers failed to create great urban centres in the face of resource limitations, locational problems, stiff competition, and adverse government, railway, and other metropolitan decisions, wringing capital gains from urban development proved risky and short lived compared to rural speculation.

The struggle for capital gains and the high rate of geographic mobility associated with it may at first glance seem to contradict what has been said earlier concerning the complex ideas that pioneers entertained about the kind of communities they hoped to establish. After all, why should anyone planning to move on care much about the nature of the community? But in fact no contradiction existed. If pioneers hoped to resell either farm or town property for a profit, it behoved them to create settlements that would appeal to potential buyers. Furthermore, the speculators also hoped to reap as many economic and social benefits as possible from their activities while they lived in the area. In that respect they resembled the stock-market investor who hopes for a capital gain some day but seeks substantial dividends in the meantime. As the next three chapters will demonstrate, most farmers looking for a resale also took considerable pains to develop valuable farms and to earn as much as possible from them.

PART II: AGRICULTURE

4
Crop Selection

Agricultural production asked Vulcan-area settlers to consider a number of basic questions: what to grow, how to grow it, and how much of it to grow. The study of agricultural production, therefore, might be best tackled by examining these basic questions in turn. Crop selection, technique, and farm size and expansion also provide convenient themes around which many aspects of prairie agriculture might be organized. Although settlers faced all these problems simultaneously, they answered the question of what to grow earliest, and hence it represents a logical starting-point.[1]

In the first year of settlement, pioneers in the Vulcan area planted mostly wheat, and every year thereafter they continued raising it, largely to the exclusion of all else. Their decision deserves close scrutiny, for conventional wisdom upheld mixed farming as the salvation of prairie agriculture, and most historical studies written since have also condemned the one–crop system.[2] Furthermore, many accounts misrepresent western attitudes towards mixed farming by implying that farmers dismissed it out of hand. But Vulcan-area settlers agonized over their decision to grow wheat. Indeed, until the great soil-drifting crisis of the 1930s no other aspect of agricultural production generated as much discussion or spread as much confusion.

Self-doubt about the one-crop system tormented Vulcan-area settlers because so many influential voices urged them to practise mixed farming. From first settlement of the area through the Great Depression, the advocates included representatives from every level of government, from corporations with interests in the west, and from agricultural experts and observers of every description. Within the Vulcan area itself a chorus of critics, ranging from newspapers editors to Mounted Policemen and clergymen, lent voices of support. Indeed, so many advocated diversification so vehemently that the mixed-farming movement resembled a crusade.

The enthusiasts usually began their exhortations by listing the sins of the wheat specialists. The Vulcan *Advocate* scolded them with a hoary cliché that served the campaign for decades: 'It does not pay . . . to have all your eggs in one basket.' Not only would crop failure or the collapse of wheat prices leave the specialist with nothing to sell, warned a provincial Department of Agriculture speaker addressing local farmers in 1912, but 'continued raising of grain was going to deplete the fertility of the soil.' 'No man has the right,' lectured the farm press, 'to leave it to posterity in a lower state of fertility than it was left to him.'³

By contrast, mixed farming not only promised the farmer protection should one crop fail; it promised great prosperity: 'There is more money in mixed farming than there is in straight grain farming,' announced the Carmangay *Sun* in 1912. A board-of-trade pamphlet issued by the town of Champion predicted huge profits for poultry, egg, and vegetable producers, and even huger ones for swine producers: 'Hog raising . . . carries a fortune for any man who cares to earn it,' it informed prospective settlers. The Vulcan *Advocate* wrote encouragingly about the big money that awaited turkey growers. Fruit trees and berry plants 'are the only part of my farm which has been a paying proposition for the past few years,' insisted John Glambeck, a local farmer who often published articles on the technique of raising such crops without irrigation; 'everything else has been grown at a loss.'⁴

More common than promises of immediate gain, however, were those that stressed long-term benefits, particularly in regard to soil conservation. Everyone agreed that livestock manure and crops like alfalfa would replenish nutrients and prevent erosion by furnishing humus. Such views found their way into government studies that recommended mixed farming as the best solution to soil drifting. A speaker visiting the Carmangay Agricultural Society suggested that raising corn might also solve the problem, and the Vulcan *Advocate* wondered if the crop might even prove a good substitute for summerfallowing. Less conventional arguments sometimes appeared. The High River *Times* explained that raising twenty-five head of cattle justified keeping a hired man year-round so that he would be available at seeding and harvest time. Mixed-farming advocates generally concluded their remarks with bold assertions of the rightness of their cause: 'You will be forced to adopt mixed farming,' a dairy expert told Carmangay farmers, 'if you are to hold your position in the agricultural world.' 'Its results are positively known to be successful,' the Vulcan *Advocate* assured readers.⁵

But the mixed-farming movement did not confine itself to preaching. The Dominion Department of Agriculture's Experimental Farm at Lethbridge raised a variety of farm products, and it seeded demonstrated plots at Carmangay and Vulcan to grass, clover, rye, and other coarse grain. The department also distributed free crop seeds to farmers; in 1912 samples of trees, field peas, potatoes, and various grains arrived in the Vulcan area. Continuing the policy of the territorial government, the provincial Department of Agriculture extended grants and loans to associations promoting various farm products. Largely to encourage mixed farming, it opened agricultural schools in the province in 1913. The nearby Claresholm school bombarded Vulcan students with courses in the raising of many crops and animals. It also distributed free samples; one year it donated eight hundred pounds of seed potatoes to Vulcan schoolchildren. Sometimes the department dispatched mixed-farming lecturers to the Vulcan area or sponsored local short courses. In 1913 it conducted seminars in Carmangay on raising horses, beef and dairy cattle, poultry, sheep, and hogs, and instructed farm wives in home food preserving.[6]

The department also promoted mixed farming by helping local agricultural societies to organized community fairs. It supplied them with grants, lecturers, judges, and exhibition forms that listed hundreds of prizes for entries of home food products, field crops, and various breeds of animals; in 1911 poultry growers alone could compete in fourteen categories. To ensure support, the department sometimes bullied local organizers. The superintendent of Fairs and Institutes chastized the Carmangay society for its poor showing in cattle and swine at its 1923 fair, and threatened to withdraw financial assistance. 'The future of your association will be decided upon the results of your 1924 fair,' he warned.[7]

The Canadian Pacific Railway actively supported many government schemes. In co-operation with the provincial and dominion Departments of Agriculture, it sponsored 'mixed-farming trains,' which toured the countryside giving lectures, demonstrations, and short courses. The first one arrived at Vulcan and Carmangay in 1912 and emphasized horse, cattle, and poultry raising. Another, ten years later, featured dairying, and hog and sheep production. The CPR also established a demonstration farm near Vulcan in 1912. Praised by the High River *Times* as an 'ideal quarter section,' it boasted a cattle and horse barn, a piggery, a poultry house, and a creamery (all pre-cut buildings that settlers might order from the company), and fields of pasture, oats, barley, and wheat cultivated in equal acreages. The company also built stockyards in the area to facilitate livestock marketing.[8]

Other corporations with a stake in a Vulcan area responded to the CPR's initiative. The Canadian Bank of Commerce supplied eight farmers with sufficient corn seed to plant experimental plots of one acre, and in 1913 the Associated Mortgage Investors of Rochester, New York, which held numerous mortgages in the area, announced that it would loan money only to mixed farmers in the future. Local merchants periodically united town councils, boards of trade, and newspapers in spirited campaigns for local creameries.[9]

Vulcan-area farmers seemed receptive to this pressure. 'The mixed farming train visited Carmangay and excited a great deal of interest,' noted the Mounted Police in 1912. Crowds of two hundred greeted the train at Carmangay and Vulcan, while the 1915 train lured five hundred visitors to Vulcan alone. 'The hall was fairly filled with a most appreciative and attentive audience,' reported the press of a poultry lecture, and talks on corn raising always drew huge crowds. Inspired by one orator at Carmangay in 1913, 'fifty farmers ... expressed their intention of planting corn on their summerfallow land the coming season.'[10]

Vulcan-area farmers channelled this enthusiasm into local organizations. Following the lead of the parent association, locals of the United Farmers of Alberta endorsed mixed farming and introduced new crop seeds to their members. The farmer-owned Vulcan Co-operative Company encouraged livestock raising and actively participated in hog and cattle marketing. Members of both the Vulcan and Carmangay agricultural societies entered a wide variety of farm products in their annual fairs, and in 1914 the Carmangay society sponsored its own short courses in dairying and beef-cattle raising. The societies also interested farm children in mixed farming by awarding them prizes for their own animals and by supporting such organizations as the boys' and girls' pig clubs. New institutions also appeared. Many farmers joined the Alberta Corn Growers' Association, and in 1918 the Vulcan Agricultural Society formed a local of the Alberta Provincial Poultry Association. Launched with fifty-two members, it solicited grants from the municipal district of Royal and sponsored annual poultry shows that awarded nearly one hundred prizes in over forty classes and often attracted forty to seventy exhibitors displaying four hundred to six hundred birds.[11]

Given the enormous pressure exerted on farmers and their own apparent enthusiasm for diversification, one might expect that the Vulcan area would have become the mixed-farming mecca of the west. But it did not. From about 1908 until the mid-1920s observers in the area reported a steady increase in mixed farming, and available statistics support some of their claims. Compared to the Ontario homeland of many Vulcan settlers, proportionately fewer farmers raised poultry, cattle, and swine, and they produced far less milk, butter, cheese, and eggs per farm. None the less, by 1916 well over half the settlers raised some livestock other than work-horses, and the production of swine and cattle per farm often exceeded the Ontario average (see Figures 11 and 12). Most Vulcan farmers also cultivated oats and barley. Some planted rye, flax, corn, or alfalfa, and a few even experimented with fruit trees, turnips, sugar

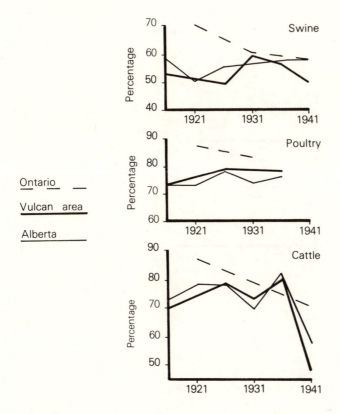

FIGURE 11
Percentage of farms raising various kinds of livestock

beets, and sunflowers. Most tended gardens, dug root cellars, and preserved vegetables and fruits.

But despite all the promotion and organization associated with these activities, they represented little more than symbolic gestures to the mixed-farming movement. The settlers rapidly developed much larger and more valuable farms than those they had left, and if the number of animals raised per farm changed little after the move west, they now represented a smaller percentage of the total value of the new farms (see Figure 13). Livestock actually raised for market represented a far lower proportional value still. To work his huge fields, the average settler required over three times as many horses as the average Ontario farmer. By 1911 horses accounted for nearly three-quarters of the value of all Vulcan-area livestock, and as tractors gradually replaced them, the

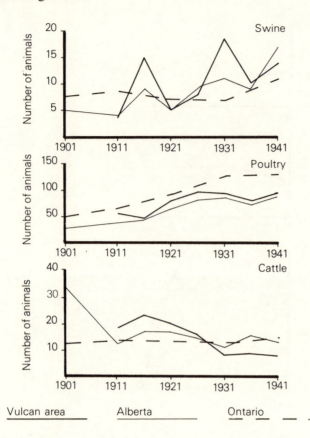

FIGURE 12
Average number of animals per farm

NOTE: The fall in Alberta cattle after 1901 reflects the decline of
ranching relative to farming; because hogs breed so rapidly,
farmers could react quickly to market changes, which resulted in
violent fluctuations in production.

value of livestock relative to other farm assets steadily declined. Between 1921
and 1941 animals and animal products accounted for only 10 to 15 per cent of
the value of all farm products raised in the Vulcan area, compared to 20 to 33
per cent for Alberta generally and 43 to 55 per cent for Ontario.

Compared to Ontario farmers, Vulcan-area settlers invested far more of
their capital in land and implements to produce field crops than in livestock, or

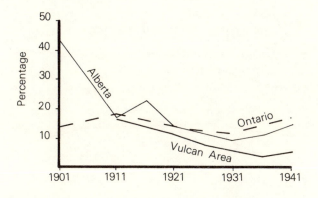

FIGURE 13
Livestock as a percentage of the total value of farms

NOTE: Total value includes livestock, buildings, land, and
implements.

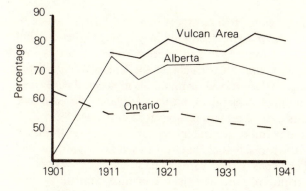

FIGURE 14
Land and implements as a percentage of the total value of
farms

NOTE: Total value includes livestock, buildings, land, and
implements.

buildings and corrals to house them (see Figure 14). And although they experimented with many crops, wheat constituted three-quarters of the seeded acreage in 1911 and increasingly more thereafter, as the acquisition of tractors
eliminated the need to raise oats for horse feed (see Figure 15). In terms of

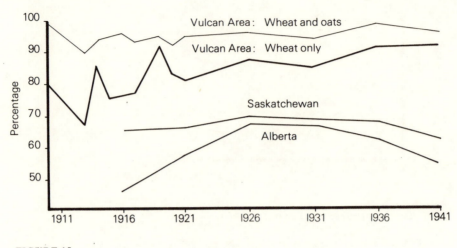

FIGURE 15
Wheat as a percentage of all seeded acreage

gross rather than proportional gains, real advances in mixed farming paled to insignificance compared to the massive increases in wheat production that accompanied the cultivation of more raw land. Within sixteen years of first settlement, settlers broke more than 80 per cent of the Vulcan area's virgin prairie. And in spite of the growth in mixed farming, the area could never feed itself. Grocers continued to import vegetables, butter, eggs, and other produce from outside, and sometimes even shortages of horsefeed developed.[12]

Most Vulcan settlers could no more accurately describe themselves as mixed farmers than could many town residents. They too raised large gardens and kept milk cows, hogs, and chickens in their yards. 'The streets are now overrun with animals of every description,' protested the Carmangay *Sun* on 25 July 1913. As practised by farmers and townsmen alike, mixed farming in the Vulcan area never developed beyond an avidly pursued hobby. After three decades of promotion an economist noted that 'mixed farming is not practised to any extent in these districts.' 'Vulcan is typical of the specialized wheat belt at its zenith,' reported another study. In 1941 the dominion government could categorize no more than 7 per cent of the farms in Census Division four as mixed (and most of those lay outside the Vulcan area), compared to 17 per cent for Alberta generally. Nor did monumental events alter wheat's position in the local economy: not the Great War, the Great Depression, the Second World War, nor the post-war boom, with its rapid advances in agricultural science and technology. Through them all, marvelled a 1955 economic report,

'Wheat production seems to have had a definite comparative advantage in the Vulcan area over all other products which might be raised there.'[13]

This variance between attitude and behaviour poses several important questions. Why did Vulcan-area settlers welcome the gospel of mixed farming, attend its sermons, and even practise its rituals, but turn to wheat for salvation? On one level the answer is simple: wheat returned a greater profit, in both the short and the long term. The missionaries of mixed farming insisted otherwise, but preparing conclusive financial statements for comparison purposes proved impossible. Before a complicated income-tax system forced the adoption of certain procedures, farm bookkeeping remained a crudely practised art. Farmers could record output, transportation rates, and market values, but despite their rhetoric about scientific management, production costs often eluded them. They did not keep complete or accurate records, and most even failed to separate all personal expenses from farm expenses. Raising many different products invited further complications. Lacking any systematic method of calculating depreciation or determining how much of a particular investment should be written off as an expense against each commodity it helped to produce, they could not discover which product returned the highest profit. 'The average farmer has a general idea whether he is making money or losing it, but ... he cannot put his finger on the vital spot in his operations and say, here is where most of my money is being made – or lost,' admitted the farm press in 1911.[14]

Given omissions in record-keeping and flaws in accounting, mixed-farming supporters tended to underestimate production costs more readily than did straight grain farmers. Mixed farming demanded a far greater outlay for buildings, corrals and fencing, wells and windmills, chopping mills and haying equipment, breeding stock, labour – and even interest charges, for although metropolitan financial institutions contributed charitably to the mixed-farming cause, most of them extended credit more readily for capital equipment to raise wheat.[15] And few farmers, if any, charged the full market value of the feeds they raised as an expense in the production of livestock, a procedure necessary to determine the efficiency of each process in a vertically integrated industry. Those who described their operations to the farm press inevitably failed to include some of these hidden expenses. Even so, many confessed that mixed-farming products took longer to show a return on capital than wheat: 'The grain crop produces the easiest and quickest money return with the least outlay of capital during the early years of settlement,' admitted the *Farm and Ranch Review* in 1915.[16]

Raising small quantities of many different products in itself ensured high production costs, since the mixed farmer realized no economies from scale. As specialized production technology appeared, he spread his capital even more thinly, and new discoveries in every branch of agricultural science continually forced him to broaden his expertise. But the skill and knowledge required for wheat farming is not useful for cattle raising, and neither talent is helpful in raising poultry. 'Farming is so complicated a business that no man can expect to know everything about its departments,' confessed one agricultural expert in 1915. 'It is an impossibility.'[17]

As in many businesses, success in agriculture increasingly depended on specialization. The hundreds of pioneers who left southern Ontario for the Vulcan area between 1904 and 1910 thought of their homeland as a mixed-farming region because each farmer there raised many different products. But they too began to specialize. Although the number of hogs, poultry, and cattle in Ontario rose between 1901 and 1941, the percentage of farmers raising them actually fell significantly (see Figures 11 and 12). But since farmers did not all specialize in the same products, southern Ontario remained a mixed-farming region. Prairie advocates of individual diversification failed to appreciate that in an increasingly efficient world trading system, specific markets could demand very specialized products. When the Vulcan *Advocate* added the sale of hides to its list of reasons for raising cattle, for example, the town harness-maker explained that local hides lacked weight and quality. He preferred Argentinian hides available from Chicago or Kansas City importers.[18] With specialization sweeping the agricultural world, any farmer who attempted to duplicate the highly praised CPR demonstration farm at Vulcan, which required a substantial investment to produce minute quantities of products suspect in quality, would surely have faced bankruptcy.

Frontier conditions especially favoured specialization over diversification. Building new communities inevitably saddled frontier societies with heavy debts, and to pay them off, settlers needed to earn quick cash in outside markets. As W.A. Mackintosh, one of the few academic critics of the mixed-farming movement on the prairies, noted: 'No large distinctively agricultural community has ever passed from primitive poverty to great prosperity except through the gateway of the "one crop" system and the export staple.'[19] Furthermore, a shortage of labour and an abundance of unclaimed land characterizes all frontier societies. Most of the mixed-farming products advocated in the Vulcan area did not require much land, but because little technology had developed to aid their production, they demanded much labour. Because of technological advances in grain machinery, however, the settlers could cultivate sprawling wheat fields with less labour.

But most Vulcan-area settlers did not need sophisticated cost accounting to see that wheat specialists enjoyed more luxuries than the mixed farmers who worked longer and harder. They soon encountered more obvious difficulties in raising a variety of products sufficient in quality and quantity to justify production costs. The physical environment flatly rejected nearly every crop imported from the midwest. The *Grain Growers' Guide* praised Wilhelm Jensen's corn-raising efforts at Carmangay so enthusiastically that it almost failed to report how early frosts often killed his crop. If the shorter growing season did not destroy midwestern crops, insufficient rainfall often limited yields; even before the drought of the 1930s, vegetable gardens at Carmangay often failed completely. 'Corn ought to grow in this district,' insisted the Vulcan *Advocate* as it pondered the difficulties, but admitted that 'experiments in the past have not been successful.'[20]

Farming with less rainfall, the pioneers discovered that they required more acres of pasture per animal in the Vulcan area than in the midwest. They also found little surface water for livestock to drink, and drainage patterns in the area aggravated the problem. Most surface water collected in shallow alkaline sloughs and stagnated; subject to long hours of sunshine and the dry winds of southern Alberta, it evaporated quickly. The expense of excavating deep dugouts to catch spring runoff awaited the sponsorship of the Prairie Farm Rehabilitation Administration in the 1930s and 1940s. Some surface water drained into the Little Bow River and the Snake Ravine, but in drought years like 1910 they too dried up completely. During the ranching era, cattle roamed to and from these streams freely, but when the pioneers erected fences to protect their crops, only farmers situated on their banks enjoyed access to the water.[21]

The lack of surface water forced settlers to drill wells and erect windmill pumps, often at great expense, for the water-table varied in depth from ten to hundreds of feet. If the pioneers struck water, alkali salts and hard minerals often rendered it useless for human or livestock consumption. But many found no water at all. Henry Krause drilled thirteen dry wells on his homestead, finally admitted defeat, and hauled even drinking water from seven miles away. 'Brother Fred and I hauled water for our stock all summer 1907,' recalled another settler. More than a dozen wells ran dry in one district in 1912, including a six-hundred-foot shaft that had cost its owner fifteen hundred dollars.[22]

Like many dryland communities, the Vulcan area periodically looked to irrigation to end such problems, and like most of them, it continually suffered disappointment. Throughout most of the Great Plains irrigation could not serve enough farmers to justify the costs involved, and the region afforded so little replenishable water that its governments could not approve many schemes without depriving downstream communities of water altogether. The promise of irrigation kept mixed-farming dreams alive, but plans to inaugurate it in the Vulcan area repeatedly failed to materialize.[23]

In communities boasting abundant water southern Alberta quickly won praise as ideal livestock country. Sunny autumns cured the native grasses and preserved their nutrients. Ranchers did not rely heavily on feed crops, as the warm chinook winds often permitted winter grazing by melting the snow and exposing the grass. But the weather could also strike cattle with the same fury that it attacked crops. The howling blizzards, deep snows, and bitter cold of the winter of 1906–7 destroyed open-range ranching in the Vulcan area. By spring thousands of dead cattle littered the prairie. Crazed by starvation, a few survivors ran wild. After settlers criss-crossed the area with barbed-wire fences, blizzards posed an even greater hazard, for cattle could no longer drift with the wind or find shelter on flat, treeless farms.[24]

Every historical account of pioneering also documents how varmints, insects, and diseases attacked wheat, but few record their equally devastating impact on livestock. Dipping cattle in hot sulphur baths to combat mange consumed long hours and invited endless trouble, and poultry and swine died readily from highly contagious infections. Farmers sometimes lost their entire stock in epidemics.[25] The rise of great hog and chicken specialty farms in North America after the Second World War depended largely on advances in veterinary medicine, on strict controls minimizing contact between humans and animals, and on immaculate sanitary conditions, many feasible only through automation. Larger enemies also attacked farm animals. On the eve of settlement carnivorous animals roamed the Vulcan area in large numbers, and early pioneers reported serious losses of livestock, especially poultry and hogs. A long, costly, and not altogether successful war against the predators ensued.[26]

Mixed farming more logically developed in districts or on farms that featured greater variety in their landscapes. The family farm of Vulcan pioneer Daniel McNiven back in Halton County, Ontario, consisted of one hundred acres of partly cleared and partly treed land of diverse quality. Dan's father seeded the best forty-five acres to grain, corn, and hay; he sold some of this produce and fed the rest to livestock. He kept hogs and chickens, and pastured cattle on the remaining land. By laboriously removing trees, stumps, and rocks, he claimed a little more land for cultivation each year. Farms or districts with such varied terrain often exhibited a predictable pattern of land use. On rich river-bottom soils, farmers intensively cultivated crops with high market values; on less fertile hillsides they raised feed crops for livestock; on thin soils or rocky hilltops they ran cattle or sheep, while such 'waste lands' as streams, ponds, ravines, and tree groves provided livestock with water and shelter. The uniform monotony of the Vulcan landscape, however, suggested a one-crop system, and those settlers truly interested in mixed farming wisely sold their expensive wheatlands and bought cheaper foothill or park-belt farms, where such features favoured variety in agricultural production.[27]

Because environmental problems (among others) hindered livestock production in the Vulcan area, the mixed-farming solution to declining soil fertility and erosion proved impractical. A New Jersey farmer visiting the area in 1913 professed astonishment at the waste of barnyard manure and the lack of alfalfa grown. But unable to raise nearly as many animals per acre of farmland as they had back home, the settlers could only spread a limited supply of manure thinly over a vast area, and in dry years it often failed to rot properly.[28] Spreading manure involved so much trouble, time, and expense for so little gain that most farmers soon abandoned the practice. And the mixed-farming movement's champion fertilizing crop, alfalfa, refused to transmit nitrogen from the air to the earth because the Rhizobium bacteria responsible for the process did not inhabit southern Alberta soils.[29] Yet these failures probably did not matter greatly, for low wheat yields more often resulted from insufficient rainfall and inappropriate cultivation methods than from a lack of fertilizer.

By contrast, much about the physical environment of the Vulcan area favoured raising wheat. Relatively flat and free of geographical obstacles, the terrain invited the extensive use of machinery, and advances in agricultural technology served wheat far better than most farm products. Best of all, wheat plunged its roots deep into the soil and survived drought more readily than did most other crops. Arid climates actually produce harder kernels of higher protein content that do humid ones, and if farmers suffered lower yields in dry years, they usually earned a higher grade.

The rapid development of new strains even more amenable to the environment ensured wheat's dominance. Until the 1880s midwestern farmers mostly raised soft varieties, which yielded a flour adequate for making pasta and sweet pastry, but the replacement of stone wheels with steel or porcelain rollers enabled millers to crush properly the harder varieties better suited for baking bread. Switching to hard wheats, pioneers from the midwest introduced winter varieties derived from Russian and Turkish strains to the Great Plains and the Inland Empire. Seeded in the fall, these grains stopped growing in midwinter but matured rapidly in the spring, permitting farmers to harvest in early summer. Settlers in southern Alberta naturally imported these familiar varieties. Like many others, E.E. Thompson raised Kansas Turkey Red on his huge Brant farm; renaming it Alberta Red, he sold the seed to settlers throughout the Vulcan area.[30]

But because winter wheat primarily suited regions where wet springs hindered seeding or blistering midsummer heat damaged growing crops, many Vulcan-area settlers preferred hard spring wheats like Red Fife, developed in Ontario in the 1840s and first grown on the northern plains in the 1870s. Seeded in spring and harvested in fall, it often took longer to ripen that the growing season would permit, but Marquis, a hard spring variety created by Dominion government scientists, ripened a week earlier, resisted drought better, and outyielded Red Fife without surrendering its high protein content and superior milling and baking qualities. Introduced in 1911, Marquis quickly swept across the Canadian prairies and the northern American plains. Farmers in the Carmangay district grew only about one acre of Marquis for every twenty-five of Red Fife in 1912, but within a few years it replaced Red Fife altogether. With the success of Marquis, farmers quit raising winter wheat. In 1910 it still accounted for about one-fifth of all wheat grown in the Vulcan area; by 1916 it had virtually disappeared.[31]

Superior strains soon followed. Red Rob and Garnet appeared in southern Alberta in the 1920s, and although they did not match Marquis for quality, they ripened still earlier. Rust-resistant varieties arrived in the 1930s: Renown, Apex, Regent, and Thatcher, which soon replaced Marquis as the dominant strain. In 1946 Rescue added a sawfly-resistant stem to rust-resistant qualities, and in 1952 Chinook married both characteristics to milling properties superior to Marquis. Provided with a near-continuous flow of improved varieties, the soil and climate of the Vulcan area produced wheat of exceptional quality, and its farmers won three world wheat championships in the 1960s and the 1970s.[32]

Ironically, the metropolitan marketplace also undermined diversification. While its communication network boomed the message of mixed farming to the Vulcan area, its transportation and marketing systems quietly rewarded the wheat specialist. The settlers could raise no commodity in huge quantity unless they exported it out of the area, for the local market for food – indeed, the entire western Canadian demand – remained small relative to the great number of farms able to supply it. For travelling long distances cheaply, wheat quickly showed its advantage over most farm products. Undisturbed by temperature changes and refusing to spoil unless wet, it tolerated lengthy shipping delays in any season. It required no delicate or expensive handling. Unceremoniously dumped from farm bins to wagons, from elevators to boxcars, from terminals to ships, it arrived undamaged. It also qualified for preferential freight rates under the Crow's Nest Pass Agreement.[33]

Most farm products, including livestock, did not enjoy the cheap freight rates afforded grain. Fruit, vegetables, dairy products, eggs, and meat also demanded more elaborate packaging and careful handling, even to be moved from farm to town. 'We carried eggs in syrup pails for a distance of eight miles to George Mark's store at Cleverville,' recalled an early settler.[34] Spoiled by excessive heat, cold, or delay, many foods required regular delivery to town, followed by expensive storage and speedy shipment in temperature-controlled warehouses and boxcars. Given these immense costs, the Vulcan area could not possibly compete with farmers who lived near the great urban markets of eastern Canada, or even with those situated on the fringes of western cities. The Vulcan area could supply Liverpool with wheat more efficiently than it could deliver many mixed-farming products to Calgary.

To justify the costs of production and transportation, and to survive the limitations imposed by the environment and the frontier, mixed farmers needed consistently high prices in metropolitan markets. They did not get them. Farm critics argued that diversification stabilized farm incomes in two ways: if one crop failed, the farmer might depend on others for high yields; if one commodity's value fell, the others would provide compensation. But the most serious environmental disasters curtailed the output of virtually all farm products, wheat less than most, and as economic studies have demonstrated, the prices of all farm commodities plummeted during depressions.[35]

This unfortunate fact became readily apparent during the 1930s. The Prairie Farm Rehabilitation Administration found ranchers in worse financial trouble than straight grain farmers. 'I'm beginning to wonder what we are going to do with our livestock,' complained one Vulcan farmer; 'They are not paying for their keep now.' 'Eggs five cents a dozen,' remembered one woman; 'twelve dozen wouldn't pay for half a pound of tobacco.' Like many others, Ken Miller threw them to the hogs because they were not worth hauling to town, and then he killed and ate the hogs because they were not worth hauling to town either. Although some argued that 'those cattle and chickens were all that kept us afloat in hard times,' in the grim crop year of 1935 animals and their by-products yielded Vulcan-area farmers no more than 10 per cent of their gross incomes and probably no net income at all.[36] More Vulcan-area farmers quit raising cattle and swine during the 1930s than in any previous decade (see Figure 11).

Even oats, barley, and rye, crops that grew well in the Vulcan environment, that benefited from the same technological developments, and that cost nothing extra to produce or transport, could not match wheat for value. In 1920 those crops collectively accounted for about 37 per cent of the seeded acreage in Alberta but represented only 24 per cent of the value of all field crops; in 1930 their seeded acreage declined to 27 per cent and their value to 17 per cent. Pioneers in the Vulcan area only raised oats because they needed inexpensive feed for work-horses, but as they acquired tractors, they quickly converted oat, hay, and pasture lands to wheat fields (see Figure 15). Because feed grains matured early and thrived in poor-quality leached soils, where wheat did not fare as well, the production of oats and barley increasingly shifted to the prairie's northern park belt, where wheat more commonly suffered from a shorter growing season.[37] Barley, rye, flax, and rapeseed did not again threaten wheat's supremacy in the Vulcan area until after the Second World War, when their prices rose in response to increased demands for alcoholic beverages and oil seeds.

Wheat also served a number of social purposes on the Vulcan frontier. It could be raised in conjunction with rampant land speculation and restless geographical mobility. Hoping to develop a farm for quick resale, most pioneers refused to invest the extra time, effort, and money necessary to establish mixed farms. Some worked full-time at other occupations; some needed winter jobs to finance improvements, and others, especially bachelors, simply loathed spending lonely winters on isolated farms. While absent, anyone who owned horses, and perhaps a few other animals, might convince a neighbour to care for them, but with its endless rounds of daily chores a full-fledged mixed farm threatened to chain the settler to his homestead all year. Many who did start mixed farms later reconsidered the decision: 'A large number of farmers have sold all their livestock and spent their winters in the east or south in warmer climates,' noted the Calgary *Daily Herald* on 9 July 1929.

If wheat easily emerged as the most logical crop to raise, then why did local farmers bother with other products at all? Sound economic reasons provide a small part of the answer. In spite of the overwhelming odds against successful mixed farming, some settlers overcame them by exploiting exceptional circumstances. Some stretches of land would not sustain a crop – pockets of thin soil that mysteriously received little rainfall, and places where rocks, sharply graded knolls, or deeply rutted ravines prohibited the use of machinery. These features did not characterize much of the area. By 1931 only 15 per cent of the farmland in the Vulcan area remained uncultivated, compared to nearly 55 per cent on Alberta farms generally. But if a farm afforded sufficient surface or well water, the settler might profit by running livestock on these unproductive lands.

To cut production costs or capitalize on some special expertise, successful forays into mixed farming also demanded a concentrated effort. Besides wheat, a few Vulcan-area farmers raised one other product in unusually large quantities. Because of prohibitive transportation costs, these slightly mixed farmers supplied only the local market. Some recognized the tremendous demand for draughthorses in the area and bred them in large numbers. F.C.C. Andrews anticipated a related market for feed and seeded nothing but oats from 1904 to 1915. The appearance of towns on the Kipp-Aldersyde line opened a tiny market for foodstuffs. One settler near Carmangay and another three miles from Vulcan operated successful dairy farms. A few others intensively cultivated a limited variety of vegetables. But because few legitimate opportunities for mixed farming arose, the number of settlers who developed sidelines with profit margins comparable to those produced by growing wheat probably remained very small.[38]

But the existence of a small local market for mixed-farm products, and of small tracts of terrain suitable for their production, cannot account for all the mixed-farming activity in the area. More importantly, these conditions do not account for the local settlers' marked enthusiasm for the diversification movement. To explain their zeal it is necessary to look beyond the raw economic aspects of the matter and into the realm of social and cultural attitudes. One important observation is that nearly all the pioneers in the Vulcan area spent their childhoods on mixed farms in mixed-farming regions. Of twelve hundred heads of families who entered the area between 1904 and 1920, about 90 per cent grew up east of the critical rainfall line of one hundred degrees longitude. In 1926 the dominion census measured the relationship between geographical origins and mixed-farming practices; European-born farmers in Alberta showed more inclination to raise livestock than any other group, followed by the Ontario-born, the American-born, and finally the Alberta-born.

This relationship between birthplace and mixed-farming practices suggests the persuasive influence of tradition even when individuals are placed in circumstances where tradition is no longer appropriate. A specific example illustrates this phenomenon. Raised on home-grown foods, many eaten fresh year-round and others from preserve jars in winter, the pioneers did not readily switch to store-bought items. In many cases they probably did not care if raising their own foods cost more than buying them. Although they could purchase cheap condensed milk, for example, one survey revealed that settlers in Saskatchewan preferred it fresh and willingly milked their own cows to get it. Although happy to sell any surplus, one pioneer woman in the Vulcan district admitted that her family dabbled in mixed farming primarily to supply their own table.[39] Between 1920 and 1940 farm families in the Vulcan area consumed over half the eggs, three-quarters of the butter, and 95 per cent of the milk that they produced.

The willingness of settlers to stock their own pantries through mixed-farming activity also depended on one social condition more than any other: marriage. During the proving-up period, twenty of the twenty-five married homesteaders in Township 17-25-4 raised cattle, compared to only four of the thirty-two bachelors. Most bachelors kept no livestock at all save horses, and most did not even plant gardens. The routine chores of mixed farming not only threatened to end their annual escape from loneliness and isolation each winter but interfered with the raising of wheat at critical times. Sod busting, seeding, and harvesting demanded a concentrated effort that left the solitary pioneer little time for other duties. His reluctance to practise mixed farming suggests how much of its workload fell to the women and children of married men. On most farms they watered and fed the livestock, milked the cows, collected the eggs, weeded the garden, and put up the preserves. Indeed, one settler claimed that some bachelors in his district refused to keep milk cows or chickens because they regarded their care as women's work.[40]

As more settlers married, however, mixed farming in the Vulcan area increased, and large families more commonly kept livestock than did small ones. Most farmers believed that raising food for a large family cost less than buying it. They also thought of mixed farming as an effective means of busying idle hands, of training the girls in the duties of a farm wife, and of inculcating steady work-habits in the boys before introducing them to field work. As a reward for her labours, the sale of non-grain produce also provided many a farm wife with spending money.[41] Mixed-farming activities seemed profitable to any farm wife who kept the proceeds from the sale of surplus food while the farm operation as a whole absorbed the cost of providing buildings, fencing, wells, and feed. And the women's ability to sell produce at all depended largely on the refusal of single men to raise any food themselves. In most rural districts, neighbouring bachelors provided ready customers for eggs, milk, meat, preserves, and baked goods.

But mixed farming also nourished psychological appetites. Even when practised in a token manner, it provided many settlers with a comforting link to home and tradition. 'Father always enjoyed horses [and] loved livestock,' recalled a pioneer's daughter. A brief look at two activities closely associated with mixed farming, building construction and landscaping, helps to explain the importance of this nostalgic indulgence. Some studies suggest that settlers in western Canada developed a 'garrison mentality,' the need to build small fortresses of familiar landscape in the unknown wilderness.[42] Much about the new environment pleased Vulcan pioneers – the vision of sprawling fields laid out in perfect geometric forms, uncluttered by geographical obstacles, and tilled with modern technology appealed to their progressive notion of scientific management. But the starkness of the landscape also unsettled them. 'While a treeless prairie invites quick, cheap cultivation, those of us who come from wooded countries miss the beauty and shade of trees and groves more than anything else in this district,' lamented the Vulcan *Advocate*, as it yearned for the 'old orchards and beautiful flowers back east.' 'When I arrived on the

Alberta prairie from the beautiful wooded state of Illinois,' remembered John Glambeck, 'I naturally missed the trees very much.'[43]

While the settlers did not intend to interfere with efficiency in the fields, they struggled to transform their farmyards into familiar havens. As early as 1908 the Mounted Police reported 'a praiseworthy desire to beautify ... home surroundings by planting large numbers of trees.' Nearly everyone landscaped to some extent, and some settlers planted hundreds of trees. Just as they promoted many non-grain farm products, various institutions provided encouragement and aid for tree planting. The dominion Department of the Interior gave away millions of trees to prairie farmers. The CPR established a flower garden at Vulcan in 1913. Town councils launched aggressive tree-planting campaigns, and Women's Institutes sponsored flower-growing contests.[44]

With a market value of zero, trees none the less emerged as one of the settlers' most prized crops. 'It is surprising to note in nearly every case the value placed by the farmers upon their small groups of trees,' reported a 1910 publication; 'to one unaccustomed to the monotonous prairie landscape, these values may in some cases seem exaggerated.' 'Settlers have come from as far away as 15 miles to look at [my trees],' boasted one settler; '[they] speak of me as "the man who has trees."' Mr and Mrs Andrew Lawrence from Scotland attracted hordes of admirers to their Carmangay home, where through herculean effort they maintained a landscaped yard of fruit trees, flowers, and a goldfish pond. As their example suggests, few landscaping projects suited the prairie environment ecologically or aesthetically. When the townspeople of Carmangay designed a park in 1912, they wanted it to look like southern Ontario: well treed, green, and stocked with domesticated eastern flowers.[45] Although the settlers tended these gardens meticulously, and even watered trees by pail when necessary, high winds, drought, unexpected frosts, and moisture-greedy native grasses inflicted heavy damage on these delicate imports. Except for the hardy caragana bush, few survived for long.

Compelled as always to offer practical reasons for spending time and money on unprofitable crops, the settlers praised trees for their value as windbreaks, snow-fences, and stock shelters. But they also cited more dubious advantages; trees would prevent soil drifting, halt the spread of weeds, increase rainfall, improve the settlers' health, and raise land values by making the area more attractive to prospective settlers. Because they associated trees and flowers with beauty and civilization, those special preserves of feminine interest, men also thought that landscaping would make farm wives more contented. To endure the frontier wilderness, women in particular, they believed, required the security and stability of a fully landscaped farmyard equipped for a broad range of traditional agricultural pursuits. Thus the married man commonly headed for the frontier in advance of his wife to 'get things established,' and the in the weeks before her arrival the task of 'fixing the place up' for her approval filled him with anxiety.[46]

The farm buildings themselves, especially the house, formed the heart of this protective bastion. That fabled architectural innovation of the treeless plains, the sod hut, never dominated the western landscape to the extent that legend suggests. As soon as they could get lumber, the pioneers happily deserted them. On the frontiers opened by railways, like the Vulcan area, sod huts rarely appeared at all. Nearly everyone built 'sawed huts' instead. Often crude, these frame shacks yielded to more substantial structures as finances permitted and the commitment to stay deepened. Although forced to forgo the stone and brick building materials often used in southern Ontario, the settlers showed no inclination to select architectural styles in harmony with their new environment. Indeed, they often duplicated eastern buildings in exact detail by ordering blueprints from the CPR or through advertisements in Eaton's catalogue or other periodicals. Roman Catholics in Vulcan selected design number 205 from the Catholic catalogue of suggested church plans. Thus, two-storey barns, originally built against hillsides in Europe and eastern America so that wagons could deliver hay directly into the loft for storage, and two-storey farmhouses with sweeping verandas, originally designed for protection against rain rather than wind, accompanied settlers to the midwest and later to the flat, arid plains.[47]

The frontier, the environment, and even the metropolis had forced the settlers to grow wheat, but they responded emotionally to this innovation by clinging tightly to the shattered pieces of a broken tradition. As they transformed the open prairie into specialized wheat fields, they struggled to convert their yards into miniature mixed farms complete with traditionally designed houses, barns, and chicken coops, surrounded by the trees, flowers, and vegetable gardens of home. But as progressive-minded people, they refused to admit any psychological dependence on tradition. Consequently, even as they poured their resources into wheat, they insisted that mixed farming not only paid better but represented agriculture's most advanced stage of development. 'Our visit was altogether instructive,' wrote *Farm and Ranch Review* reporters of a trip to the mammoth C.S. Noble farm south of the Vulcan area, 'but ended in another failure of our quest for the good grain farmer that would condemn mixed farming.' In a later submission to the provincial government Noble urged the development of small mixed farms (by others, presumably). Such attitudes survived for decades. Indeed, many of the oldest farmers in the Vulcan area still insist that mixed farming is far superior to wheat specialization, even though they themselves abandoned livestock-raising long ago.[48]

Only on rare occasions did anyone point out the stark contrast between belief and behaviour in the Vulcan area, but in 1913 the Carmangay *Sun*, frustrated that its support of mixed farming led to so little action, lashed out at its readers: 'Our enterprising farmers who sit on their ploughs and preach mixed farming have come west, as a rule, to get away from barn yards and pig pens.' On those even rarer occasions when someone openly questioned the value of mixed farming, a savage rebuttal usually silenced them. One southern Alberta pioneer wrote a lengthy letter to the *Farm and Ranch Review* outlining the disadvantages of diversified production and concluded that 'all the mixed farming preaching that can be printed will not fill [the farmer's] bread basket, swell his bank account, or put fertility into his soil.' But although the writer forced the magazine to agree with every point he raised in favour of specializing in wheat, the editor none the less denounced his conclusion. If reality needed to be faced, presenting it with a grievous sense of loss proved more socially acceptable. '[We] expect to do farming on a less diversified plan,' wrote an American midwesterner who settled in southern Alberta. 'We have left corn, hogs, cattle, horse-growing, fruit-raising, dairying, hay production and a dozen other things of that nature across the line. Like most of the other fellows, we go after wheat, wheat, and more wheat, [but] we have never been used to this one-crop idea.'[49]

Thus, while most farmers silently recognized the advantages of specializing in wheat and acted accordingly, their infatuation with mixed farming never faded. By dabbling in it and deceiving themselves about its importance, Vulcan-area settlers found a psychologically satisfying solution to a painful dilemma.

5

Technique

Having decided to specialize in wheat, the pioneers tackled the problem of how best to grow it in the new environment. They responded to the challenge of maximizing yields from minimal moisture by adopting the frequently cited but little studied dry-farming technique. The term caused some confusion at the time, and historians have described it in various ways ever since. In many accounts it means nothing more than simply allowing land to lie fallow every other year, an ancient practice rediscovered and revived in the semi-arid west. Defined more technically, however, dry farming involved tilling the soil in accordance with a particular theory of moisture conservation. And contrary to many accounts that explain it too loosely, it did not solve the riddle of western agriculture. Indeed, it aggravated the region's most serious environmental problem, and the painful experience of the Great Depression forced farmers to abandon it.

Settlers arrived in the Vulcan area with little knowledge of agriculture under dry conditions. Some had never farmed at all, particularly the British-born. 'Neither of us knew a darn thing about homesteading or farming or anything,' confessed one couple; 'we were both city people [from Liverpool].' By contrast, many North Americans boasted of extensive pioneering, as well as farming, experience. A few, like D.H. Galbraith, a former employee of the Ontario Department of Agriculture with a degree from Guelph, even possessed considerable formal training. The settlement authorities, the press, and the other pioneers (as well as most historians since) believed that Americans made the best farmers; they arrived as veterans of western agriculture with plenty of capital and management skills.[1]

But as the last chapter demonstrated, they garnered most of that experience in the relatively humid eastern counties of the North Dakota–Kansas corridor. Indeed, before 1910 few frontier communities anywhere in the Canadian prairies could claim many American settlers from that vast, dry, and still largely empty region between the hundredth meridian and the Rocky Mountains. Misunderstandings over geographical definitions account for the confusion about the nature of American farming experience in dry areas. In Canada *prairie* generally referred to the entire arable region from the Red River to the Rockies, but in the United States the term more commonly applied to the humid grasslands of Illinois and Iowa. Americans usually referred to the arid high country east of the mountains as the Great Plains. Thus many Americans with plenty of experience in 'prairie' farming encountered difficulties when they tried to farm the southern Alberta prairie. The Vulcan-area settlers most acquainted with farming in dry areas hailed from the treeless valleys of the Inland Empire, but while some districts in that region averaged 10 inches of precipitation per year, others enjoyed 20 or even 30 inches. Thus few settlers in the Vulcan area had ever attempted to farm under arid conditions. In any event, most dry-farm techniques, save fallowing, received little publicity anywhere in the United States prior to 1905, when many American settlers had already reached the Vulcan area.[2]

As the history of the mixed-farming movement demonstrates, Vulcan-area settlers did not lack for advice on how to farm. To recapitulate briefly: government publications, farm magazines, local newspapers, and even promotional literature reported on the experiences of other communities and on research conducted by western universities, departments of agriculture, experimental farms, and agricultural schools. In turn, those agencies frequently sponsored special educational trains, travelling lecturers, short courses, and farm demonstrations. Local organizations, most notably the agricultural societies, held many similar events and promoted annual agricultural fairs. In addition, the area soon secured its own demonstration farms and experimental plots courtesy of the CPR, the Dominion Department of Agriculture, and the Claresholm Agricultural School. All these educational services channelled most of their energy and resources into the mixed farming movement, and thus instructed the pioneers on subjects they already knew best. But sandwiched between lessons on the profitability of chickens and the virtues of corn, much information about wheat growing also emerged. Some educational services geared themselves specifically to the task, especially seed fairs, crop competitions, field demonstrations sponsored by machinery companies, and the touring 'Interprovincial Weed Train.'

Influential agencies also pressured the local population to take advantage of these educational opportunities; especially active was the provincial Department of Agriculture, whose influence over local agricultural societies has already been noted in connection with mixed farming. During the First World

War stringency campaign the department announced that it would not be able to supply local societies with paid lecturers but it expected the locals to sponsor their own anyway. When A. Galbraith, superintendent of Fairs and Institutes, discovered that the Carmangay society had not invited any speakers in 1916, he gave it a scolding and cut off its provincial grant for one year.[3] But local groups applied most of the pressure themselves, for poor farmers threatened to undermine the booster campaign. Local newspapers, boards of trade, and speculators urged everyone to partake of the educational services available, and they dispensed much information themselves. 'The farmer of today, and of tomorrow,' argued the High River *Times*, 'must be a man of brains as well as of muscle, or he cannot succeed.' 'Don't get the idea that a man will learn as much looking out a train window on a distant land as he will looking over a book in some cosy corner of a comfortable home,' advised the Carmangay *Sun*.[4]

Vulcan-area settlers responded to these overtures as enthusiastically as they did to mixed-farming education. Farm educators and rural sociologists throughout North America often complained bitterly about the apathy of farmers to agricultural education, and they compiled a massive literature on the process of innovation, demonstrating that in most communities only a small minority accepted it readily – usually the progressive-minded, well-educated, and prosperous farmers who thought of agriculture as a business that should be based on scientific principles and conducted in an efficient manner. Since the Vulcan area attracted many such farmers, the educators found relatively little apathy and cynicism to combat. And since the frontier lacked restraints based on local tradition, since it brought together strangers with diverse experiences and ideas, and since it imposed the need for learning quickly how to farm a new environment, it generally proved more receptive to agricultural innovation than did settled areas.[5] Furthermore, on a sparsely populated frontier, any public event, educational or not, afforded an opportunity for socializing, and thus attracted many farmers.

The local press could usually report 'splendid attendance,' 'great interest,' and 'good discussions' at agricultural seminars, lectures, and demonstrations. Excursions to the Lethbridge Experimental Farm began in 1906, and the Vulcan area always sent a large contingent. Some farmers travelled as far as Fort Macleod to attend agricultural short courses, and the Claresholm Agricultural School attracted many students from the Vulcan area. Launched in 1914, the Vulcan Agricultural Society swelled to 152 members within two years, and competition entries at the Carmangay society's annual fair peaked at 1,216 in 1913, and often drew crowds of 1,500.[6]

Information about wheat farming also circulated informally. Many settlers had lived in several states and provinces and had been exposed to a variety of farming ideas, and they frequently compared their agricultural backgrounds. 'I learned from neighbours how to farm,' recalled an Austrian immigrant.[7] The financial ability of Vulcan settlers to travel often and far further increased this exposure. And as the *Farm and Ranch Review* pointed out on 5 October 1914, purchases of automobiles by farmers greatly facilitated their first-hand knowledge of local and regional practices: 'Not long ago the average farmer knew only his own little locality . . . the automobile lifts him out into a new and wider environment. He knows what is being done in farm operations for 20, 30, and 40 miles around. He is able to see the best that other farmers are doing and pick up kernels of truth here and there which he can adapt to his own conditions. Broader vision, new ideas and ideals must come as a result.' Thus both shared cultural traditions and outside agencies contributed to agricultural knowledge, and it circulated freely throughout the area by both institutional and informal means.

The educational campaign did not impress everyone, and some openly criticized it. Several neighbours told one young man off to agricultural school that 'you can't learn farming from a book,' and even within the Vulcan Agricultural Society itself, some members derogatorily referred to experimental stations as 'book farms.' Not unexpectedly, older farmers more often resisted the advice of experts, and the return of sons from agricultural school eager to try new ideas sparked battles on many farms.[8] Agricultural educators fretted needlessly, however, about the influence of the cynics, for if they refused to learn anything directly from agricultural agencies, they often learned about new techniques by closely watching their more progressive-minded neighbours. One farmer who contemptuously dismissed all agricultural education, and even refused to consult farm magazines, none the less expressed the view that 'if a man's going to a new area, he better pay attention to those who've been farming there a long time.'[9] Indeed, such cynics often enjoyed an advantage over their more progressive neighbours. By sitting back and letting others experiment with the new techniques, they avoided costly failures and imitated only those innovations that clearly succeeded. Thus new techniques that worked percolated quickly through the community, even if only a small minority expressed initial interest in them. Unfortunately for the Vulcan area, however, serious problems developed precisely because so many listened to expert advice so willingly.

The settlers readily accepted the first great innovation in dryland farming: leaving fields dormant every other year so that the soil might utilize the meagre precipitation of two years to produce a single crop. Although historians often debate the exact origins of this practice in western Canada, the success of summerfallowing tests at the Dominion Experimental Farm at Indian Head, Saskatchewan, in the 1880s received wide publicity for fifteen years prior to the settlement of the Vulcan area. Virtually all promotional literature concerning western Canada publicized the practice, and any settler who miraculously escaped hearing of it before arriving encountered it soon enough through literature or neighbours. 'The method has the approval of science and is a case where present loss yields a future profit,' the Vulcan *Review* advised new-comers on 9 April 1912. During the first two or three years of settlement, when many pioneers desperately needed ready cash, they continuously cropped all the land they had broken – a few, oblivious of established opinion, cropped the same fields as often as seven years – but once they had established their home-steads, the vast majority commenced fallowing, as they found it 'the only way to make grain growing pay.'[10] Besides the 'scientific' reason for its ready and unquestioned adoption, the settlers discovered that it did not threaten their traditional agricultural practices; it did not ask them to do something different, but to do nothing at all.

If few questioned the value of summerfallowing, they did ponder whether to leave fields dormant every other year, or once in every three. Wheat prices often affected their decision. High prices during the First World War led many to crop more often between 1915 and 1921. Sometimes the decision rested upon the supply of moisture in the soil at seeding time; a wet winter and spring might induce more farmers to seed some fields for a second straight year. Between 1921 and 1941, for example, the ratio of cropped to fallow land fluctuated between 1.4 to 1 and 1.8 to 1 in the municipal district of Harmony. By 1921, when the settlers had learned that some parts of the Vulcan area usually received more rainfall than others, those in humid neighbourhoods tended to fallow one year in three, while those in the drier ones more often did so every other year.

Everyone's attention soon focused on how to till the land during its year of rest, for native weeds and those imported into the district with new seed grains quickly invaded the fields. Before the development of effective chemical herbi-cides after the Second World War, weeds posed a serious problem. Nothing could prevent them from flourishing in the cropped fields. They matured with the wheat, and the wind spread their seeds to adjacent fallow. In spite of the best efforts of farmers and strict municipal by-laws regarding weed control, the intruders sometimes emerged victorious. 'The future of this section of the country is seriously jeopardized,' cried the Champion *Chronicle* on 16 December 1920 when Canadian and Russian thistle, wild oats, and stinkweed overran the fields. If weeds drained the soil of moisture, then fallowing could not serve its purpose, so killing them became a primary occupation of Vulcan-area farmers.

A truism holds that pioneers everywhere in North America proceeded to till frontier soils as they had back home simply because they did not know what else to do. More accurately, they retained those practices that they could duplicate easily, while those that could be duplicated only with great difficulty atrophied. Vulcan-area pioneers fully expected to till the soil in traditional midwestern fashion, and when no immediate difficulty imposed itself on them, they made use of the same implements that they had always used, including ploughs. Although the settlers imported them in many different designs and sizes to serve a variety of purposes, all ploughs attacked the soil in the same basic manner: curved blades entered the surface at a steep angle, cutting deep into the earth, turning it over, and burying its surface. No other implement could penetrate the tough virgin sod. Breaking ploughs cut about two to four inches into the earth, and many settlers then 'backset' it by ploughing backwards and cutting about two inches deeper into the sod.[11]

But the settlers also used ploughs to kill weeds in the fallow fields, and they ploughed as deep and frequently as necessary to keep them free of all vegetation. As late as 1930 most agricultural experts condoned this practice. Deep and frequent ploughing, they reasoned, not only aerated the soil but allowed rainfall to penetrate. 'Keeping it worked up well so it will retain the moisture on the following year with minimum rainfall ... is now very much in vogue,' wrote a Carmangay pioneer to Michigan friends in 1913. The pioneers further reasoned that vegetation, buried under the surface, would rot more quickly: 'take care that all weeds are pulled under and covered,' advised the Carmangay *Sun*.[12]

The perfectly tilled midwestern field met certain aesthetic standards: it was free of all vegetation, black in colour, and velvety smooth. As one southern Alberta pioneer reminded his peers, 'thorough preparation means deep plowing, cutting up all shoddy and grassy spots, breaking up and pulverizing all clods or hard particles, levelling and dragging and in most cases packing all soils.' As the process itself suggests, the pioneers completed this task with the extensive use of harrows, packers, and various drags, which together with ploughs remained standard weapons in their arsenal of tillage equipment for decades. The midwestern obsession for clean fields included other practices as well. A Carmangay Agricultural Society speaker recommended that, if all else failed to kill the hardy tumbling mustard or Russian thistle, farmers should mow them down and burn them. Similarly, the settlers also burned off stubble from the previous year's crop, a practice recommended to the Carmangay society by the Lethbridge Experimental Farm in 1911.[13]

To these practices the pioneers added Hardy W. Campbell's dry-farming system. Campbell, a South Dakota pioneer in the 1880s, observed that crops coming up in the spring seemed thicker and healthier wherever wagon wheels had left tracks in the field. His explanation of the phenomenon and the subsequent development of the dry-farming technique evolved over two decades, but its essential features appeared in his *Soil Culture Manual* of 1902, which underwent only minor changes in many subsequent editions. Campbell explained that water moved to the surface of the soil through capillary action and then evaporated. Of no concern in the humid east, the arid west could ill afford this loss of precious moisture. Consequently, he argued, westerners should pack the soil. Pressing its particles close together would ensure good capillary action to bring water near the surface. The soil surface itself, however, should be kept loose in a 'dry mulch' that would break the capillary action and prevent the moisture from reaching the air and subsequently evaporating. The seeded crop would then draw upon sufficient moisture stored just below the surface. Campbell even developed a 'subsoil packer' to achieve the desired effect. Curiously, Campbell regarded summerfallowing as merely incidental to dry farming; his primary concern rested with the preparation of the soil for seeding. None the less, farmers quickly seized upon his system as a method of controlling weeds in fallow fields so that neither seeds nor evaporation would rob the soil of moisture.[14]

News of Campbell's system spread rapidly after 1906. That year an organizational meeting in Denver created the Dry Farming Congress, which met annually thereafter in various western cities to discuss dry farming and sponsor exhibitions and grain-growing competitions. Although the congress soon abandoned total allegiance to Campbell by endorsing other techniques, most of the new ideas simply involved variations on Campbell's precise instructions about when and how to plough, pack, and harrow. Because boards of trade, railroads, and other western boosters seized control of the congress as a promotional tool to lure settlers west, it generated tremendous publicity throughout the northern American plains and the Inland Empire.[15]

The gospel quickly spilled over the border. When Seager Wheeler of Rosthern, Saskatchewan, won the world wheat championship at New York in 1911 (and many subsequent championships), his technique became well publicized. It included plenty of deep ploughing, subsoil packing, and harrowing and dragging to maintain a shallow dry mulch. The dry-farming technique also found its way into the authoritative manuals on how to farm in western Canada by John Bracken, professor of Agriculture at the University of Saskatchewan. Farm leader W.R. Motherwell endorsed the system during the First World War, and the Alberta Department of Agriculture officially approved it in 1919. The often reprinted 'Ten Commandments of Dry Farming' included among its edicts a commitment to deep ploughing, a compact subsurface, and a loose surface.[16] By 1920 the system had received so much publicity through farm magazines and rural newspapers that it passed for conventional wisdom.

The southern Alberta press, in particular, closely followed the activities of the Dry Farming Congress, and as early as 1907 many Vulcan-area settlers flocked to a lecture in nearby Claresholm delivered by Campbell himself. When Lethbridge hosted the Dry Farming Congress in 1912, the CPR sold 240 excursion tickets to the event at the Champion and Carmangay train stations. Faith in the dry-farming technique soared when the Carmangay entry won the congress wheat championship for the second consecutive year. As early as 1911 W.H. Fairfield of the Lethbridge Experimental Farm advised members of the Carmangay Agricultural Society to keep their soil well packed but to break up all surface crusts on summerfallow. In the fields nearly everyone used some variation of the system, although confusion over definitions arose. Some farmers referred to any practice involving the tillage of fallow fields as dry farming; others used the term to describe only Campbell's recommendations, which some farmers followed very closely; and still others used it to describe any variation on the Campbell theme.[17] In any event, nearly all subscribed to the theory of capillary action of water moving upward through packed soil and stopped short of the surface by a loose mulch on top.

Farm educators often noticed that farmers generally accepted a new innovation most readily when it promised economic rewards with little risk to solve a commonly agreed-upon problem. Dry farming clearly fit into that category, for all the settlers soon recognized that a shortage of moisture constituted the new environment's most serious handicap. Because it was 'scientific,' dry farming appealed strongly to the progressive instincts of Vulcan-area pioneers, but surprisingly, it did almost nothing to challenge their traditional midwestern tillage practices. Its innovative feature lay hardly at all in its techniques but merely in the explanations and justifications for them. All the variations on dry farming urged the midwestern practice of frequent and deep ploughing. Debate centred on which plough to use, when to plough, and how deep, not on whether to plough at all. Maintaining a dry mulch satisfied the midwestern desire for a clean, smooth soil surface, and it could be maintained with implements already in common use, harrows and drags. Farmers need not even buy a subsoil packer; many already owned a disc harrow, an implement highly favoured by Campbell himself and one generally regarded as an 'excellent subsurface packer.'[18]

Most years the dry-farming technique appeared to work well, but this success proved deceptive, for in wet years Vulcan-area soils usually produced good crops regardless of the tillage method employed. Faulty technique revealed itself only in dry, windy years. The first great test of the dry-farming system came in 1910. It failed. The spring clouds refused to release rain. The Little Bow River shrivelled to snake-infested ponds, then dried up completely. Then the winds blew. On one occasion they howled with sufficient force to destroy the baseball stands at Carmangay. The dry surface mulch on the summerfallow simply blew away. The soil dried out as far down as farmers had ploughed it, crumbled to dust, and took flight. So did the soil on fields where stubble had been burned. Wind blew the seed out of the ground, and many crops never came up. Flying dust particles mowed down those that did sprout. Soil drifting on this scale did not occur again until the 1930s, but it still struck from time to time. In 1913 a dust storm swept Vulcan with blinding force. Another in 1918 made it 'impossible to see across the street,' and during the early 1920s windstorms occasionally filled homes with layers of fine dust.[19]

No other environmental disaster strikes prairie agriculture with such devastating long-term impact as soil drifting. A hailstorm or early frost can only destroy one year's crop, but topsoil blown away and piled in great heaps in ditches, along fences, and against buildings can never be properly replaced, and the natural process of topsoil formation proceeds so slowly that stretches of the Vulcan area are still largely infertile today as a result of soil lost in the 1930s. But until that decade few farmers changed their tillage practices.

The reluctance to cast off the dry-farming technique might seem baffling in view of the fact that better tillage methods and implements quickly developed. Indeed, southern Alberta spearheaded the western Canadian search for solutions to soil drifting. It became a more serious problem there at an earlier date than elsewhere because of its climatic peculiarities and a high percentage of soils especially susceptible to wind erosion. Vulcan-area settlers appreciated the problem of using packers, harrows, and drags to maintain a smooth surface – 'they leave the soil so fine and reduce the soil fibre so rapidly that severe drifting is the result,' reported the *Advocate* on 4 October 1922 – but they continued the practice because 'these implements produce a mulch which will prevent evaporation to a great extent.' Yet as early as the 1910s some agricultural scientists in Montana began assaulting the theory of dry farming. They argued that a loose surface mulch had nothing to do with preventing evaporation, because water in most western soils did not move upward through capillary action to any significant extent. In any event, the deep-rooting characteristics of wheat rendered bringing water closer to the surface unnecessary. Not until the 1930s, however, did tests at the Swift Current Experimental Farm conclusively shatter the theory of dry farming by demonstrating that most losses of soil moisture in fallow occurred because of weeds, not evaporation.

Thus in 1921 the Saskatchewan Royal Commission on farming conditions remained committed to deep tillage, soil packing, and the theory of capillary action. It did, however, question the value of the dry mulch. To prevent soil drifting it suggested a cloddier surface and the maintenance of ridges in the field. Others had already advised farmers to leave the dead weeds and stubble on top of the soil.[20]

Because ploughs, packers, harrows, and drags buried vegetation and pulverized the soil, random experiments with other implements began. The Kansas lister threw soil in opposite directions, creating steep ridges that neutralized the impact of ground winds. Like a plough, the one-way disc turned over part of the soil, yet left more vegetation exposed. Farmers occasionally experimented with both implements in southern Alberta throughout the 1910s and 1920s. Other implements disturbed the soil surface even less. Cultivators (which featured V-shaped shovels), blades (long flat strips of steel, often shaped like huge cultivator shovels), and rod weeders (long thin bars that rotated beneath the surface of the soil) all worked in a similar manner. In marked contrast to the plough, these implements entered the soil at a slight angle, penetrated to a much shallower depth, and severed weeds at the roots. They left the dying vegetation on top of the soil to wither in the sun, and left lumps of dirt intact. Tests between 1921 and 1924 at the Lethbridge Experimental Farm demonstrated the radical idea that giving up the plough would not result in diminished yields, and farmers could even judge for themselves without any commitment, for in 1922 the Claresholm Agricultural School began tillage experiments on its demonstration plots at Vulcan. It worked some of them with traditional ploughs and packers, and others with cultivators and rod weeders.[21]

By the early 1920s Vulcan-area settlers knew of these implements and understood their purpose. Indeed, they even experimented with countless varieties of cultivators and rod weeders themselves. These implements had appeared sporadically throughout the North American west but had fallen into disuse, only to be rediscovered once again. Some Vulcan-area pioneers, for example, had used them in the Inland Empire between 1890 and 1910, yet in 1913 a farmer at Nanton, just west of the Vulcan area, patented a new cultivator that 'cut about two inches under the surface of the ground, killing weeds . . . but disturbing the surface as little as possible.' Newly designed rod weeders also kept appearing – at Vulcan in 1920, at Champion a few years later, at Gleichen to the north in 1926. Many farmers simply revamped old machinery to function in similar ways. Blades did not develop quite so readily; in spite of random experimentation, an effective design did not emerge until 1935, when C.S. Noble perfected the Noble blade.[22]

Advocates of the new machinery suggested that it had other advantages besides preventing soil drifting. With shallow and less frequent cultivation, the same acreage could be tilled faster and more easily with fewer horses or less tractor power and fuel. More importantly, infrequent cultivation also promised to combat insects. Grasshoppers and cutworms periodically attacked crops throughout southern Alberta with devastating effect. 'I can remember the grasshopper plagues well; when [we drove] into town the buggy wheels would crush them by the thousands on the road, and wheat crops were wiped out completely,' recalled one pioneer. Poisoning campaigns organized by municipal districts accomplished little, for they used a dangerous but generally ineffective arsenic-based poison. Both grasshoppers and cutworms laid their eggs in fallow. When farmers left a hard crust on the soil after early August, the creatures could not penetrate the surface and many starved to death. This idea reached the Vulcan area at least as early as 1922, but received little publicity until the 1930s. Farmers in the Vulcan area also learned of another technique in the 1920s. They knew that Dutch settlers at Monarch, Alberta, laid out their fields in long alternating strips of crop and summerfallow in an effort to combat soil drifting, yet only a small number of farmers around Carmangay experimented with strip farming in that decade.[23]

The farmers of southern Alberta had actually developed most of the new techniques to control soil drifting themselves; the role of the Lethbridge Experimental Farm remained to test and improve them scientifically. By the 1930s, the assault on the dry-farming technique finally produced an entirely new set of directives from virtually every agency involved in western agriculture: give up excessive and deep tillage; do not pack the soil; do not maintain a finely powered dry mulch; do not burn stubble or seeds; use ploughs, discs, packers, harrows, and drags sparingly. Instead, the reformed experts advised farmers to till less frequently, to cultivate at shallow depths, and to leave lumps of dirt and dead vegetation on the soil surface by making more use of cultivators, blades, rod weeders, and press drills (which pushed the wheat seed firmly into the ground and eliminated the need for packers). If necessary, farmers should employ strip farming or even listing, which left high ridges and deep furrows in the soil. Indeed, so much information about how to fight soil drifting had accumulated that by the time the Prairie Farm Rehabilitation Administration began operating in 1935, it did not need to devote much energy to finding new solutions. It developed instead into a propaganda agency to encourage the use of those already available.[24]

In spite of the growing attack on the dry-farming system before 1935, none of the new implements or techniques enjoyed widespread popularity until that date; they remained mere oases of promise in the windswept desert of dry-farming orthodoxy. One survey revealed that as late as the 1926–32 period,

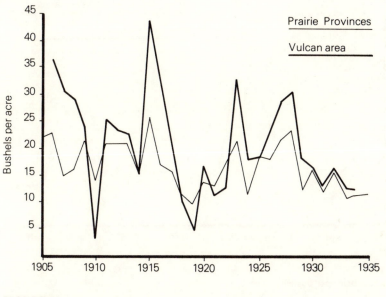

FIGURE 16
Average annual wheat yields

222 plows, 118 disc harrows, and 31 packers still remained in use on every hundred wheat farms in Saskatchewan, compared to only 31 cultivators, 6 rod weeders, and 2 one-way discs.[25]

Why did the new technology and technique fail to take hold for so long when farmers had accepted the dry-farming system so quickly and wholeheartedly? Relative prosperity clearly dampened the desire to change. The 1910 construction boom at the Lake McGregor irrigation site, on the Kipp-Aldersyde railway, and in the Carmangay townsite provided ready employment during a disastrous crop year. The memory of blinding dust storms quickly faded as yields returned to normal, and the press soon reiterated its faith in the dry-farming system.[26] From a much broader perspective, wheat yields in the Vulcan area in the three decades after 1905 surpassed those for the prairie provinces generally in every crop year but five, averaging 20.8 bushels per acre compared to 16.7 (see Figure 16). But prosperity also depended on the price of wheat (see Figure 17), and if we multiply the price by the yield to determine the gross returns per seeded acre, a more accurate picture of changing prosperity in the Vulcan area emerges (see Figure 18). Although southern Alberta farmers remained at a slight disadvantage compared to most prairie farmers in terms of transportation costs, Vulcan-area farms usually enjoyed higher returns

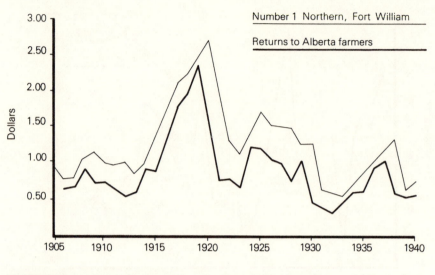

FIGURE 17
Average annual price per bushel of wheat

NOTE: Transportation costs between Alberta and Fort William account for differences
between the two price lines, but they do not differ consistently, because the Alberta line reflects
average prices for all grades and their relative proportions varied from year to year.

between 1905 and 1935 than did other communities, averaging about $18.30
per acre compared to $15.30 for the prairie provinces generally. Considered
together, price and yield could greatly exaggerate the yearly fluctuation in
income, but just as often they served to modify it. Thus, sharply declining
yields from 1915 to 1919 did not disturb farmers as greatly as they might have
because soaring wheat prices offered some compensation (see Figures 16 and
17).

Determining net farm incomes is not possible, largely because sufficient data
on expenses are lacking. None the less, while we can recognize hard times in
1910 and 1914 and the existence of some settlers perpetually in financial difficulty, the years between first settlement in 1904 and the end of the First World
War witnessed a fast-rising standard of living. The press and other observers
frequently commented on the large amounts of capital brought in by the
settlers initially and on the high yields and land expansion that subsequently
characterized farming. They reported a great increase in luxuries during the
1910s: new homes, expensive automobiles, winter vacations, fine furniture and
carpets, pianos, silver and china sets, washing and sewing machines. From the

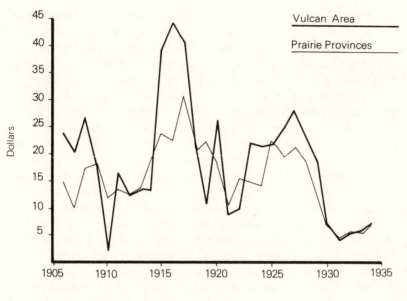

FIGURE 18
Average return to farmers per acre of wheat

lowly perspective of salaried employees like the Mounted Police, the rural settler seemed wealthy indeed. Farmers too thought of themselves as prosperous, and during the war years they boasted of crops valued between ten thousand and thirty thousand dollars.[27] In addition to rising incomes, escalating land values also characterized the period from 1904 to the end of the Great War (see chapter 2).

Fortunes declined suddenly after the war; farmers complained about hard times, and the number of applications to local government for relief suddenly swelled, yet outsiders still noted a relatively high level of prosperity in the area. An Ontario visitor reported in 1922: 'Vulcan is well settled and the majority of the farm homes are quite modern and comfortable ... There are many pretty homes in Vulcan ... The farmers all have cars as well as horses and the residents in the town also own many automobiles ... The stores of Vulcan are quite up-to-date and carry large and varied lines of goods.' And as Figure 18 demonstrates, the post-war crisis did not last long. A good yield in 1920 interrupted it, and in 1923 a stiff recovery began. One estimate for 1925 suggested that of the 50 census divisions in the prairie provinces, only 2 exceeded the farm-income range of Census Division 4; 8 others appeared in the same range, and 40 fell into lower ranges.[28]

Because of relative prosperity in the Vulcan area, and indeed in many parts of the prairie region, farmers tended to credit good crop years to the dry-farming technique and to blame the occasional bad years on adverse weather or wheat prices. Thus they based their future farm operations on the better years rather than the poorer ones.[29] 'Have not the fields in southern Alberta in times past made men rich in a year, and it has taken several to make them poor?' asked the Vulcan *Advocate* on 15 February 1922.

More importantly, perhaps, the new farming technique also failed to win popularity quickly because it challenged midwestern tradition in a way that dry farming did not. It asked farmers to abandon their favourite implements and to forget about deep and frequent tillage and clean smooth fields. The new technique, with its lumpy clods of fallow covered with dead weeds and rotting stubble, so offended farmers that they derogatorily dubbed it 'trash farming.' It asked farmers to work the land less often and less thoroughly, and since they took great pride in dutiful attention to tillage, they could not readily accept a system that seemed to condone laziness and sloppiness. They abhorred the few farmers among them who, through careless indifference, left their stubble unturned or unburned and their fields lumpy. Ironically, such farmers experienced less trouble with soil drifting than their more industrious neighbours.[30] Furthermore, trash farming suggested innovation to those who already considered themselves innovative because of their adoption of the 'scientific' dry-farming system, which, in spite of growing criticism, remained the method approved by most farm educators and agencies until the 1930s.

Thus, at first many farmers sought solutions to soil drifting that did not disturb their prejudices. They began to use different kinds of ploughs or altered their routine of ploughing. Because it functioned partly like a plough by turning over some sod and partly like a cultivator by leaving some vegetation exposed, the one-way disc became an important bridge between the dry-farming and trash-farming techniques and enjoyed popularity in the Vulcan area even into the 1930s. Since farmers could also equip it with a seeder, they often favoured it because it combined seeding and tillage in one operation. As a halfway measure, however, it did not provide adequate protection against soil drifting. In response, some farmers packed the soil even harder, which only aggravated matters.[31] When their fine dust mulch blew away, some quit using drag harrows and tried to create clumpy mulches. While providing more protection, these too eventually dried out, turned to powder, and blew away. Still other farmers began to sow wheat lightly on fallow about 1 August; winter killed it, but the dead plants prevented some drifting the next spring. Yet this solution gained them little. Since the light crop did not mature to harvest, it wasted moisture like any other weed.[32]

In retrospect, the road to better farming methods seems well marked by clear signposts, but for those who had to make the journey it more closely resembled the vast, complex interchanges of a modern freeway. Farmers did not lack alternatives; they faced too many. Patents on tillage equipment numbered many thousands. The Vulcan area boasted dozens of implement dealers, and each carried the lines of many manufacturers. Explorations into this iron jungle revealed no path of continuous improvement. Implements sound in concept might be poorly manufactured, while durable ones might perform their task inefficiently. An array of prices and varying credit arrangements only compounded the problem of selecting equipment.[33]

But even the best of the trash-farming implements exhibited flaws. The Kansas lister created ridges that not only arrested soil drifting but prohibited the use of other essential machinery that required a flat surface, especially seed drills and combine harvesters. While undeniably effective in killing weeds and leaving them on top of the soil, the rod weeder failed to penetrate hard soil. Cultivators sometimes posed a similar problem, and when rains prevented farmers from working their fallow for weeks, the heavy growth of weeds clogged the numerous standards that connected the shovels to the cultivator frame. Fields sometimes became so hard and heavily weeded that even blades refused to stay beneath the soil surface.[34]

Farmers could only discover the secret of effective trash farming after a lengthy process of experimentation, for none of the new implements alone provided the answer. They had to learn to use all of them in combination: to set aside discs whenever blades would penetrate the soil, to avoid blades when cultivators would do the job, to pull rod weeders behind cultivators where they could penetrate the loosened soil – in short, to use the implement designed to disturb the surface the least whenever soil and weed conditions permitted. They could discover only gradually the need to discard some traditional implements and to use others sparingly: to save ploughs only for breaking tough virgin sod, to abandon packers altogether and rely on press drills alone to tamp seeds into the soil, and to use harrows only for a delicate weeding job just after seeding.[35]

In addition, farmers had to learn to vary their techniques from year to year. Historians and geographers have frequently documented the cyclical behaviour of the prairie climate and recorded its impact on crop yields, but they rarely discuss how various tillage methods exaggerated or modified the impact of this variability. Rain still offered the simplest, cheapest, and most effective defence against soil drifting. No one in the Vulcan area kept official rainfall records, but those for Calgary to the northwest and Lethbridge to the southeast provide rough estimates. From 1905 to 1935 Calgary averaged 16.6 inches of precipitation per year, Lethbridge 15.6 (see Figure 19). Average annual

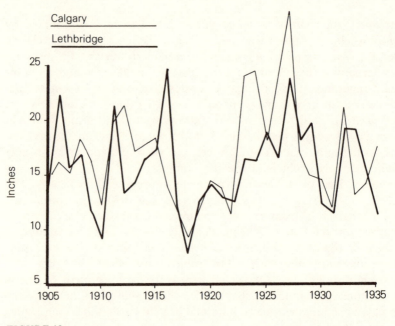

FIGURE 19
Annual precipitation

precipitation for the Vulcan area undoubtedly fell in between, but more importantly, Figure 19 charts erratic fluctuations from year to year. Almost 25
inches of moisture fell at Lethbridge in 1916, only 7.5 inches two years later.[36]

Yields depend not only on the amount of precipitation in a year but on its
monthly distribution. Growing wheat needs moisture at critical times: before
and after seeding to guarantee good germination, late in the spring to promote
the growth of long heads, and in July to ensure that the heads will fill out with
kernels. While the Vulcan area received the same amount of precipitation in
1909 as in 1919, the harvest of 1909 yielded about 24 bushels of wheat per acre,
compared to 4.5 in 1919. (see Figure 16 and 19). In 1909, however, more than
two-thirds of the 12 inches of moisture fell from April to July inclusive, while
in 1919 less than one-third fell during those months. Usually about half the
yearly precipitation will fall from April to July, but it can range as high as 72
per cent or as low as 21 per cent.[37] Crop yields also depend on when the
remaining precipitation falls. It helps if it comes in early spring, when the soil is
devoid of vegetation and most needs protection from soil drifting. If it falls in
autumn, however, it not only arrives too late to boost the yield but interferes

with harvest operations, and lowers both the weight and grade of wheat by 'bleaching it out.' If warm, moisture weather continues in autumn, the kernels may sprout; if they freeze when wet, they crack.

Sometimes even the hourly distribution of rainfall counted. Cloudbursts benefited crops far less than prolonged gentle rains, especially if farmers observed the dry-farming system. The powdered mulch quickly turned to sheets of fine mud that sealed the surface and prevented moisture from penetrating the soil. This problem plagued the Vulcan area twice in 1920, when cloudbursts transformed whole fields into shallow lakes. Evaporation swallowed up most of the water, and the rest of it eroded the soil at runoff points.[38] With its rugged surface, trash farming better facilitated the seepage of water into the soil.

Thus the amount of moisture available for crop growth did not always equal the amount that fell. The long hours of summer sunshine and the strong prevailing winds of southern Alberta have the capacity to evaporate more water than the region receives in rainfall. In all Canada, only evaporation rates in the arid interior valleys of southern British Columbia exceed those of southern Alberta. 'When we first came here, it was all s.w. winds, day after day, it never let up,' complained one early settler. But frequency alone does not explain the tremendous thirst of the winds for water. Stripped of moisture on the peaks of the Rockies, these winds grow drier and warmer as they rush down on to the plains. Called *chinooks* in winter, they delighted the rancher by clearing grasslands of snow, but they did not always treat the farmer so kindly. 'We thought this was paradise,' recalled a pioneer when a chinook interrupted the bitter cold of his first winter, but 'we learned in other years.'[39] Although the southwest winds swept the plains most furiously in winter, when they appeared in other seasons they gobbled up surface moisture, dried out the topsoil, and blew it away. In early spring they ravaged the soil in its most vulnerable condition before spring rains fell or new vegetation sprouted to check drifting.

The southwest winds affected farming in other ways too. In midsummer they dried out the grain in the stalk, or 'burned' it, before it matured. Arriving in autumn, they usually benefited harvesters by preventing the grain from taking on moisture, or growing 'tough,' thus permitting threshing to continue far into the night. If too forceful, however, they could blow away stooks and delay the harvest, as they did in 1922, or they might spread a fire started by sparks from a steam engine, especially if the engineer had removed the spark resister to increase engine draught. Prairie fires owed their destructive fury to the wind. In 1905 a raging blaze scorched a path eight miles long and four miles wide. Another in the spring of 1908 ripped through eleven homesteads, consuming farm buildings, haystacks, and piled grain. Other huge fires followed in

1909, 1910, and 1913.[40] The threat of prairie fires forced the settlers to plough fireguards around their homesteads, and town and farm dwellers alike often turned out in force to battle the flames.

Even without spreading fire, the strong wind claimed many victims besides crops. In 1906 it blew homestead shacks to pieces. In 1919 it overturned and destroyed threshing machines, wagons, and automobiles. The wind physically exhausted all who worked in it, and many found its psychological impact intolerable. 'That god awful wind blew you away,' recalled a former Champion resident; 'the eternal whine of that wind will forever haunt me.' 'The chief reason why we left Carmangay,' explained a pioneer's daughter, 'was because of the wind.'[41]

Temperature also affected evaporation rates, and it behaved just as erratically as the wind and the rain, frequently straying far from its July mean of 64 degrees Fahrenheit and its January mean of 15.7. Temperatures often plummeted below -40 degrees in winter, and it could snow or freeze any month of the year. On 10 August 1907 a heavy wet snow flattened Vulcan crops. Conversely, temperatures could soar to 100 degrees in summer and well over 60 in midwinter. Thus the number of frost-free days per year varied from 123 to 155. Responsibility for the dramatic increases in winter temperatures lay with the chinook wind. In January 1911 it raised the thermometer at Carmangay 60 degrees in a single day. On 14 February 1923 the Vulcan *Advocate* reported a temperature of -46, but after two weeks of chinooks a local resident tested the golf course and reported that gophers had come out of hibernation.[42] Sometimes the chinooks blew steadily all winter, but sometimes they failed to come at all, resulting in a season of bitter cold that killed many livestock. Although less common, cold summers resulted from prolonged rain and cloud cover associated with northerly or easterly winds. Weeks of cold weather offset the benefits of an otherwise welcome moisture supply, for wheat also requires heat and sunshine for rapid growth.

Violent fluctuations in precipitation, wind, and temperature could occur in many different combinations at various times resulting in an infinite variety of crop conditions. Nineteen ten exemplifies the worst possible combination. Following a cold, snowless winter, high temperatures and strong southwest winds prevailed throughout a dry spring and early summer, leaving almost no moisture for plant growth. Severe soil drifting resulted. A wet fall hampered the harvest and lowered the grade. Vulcan-area farmers averaged less than 4 bushels to the acre (see Figure 16). By contrast, 1915 represented an ideal year. A snowy winter gave way to a calm spring and summer when sunny spells with high temperatures alternated with periods of heavy rain. The warm, dry, breezy autumn hastened threshing and preserved the weight and grade of the wheat perfectly.[43] Average yield: 44 bushels per acre.

But even ideal weather conditions posed lethal danger, for warm air laden with moisture breeds hailstones. Thus in the great bumper crop year of 1915 hail completely levelled some crops. The record average yield of 44 bushels per acre resulted because many farmers harvested much higher yields, in one case 85 bushels an acre. Again in 1923 a combination of heat and rain produced bumper crops in the 50- to 70-bushel range, while some farmers received nothing. And although settlers could collect hail insurance under various schemes after 1905, it seldom compensated them for their full loss.[44]

Various tillage techniques could alter the impact of these weather variations on crop yield. Under dry farming, farmers worked their fallow to maintain a packed subsoil and a smooth mulch regardless of the presence of weeds. Thus in dry, hot, windy years, they increased the danger of soil drifting without obtaining any compensating benefit. Under trash farming, however, only the presence of weeds justified tilling the soil. In dry years fewer weeds grew and hence farmers might work their soil less often, leaving it undisturbed when susceptible to blowing. Furthermore, with fewer weeds to kill in dry years, farmers could use cultivators and rod weeders more often, which disrupted the soil surface less than discs or blades. In wet years, when weeds grew tall and thick, the added moisture in the soil offset the risk of more frequent tillage with heavier equipment. Thus trash farming evolved into a highly flexible technique that could take advantage of a year of good weather to maximize yields or cut losses significantly when nature conspired against the farmer. But precisely because of this flexibility it could not be adopted as quickly as dry farming. Farmers needed more time to learn how to adjust trash techniques to varying conditions.

Farmers could also benefit by altering their techniques in accordance with changing weed and moisture conditions throughout the growing season itself. The treatment of land in the autumn especially affected the severity of spring soil drifting. Midwestern settlers believed in deep fall ploughing, and dry farming confirmed this practice, but if a snowless winter followed and turned into a dry, windy spring, extensive drifting resulted. Dry farmers then aggravated it further by preparing the soil for seeding in their traditionally thorough manner. Accustomed to planting much earlier in the midwest than the climate of the Vulcan area usually permitted, farmers were only encouraged by a dry spring to take to the fields as soon as possible. In 1916, for instance, seeding in the Vulcan area began in the first week of April. But the attempt to stretch the growing season to protect against early fall frost seldom worked. Although

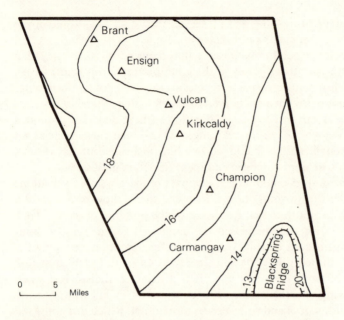

MAP 9
Average wheat yields, bushels per acre, Vulcan area, 1925–50

SOURCE: Rough estimates based primarily on shipping records
in H.K. Scott, *A Study of Crop Yields in Alberta* (Canada
Department of Agriculture, Economics Division, Misc.
Publication, 1958), 5, 16–26

often dry enough to seed by that date, the soil had seldom warmed enough to ensure good germination or fast growth. Indeed, crops sown in mid-May frequently show greater maturity by the end of July than those sown in April. Thus, at best these practices offered no advantage, and if rains failed to come immediately after seeding, drifting intensified, for farmers had now molested their soil in both the fall and the spring in the absence of both new vegetation and moisture. Under such circumstances the wind easily blew the seeds out of the ground, forcing farmers to reseed.[45] Conscious of the danger of spring soil blowing, trash farmers kept fall work to a minimum; sometimes they avoided it altogether, and even spread straw from the threshing operations over the fields. If a wet winter and early spring followed, they cultivated the soil more thoroughly for planting than if a dry spring followed, and by seeding at a later date they did not disturb the soil when it was most susceptible to drifting.

But as weather patterns varied over time, they also varied over space. Geographers often emphasize environmental differences even within the major prairie subregions, but areas as small as the Vulcan district also feature a variety of distinct environmental zones. Their presence is suggested by Map 9, which plots local differences in average long-term wheat yields within the Vulcan area. Yields gradually declined as one travelled from the northwest to the southeast, but the productivity of the Blackspring Ridge compared to the surrounding area also indicates radical environmental change within a short distance. In any given year tiny areas could exhibit even more pronounced discrepancies in yield. In 1914, for example, wheat yields within five miles of Carmangay ranged from five to twenty bushels per acre, while grades ranged from No 1 to No 4.[46]

Long-term climatic patterns in the northwestern part of the Vulcan area differ from those in the southeast. On average the northwest receives almost two inches more precipitation per year. Furthermore, the amount of rainfall there does not vary as greatly from year to year. Deviations from mean annual precipitation (expressed as a percentage of the mean) fall into the 16 to 20 per cent range in the northwest and into the 20 to 25 per cent range in the southeast. Significant differences in rainfall also occur within smaller areas; tiny pockets scattered throughout the Vulcan area consistently receive far less or far more rainfall over time than surrounding areas. Records kept in Lethbridge between 1939 and 1970 illustrate this phenomenon; at the experimental farm annual precipitation averaged 16.68 inches a year, compared to 17.53 inches at the airport. As one moves from northwest to southeast in the Vulcan area, evaporation rates increase significantly. The northwest averages about 2,100 hours of sunshine per year compared to about 2,300 hours in the southeast, where temperatures in midsummer also rise two to three degrees higher. In addition, the wind rages much more fiercely and frequently in the south than in the north. Chinooks generally raise the temperature there about 40 degrees Fahrenheit for 36 days from December to February inclusive, but for only 22 days in the north.[47]

These slight climatic differences favoured the success of different varieties of native grasses in various parts of the Vulcan area. Together, differences in climate and natural vegetation partly explain the existence of distinct soil types in the area. Others developed because of the violent geological history of the area and the differential impact of prehistoric ice and water erosion.[48] The area's most productive soils, as the yield map suggests, rest along its northern and western borders, while its least productive lie to the south and the east.

Soils can be divided into a great number of types and subtypes, depending on the characteristics selected for consideration. Inaugurated in 1963, the Canada Land Inventory provides the most sophisticated survey available.

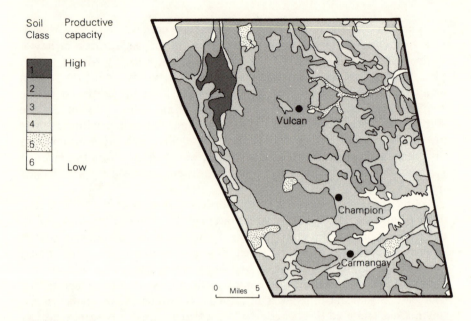

Soil Class / Productive capacity

1 — High
2
3
4
5
6 — Low

MAP 10
Canada Land Inventory soil classes, Vulcan area

SOURCE: Based on Canada Department of Agriculture, Research Branch, Soil Research Institute, 'Canada Land Inventory Soil Capacity for Agriculture,' Gleichen Map Sheet 82 I, 1969

Instead of simply classifying soils according to such traditional features as colour and texture, it ranks them according to their ability to produce crops, thus taking into account more than a dozen variables. The inventory classifies land into seven main categories ranging from the most to the least productive (Class 1 to Class 7). It also describes differences between soils in the same class. A simplified version of the inventory for the Vulcan area, portraying only the main soil classes, appears on Map 10. It revealed tremendous variety and complexity; the Vulcan area hosts representatives from six of the seven major soil classes in the prairie region. Classes 1 to 4, which are capable of 'sustained use for cultivated field crops,' cover most of the area, but Class 1 and 2 soils, 'deep soils that hold moisture well, are reasonably high in plant nutrients, and are high to moderately high in productivity,' predominate in the northern and western townships. Land to the east and south includes more Class 3 and 4 soils, which exhibit one or more problems that render them 'low to moderately high in productivity.'[49] With lighter soils, lower rainfall, and higher evapora-

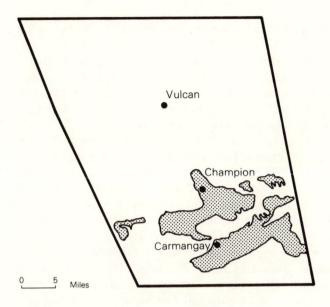

Vulcan

Champion

Carmangay

0 5 Miles

MAP 11
Land especially susceptible to soil drifting, Vulcan area

SOURCE: Based on Canada Department of Agriculture,
Research Branch, Soil Research Institute, 'Canada Land
Inventory Soil Capacity for Agriculture,' Gleichen Map Sheet
82 i, 1969

tion rates because of more wind, greater temperatures, and extra sunshine, the
southeast faced greater danger from soil drifting (see Map 11).

But in spite of the complex dispersal of land classes portrayed on Map 10,
significant variations also occur within soils of the same class, and can even
appear within a single forty-acre field. Most stem from such obvious topographical features as ravines, sloughs, rocky ridges that prohibit the use of
machinery, or slopes either too steep for cultivation or subject to severe wind
erosion, but many also result from dramatic differences in soil salinity
throughout the Vulcan area. Some heavily alkaline patches of land will not
support a single wheat plant, yet soil only a stone's throw away may produce
crops as heavy as any on the prairies. In 1935 an economist encountered an
extraordinary case that illustrates the variability of soil conditions within a
short distance and the tremendous impact it exerted on agricultural success.
Two settlers selected homesteads east of Carmangay in 1905, one on the silt

loam of Blackspring Ridge and the other on fine sandy soil only two miles away. One began with $700 in capital, the other with $500. By 1935 the Blackspring Ridge settler had expanded his farm to 1,760 acres and boasted a net worth of $78,950. The farmer on the nearby sand-flats never accumulated enough capital for any expansion, and his net worth stood at -$1,434. The economist argued that differences in management abilities and farm techniques could not account for such an enormous difference in fortunes.[50]

Settlers arriving in the area knew little of these environmental variations, nor did they seem concerned about them. They selected land for other reasons. On pre-railway frontiers settlers usually preferred land that offered a combination of open meadow and an abundant supply of wood and water.[51] On post-railway frontiers they either snuggled as close to existing steel as possible or, like Vulcan-area settlers, anticipated the path of proposed railways. Settlers crowded close to railways for many reasons, but principally to shorten grain-hauling distances. Before the completion of the Kipp-Aldersyde line, hauling grain from the Carmangay district to Lethbridge might take three days or more for a return trip, depending on winter weather conditions. Even the Vulcan-area settlers closest to the Calgary and Edmonton line reserved two days for the return journey. 'Threshing season is not the busy season out here compared with the hauling-out season,' complained a pioneer in the Brunetta district near the Vulcan area's eastern border. 'The hardships of freighting the crop twenty-five to thirty-six miles to market are fast shattering the nervous stability of the sturdy settlers,' noted another. Some pioneers in the Vulcan area even claimed that a profit could not be turned farming over twenty miles from a railtown.[52]

The social disadvantages of settling far from the railway cannot be denied, but the settlers exaggerated the economic disadvantages. Long-distance grain hauling certainly consumed much time. Travelling over poor roads in winter involved perilous hazards. It also meant the expense of staying overnight in hotels and of boarding and feeding horses at livery stables, as well as higher costs for wagon maintenance and replacement. None the less, hauling out commenced after the harvest when no other duties pressed the farmer, and these expenses paled to insignificance compared to the liability of selecting inferior land closer to town. Not only did such land yield smaller crops, but it usually carried a higher purchase price because of its location. Thus farmers on the Blackspring Ridge east of Carmangay often prospered when their neighbours on sandy soils close to town did not. But until the Kipp-Aldersyde line opened, many western settlers avoided the Vulcan area altogether. Wilfred Eggleston recalled his father's reaction when the family surveyed the area in 1909: 'It was a great shock to learn that the last of the free land in the Nanton country had been taken up four or five years earlier. There were still a few homesteads many miles east but the [Vulcan] area was not yet served by a railroad.'[53] Thus the family took up land south of Medicine Hat instead. In their desire to settle near a railroad they bypassed some of the most productive land in southern Alberta, and went bankrupt on some of its worst instead.

Having selected a district as close as possible to the Calgary and Edmonton Railway or the proposed Kipp-Aldersyde line, early settlers in the Vulcan area then proceeded to pick land on the basis of topographical features. They avoided homesteads with rocks, steep grades, dry ravines, shallow sloughs, and other wastelands. Even so, many blundered. Those who rejected high rolling land for fear of rocks and selected land in low-lying pockets found that they suffered more often from early frosts. As for picking land on the basis of soil quality, most knew nothing: 'All the land looked pretty well the same to them,' recalled one man of his pioneering parents, 'as it was covered with grass to a horse's knee.' Many did not even pretend to know good soil from poor. '[The liveryman] . . . asked me if I knew anything about picking out a quarter-section of land on open prairie,' remembered one settler. 'I confessed my total ignorance.' Such pioneers often employed 'homestead locators,' men who approached settlers arriving in the Calgary and Edmonton railway towns and offered to help them select a good homestead for five dollars.[54]

Unfortunately, neither the homestead locators nor the settlers who picked out their own land knew what to look for. Some made their selection on the basis of colour, searching for the darkest soil they could find. Although the Vulcan area lies in the sharp zone of transition that contains all three prairie soil colours – black, dark brown, and brown – most fall into the dark brown category. But colour alone proved a woefully inadequate means of determining quality. 'Black soil was common back in southeast North Dakota,' recalled one settler, 'and when we saw the brown soil here, we didn't think crops would grow very well, but we found out different.'[55]

Some settlers also looked closely at soil texture. Once again the Vulcan area furnished an astonishing range to choose from. An economic study in the 1930s identified five main categories: fine sand, fine sandy loam, loam, silt loam, and clay loam. But texture also proved a tricky means of guessing at productive capacity. During the 1930s many settlers learned to their dismay that two very different soils, heavy clays and light sands, blew far worse than a combination of the two types, a surprising fact later confirmed by experimental-farm tests and reported by the PFRA. Further research revealed more surprises. The degree of wind erosion depended on the specific structure of soil clods and the size of the dust specks. Curiously, tiny particles resisted wind erosion better than larger particles. Contrary to popular belief, drifting can also occur in soils rich in organic matter, especially if they contain high concentrations of calcium carbonate.[56]

If anyone bothered to consult the best-informed sources about soil quality in the Vulcan area, they learned nothing useful. In retrospect, the notes of the original land surveyors seem absurd. The 1879 report noted that the soil 'is very inferior, and only fit for pasture,' while the 1887 report insisted that 'no farming lands of any consequence exist.' The detailed surveyors' township plans offered no more help. They only indicated obvious topographical features that any settler could see for himself. Turning to the press for the advice of experts concerning soil quality in the Vulcan area, the settler would have discovered such vague and confused descriptions of the soil as 'not too heavy and . . . not too light. The soil consists of a quality which contains a sharpness, and ripens the grain in plenty of time.' More scientific information arrived slowly. The University of Alberta did not begin its soil surveys until 1921, and in the Vulcan area not until 1925. Even then, the value of the work was limited.[57]

Land prices in the Vulcan area reflected this ignorance. Except where wastelands lay visible, the price per acre did not vary according to soil type before 1920. Indeed, before 1910 the poorest sandy soils near Carmangay carried the highest price tags, inflated by their close proximity to the expectant little metropolis. It required fifteen years of experience before price differences based on soil quality slowly emerged. Between 1920 and 1935 light sandy soils averaged $12 an acre, compared to $39 for heavier loam soils. This price spread developed, however, not so much because of the soils themselves but because patterns in long-term rainfall distribution became more apparent.[58]

The discovery of differences in soil productivity took so long because so many factors obscured them. Variation in management skills, a crucial aspect of farm success almost impossible to measure, resulted in yield differences within each soil type. Highly skilled farmers even coaxed more grain from inferior soils than did neighbours with better land. The erratic weather variations also masked differences in quality. During the warm, wet, and relatively calm cycle that characterized most of the first decade of settlement, the light sandy soils of Carmangay yielded as abundantly as the better soils. They certainly did not lack plant nutrients, particularly trace minerals, which the rain in less arid regions often leached from the soil. Only dry, hot, windy years revealed their critical inability to retain moisture. But the slightly drier climate of the southeast also offered a few benefits that partly offset the disadvantage of inferior soils. Crops there nearly always matured before those in the northwest; farmers began harvesting sooner and worried less about early frost. A higher grade of wheat resulted and also struck less often, important considerations ignored by the Canada Land Inventory.[59]

Although generally higher yielding because of superior soils, greater rainfall, and lower evaporation rates, the northwest more often experienced wet autumns and early frosts that delayed the harvest and lowered the grade. It also suffered far more hail damage. Hail does not fall randomly; it bypasses some districts in the Vulcan area and routinely bombards others. One farmer reported hail damage in thirteen of twenty-four years. Hail strikes more readily on hot days when northwesterly winds drive rain-laden clouds across broad valleys. The clouds release their stones near the base of leeward slopes that gently rise two hundred feet about the valley floor. A broad stretch of land along the western half of the Vulcan area's northern border features such topography, and hail often mowed down the heavy yield of its superior soils.[60]

Thus, before the development of sophisticated chemical testing, only one sure method of determining the productive capacity of soils existed: observation over long periods of time. Forever moving about, few farmers anywhere in North America remained on the same land long enough to learn how it reacted to climatic cycles or various tillage techniques. Populated by no one save newcomers, frontiers like the Vulcan area required decades of settlement before a small core of stable farmers could safely vouch for the characteristics of their soil.[61]

Environmental variations posed different tillage problems throughout the Vulcan area. Faced with heavier weed growth, northwestern farmers needed to cultivate more often, using discs and blades more frequently, but because of the heavier soil and less arid climate these practices did not greatly increase the risk of soil drifting. Towards the southeast, farmers had to till increasingly less often using implements less disruptive of the soil surface. Operating on sandier soils with lighter weed growths, cultivators and rod weeders usually performed the task adequately. But because environmental variations often appeared abruptly, even the various parts of a single farm might require slightly different techniques, especially if it contained alkaline patches, which are subject to extreme drifting. In spite of tremendous efforts to provide as much detail about soils as possible, even the Canada Land Inventory warns that 'Each class includes many kinds of soil, and many of the soils in any class require unlike management and treatment.'[62]

A combination of circumstances finally led to the widespread adoption of trash-farming techniques during the 1930s. The decade dramatically shattered any remaining faith in the dry-farming system. When rain repeatedly refused to fall, soil drifting escalated to crisis proportions. The relative prosperity of preceding decades evaporated as quickly as the moisture from the soil when poor yields combined with low wheat prices in unprecedented fashion (see Figure 18). After years of clumsy experimentation by farmers, the PFRA spearheaded a massive propaganda campaign in favour of trash farming in 1935. A new weapon suddenly appeared in its arsenal. Like other trash-farming implements, the Noble blade did not disrupt the surface of the soil, but unlike them, it effectively tackled heavy weeds and thick stubble in hard soil. 'Noble saved this country,' exclaimed one Carmangay farmer. By the mid-1930s economists could record the disappearance of the plough from Vulcan-area fields. By then many farmers knew how their soils reacted under a wide variety of changing climatic and weather conditions, and they modified trash farming in ways to suit their own needs. In 1938 the Lethbridge *Herald* could report of the war against soil drifting at Carmangay that 'the methods used are as diversified as the nature of the soils operated upon.'[63]

As trash farming gradually proved itself in the Vulcan area, other alternatives to the Campbell system, notably strip farming, fell by the wayside. Dividing fields into numerous long rectangles required more turning with machinery, leaving more corners to work. It also created more 'dead furrows,' where overlapping tillage down the centre of each strip reduced the productivity of the soil. But farmers worried most about how strip farming aggravated the insect plagues that struck between 1932 and 1935. Because of their breeding habits, sawflies and grasshoppers feed heaviest along the edges of cropped fields, and strip farming greatly expanded the length and number of edges. Although many farmers turned to strip farming in desperation during the 1930s, especially in the southern townships of the Vulcan area, they happily abandoned it once sawfly-resistant wheat strains and better insecticides arrived, preferring to control soil drifting with trash farming alone.[64]

As Vulcan-area farmers groped towards better farming methods, their agricultural societies suffered a curious death. Together with membership, attendance at their functions declined after the First World War, slowly at first, then rapidly. In 1930s, when the provincial government announced that it could no longer provide them with subsidies, they folded.[65] These developments reflected a change in attitude that marked the passing of progressive idealism.When the widely heralded dry-farming technique only intensified soil drifting, farmers felt deceived. They grew increasingly suspicious of the value of agricultural research, expert advice, and farm education. As they learned more about local climatic and soil variations, they doubted whether techniques that worked on the Lethbridge Experimental Farm would perform as well on their own land.[66] That fear explains why many cynics ignored agricultural advice altogether, waited until their more innovative neighbours took the initiative, and then judged the results before committing themselves. But more farmers also tried to duplicate experimental-farm tests on their own small plots before accepting them wholeheartedly. Their lack of specialized expertise and resources limited this experimentation, but it does help to explain the variations on trash farming that appeared throughout the Vulcan area over successive years.

Ironically then, as the blind vocal faith in progressive ideas dissipated, farmers replaced it with a real but silent resolve to become more scientific and efficient in fact. Massive readjustments in agricultural technique resulted, but the dry-farming system had died hard. In 1973, when a pioneer readily admitted the evils of early ploughing methods, he none the less added nostalgically, 'but you could lay over a beautiful bunch of ground.'[67]

6

Farm Size

While farmers grappled with various tillage techniques, another aspect of wheat production commanded their attention: farm size and expansion. While lacking data for the first decade of settlement, Figure 20 demonstrates that Vulcan-area farms, like others throughout the prairies, soon exceeded the quarter-section size anticipated by the Dominion Lands Act. The average farm sprawled across three-quarters of a section by 1916 and continued to expand. A traditional and widely accepted interpretation has evolved to explain this development. To lure settlers west, the dominion government freely offered pioneers a seemingly generous acreage that exceeded the size of the average eastern farm. Pioneers responded in the belief that a quarter-section would support a family adequately, but soon discovered otherwise. Since the dominion survey ignored topographical features, wastelands reduced the arable acreage of some homesteads. Compared to the east, the arid climate meant lower yields per acre, and work-horses required more acres of pasture and haylands. The necessity of summerfallowing annually removed some land from crop production. These circumstances forced homesteaders to expand by buying adjacent quarter-sections of railway, Hudson's Bay, or school lands. Although sellers expected that late-arriving pioneers would buy those lands, historians have praised the land system for inadvertently providing for the inexpensive expansion of existing farmers. But even a half-section proved inadequate in the more arid southern parts of the prairies, and aided by mechanization, farmers began buying out their struggling neighbours.[1]

Some modifications of this scenario have appeared, and the experience of Vulcan-area pioneers suggests others. While the traditional view explains the effect of farm expansion and size, it obscures the process under which it occurred. It ignores geographical mobility. As farm size increased, pioneers arrived and left in rapid procession, and they quickly bought and sold lands in

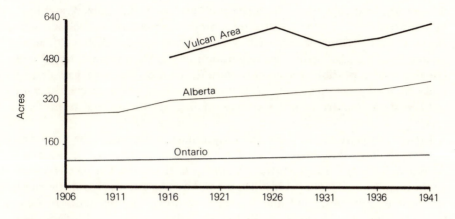

FIGURE 20
Average farm size

varying acreages. The traditional view stresses the average size of farms instead of examining the relative number of farms of each size. Thus it overlooks both the erratic rise and fall of bigger farms and the dogged persistence of smaller ones. Most of all, it overlooks the aspirations of the pioneer farmers themselves.

Invariably, scholars have assessed farm size in terms of the acreage necessary to support a single family. Some studies of both eastern and western Canadian communities suggest that most farmers expanded in accordance with changes in the size and age structures of their families. Indeed, the homestead system itself was intended to serve single families. The American Homestead Act of 1862 symbolized the victory of small northern freeholders over the huge southern landowners whose slave labour supposedly gave them an unfair advantage in the competition for western lands. Borrowed and modified, the Canadian homestead system also rested on the assumption that frontier lands should be awarded to individuals and their families, and numerous changes in the regulations all strove to ensure ownership by legitimate small farmers. The government even awarded immense tracts to railways, land companies, and ranchers in the belief that they would be redistributed to farm families when the need arose. Nearly everyone assumed that these goals coincided with those of the prospective pioneers.[2]

In the Vulcan area too, most settlers probably thought only of acquiring a farm sufficient in size to ensure a decent living for their families, yet many others dreamed of vast agricultural empires that bore no resemblance to the traditional family farm. Raised in aggressive, acquisitive societies, placed on flat, treeless landscape where stretches of cheap land lay unclaimed, and fired by the promise of frontier wealth, their progressive notions of business efficiency readily accommodated such a vision. And for the settler ultimately interested in a capital gain, land acquisition and expansion on as rapid and grand a scale as possible seemed only natural. Great corporations had already replaced family enterprises in most businesses, even those associated with other western resources: cattle ranching, mining, lumbering, and transportation.

Even in agriculture, bold men had forged huge enterprises in the past. 'The presence of large-scale ownership and giant operations have all been part of American farming throughout the long sweep of time since Europeans settled on the mainland,' notes one study. The great slave plantations provide the most conspicuous examples, but the nineteenth-century midwest also boasted bonanza farms. They arose in the Red River Valley, and even on the Canadian prairies, where mammoth enterprises like the great Bell farm and the Lister-Kaye farms appeared in the late nineteenth century. Because these dinosaurs soon collapsed, historians regarded them as transitory freaks of early western agriculture, but the vision that inspired them survived into the twentieth century.[3]

Pioneers attempted bonanza farming in the Vulcan area either by beginning small and growing big or by beginning big and remaining so. A free homestead meant nothing to a wealthy capitalist like C.W. Carman, but inexpensive railway lands did. Initially interested in large acquisitions for speculation only, he soon decided to cultivate part of the twenty-three sections he purchased in 1904. Launching the Carmangay Farm Company the following spring, he invested twenty-one thousand dollars in farm buildings, fencing, roads, wells, and livestock. By 1909 he had a five-section farm.[4]

E.E. Thompson also bought large blocks of railway land in 1904. Thompson had already developed huge farms elsewhere, most recently at Spring Coulee, Alberta, where his fall-wheat operation reportedly sprawled across an entire township. By 1907 he had broken sixteen sections in the northern part of the Vulcan area, developed an extensive seed-grain business, laid out the townsite of Brant, and inaugurated the profitable Brant Store.[5] Simon Dyment, entrepreneur, speculator, and manufacturer of gasoline engines from Barrie, Ontario, christened the mammoth Diamond Wheat Ranch in 1909 after purchasing fourteen sections of railway land. Pouring fifty-six thousand dollars into development, by the time of the First World War he often employed as many as seventy-five men operating an arsenal of equipment pulled by over one hundred horses and numerous tractors.[6]

For such entrepreneurs the Canadian frontier invited large-scale agriculture from the start, because over half its vacant lands could be purchased in unlimited quantities at cheap prices. Joe Neilson, who bought three sections in the Vulcan area, left Idaho specifically 'to find a new home where he could farm on a larger scale.' B.D. Hummon and C.W. Folk sold their Ohio farms in 1909 for $125 an acre, in the knowledge that the proceeds would finance a huge spread at Carmangay.[7]

Giving birth to such giants called for plenty of capital, and a sample of 231 Vulcan-area farmers reveals that 5 per cent began operating with more than twenty thousand dollars. Some owned their bonanza farms individually, but a corporation could best lure outside capital, accommodate changes in ownership, and facilitate rapid expansion. In the Vulcan area the Crystal Springs Ranch, the Idaho Farming Company, Mundy and Scott, and the Almire Land Company, among others, featured not only corporate organization but absentee shareholders who hired managers to run their farms. Others, like the Bow Valley Land and Colonization Company, organized in 1911 to farm three sections, remained locally owned and operated by their shareholders. Still others retained the corporate form, although lone individuals might dominate them. The Carmangay Farm Company claimed shareholders in Grand Rapids, Michigan, and Chicago, but as one of them admitted, 'C.W. Carman furnished the faith, the energy, the knowledge and most of the money.'[8]

Farmers of such size clearly constituted a small minority, yet many pioneers of modest means sought to emulate them. W.H. Fletcher and A.A. Montgomery both began as homesteaders and operated seven- and five-section farms respectively by 1923.[9] Expansion on so grand a scale involved so many difficulties that few duplicated their success. None the less, a great many built up farms larger than anyone thought necessary to support a family. In 1916, 14 per cent of all Vulcan-area farms equalled or exceeded one section in size, by 1926, 42 per cent. By then only 12 per cent retained their quarter-section size (see Figure 21).

In many parts of the prairies, pre-emptions and purchased homesteads aided such expansion. This aspect of dominion land policy allowed a homesteader to acquire a second quarter of crown land inexpensively if he observed certain conditions, but the government killed both measures in 1890 to prevent speculation. When revived in 1908 they applied primarily where railways had refused to accept land grants because they did not consider the land 'fairly fit for settlement.' In effect, then, the revived provisions applied mostly where everyone seemed to agree that a quarter-section would not support a family. In the Vulcan area only land along the eastern border met these qualifications, so most pioneers expanded by buying land on the open market at going prices.[10]

Curiously, early expansion from a quarter- to a half-section seldom repre-

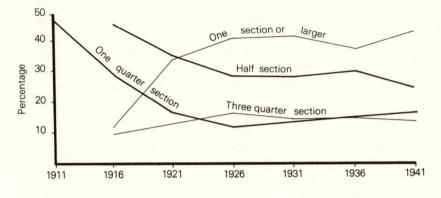

FIGURE 21
Various-sized farms as a percentage of all farms, Vulcan area

sented a true doubling of farm size. Homesteaders typically claimed all the
even-numbered sections in most districts before many odd-numbered sections
had been sold. In Local Improvement District 9-T-4, for example, settlers
occupied every homestead quarter by 1907, but buyers had taken only one-
third of the railway, Hudson's Bay, and school lands. By 1914, 90 per cent of
those lands had been sold. Thus for over a decade after initial settlement in
1904, the district contained many undeveloped sections where settlers might
pasture cattle and work-horses, freeing more of their homesteads for cultivation. When big farmers started buying those vacant lands, many homesteaders
scrambled to secure a second quarter, not to expand their operations but to
preserve a unit size that they had enjoyed for years free of charge.[11]

In spite of an aggressive campaign by financial agents who combed the
Vulcan area begging settlers to mortgage their newly titled homesteaders, a
surprising number did not resort to this classic means of financing expansion.
One-third of them never took out a mortgage at any time prior to 1935. More
surprisingly, of 152 farmers who did, only 10 per cent used them to finance
land expansion, although another 23 per cent had assumed mortgages with a
land purchase or an inheritance. Over half of them obtained mortgages to pay
off short-term debts or to finance farm operations, construction, or machinery
purchases.[12] Many settlers bought additional land on the instalment plan without mortgaging any property already owned. The largest seller of all, the CPR,
which controlled odd-numbered sections originally granted to the Calgary and
Edmonton Railway, set the standard terms of sale for the area. Before 1913 it
asked for 10 per cent down, with the balance payable in ten annual instalments

at rates of interest often well below 6 per cent. After 1913 purchasers could stretch payments over twenty years.[13]

Surviving records do not permit a precise accounting of how well buyers met these obligations, but apparently few defaulted before 1920, and of those who did, absentee speculators more often over-extended themselves than did small expanding farmers.[14] Several circumstances explain this success. Estimates of the average amount of capital brought to the prairies by settlers between 1900 and 1914 range from one thousand to two thousand dollars, yet 44 per cent of Vulcan-area pioneers may have arrived with more and many with a great deal more. These settlers usually enjoyed greater increases in net worth over the years, both in the Vulcan area and elsewhere, than did settlers of more modest means because solid financial beginnings made later expansion easier. That advantage, plus the productivity of the Vulcan area and generally high wheat prices before 1920, enabled most farmers to meet land payments. Many even avoided borrowing for land expansion altogether. In the active real-estate market of the First World War cash payments in full accounted for 42 per cent of all land transactions, in spite of sky-rocketing prices. Indeed, they accounted for nearly one-quarter of all land transactions in the Vulcan area between 1904 and 1935.[15]

With poor crops and collapsing wheat and land prices after the war, farmers experienced far more difficulty paying for land expansion. The problem even forced the province to introduce debt adjustment in 1922, foreshadowing further legislation in the 1930s. Except for the 1925 to 1929 period, paying cash for land almost disappeared in the two decades after the war, and those who borrowed faced higher interest rates. The proportion of farms under mortgage in the Vulcan area, and in the province, hovered between 35 and 41 per cent by the 1930s, when the dominion census first published such statistics, and because of their large size, mortgaged farms in the Vulcan area carried twice the debt load of the provincial average. By 1935 land payments accounted for about three-quarters of the total farm debt in the area, and most of those who started farming there any time after 1920 had suffered a decline in net worth. A mountain of debt buried some of them. One Vulcan farmer bought an $8,000 half-section in 1917. He paid $1,000 down and financed the rest at 7 per cent interest. By 1930 he had made a total of twelve payments, but he failed to make any over the next five years. By 1935 he had paid $9,858 for the land, yet with accumulated interest and penalties he still owed $5,000. The market value of the land that year sagged far below what he still owed.[16]

It became increasingly clear that regular fixed payments made little sense in an area where farm incomes fluctuated radically over time, and more appropriate ways of buying and selling land slowly emerged. During the 1920s many sellers accepted partial payments in crop instead of cash, and they accepted payments over longer periods of time. By the mid-1930s some complex financial arrangements had evolved. One scheme involved selling land, not for any set amount of money but for a specified number of bushels of wheat. The purchaser paid annual instalments equalling one-third of each year's crop until he retired the debt. By fixing neither the total cash price for the land nor the value or duration of the annual payments, both buyer and seller had bowed to the whims of the prairie environment and the world wheat price.[17]

Critics often accused farmers of courting financial disaster by foolishly expanding when they could ill afford it, but farmers often faced dilemmas that limited their freedom of choice. Each wished to acquire additional land as close to his existing farm as possible, preferably adjacent, for numerous problems frustrated attempts to farm widely dispersed lands. Early twentieth-century manufacturers did not design farm machinery for road travel. Pioneer farmers lacked hydraulics to fold machinery into compact units and lift it above the ground, and they lacked manoeuvrable tractors equipped with high-speed road gears and rubber tires, innovations that permit modern farmers to work fields twenty miles or more apart. They wasted time in busy seasons adjusting machinery for the road and hitching it awkwardly to plodding draught horses or cumbersome tractors with steel wheels that chewed up public roads. As one woman recalled, 'Jim Dew had quarter-sections of land spread far afield, and at harvest it was normal to have equipment strung out up to one mile long when moving from one location to another.' Maintaining separate sets of equipment on distant segments of the farm only increased costs, with little gain in efficiency. Most farm machinery sat idle for much of the year anyway; buying more for no better reason than cutting travel time only added to the problem.[18]

Thus, in the immensity of the prairies, the land market for farm expansion everywhere remained restricted both in area and in participants once vacant lands disappeared. When the time seemed right for a farmer to expand, he might find no land for sale in his vicinity. Faced with that problem, he might sell his farm and buy a larger one in another neighbourhood. At the same time, a farmer with plans for future expansion sometimes bought prematurely because nearby land came up for sale. He feared that if he did not buy it when it became available, he might not have a chance later. Other complications arose. Should he buy poor but inexpensive adjacent land, or a more distant quarter of higher quality? Should he buy good adjacent land even though it carried an inflated price because of farm buildings he neither needed nor wanted? Faced with these and countless other dilemmas, farmers could seldom

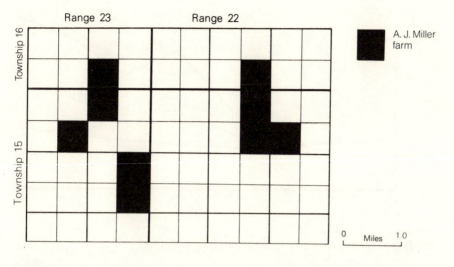

MAP 12
A typical 'fragmented farm' in the Vulcan area: the A.J. Miller farm, 1923

SOURCE: Cummins Map Company, *Cummins Rural Directory Map* no 49 (Winnipeg 1923)

time their expansion in accordance with their own capabilities, with economic conditions, with family needs, or indeed with much of anything.[19] As a result, farms often grew in a fragmented and seemingly haphazard fashion (see Map 12).

With shortages of land to buy and money to pay for it after the First World War, successful farmers turned increasingly to another method of expansion, a critically important one curiously neglected by students of western Canada: renting. The percentage of farmers in the Vulcan area who rented land from others soon surpassed provincial and national rates, escalating from 16 per cent in 1916 to 62 per cent by 1941 (see Figure 22). At any point in time about half of them rented only part of the land they farmed, the other half, all of it. Tenancy soon characterized the larger units. By 1935 wholly rented farms averaged 529 acres in size, compared to 481 acres for wholly owned farms, but partly owned and partly rented ones averaged 795 acres. Thus W.H. Fletcher's huge farm consisted of three rented sections, while he owned the other four outright. In 1931 such hybrids constituted only 18 per cent of all Vulcan-area farms, yet they accounted for 34 per cent of all the land under cultivation. Similar patterns emerged elsewhere on the prairies.[20]

Farm tenancy invariably conjures up images of downtrodden European

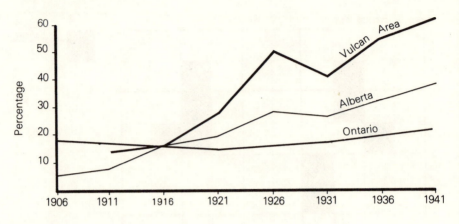

FIGURE 22
Percentage of farmers renting all or part of their land from others

peasants or struggling sharecroppers in the American south. Critics have blamed it, usually in association with speculation and absentee ownership, for everything from poor farming methods to rural poverty and community insta- bility. Recent studies, however, suggest that it did not always nurture such evils; indeed, many now argue that it served a vital function in the agricultural development of the American midwest.[21]

The role of tenancy in the Vulcan area supports that view. Figure 22 exposes the fallacy that tenancy sprang from land speculation. Before 1920, when the quest for capital gains gripped Vulcan landowners (see chapter 2), tenancy never reached the high levels of the 1920–40 period, when speculation died out. The reason for this inverse relationship is simple enough. Early speculators could find no tenants as long as cheap vacant lands remained available in the area. Furthermore, since they wanted to sell to realize a profit, expanding farmers made likely buyers. Tenancy more often results when landowners have no interest in selling or speculation, usually because they intend to pass the land on to heirs. Common examples include retired farmers or widows who rent to sons in order to assure themselves of income until their death. At that time the tenant sons assume ownership. Transfers of land from parents to children scarcely existed in the speculative periods before the war; by the 1930s they represented the bulk of all ownership changes in the Vulcan area (see Figure 6, chapter 2). In other cases, farmers who preferred ownership often sought rental agreements with retired farmers as the only means of expansion open to them. Sometimes renting gave them an option to buy at a later date.

One farmer with land of his own also rented one quarter-section from a retired man and another from his widowed mother. He eventually bought the first quarter and inherited the second.[22]

Nor did poverty in the area spring from tenancy. One man who rented for thirty-five years estimated that he prospered as much as if he had owned the land. Owners probably fared far better in boom years, but in lean ones the reverse seems to have been true. A survey of Vulcan-area farmers in 1935 revealed that owners averaged only $114 net income; part-owners, part-tenants averaged $402, and those who rented all their land, $438. A different pattern emerged from studying net worth. Tenants averaged only $1,900 in 1935 compared to $8,100 for owners, but those who combined tenancy with ownership, the largest farmers of all, averaged net worths of $9,868. That combination seemed to offer farmers the best means of expanding with the least risk. When they alternately bought in high-profit periods and rented in low ones, farm expansion, income, and net worth grew more steadily and securely. With smaller outlays of capital than purchasing involved, farmers could avoid financial traps more easily by constricting operations if necessary. The relatively short terms of most tenancy agreements in the Vulcan area, usually three years but sometimes as low as one or as high as five, contributed to this flexibility by permitting farmers to reassess their position frequently, while allowing landlords to rid themselves of poor tenants before they caused much damage to the soil.[23]

Sharecropping, another term bearing evil connotations, permitted a further degree of security and flexibility. In an area where incomes fluctuated greatly, owner and tenant shared the risks and benefits of good years and poor. A succession of lean years could not destroy a farmer renting on shares as readily as it could one saddled with cash rent payments. By 1916, renting on shares represented two-thirds of all tenancy contracts in the Vulcan area. It became increasingly common across the prairies, but especially in the south, where the climate behaved most erratically. Renting on shares commonly gave the tenant two-thirds of the crop and the landlord one-third. The owner paid the land taxes, but because renters bore all other expenses, tenancy excluded those lacking capital for machinery and operating supplies. These arrangements contrasted sharply with sharecropping practices in the American south, where many tenants began farming with no capital at all. Forced under contract to buy all equipment, seed, supplies, and most consumer goods from the local store, usually at inflated prices and high rates of interest, sharecroppers there constituted a large, permanently disadvantaged class with little opportunity to get ahead. Social class in the American midwest and on the Canadian prairies did not spring from tenancy contracts. There renting more often assisted those of modest means to enter farming, while facilitating the expansion of the largest operators.[24]

If agriculture's rising capital requirements largely explain increases in tenancy on the prairies, then larger, more mechanized farms than the regional average explain correspondingly higher tenancy rates in the Vulcan area (see Figure 22). But the large population of Americans may also account for it, since they favoured tenancy more readily than other groups. Indeed, one scholar even cites the high incidence of tenancy among Americans as proof of their transient nature and their failure to achieve their economic goals on the Canadian prairies, but in fact their previous experience in the midwest, where tenancy functioned more successfully than elsewhere, probably convinced them of the advantages it offered the expanding farmer. By contrast, the European-born usually associated tenancy with poverty and inferior social status; they more often aimed for outright ownership, both in the Vulcan area and throughout the west generally.[25]

In spite of the enthusiasm for large-scale farming in the Vulcan area and the increasing use of tenancy to realize it after the First World War, average farm size tumbled in the mid-1920s and did not recover until the late 1930s (see Figure 20). A closer look reveals that small farms showed surprising resilience; those only one quarter-section in size even became more common again, while the relative number of farms over half a section declined (see Figure 21). 'There are several large farmers around here that farm from one to three sections,' wrote an officer of the Carmangay Colonization Board to an inquirer in Oregon in 1926, 'but the general tendency is to divide up the larger farms.'[26]

Most remarkably, the biggest bonanza farms began to disappear. Some owners never intended their vast operations to last more than a decade anyway. Speculators at heart, they sought to earn as much as possible from farming while awaiting a favourable opportunity to sell out. Some even started selling off small parcels of their huge tracts soon after they acquired them. After eight years of generally good crops and rising wheat prices Simon Dyment sold the Diamond Wheat Ranch piecemeal in 1917. With land prices soaring high on war prosperity and smaller farmers around him anxious to expand, he realized $45 to $55 an acre – one parcel even went for $90 – on land he had purchased for $7 an acre in 1909. E.E. Thompson also disposed of his vast holdings, and after a restless retirement developed other huge farms in Texas and California.[27]

But the big farms did not all disintegrate profitably. Many disappeared through bankruptcy shortly after the war. The Crystal Springs Ranch, which apparently never earned a profit from farm operations, collapsed in 1921, and

Henry Marsden, the principal shareholder, committed suicide. C.W. Carman, dead by 1919, left an estate burdened with massive tax arrears on extensive holdings of farmland and town lots. These failures paled, however, beside the spectacular 1922 bankruptcy of Charles S. Noble's gargantuan forty-eight-section empire south of the Vulcan area. The event stunned the farm press, for it had not only hailed Noble as perhaps the world's largest wheat farmer but as one of its most capable and knowledgeable as well. These and other bankruptcies, both locally and across the prairies, cooled the enthusiasm of Vulcan-area farmers for huge size. 'To the minds of thoughtful men,' reported the local press in 1921, 'farming on a big scale has never been viewed as one of the drawbacks.' By 1931 the dominion census could report that 'ambitious attempts at farming on a mass-production scale which from time to time have been made in all sections of Canada, particularly the West, have almost inevitably failed and, at present, such schemes are advanced with less ardour than ever before.'[28]

Why did so many large farms fail? Historians studying nineteen-century bonanza farms in the midwest and Great Plains blamed their collapse on persistent drought, falling wheat prices, over-extensions of capital, and increased operating costs. But these problems also plagued small operators, and they lacked many of the advantages frequently attributed to big farms: the extensive use of machinery, professional management, better financing, and superior accounting systems. Why then did small farms grow in number relative to large ones after 1926? Some analysts simply explain that many uneducated, unskilled, conservative farmers, especially among the European-born, willingly accepted low standards of living to maintain a way of life that appealed to them for non-financial reasons.[29]

Considerable evidence casts doubt on these interpretations. In the disastrous year of 1935 farms three-quarters to one section in size earned the highest profits in the Vulcan area, but smaller ones averaged higher net incomes than those of two or more sections. In a neighbouring area to the east, where farmers suffered more from drought, units over two sections actually lost money while smaller ones did not. While these findings represent averages, as farmers reported wide variations in net income within each size group, they suggest that small farms better survived hard times. In prosperous periods bonanza farmers did reap an advantage from scale, but not a spectacular one. A study of an area north of Vulcan in the mid-1960s noted that although costs per acre fell as farms grew larger, they did so by surprisingly small amounts. The study concluded that the larger the farm, the larger the profits, but beyond two sections, higher profits represented increasingly lower rates of return on invested capital. The manager of a mammoth farm at Suffield, Alberta, suspected as much in 1912: 'It is not absolutely certain that bonanza farming can be made to return as much per acre as the individual farmer.' Studies of areas elsewhere in the Great Plains of time periods ranging from the 1870s to the 1960s agreed that size did not necessarily indicate financial success and that, while huge farms increased in number during prosperous times, when they operated most efficiently, they fell in number in poor years, when their relative advantages over small farms melted away.[30]

Any understanding of farm size and efficiency must emphasize the relationship between technology and labour, for in contrast to most industries, the peculiar requirements of wheat farming imposed much greater restrictions on the economies of scale. The technology of grain farming scarcely changed in the centuries before the 1830s, when the pace of innovation suddenly accelerated. Over the next seventy years, ancient single-share wooden ploughs yielded by stages to the steel mouldboards of sulky gang ploughs; hand-held cradle scythes bowed to horse-drawn reaper-binders that cut the grain and tied it in bundles mechanically, and wooden flails that knocked kernels from their shells gave way to threshing machines powered by horses on treadmills or steam engines. These and other devices drastically reduced the number of man-hours required to produce a given amount of wheat.[31]

Arriving from the midwest, where most of the innovations originated, or from the Inland Empire, one of the world's most mechanized grain-producing areas, Vulcan-area settlers appreciated what agricultural technology could accomplish. But most nineteenth-century innovations did not fundamentally alter the source of power used on farms; they simply transferred more of it from the muscles of men to those of horses. Steam and gasoline engines now promised to revolutionize agriculture further. Indeed, they inspired bonanza farming: 'It is thus, by means of mechanical power, the use of the most recent devices of machinery ... that the operation of large farms is expected to pay,' wrote an editor about southern Alberta agriculture in 1911.[32]

Vulcan-area settlers could not switch from horse to tractor power instantly. Until the 1930s they still required more horses than most prairie farmers to work their larger units, but with their superior financial resources they also bought more steam engines at an early date. 'All around could be seen the smoke of the steam ploughs turning over the virgin soil,' wrote a 1908 observer; 'one can readily see what a factor they are becoming in the development of the country.'[33] When statistics on ownership finally appeared in 1926, the Vulcan area boasted more tractors per farm than the province generally, and it acquired them thereafter at an even greater rate (see Figure 23).

In spite of the tractor's virtues, farmers seriously overestimated the role it could play in efficient farm expansion. Vulcan-area settlers derived much of their progressive idealism from the magic of technology; a generation that

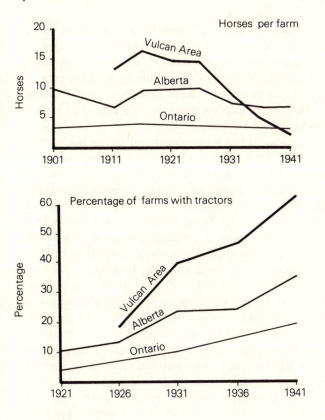

FIGURE 23
Changes in farm power

witnessed the emergence of electric light and power, motion pictures, automobiles, airplanes, and other modern wonders did not question its ability to solve any problem. Thus in 1912 members of the Carmangay Agricultural Society readily proclaimed the efficiency of tractors over horses. But complications soon challenged their bold assertion. Because steam engines in most industries accomplished their tasks while stationary, their tremendous weight posed few difficulties. In agriculture the engine exhausted so much of its power simply lumbering across rough fields that little remained for other work. The steel wheels that supported its great weight packed and pulverized the soil. It manoeuvred cumbersomely. It gobbled tons of coal and water (straw made poor fuel), sometimes fetched from great distances. It often suffered costly breakdowns.[34]

Gasoline tractors overcame many of these problems. Although they were not introduced into western Canada in significant numbers until the First World War, when the new, inexpensive Fordsons promised to relieve a shortage of horses and men, some Vulcan pioneers alert to technological change used them as early as 1910. Lighter, more manoeuvrable, and requiring no boiler crew to cart coal and water, they none the less shared the propensity of steam tractors to frequent breakdowns. They also exhibited flaws of their own; they started poorly and lacked the power of steam engines.[35]

These problems forced farmers in the Vulcan area and across the west to reconsider the relative merits of horses and tractors. 'Many styles of farming are in vogue in this section,' wrote an Ohio visitor to the Vulcan area in 1911; 'I saw power created by horse, steam and gasoline.' As one historian has pointed out, no one could predict which would triumph. Some farmers enjoyed the luxury of experimentation. In 1919 John Long hitched eighteen horses to a three-drill seeding outfit, and in the same field employed a steam tractor to pull an identical unit. But simple tests left contentious issues unresolved into the 1930s. Did the conversion of horse pasture and oat fields to wheat production justify the initial costs of switching to tractor power? How could tractor depreciation and repairs be measured against the life-span of horses, the frequency of their injuries and illnesses, and their ability to reproduce themselves? Tractor size, model, land quality, farm size, the specific task undertaken, and other considerations affected the answers to these and other hard questions. Fuel costs, for example, varied little from year to year, but the cost of feeding horses varied enormously. A government study found tractors cheaper to operate in 1930 and 1931, but with a fall in feed prices horses became cheaper over the next two years. The study offered farmers a complex rule of thumb: 'The total cost of field operations with horses, as a general rule, will be less than with tractors when it requires more than two bushels of oats to purchase enough fuel to operate a three-plow tractor for one hour.'[36]

Baffled by many such guidelines, a few farmers let personal prejudice sway them. Men like Roy Burns retained a sentimental attachment to horses and found mechanical work distasteful. Others felt differently: 'Uncle Dick ... was not keen about working with horses, so when machines came to replace them, he got the early models as soon as he could.' Most Vulcan-area farmers who switched to tractors, however, did so to liberate pasture and oat fields; in effect, they sought to increase the size of their wheat farms without acquiring more land.[37]

As it underwent considerable refinement, the gasoline tractor gradually asserted its superiority. In the two decades after the war, air and oil filters, enclosed gearboxes, and better lubrication systems appeared on some models to protect parts against dust and prolonged wear. Engines became more fuel efficient, developed more power, and delivered more of it at the drawbar. That problem had always plagued the owner of large equipment; when he used more horses to pull it, he required elaborate multiple hitches that reduced the efficiency of each animal. Early tractor owners compounded the problem by using hitches and implements designed for horses. In the late 1920s the power take-off appeared, a revolving shaft that protruded from the engine. Because threshing machines required more power than simple forward motion across a field could supply, they could only be operated when belts linked them to stationary tractors. Equipped with power take-offs, tractors could simultaneously pull and operate newer machines like the combine-harvester. After 1935 hydraulics permitted the tractor operator to adjust machinery easily without stopping. The introduction of rubber tires brought many benefits: improved traction, lower fuel costs, and more speed, comfort, and manoeuvrability. They pulverized the soil less, and by reducing vibration, they reduced wear and tractors required fewer repairs. As with tillage equipment, improvement proceeded erratically. Some major innovations appeared only on some models, others only on their competitors. Size, durability, and reliability still varied enormously, and price and credit considerations still complicated the selection of the most appropriate tractor. None the less, by the 1930s farmers discovered many suitable models on the market.[38]

But the decision to buy a tractor also depended on technological improvements in other machines. To many farmers it made little sense to acquire a tractor unless horses could be eliminated entirely. During the first decade of settlement, when early tractors still exhibited many flaws, their superiority over horses seemed restricted to breaking sod with gang ploughs and driving threshing machines when stationary. Gradually they became more suitable for other chores, but horses still reigned supreme at one task for a long time: hauling grain to town. Before the CPR proposed to build the Kipp-Aldersyde line, C.W. Carman first toyed with the idea of building an electric railway to Lethbridge, but in 1907 he decided to use tractors to haul train twenty-five miles to Claresholm, then the nearest railtown. Each immense steamer owned by his Carmangay Trackless Traction Company pulled wagons containing ten tons of grain. Fed by coal bins and water tanks at regular intervals, Carman scheduled each of them to make a daily round trip during the marketing season and offered hauling services to farmers along the route to offset costs. For a few years the clumsy engines struggled through mud holes, sandy knolls, and snow-drifts, but his expensive experiment ended with the opening of the Kipp-Aldersyde line at Carmangay in 1910. From time to time others used steam engines to haul wagon trains to town, but without consistent success.[39]

At first, trucks also failed to eliminate horses from the road. When empty, early models worked as well as automobiles, but they lacked the power to carry heavy loads of grain. Even if they moved satisfactorily on the flat, they often died on moderate grades. Poor roads hindered their progress. In 1931 dirt roads accounted for 93 per cent of the transportation mileage in the Vulcan area. Rain or snow during the hauling season rendered these trails impassable except by horse. As a result, fewer than 5 per cent of the farmers in the Vulcan area (and on the prairies generally) owned trucks in 1926. So long as they still needed horses for hauling, many farmers used them for field work as well and resisted buying tractors.[40] Although financial difficulties undoubtedly prevented even greater increases in the ownership of new machinery during the 1930s, improvements in trucks led to increased sales. By 1941, 37 per cent of the farmers in the Vulcan area had acquired them (compared to 15 per cent of all prairie farmers); as a result, the horse population declined and tractors became more common (see Figure 23).

In one important respect tractors had always held an advantage over horses: by eliminating such time-consuming chores as harnessing, unharnessing, pasturing, feeding, grooming, and stabling, they required less labour. But instead of using machinery to cut labour requirements before 1920, most farmers used it to increase farm size. Consider binders. Even though their average width doubled from five to ten feet between 1900 and 1920, most farmers did not use fewer of them, but more. On big farms steam engines pulled as many as five to seven binders each. The Diamond Wheat Ranch once employed twenty-six binders in a single field. The Thompson farm once attacked 10,400 acres of wheat with fifty binders.[41]

Operations on this scale called for a small army of men. After the binders had cut and tied the grain, another army moved in to stook the bundles. A harvest crew then descended on the field. Throughout its long development, few labour-saving innovations graced the threshing machine. Depending on its size, ten to thirty men collected the stooks, cut open the bundles, fed them to the cylinder, cleared away the straw, hauled away the threshed grain, and oiled, operated, and repaired the machinery. In the fall of 1907 Gus Spanke of Brant needed five binder operators, six stookers, and a twenty-five-man threshing crew to harvest his crop.[42] Even the smallest farms required extensive outside help at harvest time; some needed permanent hands year round.

From the beginning of settlement, labour problems of various kinds plagued the Vulcan area, and as they intensified, farmers altered their views towards both mechanization and optimum farm size. Frontiers always face labour shortages, but long after all vacant lands had disappeared, critical deficiencies remained. At harvest time the entire Great Plains region relied heavily on temporary workers imported from outside the region. Depending on employment opportunities elsewhere and extraordinary circumstances like war, the supply of those men fluctuated enormously. Between 1904 and 1920 the number of harvesters brought to western Canada by special excursion trains varied from a high of 35,334 in 1916 to a low of 9,384 in 1918. An inefficient distribution system compounded the problem. Although every town established temporary labour agencies to direct the flow of workers to various farms and threshing crews equitably, the railway often dumped too many men in some towns and not enough in others. Depending on the yield and the weather, local requirements changed from year to year, making the demand as unpredictable as the supply. In 1917, for example, the Carmangay *Sun* forecast a shortage because of the boom in war industries, but when harvest time arrived the paper discovered to its surprise 'no scarcity of men in this district at present as the town is crowded with men.' The following year, however, such an acute shortage developed that merchants left their shops to help save the crop.[43]

Farmers requiring permanent help also faced shortages, especially since they preferred single men who could live in bunkhouses. But on a frontier of unoccupied and inexpensive land before 1914, few remained content to work as hired hands for long. Even when the cost of acquiring land rose steeply, they usually preferred tenancy or a job in the city.[44]

Farmers not only decried the shortage of workers but complained about their lack of ability. In many industries technology had eliminated venerated skills and replaced them with simple repetitive tasks that anyone could perform, and at least one historian has applied that argument to wheat farming. But if mechanization rendered obsolete the art of guiding ploughs and cutting and cradling grain by hand, it also called important new skills into existence. Whereas the wheat farmer of the nineteenth century wanted brawny men who could handle horses and harness, that of the early twentieth needed workers who also understood mechanical processes. Adapting to such a change meant that workers were called upon to bridge a significant cultural gap. Complex machinery, especially if it moved across a field while it performed its duties, demanded an appreciation of its capabilities, a sensitivity to its limitations, and a keen alertness to its dangers. Workers who failed to develop those qualities caused needless breakdowns and often lost their lives or limbs in horrible accidents.[45]

But although farm work increasingly resembled urban industry, many of the old skills remained useful, and employers still found labourers raised on farms superior to others. Embellished stories about the ignorance and incompetence of eastern and urban harvesters soon blended into the folklore of the west, but they none the less sprang from real problems. When forty raw recruits from England landed in Vulcan during the harvest season, the press raised serious questions about their ability: 'They go to work entirely new to them, and absolutely unacquainted with our customs [farming methods].' 'We remember men who were raised in large cities who came to work,' recalled one couple from Bowville; 'such men did not remain in the harvest fields very long.'[46]

If these problems arose at harvest time, when foremen watched over many tasks requiring few skills and little knowledge, then finding suitable year-round workers proved infinitely more difficult. The permanent hand faced a great variety of unsupervised tasks, many requiring minor management decisions. Incompetence or negligence could cost the farmer dearly, and the most capable men soon left to become farmers on their own. Assessing these problems in 1909, Superintendent Primrose of the Mounted Police observed that Vulcan-area settlers who owned more land than they could cultivate without permanent workers seldom maintained farms in as good a condition as did smaller operators. Observers frequently cited labour troubles of one kind or another as the major handicap of the large farmer. To counteract indifference and high turnover rates among their employees, some of the largest farms even experimented with profit sharing.[47]

Most farmers adopted other strategies to cope with the twin problems of labour and technology. Often they employed contractors. Through the well-known practice of custom threshing in western Canada, specialists took on the payments for threshing machines and parts, as well as the headache of hiring, managing, and sometimes even feeding a crew. While some pioneers wrestled with a walking plough to turn over virgin sod, many others simply hired contract steam-breakers. In 1910 at least twenty of them worked in the Vulcan area. Contractors aplenty soon arose for virtually every farm operation involving men and machinery. Most also accepted a percentage of the crop in payment as readily as cash. Contracting rescued the farmer trapped in the controversy over the relative merits of horse and tractor power. If he stuck with horses, he could still realize the advantages of the tractor by contracting threshing and sod-breaking operations. Thus tractors operated on far more farms than Figure 23 suggests; it charts increases in the individual ownership of tractors but does not accurately portray their widespread use. Conversely, if a farmer switched exclusively to tractor power at an early date, he could still transport his grain by hiring contract haulers, who assembled long wagon trains pulled by teams of sixteen or more horses.[48]

Most contractors also cultivated land of their own. Small farmers sometimes bought a particular machine with a capacity that far exceeded their own needs because they looked to custom work to supplement their incomes. Their clients might be farmers of any size; small ones received the use of equipment that they could not justify purchasing, while large ones got extra help at critical times. C.W. Carman let out much of the work on his giant farm to small contractors, a practice that evolved into renting out portions of the land itself, and finally into selling it to the tenants.[49] Many farmers acted as contractors and clients at the same time, selling labour and technology for one task and buying it for another.

If many farmers turned to contractors for big jobs, virtually everyone exchanged machinery and labour informally for small ones. The practice has characterized agricultural communities the world over, but particularly frontiers where critical shortages of capital and labour encouraged co-operation. Of 280 farm pioneers resident in the Carmangay district before 1920, at least 77 had garnered considerable experience in other occupations, many in trades that could be swapped to mutual advantage. Others soon developed their own special talents. 'Mr Minty's natural inclination to mechanics kept him busy helping keep his neighbours' machinery working,' recalled one settler. Most often, however, farmers simply borrowed an implement or tool for an afternoon or called on their neighbours to turn an unpleasant task into a social occasion. Those absent from the area for various lengths of time arranged for neighbours to look after their chores and usually repaid them in kind. Informal and chaotic as labour- and technology-swapping appeared, the pioneers none the less kept mental balance sheets of debts and credits. Few risked exclusion from the system altogether by taking undue advantage of their neighbours' generosity. More commonly, farmers tried to build up reserves of credit that could be drawn upon when they most needed help.[50]

Contracting and informal exchanges wrung maximum use from machines and skills that lay dormant until the seasons, the weather, and the life-cycle of the wheat plant called upon them for a brief performance. Unfortunately, everybody needed the the same machinery and labour skills at precisely the same time. Consider the plight of the smaller farmer who finished binding and stooking his crop and then sat nervously in fine fall weather while the threshing contractor fulfilled his obligations elsewhere, only to have the clouds pour rain by the time the contractor did arrive. Hence threshing in the Vulcan area often began in late August and could last beyond Christmas. 'Where the weather permits, threshing goes on,' reported the Mounted Police in February 1912. If the want of a thresher often troubled the small farmer, large operators who owned all the machinery necessary for farming sometimes faced similar delays for lack of manpower. The two often assisted each other; the big farmer hired his impatient neighbours to help him harvest and then subsequently rented them his thresher, but such tactics did not always save everyone's crop from damage.[51]

In spite of delays and other difficulties, farmers large and small struggled on

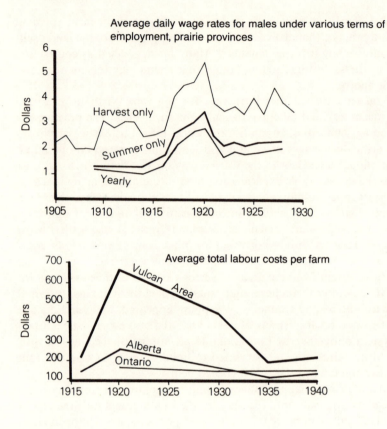

FIGURE 24
Changes in labour costs (wages and board)

– relying on contracting and informal exchanges to supplement their machinery and hired labour – until a crisis forced them to make major readjustments.
Farmers always found themselves short of cash at harvest time, when their
labour requirements rose, and they frequently failed to pay wages on time.
Sometimes the delay dragged on indefinitely. Wages soared during the First
World War, and with farms expanding and thus requiring more workers, total
labour costs per farm in the Vulcan area sky-rocketed from just over $200 a
year to more than $650 (see Figure 24). With good yields at war's beginning
and high wheat prices at its end, most farmers managed to meet the cost.

Wages dropped after 1920, but they still hovered far above their pre-war level. With poor harvests and a collapse in wheat prices, farmers now found the burden of wages onerous, especially the largest ones, who employed the most labour. When they slid into bankruptcy, staggering labour costs shouldered much of the blame.[52]

Farmers tried to deal with the labour crisis head on. They banded together with threshing contractors in the spring of 1921 in an attempt to fix wages. 'They agreed on $40 a month as the price they can afford to pay farm help from seeding up to harvest,' but in an industry of many employers and few employees they soon found themselves paying $50, then $70.[53] High wages, labour shortages, and the fear of labour radicalism prompted the formation of local colonization associations in the area. In co-operation with the CPR they hoped to import farm workers directly from Europe through the Railways Agreement. The CPR initially supplied them with hands from 'Czecho-Slovakia, ... a clean looking lot of men,' the company assured them, 'and once people get to know the class of men they are, they will be glad to have them.' But the community was not glad to have them; farmers grumbled about the language barrier and declared the workers incapable of adjusting to mechanized wheat farming. The immigrants themselves complained about prejudice, low pay, and poor working conditions. They soon fled the area.[54]

Unable to solve their labour troubles directly, farmers began looking to mechanization, not as a means of expansion but as a means of eliminating labour. As one student noted in 1923, 'There is a decided re-action against the large farm, labor costs and the difficulty of securing a suitable class of labor being largely responsible for this.' In consequence, the local press reported, 'farmers will only cultivate wheat land they can take care of themselves,' and the provincial minister of Agriculture added that since 'there is no farm labour class in this country such as one finds in Britain, ... this makes the family-operated farm the one most satisfactory.' Increasingly, then, farmers aimed to acquire machinery that allowed them to cultivate the greatest possible acreage without need of any labour save that of the farmer and his own family. Given the technology available after the First World War, that goal could not be realized without a reduction in average farm size in the Vulcan area. Indeed, it did begin to fall by the mid-1920s. The proportion of farms three quarter-sections or larger declined slightly, while those only a quarter- or a half-section in size regained some of their lost popularity (see Figures 20 and 21). No standard farm size could emerge from the process of maximizing production while minimizing outside labour, however, for much depended on the size, age, and sex structure of the farmer's family, on the amount of wasteland that claimed his farm, on soil type, and on other conditions, but a pamphlet promoting the Vulcan district in 1920 did suggest the most efficient range of farm sizes: 'One man with a good outfit can easily work a half section of land and with very little help can handle a large tract ... The ideal farm, though, is generally considered to be about a half section to a section.'[55]

Because tractors liberated agriculture from the 'tyranny of chores,' farm editors now began promoting them as 'a partial solution to the hired help problem.' But they could save labour in other ways too. As tractors became more powerful, farmers combined several field operations, using tractors to pull cultivators, seeders, and harrows all at the same time. Tractors also used labour more efficiently to complete jobs quickly at critical times: 'the tractor never tired like the horses, so we ran it 24 hours a day for weeks at a time,' recalled one Vulcan farmer who discovered the usefulness of headlamps.[56]

But changes in harvest technology promised even greater savings in labour. During the 1920s farmers gradually abandoned the contractors and bought their own small threshing machines. They required fewer men to operate, while individual ownership guaranteed the farmer access to a rig as soon as harvest commenced. By 1931 about one in five Vulcan-area farmers had acquired his own threshing machine, but then a far more important labour-saving device began outstripping it in sales: the combine-harvester. Pulled by tractors, these mobile units 'combined' the reaping and threshing processes. They moved through ripe standing grain, mowed down the stalks, and mechanically fed the grain unbundled into the separating mechanism, thus eliminating the need for binder operators, stookers, teamsters to collect the stooks, and spikepitchers to cut bundles and dump them into the thresher. Models available in the 1920s reduced harvest gangs of twenty or more men to about four or five.[57]

Surprisingly, prairie farmers had ignored this labour-saving machine for decades. Horse-drawn combines had developed in the late nineteenth century and soon became popular in the wheat-growing valleys of the Pacific slope. In the Inland Empire future Vulcan-area pioneers like Daniel Orcutt and Frank Massey had even driven the great thirty-six-horse teams that pulled the largest units. Some of them used combines in the Vulcan area at least as early as 1910, when a claim for western Canada's first combine emanated from Saskatchewan. Random experimentation continued up to 1923, when the Canadian Department of Agriculture insisted that no more than five combines existed in all western Canada. By 1931 about 12 per cent of the farmers in the Vulcan area owned combines; proportionately, they owned three times as many as prairie farmers generally, but widespread acceptance still clearly eluded the combine.[58]

Numerous problems slowed its adoption, including the controversy over horse, steam, and gasoline power. To pull the earliest models a farmer needed anywhere from sixteen to forty-four horses, more than he required for other tasks, or else an enormous steam tractor. This dilemma complicated experiments in the Vulcan area; as early as 1916 the Clever brothers pulled their small combine with a gasoline tractor, while as late as 1934 horses pulled the Holt machine used on the L.M. Groves farm. Before sawfly-resistant wheat stems appeared, farmers feared attacks if they left the grain standing until fully ripe, and in wet autumns, green weeds sprang up in the crop and jammed the threshing mechanism. The green weed seeds mixed with the dry wheat kernels, 'heated' through spontaneous combustion, and spoiled the grain. Because of its mobility the combine took a terrible pounding; its life-span did not exceed eight harvests. It suffered frequent breakdowns, and a shortage of parts delayed repairs. It seemed to dump as much threshed grain on the ground as into the storage hopper.[59]

In spite of these problems, the labour-saving potential of the combine appealed to farmers on the southern American plains, in Australia, and in Argentina. While the Massey-Harris Company steadily expanded sales in those countries after 1910, it failed to convince its own western farmers of the combine's practicality. But the Canadian prairies and northern American plains faced one problem that other wheat belts did not – a shorter growing season. To hasten ripening, farmers cut their wheat early and set in watershedding stooks exposed to the drying wind. They feared damage from frost if they prolonged the ripening process by letting the wheat stand connected to its moisture-supplying roots. 'The risks encountered in the use of the combine harvester are of great consequence,' warned a government report. 'The losses in some years may be so large that harvesting by this method may prove more costly than when binders ... and threshing machines are used.' And even when warm, dry autumns did ripen the standing crop, high winds often knocked the brittle heads together, shelling out the kernels.[60]

With hindsight, the solution seems simple. Instead of cutting the grain with the combine itself, or 'straight combining,' farmers could first swathe it. The windrow harvester, or swather, cut the wheat and left it to ripen quickly in rows supported above ground by the crop's own stubble. The combine's reel and cutting bar could then be replaced by a 'pick-up,' which mechanically lifted the swath into the cylinder. At first glance this method seems little more labour efficient than the binding–threshing-machine process, but it did eliminate stooking, stook collecting, twine cutting, and spikepitching. In addition, swathers downed the crop before the sawfly season began and allowed green weeds to dry out before combining began.[61]

In spite of its simplicity, the swathing-combining technique remained relatively unknown until the late 1920s. Its delayed appearance demonstrates how simple technological solutions are often overlooked because of the nature of those that preceded them. In effect, swathing asked farmers to return to an old technique that had disappeared. The earliest reapers had simply cut grain, but later improvements modified them almost beyond recognition. When mechanical knotters appeared to tie the cut grain into small bundles to facilitate stooking, the reaper had evolved into a binder, and dispensing with that part of its function did not readily occur to anyone. Note how both farmer and manufacturer groped around the solution to the problem of combine use on the Joe Neilson farm in 1913: 'The great drawback [to combines] is that the grain has to be cut too green here and in consequence is not in shape for threshing until it has had time to dry out in the stook for a few days. However, the company [that manufactures combines] hopes to overcome this difficulty by using the machine in combination with a sheaf loader ... Mr. Neilson has invented ... Next week the combined harvester and the sheafloader will be worked together and if the experiment is a success the company will buy the patent.'[62] By needlessly retaining the binding and stooking process, this method eliminated only the task of transporting bundles to the threshing mechanism.

Experiments with 'headers' further delayed the adoption of the swathing-combining method. The header moved through standing grain, cut off only the heads, collected them in a barge, and dumped them in piles to ripen before farmers fed them to threshing machines. But the farmer was left with a field of straw that still required levelling, and the heads seldom dried out sufficiently when heaped in piles.[63] As a result, less than 5 per cent of Vulcan-area farmers ever acquired headers, but they did complicate the discovery of the most efficient method of harvesting.

Tests conducted at the Swift Current Experimental Farm between 1922 and 1928 finally publicized the effectiveness of using swathers in conjunction with combines equipped with pick-ups. Although the method cost more than straight combining, it proved significantly cheaper than the binder–threshing-machine process, largely because it eliminated so much labour. Testing also confirmed that combines threw no more shelled grain on the ground than did threshing machines. These discoveries helped to popularize the combine, but so did the technological advances that soon followed. Only the forward advance of horses or tractors powered the works of most early combines. Large models demanded so much power, however, that they acquired their own engines to operate the threshing mechanism independent of the tractor, which merely pulled the machine along. During the 1930s the newly developed power take-off enabled tractor engines simultaneously to pull and operate large combines. By decade's end the appearance of a fully self-propelled, self-powered model eliminated the need for a tractor altogether. Further reductions in labour requirements accompanied these developments. The self-propelled combine required only a single operator. A truck driver to haul away the threshed grain completed the harvest crew.[64]

These advances encouraged farmers to buy swathers, and the number of combines in the Vulcan area nearly doubled during the 1930s. Although just under one in four farmers owned them by 1941, contractors had transformed combining into the most common method of harvesting. But as one contractor noted, most farmers bought their own machines as soon as finances permitted. Although a few sought to expand farm size by buying more than one combine, the vast majority now avoided acquiring more machinery if it also forced them to hire more labour. As a 1935 study noted, the combine won popularity in the Vulcan area for 'enabling a single operator with a small amount of labour to harvest a large area.'[65]

Whereas Vulcan-area pioneers had once hungered to farm as many acres as possible, the collapse of bonanza farms and high labour costs after the First World War forced them to modify their goal. Increasingly, they sought to realize two closely related ideals: the acquisition of machinery that would permit them to farm the maximum acreage without relying on labour outside their own families, and the individual acquisition of all the machinery necessary to farm independent of contractors. Technological difficulties in the 1920s, financial ones in the 1930s, and the conversion of farm-machinery factories to war production in the 1940s all hindered the full realization of those goals. None the less, the ownership of tractors, trucks, and combines all rose significantly in the quarter-century after the First World War. As a result, the demand for farm labour tumbled, although it failed to disappear entirely. During the 1930s, when detailed statistics on farm labour first became available, Vulcan-area farmers cut the average weeks of hired labour per farm from about 31 to less than 16. The number of farms requiring permanent employees fell from 15 per cent to less than 10 per cent, and the number of temporary labourers per 100 farms dropped from 200 to fewer than 40. Total labour costs per farm plummeted dramatically; aided only in part by falling wage rates during the Depression, by 1935 they stood at less than one-third of their 1920 level (see Figure 24). Since the level of technology available would not permit farmers to operate huge units without outside help, farm size drifted downward in the mid-1920s and did not rise again until the late 1930s. That small increase foreshadowed the great technological revolution that would occur after the Second World War, when powerful sophisticated tractors, trucks, and combines would permit farm size to climb steadily without increasing labour requirements.

The relationship that developed between farm size, technology, and labour in the Vulcan area suggests some modification of traditional views. Farm size did not increase initially merely because the homestead system failed to provide settlers with enough land for survival. Expanding farms and big farms reflected big ambitions. Furthermore, they had little to do with financial success or even financial survival, since huge farms collapsed as readily as little ones. The family-operated unit emerged triumphant not because pioneers nostalgically dragged an outdated economic organization into the industrialized world of great corporations but because it constituted the most efficient form of production in an industry where technological and labour requirements severely limited the economies of scale. In large measure, our understanding of this development is obscured by faulty concepts. We insist on calling the half-section unit of 1915 a family farm even though dozens of contractors and labourers swarmed over it. We bemoan its demise in recent years and refer to the modern four-section corporate farm as an 'agribusiness,' even though it may be wholly owned and operated by a single farm family. The experience of Vulcan-area settlers with farm size and expansion should challenge those perceptions.

PART III: SOCIAL LIFE

7

Activities and Institutions

While many historians might concede some environmental or even frontier influence on the agricultural activities of newly settled places, they often point to the social side of frontier life as the strongest evidence of transplanted tradition.[1] And superficially, little seems to distinguish the social activities of the prairie frontier from those found in the mother societies of the pioneers. Yet close examination in a limited setting like the Vulcan area reveals that they too underwent some important alterations because of the new setting, even when the pioneers consciously and deliberately attempted to transplant them intact. Precise comparisons with social life in the home communities are difficult to draw, for no comprehensive body of readily comparable statistics exists, as it does for the agricultural economy. But if conclusions must be more tentative, important differences are none the less discernible.

When not working or alone with families, Vulcan-area settlers indulged in a myriad of social activities. 'We did have good times while we lived in Vulcan,' recalled Mrs James Craig, 'fishing . . . , horse racing . . . ; the games of baseball, horseshoes, water fights, Easter egg hunting; candy making, and many more things like meetings, concerts, dances, etcetera.'[2] Others could compile equally long lists without fear of duplication, for the variety and sheer number of social activities seem remarkable. More than a dozen sports, a like number of well-known fraternities and lodges, and an even greater number of local organizations devoted to cultural, recreational, service, economic, and political purposes proliferated in the area. In addition, scores of special events devoted to one or more of those purposes, whether organized locally or by touring groups, cluttered the announcements columns of local newspapers. Furthermore, such work-related activities as agricultural education, booster campaigns, harvesting, or buying supplies provided countless additional opportunities for socializing. And in between such events, casual visiting – to eat, play cards, or simply gossip – occupied most Sundays and occasional evenings.

The number and frequency of social activities implies much leisure time, which seems incredible considering the quantity of documents that also tell of the endless hours involved in building frontier communities and sustaining the agricultural economy. But while valid, these accounts are also misleading. Farming, of course, is a seasonal activity, but grain-growing in western Canada became one of the most seasonal agricultural systems in the world. Few others operated within as short a growing season, and only recent advances in science and technology permitted the cramming of essential work into such a short span of time. While critical periods like seeding and harvest called for mighty, concentrated efforts, long stretches in midwinter left many farmers with little to do save a few routine chores, since they kept little livestock. 'A working day then was from about 4:30 a.m. to 11 o'clock at night,' recalled one pioneer, 'but this was only in seeding and harvesting time. In the winter we used to really have fun.'[3] Less obvious are several important lulls in farm work that occurred during the growing season itself, the most lengthy coming just before the grain ripened. Once the fallow lay cultivated and the crop still awaited the binder, farmers could steal away for hours, or even days at a stretch. 'Seeding operations are now over and farmers are taking it easy after a very strenuous season,' reported the Vulcan *Advocate* on 1 June 1921. Again, with little livestock, such traditional midsummer activities as haying and repairing buildings and fences demanded little time. And rainy weather, of course, could create leisure at any time during the summer.

While it ebbed and flowed with that of farm operations to some extent, the work of farm wives followed a more relentless routine, yet clearly women stole time for many social activities. 'The women were extremely sociable and got together quite often,' remembered Carrie McIntyre. 'Men were left to cook their own supper on [Women's] Institute days.'[4] If most frontier women worked as unceasingly as some studies suggest, then the frontier would have had no women's organizations of any kind – no dances, card clubs, dinner parties, and practically no churches or cultural organizations. But these activities did appear on the frontier, and in the Vulcan area they played a major role in the area's social existence.

This whirlwind of activity also seems to belie repeated observations about the isolation and loneliness of frontier life. Such testimonials abound in the Vulcan area as well: 'I sure wanted to see some one from Washington or anyplace else for I was very lonely,' remembered Albert Miller. Again these complaints are both valid and misleading. They tended to come from those who settled particular districts in advance of others, but such situations rarely lasted beyond a year or two. As on most post-railway frontiers, extensive settlement quickly followed. For women, the sense of social isolation might last longer because bachelors so dominated the early settlement of many districts. 'I never seen a woman for two years once I was on the homestead,' said one woman. 'Mother was very lonesome and homesick on the homestead, as there were no families for miles around – only bachelors,' remembered another. Even so, most districts had some families at early settlement, and others quickly arrived.[5]

Yet in a very different but none the less real sense, isolation persisted for both men and women in spite of the presence of neighbouring families, for the organizational structure of wheat production itself imposed solitude on everyone. Most days the farmer toiled alone in the field, his sons or hired men (if he had them) alone in other fields, his wife alone in the house or yard, and if younger children worked alongside her, she none the less missed adult company. And when vital work demanded attention, everyone worked long hours indeed. Then adults converged only briefly at meal time, and when especially busy, men might even take their meals to the fields. They often toiled so late into the evening that families spent practically no time together before collapsing into bed. This daily isolation in work sprang first of all from the tradition of sexual specialization common in most commercial agricultural societies and secondly from the technological revolution that made grain-growing the most mechanized agricultural process in the world, a process that consistently sought to facilitate the completion of each task by the lone individual. The solitary nature of grain farming partly explains why the exhausting harvest season is often recalled with fondness; it brought together family members, neighbours, contractors, and workers in a co-operative venture rarely experienced at other times of the year.

Deprived of social contact during their work day, these pioneers more readily sought it when they did not have to work, and they willingly invested considerable time and endured extraordinary hardships in the process. They routinely caught and harnessed horses in the dark, rode ten, fifteen, even twenty-five miles over poor roads in open wagons in bitter cold to attend concerts, meetings, and other events. The danger involved should not be underestimated. 'There was an awful blizzard on the 5th of December,' recalled one pioneer. 'It came so sudden that some that were on the road could scarcely get to shelter. One farmer at Champion got lost in it and perished.' Almost every winter coroners' files and local newspapers reported the deaths of those caught in blizzards. None the less, pioneers took the risk. In 1911 some settlers travelled twenty-five miles to see a schoolhouse play at Blackspring Ridge, and for decades the Priscilla Club of Carmangay, a women's recreational organization founded in 1910, routinely attracted members up to fourteen miles distant. 'The sleighing being good,' reported the Champion *Chronicle* on 3 February

1921 of a costume dance at the Bow Valley School, 'Champion, Carmangay, Stavely, and Vulcan districts were well represented.' Sometimes it did not take much of an event to attract a crowd. Joe McNaughton recalled that about 150 people gathered at his father's farm to watch a boastful hired man ride an ornery mule.[6]

This powerful urge for social contact most afflicted those who experienced the greatest isolation in their daily lives – not farm wives, as some studies suggest, but male bachelors, who worked, ate, and slept alone each day. Loneliness drove many of them out of the area entirely each winter, and those who stayed often moved in together, sometimes in groups as large as six or eight. They often endured amazing hardships just to see one of those rare specimens of the early frontier: a single woman of courting age. When Otto Hagg began homesteading he had little cash – no money for a riding horse and very little for machinery. He broke his land with a walking plough, work of the most physically demanding sort. Yet once a week after finishing for the day, he walked ten miles to attend a dance. (The draught horses needed rest for the next day's ploughing, so they could not take him.) He then danced most of the night, and by the time he walked home again, dawn had broken – just in time for another day behind the walking plough. Sometimes exhaustion and inebriation overcame him on the way home, and passers-by found him lying unconscious on the prairie. Once, icicles had formed on his chest during the chilly dawn. People with social contact in their daily lives, who live in settled places where normal age and sex structures prevail, are not as likely to suffer such difficulties just to attend a dance.[7]

Critics in both western Canada and the United States often blamed the homestead and survey system for needlessly imposing such difficulties, for it widely dispersed pioneers when settlement in central villages would have insured social contact. But such criticism is misplaced. Farms in the Vulcan area grew to such size that daily commuting from village to field would have proved impractical, if not impossible. Furthermore, there is considerable evidence that the settlers themselves did not prefer such an arrangement, for even within the existing survey system the opportunity arose for many settlers to build farmsteads adjacent to each other. They rarely did so. Many even built their homes considerable distances back of the road allowance. They did so not to avoid contact with others – which they clearly sought with eagerness – but simply to reinforce a distinction between private and public life. They desired both intensely, but as 'modern, progressive-minded' people they lacked the peasant's sense of community, whereby private and public life are virtually indistinguishable. Besides, building adjacent to each other would have increased the distance to still other neighbours while doing nothing to lessen the distance to town. Indeed, given the farm sizes that emerged, any other settlement scheme would have created as many communication problems as it solved. Given the obvious primacy of agricultural production over all other activities, the existing system best served it by placing settlers directly upon the land they worked.[8]

If pioneers more readily sought out social activities than they had back home, and endured greater hardships to attend them, it should nevertheless be noted that the activities themselves were virtually all imports, most from the settlers' former communities. The exceptions, like rodeo events or new political or religious organizations, all arrived from other western communities. Indeed, 42 per cent of those formal organizations that appeared in the town of Vulcan in the two decades after its founding were actually affiliates of larger organizations originating outside the area. Some, particularly the fraternal orders, stretched across the continent and even to Europe.[9] None the less, these imported activities appeared on the frontier in new combinations. Settlers from Ontario brought hockey and chapters of the Orange Lodge, and if those institutions were alien to many American midwesterners, they in turn imported baseball and the Oddfellows. At the same time, settlers abandoned certain traditional activities because the frontier population proved too small or financially incapable of sustaining highly specialized social activities of limited appeal, especially if they also required a particular environment. No one, for example, tried to establish a canoe club in the area. The small number of scattered European-born settlers, in particular, abandoned many activities linked to culture because so few others of the same nationality settled near them. Thus, while not in themselves unique, the social activities of the Vulcan area probably appeared in a unique range and number, for every settler could find some activities familiar to him and others entirely new, while some familiar ones never appeared at all.

Out of this range of social activities, some emerged more predominant than others simply because of the weight of human numbers. Since soccer was played 'for the most part by the English, Irish, and Scotch, and some Canadians,' it could never equal baseball in popularity, as American settlers outnumbered British ones by a wide margin. The local press often noted that soccer, along with hockey, lacrosse, polo, and other equestrian events more commonly appeared in the neighbouring High River area than in Vulcan. But a British and eastern Canadian ranching elite founded the much older community of High River, and it lacked the proportional domination of the more recent American immigrants.[10]

Yet the number of settlers from a particular ethnic group, class, or region did not alone determine the prominence of various social activities. Local circumstances imposed by the frontier, the environment, and the resulting economic, demographic, and social structure also played a critical role in dictating their fate; they thrust some activities into the background and elevated others to greater importance than back home. Three groups of activities soon acquired an unusual prominence: politics, sports, and a special category of contentious activities that included drunkenness, brawling, gambling, and prostitution.

Many have observed and analysed the enthusiasm for political activities in the rural west generally,[11] and it requires only a brief review here. Agricultural settlement in the Vulcan area began when ranchers still dominated huge, sparsely populated ridings, both provincially and nationally, and hence the farm pioneers arrived with Conservative representatives incumbent at both levels of government. As agrarian newcomers swelled and then subdivided these old ridings, new favourites quickly appeared – and disappeared. Provincially, the area elected Liberals from 1909 until 1921, United Farmers of Alberta (UFA) until 1935, and Social Crediters thereafter. Nationally, it went Liberal in 1911, Union in 1917, Progressive or UFA from 1921 until 1935, and then Social Credit until the Diefenbaker Conservative sweep of 1958. In addition, sizeable minorities in the area supported a variety of other political parties, organizations, and pressure groups. The area also readily joined in co-operative enterprises both local and regional in origin, movements often as political as economic in nature, as the histories of the Grain Growers' Associations, the Wheat Pools, and the UFA exemplify.

This proliferation of political organizations sprang from the cross-fertilization of political ideas among eastern Canadian, American, and British settlers, and from the profound disillusionment that accompanied the failure of each new political party in turn to control the most important determinants of economic success: weather and climate, international grain prices, and national economic policies. And because the Vulcan area experienced even greater economic instability than many prairie communities because of its especially erratic climate and its extreme reliance on the price of wheat, it more freely abandoned old parties for new ones whenever both yield and price conspired against local prosperity, as they did in 1921 and 1935. Thus, repeated crises springing from the interaction of local, national, and international circumstances kept the area in perpetual political turmoil.

Similarly, others have frequently noted how the imbalanced sex, age, and marital structure typical of frontier populations commonly resulted in a high incidence of prostitution, gambling, drinking, and brawling.[12] Such activities especially marked the Vulcan area's earliest and most demographically imbalanced years. Extensive gambling – on real estate, oil stocks, wheat futures, baseball, and cards – has already been noted in another connection. In addition, gambling influenced the popularity of other sorts of activities. Sports and games thrived in the area partly because they lent themselves so readily to gambling. Those most amenable to gambling survived best. Frequent references to the card game of euchre, for example, especially among pioneers from southern Ontario, appear for the early years of settlement, but references to it soon disappear altogether, while poker enjoyed both early and enduring popularity.[13]

Heavy drinking and brawling (the two seem inseparable) frequently attended gambling, and most other public functions as well. 'It was a young man's country and it was a drinking country,' remembered Oscar Hagg, 'and most of the young fella's did drink.' At every dance 'there was usually a few fellows who had a bit too much,' recalled Mrs J. Smith, and 'once in a while a few fists would fly.' Indeed, drunken brawling erupted frequently enough at the earliest bachelor-dominated dances that an orderly gathering occasioned newspaper comment and praise. Of the 259 convictions reported in the files of Carmangay's justice of the peace from 1910 to 1915, nearly half involved drunk and disorderly conduct, and many others involved closely related offences.[14] The high incidence of drunkenness and brawling locally – not some tirade against the wickedness of distant cities – largely accounts for the rise of the prohibition movement in the Vulcan area. Scores of documents attest that the introduction of prohibition in 1916 did little to curb these activities, but as a youthful bachelor society gave way to an older, family-dominated one, such behaviour subsequently declined, both in the opinion of contemporary observers and in court records.

So too did prostitution. It remained a more secretive and less contentious issue, as no doubt the red-light districts of Calgary and Lethbridge drew many of their clients from small communities and away from local scrutiny. None the less, a brothel operated intermittently in Carmangay, and itinerant prostitutes regularly visited the hotels of other towns on the railway.[15]

Less commonly recognized, and virtually unstudied, is the surprisingly large number and variety of sports and games played on the rural frontier. Again, a young, male-dominated society explains much of this activity. More significantly, local circumstances also determined the relative popularity of each sporting event. The pre-eminence of baseball as a spectator sport has already been noted. During the season it often dominated front pages of the local press, spilling over into the letters-to-the-editor section and even creeping on to the editorial pages. Few events compelled local merchants to shut down business, but in 1910 Carmangay shopkeepers closed at midday so that everyone could attend the season opener against Cleverville. Other towns followed suit: 'Very near all of Cleverville drove down to Barons to witness the baseball games,' noted the Carmangay *Sun* only two weeks later. 'A 40 or 50 mile jaunt either to play or see a game is nothing to the fans,' wrote an astonished Ontario visitor. Sometimes, Vulcan-area fans even outnumbered home-town supporters in much larger centres like Lethbridge.[16]

The huge size of the American contingent of settlers only partly accounts for baseball's popularity. Others grew just as obsessed with it, largely because it blended perfectly with two other passions discussed earlier: boosterism and gambling. While a connection with those two activities reflects the initial popularity of the game, they in turn bolstered it considerably. With civic pride at stake, with individual bets as high as five hundred dollars or a quarter-section of land, with a thousand-dollar purse to a series-winning team, or with the rumour of a fix circulating, even those initially apathetic about the sport became inextricably involved.[17]

Baseball also thrived as a participation sport. Even isolated rural districts cheered their own teams, often sponsored by the UFA locals, and the towns had both amateur men's teams and women's softball teams. Special games often pitted half of a town's streets against the other half, or its fat residents against the lean. The more serious participants who lacked the talent to play on the semi-professional teams created an all-amateur league in the area in 1918.[18] As a participation sport, baseball suited some requirements of the local population and economy well. It required no elaborate playing-field and little equipment. Its athletic demands were not so onerous that it could not be played without some pleasure by even the rankest amateur. By contrast, hockey imposed one severe limitation: those lacking experience on skates could not even stand up, much less play the game, and because that skill required a long apprenticeship, hockey generally excluded all settlers save those from eastern Canada. As the Carmangay *Sun* reported on 17 January 1913 of the town's first hockey game, organized by recently transferred Ontario bank employees, 'the game was witnessed by a good crowd, many of whom had never before an opportunity of seeing the game played.' Furthermore, hockey required a more elaborate playing surface than baseball, and one often ruined by chinooks. The sport survived in the area because of the initial passion of some eastern Canadians and the willingness of children to take up skating, but it never rivalled baseball in popularity.

Some sports actually thrived in the area in spite of serious handicaps. Curling, for example, demanded an even better-groomed surface than did hockey, and chinooks victimized it just as often. As with hockey, many settlers had never seen the game before arriving in the Vulcan area. Yet curling finally emerged as the most widely played and enduring participation sport in the area, as it did across the rural prairies generally. Ultimately, it also stimulated the highest level of skill of any sport played in the area. For decades the Canadian prairies produced the world's best curlers, and Ron Northcott, three-time world champion in the 1960s, learned his craft at the Vulcan Curling Club. Of no more importance than a dozen sports in the early years of settlement, curling's popularity rose slowly but steadily. By 1921 curlers on the Kipp-Aldersyde line had formed an interlocking league, and the next year the ratepayers of Vulcan voted 91 per cent in favour of supporting the construction of an indoor rink, even though several years of drought and falling wheat prices had eroded their ability to pay for it.[19]

An understanding of curling's burgeoning popularity in spite of the problems it faced requires a reminder of the basic function of all social activities in the area. Regardless of their avowed purpose, they all provided the opportunity for people who worked alone on isolated farmsteads to socialize. The huge crowds noted in earlier chapters that attended agricultural education sessions did so as much for social as for economic reasons. The Hicksburg district formed a soccer club in 1907 'for the purpose of spending sociable evenings during the summer months.' The hamlet of Brant formed a drama club because 'it helps to while away the long winter evenings and gives Brantites something to do.' The Berrywater Literary Club aimed 'to make the people around this district meet each other more frequently and create a greater friendliness and a more sociable surrounding.'[20]

Most organized activities afforded equal opportunities for informal socializing. Many participation sports, however, did not. Those that required so much running and puffing during the play that conversation became impossible, like soccer and tennis, died out altogether; those that encouraged a lot of casual chit-chat during the play, like baseball and golf, survived. But none rivalled curling as a forum for idle chatter. Frequent lulls between throws provided ample opportunity for eight people to discuss strategy or gossip. Curling also accommodated itself to an unlimited number of teams. It could be played equally well by both men and women, who could play together on mixed teams or separately on segregated ones. Advancing age did not prevent continued participation, nor even diminish skill much – all important considerations as the population aged, as sex ratios balanced, and as marriage rates rose. As the Champion *Chronicle* pointed out on 11 November 1920, 'from a social point of view [curling] provides a mixing place that cannot be equalled.' In addition, the season began in midwinter, when both farmers and townspeople enjoyed more leisure time. By contrast, even the enormously popular baseball season closed on the first of August because of the upcoming harvest.

Local circumstances not only dictated the number, variety, and relative prominence of various social activities imported into the Vulcan area but the manner in which they functioned. By definition, frontiers have low population densities; indeed, they all begin with zero people per square mile. But in the Vulcan area large farm sizes ensured that population density would remain low. At their peak density in the mid-1920s, most townships sustained only five or six rural people per square mile. By then average farm size approached one section, so ironically the density of households reached a new low, scarcely exceeding one per square mile. The peak in rural population density therefore resulted solely from increases in household size, as the proportion of bachelors and childless couples declined and as marriage and birth rates climbed. Thus by the mid-1920s hardly a stretch of road in the Vulcan area could boast three farmsteads per linear mile, and most averaged only two. By contrast, most Ontario farm communities sustained rural populations exceeding twenty people per square mile, and many a good deal more, at the time they contributed settlers to the Vulcan area.[21] The size of their service towns and the density of their distribution were proportionately greater as well.

Low population density little affected agricultural production in the Vulcan area (although it certainly affected the transportation of agricultural products), since farming did not require the frequent convergence and dispersal of large numbers of people from different households. But every community activity did make such a demand. Low population density therefore tended to curtail spontaneous, informal socializing. This may seem surprising, considering all the testimonials about neighbours who dropped in unannounced: 'We didn't need an invitation,' remembered Georgina Thomson; 'we could arrive at a neighbour's without warning to visit and have dinner, just as they were welcome if they arrived unexpectedly at our place.'[22] But consider the problem involved. People did not live close enough to each other to do much visiting on foot. Social contact usually meant wrestling with horses, harness, and hitches first. Pioneers did that willingly, but having done so, they wanted a guarantee that a desired social activity would justify the time and effort involved. They would not spend hours roaming the vast countryside hoping to stumble upon some gathering.

Assured social contact on an informal, casual basis usually meant a trip to the nearest railtown. But to justify the time and effort involved, it had to be limited to infrequent trips, rarely more than once a week and often much less, and it had to be combined with essential economic tasks. To serve the social as well as the economic purposes of the trip, unspoken mutual agreement established a particular day when a farm family might meet friends and neighbours informally. Thus the tradition of Saturday-night shopping, common in the American rural midwest, reappeared in the Vulcan area. On that night the towns buzzed with congestion and activity: 'Saturday night was a big night in

Vulcan,' commented the Vulcan *Advocate* of a typical weekend. 'There were hundreds of people in, all on business.' On other days the towns seemed virtually abandoned. Following essential shopping, rural visitors often took in a movie, and then sat eating and visiting at the cafés far into the night.[23]

Mutual consent also established one other day for informal socializing. If the laws prohibiting Sunday work originally sprang from religious dictate, they also served a social purpose. For some, going to church provided sufficient justification for overcoming transportation difficulties, and once there, the opportunity to extend or accept a sudden dinner invitation arose. Or, since the team had been hitched anyway (or the Model T coaxed into operation), an afternoon's outing could be planned and might include an unannounced visit to distant friends. If absent, the outing itself justified the investment of time. Thus, long before the weekend became ritualized in the modern city, it served an important function on the rural frontier.

Attempts at informal visiting at other times proved too time-consuming, too troublesome, and too likely to end in failure. In response, the pioneers soon pre-planned most social activities and gave them prior announcement. That in turn called for formal organization. The pioneer press soon complained that 'we have meetings without end for organizing and reviving different movements.' Even the farmers who seeded a sick man's crop one spring called a formal meeting to organize the work. To avoid the constant organization demanded for every pre-planned event, permanent structures soon assumed much of the responsibility. Thus frontier social life became institutionalized to a remarkable degree. In the two decades after its founding, the town of Vulcan alone became the meeting place of at least sixty formal, standing organizations, not counting numerous organizations within organizations (such as church auxiliaries), even though its own population never exceeded eight hundred. Three-quarters of those organizations appeared in the town's first decade, and most of those within a year or two of its founding. Only three years after the founding of Carmangay, a newcomer so marvelled at the array of formal organizations that he felt compelled to comment on the phenomenon in a letter to the Carmangay *Sun*, 24 June 1913.[24]

While towns and villages made logical centres for formal organizations used by rural people, farm families situated too far from a town to partake conveniently of all its activities on a regular basis created formal organizations in the countryside itself. The rural district known as Alston, for example, twelve miles from the nearest railtown, formally organized its own baseball team and card club, and featured its own locals of the UFA, the Women's Institute, and the Red Cross. It had its own school-board and its own formally structured ward within a larger municipal district. And it boasted all these organizations when no public facility existed in the district except a one-room schoolhouse. Rural districts centred on tiny off-railway hamlets featured even more formal organizations. No precise boundaries delineated these rural neighbourhoods. The boundaries of formal organizations rarely coincided, and indeed many of them recognized no geographic restrictions to membership at all. Thus, rural neighbourhoods existed largely to the extent that informal and formal social boundaries coincided to a degree sufficient for both residents and outsiders to think of an area as a particular district. Such readily recognized examples as Alston, Reid Hill, or Loma inevitably evolved in areas most distant from the towns. As distance to a railtown decreased and it became increasingly convenient to partake of its organizational activities, the rural neighbourhood finally disappeared altogether, replaced by the 'rurban community,' a single web of social organization that united town and surrounding countryside.[25]

Although formal organization on rural frontiers has not been studied much, the Vulcan area does not seem unique in this respect. As Jean Burnet later observed of a ladies' church group in Oyen, Alberta, 'although they seldom do anything more significant than drink tea, they do it as a formally organized group.' Some studies suggest that agrarian frontiers in general, and wheat-growing areas in particular, may have been more highly organized than older, more densely settled communities.[26] Throughout much of Europe and the Third World rural people commonly worked side by side – often they lived in centralized villages – but regardless, a brief walk brought them to public places and social contact. Little need arose for pre-planning and prior announcement when everyone in a community lived within earshot of a village bell or animal-skin drum. They could be gathered together quickly without warning for almost any purpose. The more dispersed but none the less densely settled rural areas of eastern North America fell between these two extremes.

Nor did the early introduction of automobiles and telephones to the Vulcan area erode the need for formal organizations and restore the ancient informality of rural life, as might be expected and as some local residents anticipated. The press thought that the auto might revolutionize rural social life: 'How can you measure in dollars and cents the value of the motor car on the farm?' asked the *Farm and Ranch Review* on 5 April 1916. 'What is the universal complaint today in respect to farm life? Loneliness, isolation.' But although the prosperity of the Vulcan area permitted its residents to acquire more autos per capita than most prairie areas, by the time of the Second World War over a third of all families still did not own one (see Figure 25). Furthermore, early autos proved as unreliable as early tractors, and the roads remained poor even for summer travel. A sixteen-mile trip to Vulcan during a rainstorm in 1927 took a Model T two hours.[27] Winter, the high season of social activity, rendered the

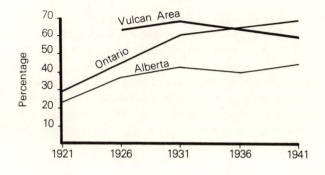

FIGURE 25
Percentage of farms having automobiles

car almost useless. Reliable cold-weather cars and all-weather roads evolved over long decades, and as they did, ever larger farm sizes, and hence greater distances between farmers, offset their advantages to some extent.

Similarly, the telephone did little to eliminate the need for formally organized meetings. Although telephones appeared almost simultaneously with first settlement, the earliest lines only linked a few neighbours. Co-operatively owned and built lines next joined together a dozen or more farms, but not until the new railtowns appeared and established central exchanges in the early 1910s could these local networks contact each other. Even so, some communities did not have any phone service at all until the late 1910s, and some had no connection to the larger railtowns until the 1930s. The telephone did increase the incidence of informal visiting – although without face-to-face contact – and as all phones operated through party lines, they gave rise to the popular activity of 'rubbernecking,' or listening in on other people's calls. But instead of eroding the need for formal, organized gatherings, telephones more often served as an additional tool, together with the postal service and the columns of the local newspapers, for giving prior announcement to pre-planned events. More importantly, once the tradition of formal organization became entrenched, subsequent improvements in transportation and communication technology did little to shake it, as a 1961 survey of formal organizations in Biggar, Saskatchewan, revealed.[28]

Furthermore, institutionalization suited other community requirements besides the need to overcome distance and low population density. Frontier societies are initially composed of many strangers, and in the Vulcan area, as elsewhere, high rates of geographic mobility provided a constant stream of newcomers. Rural sociologists over the decades have almost unanimously agreed that constant population turnover led to the deterioration of rural communities in general and their organizations in particular. Social experiences in the Vulcan area do not support this generalization. The formally organized frontier provided newcomers with an instant entrée into local society, and provided as well for equally easy withdrawal if they moved away. Indeed, such huge, continent-wide organizations as fraternities provided for readily transferable memberships. Thus items like the following commonly appeared in the frontier press: 'Jack has been in Carmangay for eight months and has played an important part in the . . . social life of the town.' The huge number and variety of organizations also permitted newcomers to participate either as much or as little as they pleased in community social life, and in ways that particularly suited them. Social pressures sometimes trapped them into uncomfortable situations, but the options available seem far greater than the common literary image of small-community life suggests. Because of its suitability to rapid population turnover and its flexibility in permitting varying degrees of commitment to local society, the institutionalized frontier fits neatly into the concept of 'communities of limited liability,' an idea originally developed from studies of big-city neighbourhoods. Indeed, institutional structures are generally believed to be a distinct characteristic of the city, and while the generalization is perhaps justified, clearly they were as prominent a feature of the rural frontier, and perhaps more vital to it.[29]

While the role of local circumstances in explaining the institutionalization of social life has been stressed here, it should be noted that this process was also nurtured by other, continent-wide influences. The proliferation of institutions in early twentieth-century North America sprang in part from a progressive ethos that sought greater efficiency in human affairs through planning, organization, and bureaucracy. Thus the institutionalization of social life also blended nicely with the settlers' progressive outlook.

While low population density, long distances, and poor transportation initially played an important role in the institutionalization of social life, they had other consequences as well. Each organization, regardless of its avowed purpose, assumed responsibility for a wide range of diverse activities. Thus literary societies often organized sporting events; UFA locals sponsored motion-picture nights at the rural schoolhouse, and the rural baseball team organized the annual New Year's dance. Multi-purpose organizations appeared in densely populated places too, yet they better served the thinly settled frontier, which forced fewer people to administer relatively more organizations. Multi-functionalism simply saved time and effort.

Multi-functionalism also sprang from another consequence of low population density: long periods of travel encouraged people to spend far more time at each social gathering than they had back home. Having shivered for an hour in an open sleigh to attend a function, they did not drop in for a few minutes and then leave. They stayed. Dances in the area almost never ended before 4 a.m., and often much later. Similarly, people would not endure transportation hardships merely to attend a short business meeting of the political party or fraternity. Thus multi-functionalism provided the variety necessary for lengthy outings, and indeed these two consequences of low population density usually operated in tandem. At one meeting of the Reid Hill Women's Institute in 1916 the ladies quickly dispensed with the organization's business. A sing-along session followed. They heard solo piano pieces, then solo songs. Next came a lecture on gardening and canning, followed by poetry readings. A member then read a letter from a local boy at the European front. Lunch followed, then informal visiting. As one man recalled, 'UFA meetings were well attended as they were usually followed by cards and other games and the inevitable abundant supply of sandwiches, cakes, and coffee.' UFA picnics frequently featured half a dozen different activities over a twelve-hour period and might include several sports, a band concert, a play, and a dance, as well as political speeches. Special holidays, like the joint 1 July and 4 July celebrations, often turned into gruelling marathons that collapsed even the hardiest socializers.[30]

The activities offered by each organization often bore little relationship to each other. Consider the agenda for an afternoon meeting of the Berrywater Literary and Social Club. A sit-down lunch was followed by a gopher-snaring contest. Next came a swimming regatta – for the snared gophers. Afterwards, everyone went indoors to hear a guest lecture on economics.[31] Yet very little distinguished the range of activities offered by each organization, except for its avowed purpose and sometimes not even that. This multi-functionalism explains why the same sets of formal organizations did not appear in neighbouring communities otherwise socially similar; all organizations, regardless of their supposed purpose, sponsored the same activities anyway. Again, this oddity is not so surprising considering the real purpose of all formal organizations: simply to facilitate social contact itself. Thus the various activities sponsored by prairie political organizations were not merely clever tricks to attract more converts to the cause, as political historians sometimes imply, but integral components of all rural prairie organizations.

But less pleasant consequences also stemmed from transferring social traditions to an area of low population density. In an important essay A.H. Anderson argued that whenever such movements occurred, one of two problems ensued: either the economic cost of social organization rose or the quality of the institution fell. Usually, he argued, both problems attacked simultaneously, resulting in what he called the 'social cost of space.' This problem plagued every aspect of local social organization, especially during depressions, but it always affected public facilities and services the most. Good roads, for example, so vital to commercial agriculture and the primary concern of rural municipal governments, proved impossible to provide. Even though per capita costs surpassed those of densely populated agrarian communities, as late as 1931 dirt roads still accounted for 93 per cent of all mileage in the Vulcan area. In rural southern Ontario at the same time, all-weather surfacing of some kind covered most roads.[32]

Or consider medical care. How could such expensive facilities as hospitals be built and maintained so as to be readily accessible to everyone? Indeed, the area had no hospital facilities of any sort until a privately owned four-room unit operated by a lone nurse opened in Vulcan in 1917. And although the provincial Municipal Hospital Act of 1917 paved the way for the creation of hospital districts, the enormous costs involved prevented the building of any publicly owned facility until a twenty-bed unit appeared in Vulcan in 1928. As for medical doctors, the area could not attract even one until after the new railway towns arose, even though some communities offered free space to any that would come. And once the doctors had arrived, rapid communication with them awaited the drawn-out process of linking rural telephone systems to central exchanges – another utility that suffered high per capita costs and halting service. The first farm families linked to Carmangay immediately petitioned the town for a night operator in case the doctor needed to be summoned. And for some time after the new railway towns arose, the area relied only on the services of an itinerant practitioner for dental services.[33]

Thus, until after 1910 settlers lived fifteen to fifty miles from professional medical services of any kind and enjoyed only widely scattered and limited services thereafter. They coped with the problem as best they could. 'The first thing I did when I went on the homestead,' recalled Elizabeth Akitt, 'I paid $10 for a doctor book.'[34] Nearly every home library had one, and each district relied on amateur healers and midwives for much medical aid. Yet the area badly needed professional medical attention. Farm families worked with surly draught horses and dangerous machinery. Each summer the local newspapers reported dozens of grisly accidents, injuries of the sort that early twentieth-century medicine could best treat. Deaths sometimes resulted from lack of prompt medical attention.

The pioneers tried to reduce the costs and maintain the quality of public services through a variety of means. They volunteered labour and materials, and lent wagons, teams, and tools. They formed co-operatives and joint stock companies, issued debentures, borrowed money, solicited donations, and hounded the provincial government for funds. But these tactics failed to cut institutional costs; they simply deferred payments, replaced cash outlays with indirect payments, or else transferred costs to outside agencies. Better results came from using physical facilities for a variety of functions, just as formal organizations served a multitude of purposes. The rural schoolhouse offers the most obvious example of a multi-purpose community centre, but even private buildings were summoned to public duty. In the hamlet of Kirkcaldy the pool hall headquartered a variety of organizations and hosted a variety of events, including religious services, a remarkable development given contemporary church views of pool halls.[35]

Some multi-functional applications showed great ingenuity. Early barbed-wire fences in the area, for example, served three wholly unrelated purposes. They kept livestock out of the crops; they carried the messages of the area's first telephones, and they served as nets for the area's first tennis players. Another ingenious solution set institutions on wheels; instead of forcing the public to travel to the service, the service travelled to the public. The provincial Department of Agriculture inaugurated a successful travelling library, but few practical applications of this tactic emerged. Using all these strategies, the pioneers sometimes cut institutional costs and sometimes maintained the quality of services, but try as they might, they rarely conquered both problems simultaneously. Low population densities simply rendered their high level of individual prosperity impotent.

When A.H. Anderson presented his views on social costs, he assumed they were an inescapable consequence of low-density living, but he failed to consider another possibility: radical innovation that simply rendered the problem irrelevant. Innovation on that scale, however, would have transformed the imported activity or institution into an unrecognizable mutant. Schools, for example, would not have arisen on the frontier; instead, some wholly unknown, indescribable process for educating the young would have replaced them. In short, new cultural forms would have arisen. That did not happen. The Vulcan area clearly retained the institutional structures of Anglo-American culture. They could not, however, remain exact replicas. The frontier and the new environment not only gave rise to a unique combination of activities and not only rearranged their relative importance, but its low population density led to the proliferation of formal organizations, altered their purposes, expanded their functions, demanded greater investments of time, raised their costs, and lowered their quality.

Furthermore, the cumulative impact of these processes also altered the basic nature of the activities themselves. So while an Ontario newcomer to the area could clearly recognize its activities and institutions, he found his participation in them a notably different experience from what he had previously known. An adequate demonstration of that change, however, requires a different approach than the one taken here. Here examples have been drawn deliberately from many activities and organizations to illustrate various points. But to observe the cumulative impact of those modifications it is necessary to concentrate on single institutions. The following chapter focuses closely on two institutions long regarded of vital importance to the prairie community: schools and churches.

8

Schools and Churches

Building schools obsessed settlers in the Vulcan district. 'Nearly every man and woman I met mentioned the subject,' noted a traveller through the area in 1906. Early arrivals scrambled to form school districts, since many refused to bring their families into the area until schools opened. Together with post offices, schools rose on the frontier long before other public institutions; dozens appeared before the area could boast a single church, railtown, or even many roads. As soon as the new town of Carmangay mushroomed from the prairie, it begged the province to act quickly on its bid for municipal incorporation because it wanted to settle the question of a school location immediately and begin construction. Many rural pioneers boarded older children in the towns at considerable expense so that they might attend high school. Others relocated the whole family each winter. 'Hardly a day passes but enquiries are made regarding the possibilities of renting a house in town,' observed the Carmangay *Sun* in 1910; 'these enquiries come from farmers who want to move to town so that their children can attend school.' Some families even fled to the city in winter to provide their children with a better education.[1]

Behind this desire to build schools lay a conscious attempt to transmit cultural traditions to the young. As John Charyk has observed, the prairie schoolhouse hoped to plant 'the bulwark of civilization in a new and primitive land. Under its roof devoted and knowledgeable men and women, steeped in the traditions and cultures of the old world, passed on to children the fundamentals of an education that had taken mankind centuries to garner and learn.' If the pioneers wanted a school system that implanted Western civilization generally, and British culture in particular, then Ontario provided a ready model, and the early Alberta school system freely copied it. Besides the classics, it offered the literature, history, and geography of Britain and the empire (including eastern Canada). Ontario's system represented not only an imported institution but one reinforced by metropolitan control. The provincial government retained the power to dictate both the curriculum and the general administrative structure through which local school districts would implement it. The large contingent of American settlers did not complain about this eastern Canadian import. In spite of the heavy American content of most school curriculums in the United States, cultural institutions there none the less recognized and accepted the British origins of their heritage, and they further accepted that moving to the Canadian frontier meant even greater emphasis on that tradition.[2]

But even with the immense weight of transplanted tradition and metropolitan control behind it, the attempt to re-create the Ontario school system only partly succeeded. Within it lay the seeds of its own modification, for it permitted local boards to carry out the actual administration. Of necessity they soon bowed to a myriad of local circumstances. Low population density and crude transportation imposed even more restrictions on children than adults. For many families that could not spare riding horses or the time to take children to school by wagon, walking provided the only means of getting to school, and the youngest could not walk far, especially in bitter cold or stormy weather. The provincial government soon recognized this necessity; no school district could exceed five miles in length or width. It strongly urged that none exceed twenty square miles, and it instructed school-boards to build as close as possible to the centre of the district. Thus schools became the most decentralized formal institutions in the Vulcan area and across the prairies generally. Even so, the problems of time and distance led to local squabbles over school location, as each family wished the school built as close as possible to its own homestead. Many even selected their land solely because of its proximity to a school.[3]

The province assumed that a school district of recommended size would contain at least eight children of school age and stipulated that ratepayers could not petition for a school district otherwise. But since a preponderance of bachelors and young childless couples characterized early settlement and since some land lay vacant for years, many districts lacked even this minimal number of school-age children. As elsewhere across the west, parents submitted fictitious names on school-district petitions in order to receive the approval to proceed. Thus the number of students in a school district might be so low that the fate of the school hinged on the movement of a single family in or out of the district. Enrolments at the Mayview school fluctuated wildly over the years from seven to thirty-six pupils, and in some years rural schools closed altogether for lack of students.[4]

Under such circumstances, no thought could be entertained of such luxuries as local private schools, sexually segregated ones, or even separate schools based on religion. Given transportation difficulties and the problem of low population density, Catholics in the area did not even consider exercising their legal right to have separate schools. Most historians of the 'schools issue' have too easily dismissed western Canadian complaints about the inefficiency of separate schools as mere masks for bigotry. As it happened, the problem of providing a single public school for everyone overwhelmed many communities. Massive decentralization coupled with low population density meant substantial costs per pupil, difficult to meet for frontier communities that had to invest huge capital sums in virtually everything else as well. So even though the province awarded grants (which came in turn from the invested proceeds of the sale of dominion school lands), local volunteers gave land, labour, materials, and money to build many schools, and still resorted to long-term debentures and short-term loans, as well as local taxes, to raise funds for schools. None the less, financial crises struck swiftly. Within three years of opening the Boyne School District lacked operating funds and turned over the collection of back taxes to the Department of Education. Schools often closed temporarily for lack of funds, especially when drought or depression struck.[5]

Paying a teacher represented the highest and most unavoidable expense. The sudden settlement of the prairies, with its proliferation of countless tiny schools, created a demand for teachers that the nation could not meet. Luring them to frontier communities at all forced school-boards to pay higher wages than the national average, and even so schools sometimes shut down temporarily because of the failure to secure a teacher. The Fireguard School District so worried about the failure to secure another teacher that it threatened legal action against one who refused to fulfil her contract. By the war years anywhere from 60 to 90 per cent of the schools' total expenditures went towards teachers' salaries, a ratio that often fluctuated but none the less remained high even when school-boards slashed wages by a third or more during the 1930s. The expense of a teacher left little money to cover such essentials as heating, much less anything to retire debt or supply furnishings, books, and instructional materials. In 1937 the Buffalo Hills school had twelve dollars left in its budget to cover all other costs after paying the teacher.[6]

As well as high per capita costs, schools also suffered the other consequence of low population density: lower quality. Although provincial regulations stipulated conditions for school sites, their grounds, their design, and their care (and even supplied architectural plans for one-room schools), local boards rarely provided a physical environment conducive to learning. Financial constraints resulted in many substandard schools with inadequate lighting and ventilation, poor sanitary conditions, and faulty heating systems. Much nostalgic nonsense about pot-bellied stoves and frozen inkwells had been published, but experiencing them was scarcely romantic. As Mary Boose recalled, 'the backs of the pupils might be roasting while faces were cold and always the feet were freezing. In this particular school [Auburn, near Vulcan] the water for drinking or washing had to be carried one half mile in a pail. Therefore no one drank or washed much ... As school was conducted in daylight, the lamps on the wall were never lighted.'[7]

Secondly, beyond the few textbooks purchased by their parents, the students had little in the way of materials or books. When the Boyne school opened in 1910 the school-board spent $3.83 on library books, and not another penny over the next decade. Even after twenty years of operation the relatively large and better-financed high school of thirty-two pupils in Carmangay faced similar problems. School inspectors reported that 'the teachers have not sufficient supplies and apparatus, [and] the reference library is rather meager.'[8]

The quality of teaching itself likewise suffered. Even though rural school-boards offered higher wages than might be obtained back east, the teachers seldom gained, for they also faced proportionately higher living costs. Many did not wish to work in an isolated frontier schoolhouse in any event. And even in prosperous times school-boards did not always pay on time and in full. Luring experienced teachers proved especially difficult, and frontier communities mostly received young, single teachers fresh out of training school. But many did not have much, if any, teacher training. Although the province established standards for the certification of teachers, intense pressure from desperate rural communities forced it to lower standards and even to permit uncertified teachers to teach.[9]

Upon arrival these inexperienced, untrained teachers faced a near-impossible task. In uncomfortable, ill-equipped schools, they faced a dozen students of different ages and might be asked to teach any or all grades. The best-planned method of proceeding might fall astray because of unpredictable problems. Teachers could only guess at the length of the school year. Financial crises and environmental calamities resulted in the cancellation of many school days. Thus rural schools in Alberta averaged 160 days of instruction a year between 1905 and 1910, compared to 190 days for urban ones, but the school term varied enormously from year to year. Erratic attendance by pupils compounded the problem. Critical labour-intensive farm operations, like threshing, often kept children from school. In September 1915 the Sanderson school operated for only fifteen days because of the harvest, and the pupil with the best attendance record that month only appeared for six and one-half days. The absence of one child might postpone the teaching of an entire grade, and the movement of families in and out of the district might mean the sudden addition or deletion of entire grades in the middle of the school year.[10]

Nearly all former students of the one-room school agree that discipline posed a severe problem. Although school-boards and parents alike sanctioned harsh corporal punishments, eighteen-year-old female teachers with no other adult to help them confronted rowdy boys nearly their own age and twice their size. Few teachers endured these conditions for long. They quit at an alarming rate. The one-room Alston school employed nineteen teachers between 1906 and 1929, averaging almost a new one per year. Not as lucky, the Burwash school employed thirty-four different teachers during its twenty-five years of operation. At the Auburn school teachers rotated every few months between 1910 and 1915. As the Lethbridge *Herald* noted of a teacher who taught fifteen years in the area in the same one-room school, 'perhaps his case is without parallel ... in all Alberta.' Several escape routes facilitated this high turnover. Some found employment in large city schools. The Great War claimed many of the area's male teachers, the men doubtless convinced that the horrors of the trenches could scarcely equal the battle of the classroom. The more numerous single female teachers found less hazardous escape as the area's many bachelors bombarded them with marriage proposals. Thus a steady turnover of teachers aggravated the already severe difficulty of getting them in the first place.[11]

While still on the job teachers responded to their onerous task in a variety of ways. Some worked long, hard, and conscientiously to fulfil all that school-boards asked of them, but many eased the burden by cutting out some subjects and concentrating on a favoured few. Others gave up entirely and simply marked time: 'Mr Bradley was a good teacher, but a casual one,' recalled Mrs J. Smith; '[he]had a nap occasionally, feet on desk, ... when he snored he awakened himself or if we became too noisy we awakened him.' The provincial system for the inspection of schools and teachers was far too inadequate to police such problems. Inspectors complained that they 'did not see how an Inspector could inspect a school and do justice by staying only one and a half hours.' But communities often reluctantly accepted a bad teacher rather than no teacher at all.[12]

Even under the best of conditions, many students in the Vulcan area did not absorb the cultural heritage so eagerly foisted upon them. One former student remembered that 'the work in all the grades was sketchy due to a lack of proper or interesting texts. There was an English history and a Canadian history text which seemed to have little meaning for the pupils. [They] memorized how many wives Henry the 8th had and something about the Druids.' Since adults donated most of the books in the sparse libraries of one-room schools, 'few books of interest to children cluttered the shelves ... and were seldom if ever borrowed and taken home.' While students everywhere have always doubted the need for learning strange and difficult material, those in one-room prairie schools often sat in utter mystification. They heard an imported message delivered by a teacher fresh from eastern Canada who knew far less about the new western society than did the students themselves. Thus essay competitions often asked children to write on subjects wholly beyond their experience. In 1913 children who might never have seen a forest wrestled with the topic 'A Picnic in the Woods.'[13]

Complaints about the curriculum surfaced occasionally among adults in the Vulcan area and throughout the province. The UFA minister without portfolio, Irene Parlby, criticized the curriculum for its failure to deal with the 'life and environment of the child outside the school.' A few teachers grappled with this problem. One even carved the schoolyard into tiny 'homesteads' and had the students raise grain and vegetables and pass inspection before he issued them 'patent,' an educational tactic that had been tried elsewhere in prairie schools. Such experiments were not only rare but anachronistic, for homesteads rapidly disappeared after 1912 and scarcely existed by the time most children reached legal homestead age.[14]

But the settlers did not want sweeping changes; for them the schools still remained an important link to a heritage that needed to be preserved on the frontier and passed on to new generations. Thus province-wide curriculum change proceeded slowly, and not until the late 1920s did texts more attuned to the occupational and regional setting of rural prairie students appear. Curiously, however, new courses in agriculture and other technical skills only appeared in the larger urban schools. Major curriculum change did not arrive until the introduction of William Aberhart's progressive reforms in the late 1930s. But while those innovations attempted to make the curriculum more relevant to the child, they little disturbed the emphasis on the cultural heritage of Britain and the empire, in spite of the growing use of American texts and methods for many subjects.[15]

Local school trustees concentrated instead on resolving the various administrative, financial, and physical problems plaguing education. Larger, more centralized schools, some reasoned, would eliminate multi-grade teaching and the duplication of many costs, while providing superior facilities and more specialized instruction. While the horse-drawn 'school van' made larger school districts possible from the beginning of settlement, they rarely appeared, since most settlers assumed that population density would rise with the occupation of vacant lands and the marriage of bachelors. As farms swelled in size and settlers realized that low population density would remain a permanent feature of local society, voices favouring centralized schools grew louder, especially after 1913, when the province introduced legal changes to facilitate consolidation and when gasoline school buses became available. In 1917 ratepayers of three rural school districts held a joint meeting to consider consolidation because 'small attendance and the existence of eight grades makes it impossible for one teacher to do effective work.' As logical sites for the new, larger schools, the towns also favoured centralization. 'Did you ever think of the waste of money and lack of efficiency resulting from four or five small schools contiguous to Ensign, some having as low as six pupils attending?' asked the Vulcan *Advocate*, which also hinted that a consolidated school in the town might help to secure the trade of hinterland families.[16]

But although consolidation promised long-term reductions in costs, it initially threatened to raise them. Parents now balked at the expense of purchasing and running school buses. Having already borne the burden of building one-room schools, they remained reluctant to close them – especially since they served so many other social purposes – while they were also shouldering the expense of newer, larger schools. Furthermore, the lack of all-weather roads and the slow evolution of reliable vehicles meant even more winter days when school would be cancelled or arrivals delayed. Many children faced long rides, and while the oldest could endure them better than the youngest, they would none the less lose time needed for chores.[17]

Thus, consolidation proceeded slowly in spite of its admitted virtues. The earliest consolidations did not involve the building of expensive new schools but the combining of students from two half-empty ones. Not surprisingly, centralization consolidation proceeded most rapidly at the higher grade levels. The one-room school was least equipped to deal with them, and since few children went on to secondary education anyway, centralization seemed the only practical solution to the problem. In 1925 the town of Vulcan erected a new four-room brick school that drew many students from distant farms. In the 1930s, when rural schools began to close at an accelerated pace in the surrounding districts, the school sprouted new appendages and soon housed ten teachers and over three hundred pupils. Schools in other towns also ballooned in size, although they remained much smaller. Consolidation therefore proceeded slowly and piecemeal before 1935. It resolved only some of the problems, and raised new ones in terms of initial costs and transportation problems.[18]

While the difficulties outlined thus far seemed horrendous if inappropriately judged by today's standards, it must be added that contemporaries also thought them extraordinary. Although many of the problems plaguing frontier schools in the Vulcan area also afflicted rural education in Ontario and the

American midwest, they did not strike there with the same frequency and severity. Furthermore, it must be remembered that the pioneers attached enormous importance to schools and tried to provide their children with the best education possible. Evidence of this effort is that by the mid-1920s parents in the Vulcan area kept a higher percentage of their children enrolled in school than did either the province as a whole or the province of Ontario generally.[19]

But in spite of their best efforts they succeeded marginally at best in providing the kind of education they had first envisioned. True, the schools did produce a generation vaguely familiar with the rudiments of British and Canadian culture, whose loyalty to that tradition would pass the great test of the Second World War, yet much of the acculturation process seems to have been experienced outside the classroom. Frontier schools hardly represented a perfect replication of an imported cultural institution when untrained and inexperienced teachers knew little of the heritage they supposedly implanted, or if they ignored some important aspects of it, or if they slept instead of presenting it, or if they spent most of their time maintaining order, or staying warm, or dividing their attention among children of many different ages and levels, or if the recipients often missed school for a variety of valid reasons, or if a few books and materials aided the process, or if lack of funds, teachers, or students forced temporary school closures, or if the messages conveyed held little meaning for children of the prairie frontier.

Churches offer many parallels with schools. Like them, churches represented imported institutions that nominally remained under metropolitan control with respect to organizational structure and 'curriculum,' but left administration in local hands. As settlement spread west, most eastern-based churches followed a similar plan for expansion. Each carved the frontier into huge geographical units such as dioceses or presbyteries. At first almost no one lived in them, but as settlement spread, the parent church sent missionaries into the new communities to locate members of the faith and test the waters by holding a service. If the community showed interest, it became a mission station on the route of an itinerant minister supplied by the church on (it was to be hoped) a regular basis. A pioneer's home, a school, or some other public building served as meeting-place. Eventually the congregation would support itself, building its own church and hiring its own minister. Parent churches pushed congregations into this final organizational phase as quickly as possible, for the opening of the west rapidly drained them of mission funds.

As had the schools, however, the churches soon found that local circumstances dictated modifications. Immediately they faced the same problems of low population density and crude transportation. While adults could travel further once a week than children could five days a week, denominational splits that greatly lowered the population density of each faith offset this advantage. Some churches found their members so scattered that they could not even form congregations in many districts. In other cases the parent church stretched its financial and clerical resources so thin that it could not maintain missions everywhere than demand for them existed. But most of the preaching points established under the mission systems never achieved self-sufficiency anyway. And those that did erected their own churches with painful slowness. No churches appeared until 1912, and Vulcan, the largest town in the area, did not have one until 1917, even though a Methodist mission congregation had been established there as early as 1906 and a building fund as early as 1912.[20]

In all, only thirteen church buildings arose in the entire area before the Second World War. Small, crude, and soon in need of structural repairs, most of those became self-sufficient in name only. Vulcan's interdenominational Union congregation, under the auspices of Presbyterian administration, declared itself self-sufficient in 1914 but could not actually support itself without outside help until 1919. The Anglican Church failed to do as well. 'Far from being self-supporting,' complained its clergyman in 1931, 'Vulcan, with great effort, could possibly sustain about two white mice and a canary.' Even though donations of materials and labour helped raise many churches, building debts saddled them for years. In 1927 Carmangay's Union Church retained a 'long-standing debt' of $730 and predicted that it would never be paid unless the bank dropped interest charges. A loan of $1,500 taken out by Vulcan's Roman Catholic Church in 1922 still had an unpaid balance of $651 in 1938. Churches also collected insufficient funds for building maintenance and ministers' salaries. Parent churches saved some self-supporting congregations with temporary bail-outs, but those crushed by heavy debt reverted back to mission status. Others came perilously close to doing so. Financial woes and worries dominate virtually every document relating to religious organizations in the Vulcan area, even though the largest congregations sometimes enjoyed a few years of financial health.[21]

Those congregations most likely to build self-sufficient churches did so largely with the aid of geography. If chance placed enough adherents of a particular faith close enough together, or if it won enough converts within close proximity of each other, then success might follow. If not, no church appeared. This helps to explain why two Baptist churches arose in the area, while the Lutherans, with twice as many adherents but spread much more thinly throughout the area, could not erect even one church. The largest denominations, however, enjoyed the best chance of developing self-sufficiency. Before 1925, almost one-quarter of the Vulcan-area population claimed allegiance to the Presbyterian church and almost another quarter to the Methodist. After their merger created the United Church of Canada in 1925, it claimed more than one-third of the local population. Of the remainder, Anglicans accounted for about 15 per cent of the population, Roman Catholics and Lutherans about 10 per cent each, and Baptists about 5 per cent. All other religions combined rarely accounted for as much as 15 per cent of the population at any time prior to the Second World War.[22]

To overcome distance and low population density, the settlers soon seized upon the solution ultimately applied to the schools: consolidation and centralization. But in addition to consolidating congregations of the same faith, they also achieved this purpose through interdenominational co-operation and church union. From the beginning parent churches had struggled without success to supply preachers to every rural district on a weekly basis. Thus, in a particular district on any given Sunday, services might well be administered by any one of half a dozen faiths. At the Berrywater school, 'church services did not follow any particular denomination,' remembered P.J. Haslam. Wallace Miller recalled that before 1910 American Methodists sometimes attended Anglican or even Roman Catholic services. A Presbyterian minister who held a service in 1905 found members of five different faiths in attendance and even 'one or two avowed agnostics.'[23] Thus some settlers preferred attending services in any faith to attending none at all. By the time census takers entered the Vulcan area in 1910, many settlers could not accurately report their religious affiliation. Some undoubtedly listed their traditional faith, although they more often attended services of a different church, while others named the church they usually attended. Still others probably suggested that they now belonged to an interdenominational Christian faith – a category missing from the census check-list.

The parent churches themselves unwittingly contributed to this crumbling denominationalism. With their resources spread thin in 1905, Anglican, Methodist, and Presbyterian ministers agreed to take regular turns preaching at the Ferrodale school, services that soon attracted settlers of all faiths. Presbyterians and Methodists, however, achieved the greatest co-operation. At first both churches attempted to extend their separate mission systems into every district of the Vulcan area. But the financial burden and the personnel problem soon brought them to an understanding. They quit competing throughout much of Alberta, and in 1911 they met to carve up the south between them. In the Vulcan area the Presbyterian Church agreed to abandon several towns and one-half of the rural districts, while assuming full responsibility for the other half and for the town of Vulcan itself. The Methodists withdrew from those localities, taking full charge of the rural districts vacated by the Presbyterians and assuming complete responsibility for the towns of Carmangay and Champion. The two churches even swapped lots purchased in each other's towns. Like the parent organizations, Vulcan-area settlers approved of the scheme in the name of efficiency and economy, and because a shortage of ministers made it imperative anyway.[24]

But the settlers themselves demanded more than interdenominational co-operation; they wanted a full merger, something the parent bodies had been discussing for years. At Carmangay and Vulcan members of both faiths joined the existing church almost unanimously, and their locally elected church administrators declared the congregations fully interdenominational. Both christened their new meeting-places the 'Union Church,' although technically each remained under the separate institutional umbrellas of the Methodist and Presbyterian churches. A vote taken among Vulcan Union Church members in 1915 revealed that only one person opposed the formal merger of the parent bodies. Meanwhile, a vote held throughout the High River presbytery (a larger administrative unit of the Presbyterian Church that included the Vulcan area) revealed that 90 per cent of its church members favoured a nation-wide merger. Clergymen of the two churches did not respond quite as enthusiastically, yet as early as 1910 five of the seven ministers in the presbytery favoured it, as did a majority of Methodist ministers in a 1918 vote.[25] While discussions between the parent churches in the east obviously influenced those results, the innovation enjoyed quicker acceptance on the frontier, where circumstances favoured it and where no entrenched interests or established traditions stood ready to oppose it. Thus, of the three thousand preaching places that had already taken the interdenominational plunge before the union of 1925, 70 per cent hailed from the prairie provinces.[26]

But interdenominationalism in the Vulcan area extended far beyond the merger of Methodists and Presbyterians. As the Presbyterian Reverend D.K. Allan noted of the Union congregation at Vulcan in 1914, 'While the agreement is only with the Methodist Church, the members of other denominations favour the idea of one church. They are, Anglican, Baptist, Lutherans, etc.' Anglicans who had attended Methodist and Presbyterian services in the district for years participated in the organization and building of the Union Church at Vulcan, 'as much as if it were an Anglican Building,' and even Roman Catholics contributed to the building fund. Members of both groups undoubtedly believed that churches of their own faith might never be built in the town. The Anglican and Roman Catholic authorities abhored this interde-nominationalism, condemned it, and forbade it, but many settlers defied such decrees whenever their own churches failed to supply them with fully funded missions and financial aid leading to self-sufficiency. The interdenominational magnet of Vulcan's Union Church explains why both the Anglican and

Roman Catholic churches burst into a sudden flurry of activity that led to the building of two new churches in Vulcan within five years of the erection of the Union Church. But all churches could not offer services to all adherents in all the outlying districts. When none but the Baptists seemed willing to build a church in the Reid Hill district, settlers of many faiths decided to support it. As Mrs V.B. Budd recalled, 'this denomination was not the choice of all present,' but they recognized the practical necessity of having one church accept the responsibility of supplying ministers and funds. After all, the irregular itinerant missionary system had already conditioned Vulcan-area settlers to interdenominationalism long before any churches rose.[27]

Mixed attendance affected the sermons delivered to Vulcan-area settlers. No clergyman could dwell on the particulars of his own denominational background without offending some members of the congregation. While a basic choice remained between Protestantism and Catholicism, within the Protestant churches wise clergymen served up a bland, innocuous diet of Christian values unlikely to offend anyone. Those who won acceptance most easily leaned towards a moderate 'modernism,' delivered in a style more reasoned than impassioned. If we are to judge from the summaries of sermons occasionally printed in local newspapers, preachers often took a passage or story from the Bible and treated it as an allegory or parable that revealed some universal moral truth relevant to contemporary life. Thus, they eschewed a literal interpretation of Scripture and accepted the validity of most scientific discoveries. They usually ignored thorny problems such as the Creation or else smothered them under vague assurances about the existence of God. As a result, serious theological discussion rarely crept into any sermon. This approach to religion constituted the regular diet of the Union churches in particular; its interdenominational audiences could easily digest it, and it nicely complemented their secular progressive fare.[28]

The prominence of this brand of religion in the Vulcan area belies two somewhat contradictory impressions that scholarship has foisted on prairie Protestantism: either that evangelical fundamentalism ran wild on the frontier, or that the social gospel spewed from every pulpit. Some imply that Alberta became the hotbed of the former and Saskatchewan and Manitoba the latter, although no one has satisfactorily explained this curious anomaly.[29] Frontiers have always attracted religious sects and cults because they provide the isolation necessary to escape hostility back home or to avoid contact with an evil world, and plenty of them appeared in Alberta. None the less, two-thirds of the provincial population subscribed to the Anglican, Roman Catholic, Presbyterian, and Methodist faiths between 1901 and 1921. These traditional churches claimed an even greater proportion of the Vulcan area since no religious-based bloc settlements established themselves in the area. Some clergymen and adherents of sects and cults arrived independently, won new converts, and established at least half a dozen new religious organizations, most of them in the 1920s. But they never attracted as much as 10 per cent of the area's population.[30]

Fundamentalism, especially when emotionally charged with scriptural literalism and hell-fire, rarely invaded Union churches in the Vulcan area either. When it did, audiences grew restless. When one evangelical preacher arrived at the Carmangay Union Church in 1911, an Anglican layman wrote: 'From what I can gather, the people are not satisfied with the shouting and waving of arms.' Fundamentalism simply did not suit the outlook of a people steeped in progressive rhetoric. Although nothing about progressivism necessarily collided with any religious faith, its stress on efficiency presumed that rational, scientific reasons accounted for the way in which the world worked.[31]

In their rejection of fundamentalism, and of sects and cults generally, Vulcan-area settlers also overlooked the suitability of the sects' organizational structure to frontier conditions. Tiny, virtually autonomous congregations could avoid the expense of a church, as meetings could conveniently rotate among members' homes. No minister need be paid if a congregation accepted the cult's faith in lay preachers. But such was fundamentalism's lack of appeal on theological and social grounds that pioneers turned instead to another solution to distance and thin population: centralized interdenominationalism. (More will be said later of an extremely cost-efficient alternative that become available in the 1920s: radio evangelism.)

At first, social gospel rarely appeared, either. Sermons served more as guides to personal conduct and faith, and if society should be reconstructed along Christian principles, that would come about through changes in the attitude and behaviour of many individuals. True, most of the Union preachers called for political action to abolish drinking, gambling, and prostitution, but such demands hardly represented a distinct social-gospel outlook. None the less, social gospel better suited the progressive attitudes of the area, and as Richard Allen has pointed out, agrarian-reform organizations crusaded for economic and political change with a moral fervour often specifically Christian in nature. Social messages of that sort occasionally appeared. In 1916 Vulcan's Union preacher spoke on the subject of 'Applied Christianity' for a special UFA Sunday service. The Vulcan *Advocate* nodded its approval: 'Too long has the Church appeared as something apart from the general life of the district.' Such attitudes did not appear consistently, however, for a few years later the paper complained that 'too many people are busy laying at the church's door the responsibility for the sins of government or the business manager.' When the hardship of the Great Depression struck, more ministers raised the banner for social action; in 1932 United Church clergymen in the area endorsed the aims of the socialist League for Social Reconstruction.[32]

But a growing social concern among the clergy did nothing to bolster membership, attendance, or financial contributions to the church. Indeed, neither social gospel, moderate modernism, evangelical fundamentalism, nor anything else religious excited the community. Except for a small minority, the settlers cared little about theology. When a lay official of Carmangay Anglican Church wrote to the archdeacon in 1913 concerning the hiring of a preacher, he noted that 'it would not matter very much whether he were "high" or inclined to be Evangelical, so far as he knew how to be tactful and could compel respect.' The layman considered a 'strong' man with good oratorical skills far more important for sustaining the church than any message he might deliver.[33]

Indeed, the very popularity of interdenominationalism in the Vulcan area, while carried out in the name of efficiency and economy, reflected this lack of concern about theological postures. While the settlers considered themselves good Christians at heart, religion seldom intruded on their thoughts or played a vital role in their daily lives. In the great mass of documents left by the settlers almost never do they refer to God, and hardly anyone invoked his name to explain the ebb and flow of individual or community fortunes. In short, the settlers were secular minded and thus preferred a diluted Christian universalism. The clergymen themselves complained endlessly about this spiritual apathy. 'The shallowness of conviction,' observed Rev. J.T. Ferguson of the Presbyterian Church in 1913, 'is a noteworthy sign of the state of religion on our mission field.' Two years later he added, 'The story of our mission fields is one of spiritual perturbation.'[34]

While it is perhaps natural for clergymen everywhere to fret about the spiritual condition of the flock, those in the Vulcan area offered hard evidence for their complaints. Clearly the financial woes of the churches cannot be explained solely in terms of low population density and transportation difficulties. In spite of similar difficulties, other institutions and organizations arose more quickly on the frontier and encountered fewer financial problems, even when they lacked the outside funding that the mission system provided. The pioneers did not think the church important enough to support wholeheartedly, and extracting funds from them exasperated the hardiest clergymen. When Methodists organized a congregation in the Brant district in 1906, total contributions that year barely reached fifteen dollars, even though thirty-seven members had joined. Presbyterian fund-raising in the Vulcan area between 1907 and 1912 yielded meagre returns of six to seven dollars per family per year. 'Mayview ... will have to be cut out very soon,' reported Carmangay's

Anglican clergyman, Thomas Melrose, of a mission station in 1911; 'I cannot get them . . . to pay anything beyond a very small collection averaging about 60 cents per fortnight.' The records of the Methodist preaching circuit east of Vulcan are sprinkled with such comments as 'no money raised recently,' '40 cents in the treasury,' 'mortgage payments behind,' 'little money raised for districts.'[35]

Perhaps the settlers deliberately curtailed contributions in the knowledge that parent churches would continue to pick up additional costs through their mission systems, but even when the parents pushed some of them into independence, the situation scarcely improved. Church-goers told ministers to 'wait until harvest,' and then gave little because of 'poor crops' or 'low grain prices.' Drought and depression did reduce the take. Contributions to the Champion United Church and its four circuit stations averaged $1,920 to $2,962 annually before 1932, but fell to $542 to $800 annually during the late 1930s. Yet prosperous years did not always mean increased contributions. The Carmangay Union Church complained that it collected less money in 1915 and 1916 than in previous years. At the same time clergymen repeatedly noted the money spent on farm expansion, on luxuries like automobiles and vacations, and for the support of other organizations.[36]

Unlike those of most institutions in the area, church building and maintenance funds flowed chiefly from the largesse of a very few generous patrons. In 1916 over half the contributors to the Carmangay Union Church gave sums of five dollars or less for the entire year, while five members donated fifty dollars or more each. In several cases a single patron determined the financial fate of a local church, which helps to explain the somewhat chaotic spatial distribution of churches in the area compared to schools. It is unlikely that an Anglican church would have arisen in Carmangay without C.W. Carman's gift of eighteen town lots at the height of the real-estate boom. Indeed, he made the donation conditional on the erection of a church. The Presbyterian presbytery greatly feared the consequences for its congregation in Brant when its chief benefactor sold his business to a Roman Catholic and moved away. In 1938 the Catholic priest at Champion complained that 'this Mission was for many years practically a one-family affair and this family built the original Church and virtually "ran it" long years.' The Catholic priest at Vulcan reported a similar case: 'If it were not for the Stacks, I don't know where Vulcan would be, for, not only are they responsible for about one-third of the income, but they do more real work than the rest of the parish put together.'[37]

Complaints about attendance matched those about stinginess. Many settlers almost never attended services. The size of this group is impossible to determine accurately, but one estimate in 1911 claimed that only half the settlers in the Alston district ever went to church. Even church members failed to attend regularly. Of seven Anglican families in one district, a priest moaned that 'although visited and urged to attend, but one family came *once* to any of the services. I went several times and had absolutely no one out for service.' A Presbyterian cleric grumbled, 'I get a little disappointed at times after making a journey to find few or no one present.' Although clergymen rarely experienced rejection to such an extent in the larger towns, they still faced empty pews. By 1914 attendance at Vulcan's Union services averaged 50 per cent of membership, and the Methodist Church claimed about the same attendance rate for the province generally. After 1920, as more churches and preaching circuits established themselves in the area, as better roads and more autos appeared, and as more children reached Sunday school age, the churches reported slightly better attendance, but complaints still persisted. Priests noted that Catholics, because they had rarely had the opportunity to take communion in the earliest days of settlement, no longer feared the grave strictures about skipping mass once the Church did establish itself in the area.[38]

Clergymen also complained about the reluctance of people to stand for election to church administrative positions or to work for church organizations and projects. The settlers offered time, distance, and transportation problems as excuses for lack of participation, yet they readily bore such difficulties for other events, and other institutions routinely reported good attendance. The largest crowd ever recorded at the Vulcan Union Church, for example, assembled not to worship but to organize a wheat pool. 'They will drive 20 miles to a dance who would not go half a mile to church – that is the actual truth,' reported Dr W.W. Upton, an active layman in Vulcan's Union congregation. 'Although the religious meetings at Loma were not well attended,' observed another layman, 'I notice the same district had a large attendance at the various dances held there.' When the Carmangay Union Church held its cornerstone-laying ceremony on 1 July 1910, almost everyone in the congregation attended the Dominion Day celebrations instead.[39]

The low esteem in which many congregations held their ministers contributed greatly to this apathy. The settlement of the prairies placed an enormous strain on churches to provide ministers for thousands of new communities spread thinly across a vast region. When the Vulcan area secured any ministers at all, they inevitably equalled schoolteachers for youth and inexperience and for their lack of knowledge about western and local conditions. Many were still theology students, and if schoolteachers had trouble commanding the respect of children scarcely younger than themselves, these prospective clergymen had little chance of succeeding with 'pupils' older than themselves.

An active Anglican layman, R.A. Mowat, complained to the archdeacon in

1913 that the church in Carmangay suffered from 'one weak clergyman after another.' He pronounced the last two 'good Christian men' with whom he had no personal quarrel, but 'as missionary priests they are sorry misfits.' Although he felt comfortable with the settlers, a Methodist minister at Champion later recalled, 'I realize now that my pulpit and administrative abilities left much to be desired.' His successor also described himself as a 'green' probationer: 'What foolish things I did or tried to do,' he recalled. Years later the United Church even admitted that inferior ministers often ended up in isolated rural areas. Thus prominent laymen told their churches that attendance depended very much on the qualities of the minister. 'There would be between 25 and 35 people who would attend services,' advised an Anglican at Vulcan, 'and it would depend upon the clergyman himself how many more could be added to the above numbers.'[40]

Fresh from theological training in eastern Canada or Britain, clergymen often first erred by insisting on denominational purity out of loyalty to their chosen faith and church. In his sharp criticism of the new young Presbyterian minister, Dr Upton complained that 'his ideals, and plans are more suited to an old church of rank Scotch Presbyterians, but here we have to abandon prejudices and conventionalities and be darned glad to get a small mixed bunch together.' Since the frontier sex structure and low population density severely restricted the marriage market, romance often flared between Protestants and Catholics. 'I regret that so many of my marriages are of the Mixed variety,' complained Father Beausoleil, 'but each such case that I have had seemed inevitable.' Clergymen who did not accommodate themselves to interdenominationalism, however reluctantly, faced a chilly reception. When a Catholic priest at Vulcan refused to conduct a funeral for a young man who had attended Protestant services, the community ostracized him: 'A section of the parishioners are saying hard things about poor me,' he moaned.[41]

Nor did the clergy wield moral authority on other matters. A congregation refused to pay a young minister his wages when he pressured police into arresting forty-five men for cutting grain on the Sabbath at harvest time. When the Rev. S.W. Hann decided to expel Mr and Mrs J.F. Synder from the Union Church at Carmangay for some undocumented reason, the locally elected Quarterly Official Board promptly reinstated them and officially 'deplored the action' of the minister. When Methodist clergymen in the area urged Bible study in public schools in 1914, the community and the local press sharply rebuked them. Given these and like episodes, it is little wonder that attendance and co-operation depended more on the character of the preacher than anything else.[42]

In their defence, the youthful clerics carried burdens that might have broken wiser, more experienced preachers. The horrors of circuit riding are described in every surviving memoir of the Vulcan-area clergymen who experienced it. Nor did the situation improve greatly once churches rose in the larger towns, for they expected resident clergyman to continue to visit isolated congregations. Consider the itinerary of one Catholic priest in 1914: 'When there is a fifth Sunday in the month, Mass at Mr. J. Fath's, five miles west of Carmangay. The Friday before that 5th Sunday, Mass at McDonald brothers at Brant at 8. The Saturday at Vulcan at 10:30. Mr Fath comes for the priest at Vulcan. The priest stays at Vulcan at Conlin's ... Barons, at the Arnold Hotel; Carmangay, at Mr. G. Buckley's, ... Mass on week days at Barons, Carmangay, Vulcan and Reid Hill.' Churches constantly changed the circuit routes, but they always remained vast in size. Anglican priests of the Calgary diocese (which encompassed the Vulcan area) preached at anywhere from six to ten different locations before 1920, and for years the diocese expected a single priest to cover seven hundred square miles within the High River Church Mission area.[43]

Road and weather conditions frequently upset schedules: 'Mr. Stack came along with me and fortunately he brought his two bays along. They had to dig us out eight times,' reported Father Ritter to his bishop of a trip from Vulcan to an outlying preaching point. 'By the time we reached Lomond we were so late that the few people who had been able to make it had left for their homes.' Clergymen routinely begged their churches for a car, but Father J. Bidault was denied even a horse: 'I had no other way of transportation but the good will of the people, who would take me with their horses and wagons from one farm to the next. Often when I had no one to take me I walked with my suitcase in which I had my chapel. In 1913 I bought my first car, a Model T Ford, but roads were deplorable.'[44]

Once arrived, new clergymen undoubtedly expected the respect and status commonly accorded their fellows back home. Instead they faced tiny audiences, meagre collection plates, and outright hostility if they adhered to denominational strictures. Rarely could they turn to other clergymen for advice and sympathy: 'In Ontario population is thick and the Ministers touch elbows with one another,' complained one sky pilot in 1927; 'how different is our situation.' And as beginners, perhaps still students, clergymen suffered such hardships for lower pay than preachers in settled, densely populated areas. Unlike the school-boards, churches lured clergymen to the rural frontier not by offering higher pay but by stressing the nobility of mission work. One circuit rider who served a vast area northeast of Vulcan from 1917 to 1920 rented an isolated shack in the countryside because he could afford nothing else. To sustain himself he kept a few turkeys and chickens and raised a garden which the gophers usually ate. He searched for odd jobs on farms to earn a few dollars and honed a talent for wangling free dinner invitations.[45]

Nor did the young and inexperienced have much opportunity to earn the respect of the community, especially in the early circuit-riding days, when they spent no more than two hours a week in any district. Student ministers soon returned to their studies, and graduated missionaries faced repeated changes in their circuits and frequent transfers to entirely new mission fields. Many quit in desperation. If they failed to find more financially stable congregations in more densely populated places, they abandoned the cloth altogether. Thus most mission stations welcomed a new minister every year before the First World War, as did the smallest rural congregations thereafter. Even the larger town churches experienced rapid turnovers. The Union Church at Vulcan greeted only six new ministers between 1910 and 1942, but over the same period Carmangay faced at least fourteen. Cleverville-Champion had at least eleven between 1906 and 1920, although only three from 1920 to 1955. Such transient ministers could hardly emerge as community leaders. Missionary branches of parent bodies and self-supporting congregations repeatedly failed to attract hardier, more determined recruits. Indeed, they struggled to attract anyone at all.[46]

Poor attendance, meagre financial support, and spiritual apathy combined with a demand for interdenominational universalism all support the conclusion that neither church nor religion mattered much to the population. Vulcan may be an isolated case in this respect, yet many studies at the time and since, both of western Canada and of rural North America generally, have also cast doubt on the matter.[47] Why, then, did churches appear in the Vulcan area at all? Clearly, the parent bodies provided the initial impetus. All feared losing their flocks on the vast frontier. 'Living often 30, 40, and 50 miles from a Catholic chapel, these settlers drift away from the authority, teaching, and sacraments of the Church,' claimed George Daly in 1921. In particular, churchmen worried that children of the frontier would grow up without benefit of proper religious training. Rev. J.T. Ferguson feared for their souls when he discovered that out of a Sunday class of twenty teenage girls only six had 'any acquaintance with the parable of the Ten Virgins.' Thus a Methodist edict of 1906 threw out the challenge: 'Devise all means within your power to help hold these young people for Christ, the Church and home.'[48]

But concern that pioneers and their children might drift from God altogether paled beside the fear that some other unpalatable faith might engulf them simply because it pursued frontier missionary work more aggressively. Ferguson recoiled in horror from the thought that the monster of Mormonism would swallow up the faithful and convert them to polygamy unless strenuous missionary efforts prevented it. Daly worried about how 'social relations often bring our Western Catholics in very frequent contact with the different Protestant churches and their tremendous activities ... God alone knows how many of our Catholic boys and girls have been lost to the faith through mixed marriages,' he added grimly. 'The reason for starting services in Mayview was in the hope of getting hold of the children,' reported an Anglican lay preacher in 1911, 'but a Methodist was sent when they found me there.'[49]

But if churches took the initiative in moving into the area to build their own western empires, the pioneers themselves lent some support, however grudgingly. They agreed that children needed structured religious training, even if they themselves did not. They conscripted huge numbers of their offspring into Sunday schools. Enrolments at Union Church preaching stations commonly outstripped adult church memberships by ratios of three to one. In the towns, adults could easily shunt children off to Sunday school alone. Thus attendance at the Vulcan Union Church school ran a respectable 74 per cent of enrolments in 1915. Rural parents faced a greater dilemma, since it was troublesome to take children to services unless the parents planned to attend themselves. Thus, in rural preaching stations Sunday school attendance ran at only 50 per cent of enrolments, even in fine summer weather.[50]

And although moving to a frontier freed many settlers from social duties they could not escape at home, such as going to church, some adults in the Vulcan area still attended out of a sense of social obligation, especially if they held a position in the community, like schoolteacher or school-board member, in which the correct moral posture seemed important. As the custodians of frontier morality and respectability women more often attended and supported the church than men. 'The women-folk had a deeper desire for the niceties of Christian culture,' reported one minister, and men more readily conceded leadership to them concerning church affairs. Women's church clubs played the most important role in fund-raising campaigns through their dinners, teas, bazaars, and plays.[51]

For most settlers, however, church-going had little to do with religion. Like all organizational gatherings in the area, it became a social occasion – a chance to meet friends after the service and to arrange Sunday dinner invitations and afternoon visits. Some went for the music. As one participant observed of an early service in 1905, 'Some of them went just to get out and have a chat with their neighbors, and a few to get the minister to post letters for them in town.' Should a newly arrived, single lady teacher start frequenting services, attendance among bachelors inevitably improved; some might attend anyway because an invitation to dinner would provide them with their first decent meal in a week. But one minister who recognized the social significance of rural churches knew that other means of socializing drew bigger crowds. He explained that farmers visited the towns for many economic as well as social reasons, whereas on Sunday they could only go to church, 'and this did not operate as powerfully as the combination of motives which brought them into town for business [and] pleasure.'[52]

But even those who rarely attended or supported churches still thought them necessary. Ancient rituals like baptisms, marriages, and funerals needed a shrine and a master of ceremonies. Indeed, one student concluded that by the time of the Second World War this had become the principal function of churches in rural Alberta. But some also believed them essential for preserving heritage. English settlers at Carmangay, in particular, wanted an Anglican church to help them to retain ties with the Motherland. Nearly everyone also thought churches a necessary mark of a civilized and respectable community. Thus boosterism also embraced church building. Before 1917 Vulcan merchants complained that churches could not be included in the town's promotional literature. 'It is hardly to the credit of the district that we have everything save a Church,' lectured the Vulcan *Advocate* on 22 September 1915. The ensuing Union Church building-fund drive sprang as much from civic spirit as from any other motive. Both the merchants and the local press protested the simple architectural style first chosen and successfully lobbied for a change of plans. The adding of 'pillar embattlements and tower' provided them with something more impressive to photograph for advertising campaigns.[53]

At the same time, churches could not be allowed to interfere with business itself. They should occupy a position of prominence in the promotional literature rather than in the townsites. As the Carmangay *Sun* reported on 4 March 1910: 'The Methodists are preparing to build a church on Grand Ave. nearly opposite the Post Office and some of the businessmen are objecting. They say that a church is an impediment to a business street and a petition is in circulation asking the Methodists to select another site.'

One final puzzle about the role of church and religion in the Vulcan area remains. In 1935 local residents elected two clergymen to major public offices, Rev. Ernest Hansell of the Vulcan Church of Christ to the House of Commons and Rev. Peter Dawson of the Champion United Church to the Alberta legislature. Both represented the Social Credit party. That result seems to contradict much of the preceding argument about the relative unimportance of church and religion in the area, but the paradox is far more apparent than real. The preachers won, not because of their religious beliefs or occupational status, but in spite of them.

Religion itself did not gain ground in the area because of the Depression. It is sometimes assumed that people turn to religion in times of great hardship, but hardship just as often yields the opposite result. As United Churchman Rev. R.J. McDonald reported of southern Alberta in 1938: 'Then came a crop failure, the worst yet. Is it any wonder that people said, "What's the use?" and for many even their faith in God was shaken.' The Catholic priest at Vulcan concurred with this judgment: 'With the exception of just a couple of families,' he reported, 'the people who really built the parish have all gone, and those who are here now have little enthusiasm, either spiritually or otherwise.' The United Church reported declining membership in most congregations in the area during the 1930s, and Dawson's own large ministry, which included Champion and several country preaching points, claimed 525 people under pastoral care in the year of his election, but never more than 450 thereafter. Hansell's Church of Christ at Vulcan never claimed more than 230 adherents throughout the Depression. Thus neither Dawson nor Hansell took political advantage of a sudden surge in religious sentiment.[54]

Nor did Social Credit leader William Aberhart win support in the area on religious grounds. His personal magnetism certainly captivated the local population, as it did others in the province. When a political opponent attempted to question Aberhart following a speech in Vulcan, the crowd silenced him with a tremendous roar. But his radio show occasioned no comment in the local press or other surviving documents until he introduced Social Credit economic theory into his sermons. For that matter, no religious radio programs ever commanded the attention paid to radio comedies. No branch of Aberhart's Prophetic Bible Institute took root in the area, except at one rural schoolhouse, and even it withered in 1936. Indeed, most of the local propaganda favouring Social Credit theory spewed from the avowedly secular, Douglasite 'New Age Club,' led in Vulcan by merchant George Whicher. Long-time Social Credit organizer in the Carmangay area Rena Burns, who did join the party partly for religious reasons, none the less thought religion of little significance in the movement's success locally. Neither Hansell nor Dawson mentioned God or religion once in their campaign speeches of 1935, although Hansell sometimes incorporated Social Credit ideas in his sermons.[55]

The Vulcan area, then, embraced Social Credit for secular reasons. Its attack on bankers found ready acceptance in an area long accustomed to criticism of the financial and monetary structure. Midwestern settlers arrived with notions culled from the Populist silver crusade of the 1890s. In the 1910s local Non-Partisan workers in the area attacked the monetary system as vigorously as they did the tariff. The Vulcan area's MP from 1921 to 1936, George Coote, served as chief financial critic for the 'ginger-group' wing of the Progressive party. Aberhart's promise to hire experts to implement a scientific monetary system also appealed to the area's long-standing infatuation with progressive efficiency. Most of all, however, support came from the failure of the existing governments to deal with the Depression effectively, and from the Social Credit promise of twenty-five dollars a month in additional purchasing power.[56]

It still remains to explain how two clergymen ever got themselves nominated by the community in the first place. It must be remembered at once that Social Credit did not select candidates through the traditional process of leaving the matter solely to local constituency associations. Instead, each submitted a list of four or five acceptable names, and Aberhart and his associates picked the successful candidate from the list. Thinking that Aberhart would be sympathetic to clergymen, the provincial Little Bow constituency association may have included two tolerable clergymen on their list of four names to ensure that Aberhart would not reject them all. The Macleod riding association then included Hansell on its list of three names for the dominion nomination once Dawson had been picked for the provincial campaign. Aberhart may have persuaded Hansell to seek nomination, for they had been close associates at the Westbourne Baptist Church in Calgary in the 1920s. But certainly neither man made the list because of long-standing positions of leadership in the area. Dawson moved there in 1930, but Hansell arrived barely a year prior to his nomination. Neither man had previously held any elected position in the area.[57]

Although Dawson claimed that friends persuaded him to let his name stand for the provincial contest, there may have been good reasons for both clergymen to have wanted the nominations. Social Credit may have impressed them as a Christian crusade, even if lay supporters thought of it in other terms. Secondly, considering the difficulties and hardships that clergymen faced in the area, politics provided an attractive escape from the pulpit. Certainly the salary could not be overlooked, for even Dawson, who headed one of the largest congregations in the area, survived the Depression only because a general store continued to give him credit. As Mrs Dawson recalled: 'Came the dry years, no crops, and the dust storms . . . Often there would be thick layers of dust in the Church . . . there was very little money coming in – no one had much – so of course the minister's salary dwindled. Sometimes we went for months with very little salary.' In addition, politics, with its emphasis on oratorical skills, naturally suited the training and inclination of clergymen. But regardless of the reason for placing clergymen on the nomination lists, it seems clear that the Vulcan area would have voted for anyone representing the Social Credit party in 1935. Thus evidence from the Vulcan area strongly supports the contention of David Elliot and other revisionists that Social Credit support came largely from members of established churches and not from sects, that religion played little part in its success, and fundamentalist religion even less.[58]

The role of church and religion in the Vulcan area differed slightly from that of school and education. The pioneers considered the school more vital, although they bestowed symbolic importance on both institutions. They also showed greater reluctance to alter the school, perhaps because decision-making adults did not have to endure its classrooms. When seated in the classroom of the church, however, pioneers more readily used their power to modify the curriculum. Even so, similarities between the two institutions are more striking. Like the school, the church had difficulty luring competent 'teachers' who could command the respect of apathetic 'pupils' who frequently failed to attend 'classes.' Transportation problems also plagued the church, and it too faced financial burdens only partly resolved through consolidation.

Church and school both embodied the attempt to transplant eastern institutions faithfully. Nurtured by metropolitan support, both took root in the new setting. But both immediately began evolving when cross-bred with frontier conditions in a new environment. Low population density left both to blow in the dry financial winds of the open plains. Even the larger and hardier specimens survived only by spreading roots over vast distances to tap the precious supply of nutrients: people and money. In the process their genetic structure changed. Both evolved, if not into new species, then into particular varieties of still-recognizable forms.

PART IV: SOCIETY

9

Social Structure

Scholars have differed widely in their assessment of social stratification in the rural North American midwest and on the Great Plains. Many have pronounced it largely absent or insignificant, especially during the frontier era.[1] Others have insisted that the egalitarianism of the frontier never existed – that important social distinctions based on class and wealth appeared either from the beginning of settlement or soon after.[2] Some researchers have reported significant social distinctions in addition to those based on social classes (or sometimes instead of them), distinctions based on ethnicity, religion, age, years of settlement in the community, place of residence, education, institutional memberships, occupations, and other criteria, which in various combinations produced important elites, as well as other groups that engaged in ongoing conflicts.[3] The great range of scholarly opinion on these matters derives from the variety of definitions of class and status employed, from the presence or absence of community conflict and the significance attached to it, and from the ideological orientation of the scholar. In many cases it even stems from the scholar's fastidiousness, for in every society groups of individuals tend to set themselves apart from others on the basis of real or imagined characteristics.

Rural society in the Vulcan area can be dissected into many fragments using any or all of the criteria employed elsewhere by others. Yet such distinctions held relatively little significance for local society. An elite failed to develop in any meaningful sense. One huge group dominated local society, and its membership enjoyed a rough egalitarianism. Distinctions based on class, wealth, and other social characteristics played some role in forging the social structure, but local conditions all conspired to render them less important than in the pioneers' home societies.

If we accept the classical Marxist definitions of social class, the 'petite bourgeoisie' – celebrated as the backbone of prairie society in C.B. Macpherson's famous *Democracy in Alberta* – dominated the area numerically, increasingly so as the frontier disappeared. These self-employed farmers, merchants, tradesmen, and professionals owned their 'means of production,' did most of the work themselves, and employed little or no labour. Within the category of independent farmer, however, varying degrees of ownership soon appeared. Some farmers held title to all the land they tilled; some rented part of it, and some rented all of it. The last none the less qualify as 'petits bourgeois' because they owned virtually everything else needed for production, and they independently controlled and managed their own business operations. As Figure 26 shows, the relative number of wholly owned farms soon plummeted, falling from 86 per cent of all farmers in 1911 to less than half by the Second World War, while the proportion of renters increased. In the towns no distinction arose between the self-employed who owned all their means of production and those who owned only part of theirs. Tax rolls demonstrate that nearly all businessmen owned the buildings and lots on which their enterprises stood. The early speculative frenzy in town lots, as in farmland, pertained almost exclusively to undeveloped land, and thus few commercial landlords appeared.

Always small in number, those without any property at all soon declined further. The great trainloads of itinerant harvesters employed in the early years evaporated as farmers acquired their own small threshing machines or combines. By 1931, when the Census first collected reliable statistics, Vulcan-area farmers employed about 200 temporary workers per 100 farms, and by the end of the decade fewer than 40. The average weeks of hired labour per farm fell from 31 to fewer than 16 over the same period. Yet most of those workers cannot be considered members of the local social structure anyway, since few lived in the area. But the number of year-round, permanent farm labourers also declined, especially after the First World War, when the largest bonanza farms collapsed and small farmers began to abandon labour-intensive horse power. By 1931 only 15 per cent of the farms employed permanent labour; by decade's end less than 10 per cent. And most of those only employed one labourer each.

Town labourers also declined in number. Employment opportunities peaked between 1910 and 1912, when the area's biggest construction projects began: the railway, the towns, the grain elevators, and the reservoir at Lake McGregor east of the area. Never again did such massive projects draw so many labourers to the area. In 1912, 58 per cent of those earning a living in Carmangay worked primarily for wages. While no reliable statistics exist for the period thereafter, wage-earners in the towns may have fallen to 25 per cent of the gainfully occupied population by the 1920s, for like farmers, merchants employed little

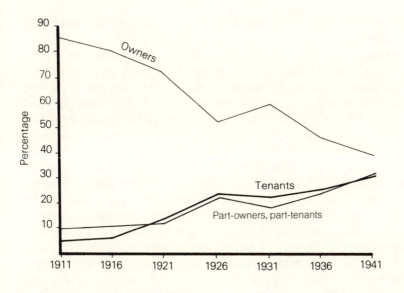

FIGURE 26
Percentage of farmers operating under various forms of tenure, Vulcan area

labour outside their own families. Statistics first available for 1930 indicate that local businesses averaged fewer than one employee per workplace, but many employed none at all. A few labour-intensive enterprises housed most of the workers: the largest stores, hotels, restaurants, banks, lumber yards, and the railway.[4] Rather than widening the social gap, as many researchers suggest it did, the disappearance of the frontier served instead to narrow it, both in the countryside and in the towns.

No precise rendering of the relative proportions of self-employed and salaried workers over time has been presented here. But such knowledge would not clarify the nature of the social structure for the two groups often blended together anyway. During the settlement era most pioneers were 'petits bourgeois' in summer and 'proletarian' in winter. In Township 17-25-4, 80 per cent of the homesteaders worked for winter wages during the proving-up years from 1904 to 1908. As late as 1940 perhaps as many as a quarter of the area's farmers continued to work for wages part of the time, if only for a few weeks a year.[5] Similarly, some salaried workers functioned as independent contractors or self-employed tradesmen part of the time. These caveats aside, however, Macpherson's monolithic characterization of the prairie class structure stands up well as a social description of rural farming communities like the Vulcan area, although it is wholly inappropriate for prairie cities and non-agricultural resource towns.

The predominance of the middling class can be explained in several ways. Typically, the frontier did not draw many people from either the upper or lower tiers of the donor societies. Secondly, cheap frontier land, combined with government and railway policies of distributing it in small parcels, permitted pioneers of moderate means to acquire and develop property, either for business or for agricultural purposes. Shortages of both labour and services on the frontier allowed many former workers to establish small businesses. A variety of local circumstances perpetuated these frontier conditions. As we have seen, the economics of wheat farming rendered the independently owned and operated family farm the most economically efficient one, thereby avoiding the huge social chasms of plantation agriculture. The low population density of wheat farmers called for decentralized services, perpetuating the need for small-scale business enterprise. The lack of natural resources, except farmland, meant that class-ridden extractive industries never appeared. Other big enterprises that drove the sharp wedge of class into prairie society – wholesaling, manufacturing, and major transportation functions – gravitated to a few large cities, ignoring the vast majority of wheat-production centres like Vulcan.

Because it lacked permanent employment opportunities, workers shunned the area to such an extent that a chronic shortage of labour persisted for the little need that did exist, which explains the need for outside harvesters. But year-round positions remained vacant as well. 'We are having difficulty in getting domestics,' complained the secretary of the Carmangay Colonization Board in 1926. 'Very few indeed are coming out and the demand in the East is so heavy that it is practically impossible to get any this far west.'[6] In turn, the shortage of labour further discouraged the establishment of large-scale enterprises in the area.

If we shift the focus from social class to wealth, much greater divisions appear in local society. The most obvious gap occurred between the totally destitute, whose applications for municipal relief routinely appear in the records of both town and rural municipalities, their numbers greatly swollen in times of depression but always present, and those successful merchants and farmers who drove expensive cars, vacationed frequently and far, and lived in large homes appointed with conveniences and luxuries. But striking differences in wealth also appeared within the petite bourgeoisie itself. In the towns they can be readily quantified through the listings of the R.G. Dun credit-rating company. Although the company never rated some local enterprises, Figure 27 demonstrates that from their founding, the towns featured some locally owned businesses with estimated net worths of less than $500, while others exceeded $10,000 in value. The margin continued to widen, for by 1930 roughly 10 per

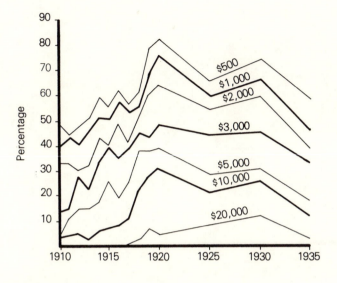

FIGURE 27
Percentage of locally owned Vulcan-area businesses with net
values exceeding various amounts

NOTE: Rough estimates based only on those businesses given
ratings: 27–117 businesses per year, or 40–80 per cent of all those
listed

cent of all locally owned businesses surpassed $20,000 in net worth, while more
than a quarter remained below $500.

By the First World War these discrepancies began appearing in different
categories of businesses (see Figure 28). Although some billiard parlours and
livery stables became valuable, most service businesses failed to match the
success of retail stores and automotive dealerships. Receipts in 1930 averaged
only $1,651 per service business, while net sales per store averaged $13,903.
The general store, which mainly sold goods for both consumer and agricultural
purposes, emerged as one of the most profitable as well as the most numerous
of all businesses. Retailers offering general supplies, groceries, motor vehicles,
clothing, and lumber in 1930 averaged sales of $17,000 to $35,000 per store by
type. Stores, of course, tied up greater amounts of capital in stock on hand and
needed expensive space to store it, while a tradesman with only a few tools and
supplies could easily operate out of a tiny shop. Thus the gap in profits
between service businesses and stores may not have been as large as that in net
worth.[7]

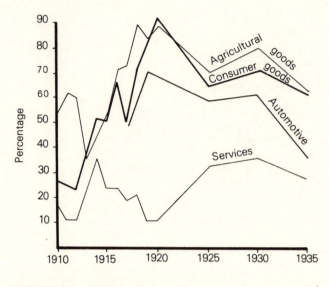

FIGURE 28
Percentage of locally owned Vulcan-area businesses, by type, with
net values exceeding $2,000

NOTE: Rough estimates based only on those businesses given
ratings: 27–117 businesses per year, or 40–80 per cent of all those
listed

Great differences in wealth also appeared among farmers, but consistently
measuring them over time is not possible. No credit-rating agency assessed
individual farmers, and bank records are lost or closed to researchers. As
previous chapters have demonstrated, farm size is hardly a reliable guide to
either income or net worth. Tax rolls are poor indicators of wealth, since
assessors once valued nearly all land the same (often local by-laws required
them to do so), and even today assessments only partly reflect differences in
soil productivity. Besides, individual management techniques drastically
affected wealth, and many coaxed far more or less from the soil than any
assessment based on potential might suggest. The range of wealth indicated by
wills offers no help, for some farmers commonly began disposing of property
to heirs before they died, while others did not.

Thus any assessment of differences in wealth depends on records compiled
individual by individual for specific times. Few exist, but they do suggest a
great range of wealth, confirming the impressionistic accounts of local newspapers and other observers. Studies sponsored by the Prairie Farm Rehabilita-

tion Administration in 1935 determined the net worth of 231 Vulcan-area farmers at the time they began farming in the area:

$	0– 500	27%
	501– 1,000	13
	1,001– 2,000	16
	2,001– 5,000	18
	5,001–10,000	15
	10,001–20,000	6
	over 20,000	5

The table reveals that while 40 per cent of the sample began with net worths of less than $1,000, 5 per cent began with more than $20,000. The range is exaggerated here, for these farmers entered the area throughout the 1904–35 period, and it certainly cost much more to start farming during the inflationary boom years of the First World War than in 1904, when homesteads remained plentiful, or in 1935, when land prices fell.[8]

The patent applications of homesteaders suggest differences of wealth within a much shorter-time frame, usually between 1907 and 1910 for most districts. Unfortunately, they mostly list only the homesteader's evaluation of his buildings and fences, and they reveal nothing about debt. They also include short-term speculators who put as little as possible into homestead development, and exclude big farmers who bought land instead of homesteading. None the less, they at least imply major differences in wealth and thus confirm newspaper accounts of settlers who arrived with boxcars of goods and plenty of cash while others arrived virtually penniless. In Township 17-25-4 one homesteader valued his buildings and fences at a mere $75, another at $1,535. Of 56 homesteaders in the township, 71 per cent valued buildings and fences at less than $500, 25 per cent at $500 to $1,000, and 4 per cent at over $1,000.[9]

Aside from statistics relating to capital at, or soon after, the commencement of farm operations, only the PFRA-sponsored studies pinpointed differences in wealth for a specific year. A survey of 232 Vulcan farmers for 1935 revealed the following range of net worths:

$–10,000 or more		.4%
–9,999– –5,000		3.0
–4,999–	0	17.3
0–	5,000	35.0
5,001–	10,000	17.3
10,001–	20,000	14.2
over 20,001		12.9

The study concluded that 'the picture at present is one of many farmers living side by side, some of them are successful financially or at least are holding their own, whereas others are helped to remain by means of the relief that is, in essence, extended to them by their more fortunate or astute neighbours.'[10] Again, this picture in confirmed by many contemporary observers.

If a statistical profile existed for a more prosperous year, it might reveal even greater disparities in wealth, given the huge capital gains reported by some farmers during the First World War and the massive debt acquired by others for expansion. But although the 1935 range is wide, it does conform to a bell-shaped curve, with over 52 per cent of the farmers clustered within $10,000 of each other and nearly 70 per cent within $15,000. By urban standards, of course, the range of wealth in the area seems narrow, yet it clearly surpasses that suggested by most prairie studies, which assume or imply that because self-employed small businessmen predominated, a rough equality in wealth also prevailed.

An enormous variety of variables account for these divisions in rural wealth. While some of the ingredients for success depended on the qualities of the pioneer himself, much depended on sheer luck. Those who began with considerable capital had the best chance of multiplying it, but the selection of productive land in a favoured micro-environment, preferably close to a rail-town, helped enormously. Farming ability did not matter much initially when prevailing wisdom failed to account for the new environment, but the willingness to adopt appropriate new methods rapidly did. Financial and managerial ability, as distinct from production skills, certainly made a difference. Successful farmers used credit shrewdly. They drew distinctions among capital, operating, and living costs and balanced them judiciously. They predicted market trends and acted on them appropriately. Finally, they possessed a quality of immense, if immeasurable importance: determination. Townsmen needed the same entrepreneurial skills and drive as farmers, and like them also needed luck, particularly in selecting a town destined to experience sudden growth and in arriving there before it did so.

Vulcan-area pioneers attached great importance to money. As earlier chapters have demonstrated, it drew them to the frontier in the first place and it subsequently stoked the fires of boosterism. Yet ironically, divisions of wealth failed to produce a social elite. Consider the two most prestigious positions of leadership within the area, election as an MP or MLA. Only five men from the Vulcan area itself served in these capacities from 1904 to 1940. Little distinguished them in terms of wealth or class. The press considered three of them prosperous, self-employed businessmen (two farmers and one hardware merchant), yet the other two, both salaried clergymen, were no wealthier than the proverbial church mouse. Social characteristics seemed more important. All sprang from British stock; two were born in Ontario, two in Britain, and one in the United States. All were Protestants: three Unionists, one Anglican, and one fundamentalist sectarian. But ethnicity and religion aside, they shared little else. Two lived in the area more than fifteen years prior to election, three of them for less than five years. Four had some prior involvement in local organizations, one very extensively, but the fifth had virtually none. Thus they represented a cross-section of local society in most respects save one: four of the five, including the two farmers, had at least some university education.[11]

Without question, the sample is too small to reveal much of the relationship among class, wealth and social characteristics and positions of status and influence, but analysing other leadership roles reveals similar patterns. Seats on town councils during the 1910s constituted the next most prestigious positions. With boosterism in full swing, many candidates contested these seats, and voters turned out in droves to elect them. Carmangay's first village election in 1910 inspired six men to seek three council seats, and the 157 ballots cast represented nearly every eligible voter. The following year twelve men battled for the seven positions required by the new town status. Champion's first election attracted eight men to three council positions, while the second contest produced five candidates. When 208 voters selected three of five aspirants to Vulcan's first council, the High River *Times* claimed that nearly everyone with a franchise and 'many without' had voted. The next election again produced five candidates. Hence, many welcomed the challenge of town promotion, and voters seemed anxious to select the best men for the job.[12] Town councils during the 1910s, therefore, indicate the kind of people considered suitable for leadership.

Of the 44 men who served on town councils from 1910 to 1921 (no women sought election), the occupations of 38 can be determined. All but 3 were self-employed, although it is probable that some of the 6 unknowns earned wages, for employees are far more difficult to trace in existing documents. None the less, the petite bourgeoisie dominated town politics to an even greater degree than they did society at large, no doubt aided by the property qualifications required for office. Among the self-employed, merchants were over-represented; 27 of them won election, compared to only 7 self-employed tradesmen and 2 professionals. The range of their wealth at the time of their election was also much wider than that of businessmen at large. The R.G. Dun Company estimated the net value of the businesses of 26 of them during their terms in office:

under $500	5
$ 500– 1,000	3
1,000– 2,000	3
2,000– 3,000	4
3,000– 5,000	1
5,000–10,000	5
10,000–20,000	5
total	26

If we compare these results with Figure 27, it is evident that elected town officials possessed slightly more wealth than businessmen at large. About 58 per cent of them ran enterprises with net worths exceeding $2,000, whereas in 1915 only about 40 per cent of all businesses in the area surpassed that value.

All but 4 of the 44 sprang from British stock, whereas only two-thirds of the population did so. Yet this predominance is of less significance than it seems, since most of the non-British people in the area had already been anglicized to some extent before arrival, as had all 4 exceptions on the town councils. The birthplaces of only 13 are known, but they hold no surprises: 6 in Canada, 3 each in the United States and Britain, and 1 in Norway. Religious affiliation is much harder to determine, but Union Protestantism appears to have appealed to most of them. None the less, Catholicism did not prevent the elections of at least 3 of them. Time of arrival and number of years in the community little affected their success. Of 18 whose dates of arrival are known, only 4 had arrived before 1909, when plans for the first railtown became known. Thus, the cult of the pioneer represented symbolic status in the community, but it did not readily translate into leadership. Unlike the five MPs and MLAs from the Vulcan area, the councillors did not stand apart from the rest of the population because of education. Few professionals – lawyers, doctors, teachers, or clergymen – ever won election, belying the mantle of community leadership thrust upon them by most scholars, while confirming the evidence presented in the previous chapter.[13]

In terms of ethos or values, the councillors seem to have been largely of one mind with each other and with the population at large. They considered themselves liberal minded, progressive boosters with a common-sense, businesslike approach to public affairs. Their supporters vouched for their honesty and personal integrity far more often and more openly than do political campaigners today. In terms of public goals they hardly disagreed at all, neither in the few surviving views that they expressed prior to their election nor in the council minutes recorded thereafter. All of them worshipped the goddess of growth and vowed to do everything possible to promote it. At the same time they also stressed the importance of creating respectable and civilized images for their towns. Bickering between them arose almost solely over administrative procedures or personal animosities. It seems clear that attitude, character, and behaviour counted far more in the determination of local leadership than class, wealth, or other social attributes.

Not only did the town councillors fail to exhibit many extraordinary social characteristics, but no clique of individuals emerged to dominate local government during the period, either. The first councillors elected after municipal incorporation did not hold their positions for long. Carmangay, with a council of seven men after its first town election, replaced five of them in the 1914 election and five again in 1916. Vulcan, with a village council of three in 1913, replaced two of them in 1914. All of them were replaced by 1915, and all those by 1917. At Champion, the three-man council averaged a turnover rate of almost two per year from 1911 to 1917.[14]

Town councillors became even more representative of the general population after the First World War. With boosterism a hoarse whisper of its former bluster, residents no longer coveted positions in local government. Councillors faced no exciting new challenges, only the unsavoury task of collecting back taxes, paying off old debts, and foreclosing on friends, family, and neighbours. Voter apathy and election by acclamation resulted. Almost anyone who wanted it could have a seat on town council. In Champion, the school janitor served a number of terms on both the school-board and the town council between 1928 and 1946. The uncontested election of W.E. Butchart as mayor of Vulcan in 1921 signalled the change. A British-born, self-employed tinsmith, he had never been counted among their numbers by the more prosperous businessmen. The net worth of his business stood between $1,000 and $2,000 upon his election in 1921, and it fell to less than $500 during his term in office. During his long administration the laziness, incompetence, and corruption examined in an earlier chapter smouldered undetected until 1929. In the 1930s apathy reigned supreme. When the town of Carmangay reverted to village status in 1936, regulations also required that the school-board reduce its membership from five to three. The Department of Education asked for the resignation of any two members. In reply the board complained of an insurmountable difficulty – they all wished to resign.[15]

A large body of comparable information does not exist for rural municipal councillors, but nothing in the random data available contradicts the general pattern that emerged in the towns, either before or after the Great War boom. If anything, rural councillors varied even more in wealth, a reflection, perhaps, of the fact that farm tenants could vote in local elections while town renters could not. None the less, one long-time secretary-treasurer of rural municipalities in the area who held an appointed, paid position rather than an elected post believed that good farmers tended to win most elections, and in his view they also made the best councillors.[16] Education, age, and time of residency in the community scarcely mattered, but as with town councillors in the 1910s, Protestants of British stock seemed to have enjoyed a slight edge over other groups at the polls.

As many scholars have pointed out, however, elites commonly eschew public office while still wielding considerable power indirectly.[17] After all, the wealthiest residents often abdicated positions of authority by leaving the Vulcan area each winter. But the available evidence will not support the argument that an unofficial elite controlled this area. As Carmangay's founder, largest real-estate developer, biggest farmer, and probably its wealthiest resident before the First World War, C.W. Carman would seem to qualify as a member of an influential elite even though he never sought public office. Yet on the only recorded occasions that he tried to use the Carmangay town council for personal gain, it rebuked him. When council held court in 1910 to hear appeals on property assessments, they lowered the evaluations for many complaining individuals, but not for Carman. They even hiked the assessment on one of his lots from $850 to $2,000. That same year the town purchased property from Carman for a nuisance grounds, a cemetery, and municipal buildings. Carman said that the town could forget the $2,500 purchase price if it gave him a monopoly franchise to supply electricity. But council refused to 'consider it at all.' Instead it paid Carman off with borrowed money and spent $4,000 more acquiring the existing light plant for itself. It then introduced subsidized rates in order to attract industry. In these instances the council was not seeking revenge against a hated despot. All who remembered Carman in later years did so with considerable fondness. Big entrepreneurs like Carman or like E.E. Thomson of Brant frequently won praise for their early contributions to community development.[18] But they were not permitted to threaten the aspirations of other members of the dominant, self-employed class.

If no elite minority based on wealth dominated local politics, either directly or indirectly, then perhaps one emerged in a more purely social sense. If so, one would expect its members to coalesce in particular organizations. But aside from certain lodges and orders that limited membership to a particular religion or sex, voluntary organizations do not reveal sharp differences in their social compositions. Of those with surviving membership lists that permit analysis, the Vulcan Curling Club might be considered a partial exception. Its by-laws stated that new applicants needed the approval of members before they could join, yet the minutes do not record a single case where admission was refused to anyone. While the occupations and wealth of only 60 per cent of the founding members can be traced, it appears that prosperous merchants may have been over-represented. But the charter group also included professionals, farmers, self-employed tradesmen, and salaried white-collar workers. And among the self-employed townsmen, the same wide range of wealth found among town councillors prevailed. Curling soon became even less exclusive as its popularity soared, especially among farmers.[19] Higher degrees of social segregation undoubtedly prevailed among small, unchartered groups, like card clubs or supper clubs, for non-members sometimes made disparaging comments about their 'snobbishness.' An insider considered such attacks unjust, however, and dismissed the critics as unsociable souls who begrudged others their good fellowship.[20]

But the most striking difference between the social composition of town councils in the 1910s and that of other institutions is the inclusion of far more women in voluntary associations, both on membership rolls and in positions of leadership. Indeed, women overwhelmed the composition of some organizations that admitted members of both sexes, especially those related to culture, religion, or service. Women, for example, composed 64 per cent of the fifty-three-member Alston Red Cross Society. One study even argues that rural men consciously avoided positions of responsibility in such organizations, while women eagerly sought them. 'The jostling for positions involving prestige seems related to the limited opportunity afforded women for the expression of ambition outside the household,' reported Jean Burnet, but perhaps it also relates to the sex roles commonly agreed upon by both men and women. Sexual specialization in establishing the frontier community accorded women precedence in matters pertaining to refinement, respectability, and charity – attributes regarded by frontier men as essentially feminine in nature. As in many agrarian societies, as well as in most hunting and gathering ones, distinction based on sex often proved more significant than those between classes or other social groupings.[21]

Rather than searching for a social elite among community leaders and club members, it might be more fruitful to ask if local society excluded anyone from public affairs altogether. Two groups repeatedly suffered such ostracization. An ill-defined crowd variously described as drunks, kickers, knockers, or more often as 'ne'er-do-wells,' inhabited the dilapidated shacks and boarding-rooms of the towns. They occasionally worked as general labourers and lived a hand-to-mouth existence. But physical circumstances alone do not explain their lowly status. Just as character, attitude, and behaviour counted more than wealth in winning positions of community leadership, so too did personal qualities brand the ne'er-do-wells. They reportedly abused or neglected their families, if they had them, and they actually preferred loafing about the towns to honest work. Pool halls, bars, cafés, and livery stables became their favourite haunts. They openly ridiculed the booster campaigns and delighted in flouting community standards of conduct through boisterous drunkenness, tobacco spitting, cursing, and fighting. Though apparently tiny in numbers, this amorphous group aroused considerable concern and incurred the special wrath of reform movements like prohibition and women's suffrage. Presumably, they would have shunned participation in community affairs even if anyone had offered it to them.[22]

The ne'er-do-wells shared the social basement with another group: the Chinese. If a single member of that minority ever belonged to a local organization, the fact has gone unrecorded. Their exclusion demonstrates that neither wealth and class nor character and behaviour are sufficient indicators of social acceptance. As self-employed businessmen who dominated the restaurant and laundry businesses of the area, the Chinese could not be criticized for lack of industry or of sobriety. Racial and cultural prejudice alone, most of it directed against them in discriminatory fashion by the white population but some arising from their own desire for cultural isolation, explain their exclusion from community social life. Exclusively male and highly transient, they anticipated a short stay in the area before earning enough to return to China. Hence they felt little compulsion to accommodate themselves to an alien North America society.[23]

Thus, in contrast to most communities, where studies have suggested that the social structure resembles a pyramid, Vulcan more closely resembled an inverted one, with the most stratified layers appearing at the bottom rather than at the broad and heavy top.[24] Why did an elite apex fail to crown the social configuration? In part, it failed because of a weak correlation between wealth and social class. As the 1935 net worths of farmers shows, many self-employed individuals mired themselves in debt. Every propertyless labourer, therefore, enjoyed a healthier net worth than many land-titled farmers. Big farmers with big debts might still enjoy a higher standard of living, at least until the day of reckoning, simply because they could siphon funds from their larger cash flows, but no matter how much wages dropped, a hired hand could not, under the prevailing conditions of credit, bury himself under a mountain of debt. Sharp differences in wealth also appeared within the salaried class, especially between casual day labourers and the local managers of large corporations but also among employed professionals like teachers and clergymen, clerks in banks and stores, and maids, cooks, and waitresses. When their wide-ranging incomes are compared with the even more wide-ranging wealth of town businessmen and farmers, the relationship between social class and prosperity is often blurred.

The extent of property ownership among farmers themselves likewise bore little relationship to wealth. The largest landowners did not always reap the greatest rewards, as the bankruptcy of bonanza farms after the First World War attests. Farmers who owned all their own land did not necessarily garner the most wealth, either. As an earlier chapter demonstrated, the highest financial rewards usually went to partly owned, partly rented farm operations. In many cases the landlords from whom these farmers rented owned less property than they did. Most landlords were retired farmers or townspeople who let their small parcels of land to large, expanding farmers. In certain situations, wholly rented land produced the most farm income, especially when owner-operators faced both debt and tumbling land values. Even sharp differences between net wealth and income existed. Many pioneers suffered tremendous hardship while struggling to develop a farm, yet realized substantial profits by selling out during the Great War. For all these reasons farmers increasingly cared little about the outright ownership of land; it guaranteed neither prosperity nor social status.[25]

Not only did social class often fail to indicate wealth, but rapid social mobility continually altered class memberships. The concept of an 'agricultural ladder' has often been employed to describe social mobility in rural societies; penniless newcomers first work as farm-hands, then become farm tenants, and finally acquire their own land.[26] Although some newcomers to the Vulcan area progressed in that fashion, most braved a more chaotic course. Rather than climbing an agricultural ladder, they rode the roller-coaster economy of the Vulcan area and frequently changed both occupation and social class along the way. Not many arrived penniless, but even for some who did, cheap frontier land allowed them to vault the hired-hand and tenant rungs altogether. If successful in proving up a homestead, they might leap ahead by expanding through renting rather than buying, thus becoming part tenant. Crises plunged some of them back to the category of wage-earner. Many of those soon acquired a business in town or another farm. Thus settlers experienced the social mobility bragged of in the booster literature, but discovered that it sometimes tilted them down as readily as up.

They also experienced dramatic changes in wealth, even without any shift in occupation or social class. The settler who never altered the size of his farm or the nature of his tenure none the less watched his income soar and dive with the price, grade, and yield of wheat. The fortunes of the town businessman swung rhythmically with those of the farmer, particularly if he also indulged in real-estate speculation. Not even the self-employed professional escaped this ride; in the Great Depression doctors and lawyers went unpaid, and joined many of their patients and clients in common poverty.[27] Indeed, the rising and falling prosperity of the community as a whole often overshadowed differences in individual fortunes, and thus in itself blunted the social significance of wealth.

But shifts in community fortunes also altered the relative wealth accruing to each social class. Moving into a boom, the property owner prospered far more than the wage-earner, for capital gains significantly outstripped rising wages. The expanding farmer who possessed all the land he farmed also grew richer than his tenant neighbours. As Figure 28 suggests, merchants tied directly to the agricultural economy enriched themselves far more quickly than did those who offered general services to everyone. On the downswing, positions reversed. Big property owners with big debts faced big trouble. The farm tenant with no property and no debts fared better not only relatively, but absolutely.

Exceptions to the general pattern further altered the distribution of wealth. Some farmers went broke at the height of prosperity, usually because of recurring hail damage. And for the few who entered the 1930s with cash in hand, even the Great Depression offered an unparalleled opportunity to expand operations. As the price of prime farmland slumped, deflation swelled the purchasing power of their money. If they bought and hung on through the Second World War, they reaped enormous benefits from the return of prosperity. Thus William Christensen came to the parched Carmangay district in 1936 and bought two sections of dust, probably for almost nothing. He studied land reclamation, experimented with the new techniques, and worked out special arrangements with machinery companies. By allowing them to use his farm to test and demonstrate new equipment, he obtained the use of the implements without buying them himself. By 1942 Christensen owned and leased six and a half sections of land, and soon enjoyed the rewards of better times.[28]

If the retention of wealth proved difficult at all times, it follows that inheritance did not lead to family dynasties. Furthermore, the nature of inheritance made the transmission of large blocks of wealth particularly difficult. The Vulcan frontier followed the pattern already well established in southern Ontario and the American midwest during the nineteenth century. Benefactors there realized that farms could not be subdivided and remain economically viable, so they bequeathed their land to a single son, yet to ensure an equitable distribution of the estate among their children, they saddled him with annual cash payments to his siblings.[29] Thus the frontier could have no prominent 'old families' to begin with, nor could the pioneers readily lay the basis for future ones.

Yet another factor complicates this picture of shifting occupations, classes, and wealth. Geographic mobility, especially before 1920, frequently accompanied other changes. It also explains why entrenched cliques failed to dominate local politics during the settlement era. But geographic mobility also altered the social structure of the area bit by bit. Unable to find big buyers, the bonanza farmers who moved away, like Sigmund Diamond, C.W. Carman, or E.E. Thompson, frequently sold their land in parcels to much smaller farmers. Conversely, the small farmers who left often sold to large, expanding farmers, thereby contributing to the big-landholder group. Or, if retiring out of the area, small farmers might rent their land out, thus contributing to tenancy.

All these sweeping changes in social circumstances can be observed through the experiences of single individuals. D.O. Jantzie, a wage-earner with Ontario Hydro, came to Vulcan on borrowed money in 1912 and arrived with two dollars in his pocket. He worked at a variety of unskilled jobs but saved enough to begin homesteading on a neglected quarter-section in the arid country far east of town. Now a petit bourgeois rather than a proletarian, he proceeded to live more poorly than ever before. To save money on coal oil he spent most of his evenings sitting home in the dark. He struggled on, proved up the homestead in 1916, sold it for a small profit, and returned to Ontario. Finding no opportunity to his liking, he returned west, worked in a British Columbia lumber camp, and saved a little more. He bought a small farm and rented additional land in the Vulcan area in 1917. Having elevated himself once more to the status of petit bourgeois, he soon sank deep into debt. Realizing the poor quality of his land, he sold it and acquired a better farm. In the late 1920s he prospered, living in a 'modern twelve room house, [with] inside plumbing and hot and cold running water and [a] central heating coal furnace.' The Depression brought declining fortunes, but he still lived far better than he had in the booming 1910s.[30]

The specific changes in Jantzie's life were, of course, unique, but their chaotic pattern was not, as even a casual reading of local biographical sketches makes clear. Consider another case. Frank Shaw arrived west from Ontario, where he had been an unskilled labourer. He worked here and there as a hired hand on farms, railways, and lumber camps. He continued those pursuits in British Columbia during the winters while he proved up an Alberta homestead. He sold out, and came to Vulcan in 1910, where he built a boarding-house. In 1912 he tried his luck as an independent grain dealer. A year later he was back farming. In 1917 he bought a threshing machine and made custom harvesting his primary occupation. Thus, within a decade he lived at various times, and often simultaneously, as an unskilled labourer, a contractor, and a propertied farmer; as a landlord and a renter, an employer and an employee, a resident and a non-resident, a townsman and a country dweller. And through it all he never grew particularly rich or poor.[31] Given such chequered experiences, it becomes easier to understand why social class, occupation, and wealth carried relatively little weight in the selection of community leaders and why personal qualities counted far more.

But even if we concede that some individuals experienced no change in their social class and relatively little in their level of wealth over the decades, forces still conspired against the emergence of an elite. The sheer numerical dominance of the petite bourgeoisie itself acted as a brake on the exercise of power. In marked contrast to most resource-based communities, the Vulcan area's biggest entrepreneurs garnered wealth not by acquiring more property and putting more men on their payrolls but by selling off their holdings, ridding themselves of employees, and creating other independent entrepreneurs in the process. Since the biggest developers could not exert direct economic pressure on other independent operators, they could not control them politically, either. Thus Carmangay's wealthiest resident failed to secure a monopoly franchise on the town's electricity; council could not be persuaded to grant concessions to one independent entrepreneur to the disadvantage of so many other independent entrepreneurs.

But elites also failed to develop because the low population density of the area created decentralized institutions and therefore demanded decentralized leadership. Within the thousand square miles of the Vulcan area over a dozen units of local government emerged. Even after the extensive consolidation of local-improvement districts during the 1910s, four rural municipal districts survived in the area until the inauguration of a single county government in 1952. In addition, three village and town governments persisted throughout the period, as well as dozens of school districts. A vast array of voluntary organizations appeared in every neighbourhood. This huge collection of formal institutions could not afford to exclude many on the basis of social class, wealth, or much else if they hoped to attract enough members to sustain themselves. Even the Vulcan Tennis Club, which promoted a game traditionally associated with social elites, cried out in desperation, 'All interested in the game are requested to join the club.'[32] But not even this open invitation saved the organization from death.

With its myriad of formal institutions and its low population density the area offered opportunities for leadership to practically anyone willing to seize them. The Vulcan Agricultural Society commenced operations with five officers and fifteen directors. A congregation of twenty-two Methodists struggled to fill eight elected positions, and the Vulcan Tennis Club, nine. The Vulcan Ladies Community Society maintained a public rest-room for farm women visiting the town, and elected three executives to look after it. The Carmangay baseball team even selected its manager and secretary-treasurer by election.

Given these requirements for elected officials, organizations filled executive positions only with great difficulty.[33]

Not surprisingly, those deemed worthy of leadership by their peers often found themselves swamped by positions of responsibility. B.D. Hummon belonged to at least eight organizations and served as chief executive on five of them. Sometimes even the grossly incompetent had to be included. 'You were expected to take your turn as trustee,' recalled Harvey Beaubier of his rural school district. Rather than rejoicing in a generous measure of political democracy, rural frontiersmen often suffered from an excess of it.[34] And yet the vast political training-ground that local communities provided undoubtedly gave the rural west the confidence, experience, and administrative skills necessary to launch regional protest movements and new political parties.

Thus Vulcan society featured a degree of social stratification in which class, wealth, ethnicity, and religion played minor roles, but the area did not replicate the highly structured social order of older, more densely settled rural communities.[35] In spite of significant differences in wealth, a rough social egalitarianism prevailed, dispersing leadership widely and preventing the emergence of an influential elite. The frontier contributed to this egalitarianism by attracting a self-employed middle class, thrusting it into a social vacuum where it need not accommodate itself to any pre-existing social order, and creating the conditions necessary for its maintenance. The local, national, and international forces that dictated the nature of the local economy perpetuated the dominance of this petite bourgeoisie. Low population density, high rates of geographical and social mobility, fluctuating incomes (both collective and individual), and a weak correlation between property ownership, income, and net worth all eroded the social importance of those differences in wealth and class that did arise. Indeed, their social significance became so obscured that the pioneers refused to believe in the existence of such distinctions at all. Contemporary documents and memoirs refer often to a complete absence of class differences, and even deny great variations in individual wealth, especially during times of hardship. 'We were all in the same boat,' shares the honours with 'nobody had anything and we all shared it' as the most overworked cliché in the area's historical records.[36]

For that reason specific occupations afforded little prestige. As the previous chapter demonstrates, neither clergymen nor teachers enjoyed high status. Doctors and lawyers fared better, but no one paid them much deference or tolerated any social pretensions from them. The pioneers hung the epithet of 'Doc' on every medical man in the area. They even made professionals the butt of good-natured jibes and jokes. Carmangay lawyer A.B. Hogg was a tall man who employed a very short assistant, and for years local residents referred to them as the 'Big Hog' and the 'Little Hog.' Those of exceptional wealth or education wisely took such barbs good naturedly, for of all the social sins one might commit, pretension seems to have been the one least tolerated. One woman who took in a neighbour's laundry soon quit because 'his mother . . . thought she was somebody a little bit above my class.' In some cases traditional layers of social status even folded over. The imported stars of semi-professional baseball basked in local glory despite the fact that virtually all of them supplemented their incomes by working as unskilled labourers.[37] But the blurring of status and the denial of differences in wealth and class arose for even more important reasons, as the subsequent chapter will demonstrate.

10

Social Relations

Instead of asking if an elite dominated local society, we can determine the significance of social groups by applying a different acid test. Rather than examining the social characteristics of community leaders or the memberships of organizations, we might focus attention on local conflicts to see if particular groups consistently aligned themselves against other groups. In the Vulcan area they rarely did so. Indeed, internal conflict seldom racked the area at all. The social glue of a common ethos usually held strong against underlying tensions, and the area shared the same set of outside enemies, which it regarded as more menacing than any internal group. But when trouble did erupt, each controversy pitted different combinations of social groups against each other or else cut across social distinctions entirely.

The Vulcan area did not entirely escape the class conflicts of Marxist lore. Tensions between farmers and hired men and between threshing contractors and the gangs they employed surfaced occasionally. They flared most dramatically during the First World War, when labour shortages fattened pay-cheques, much to the dismay of the farmers and contractors who conspired unsuccessfully to thin them. At the same time, farmers feared the influence of radical labour organizations. The Industrial Workers of the World attempted to unionize migrant American harvesters through the creation of the Agricultural Workers Organization in 1915. Because of the war-induced labour shortage, western Canada resorted to importing American harvesters, and the AWO dispatched an organizer to the Champion district in 1917. When this recruiting campaign failed, the One Big Union launched a new one in the Vulcan area in 1919.[1]

Although the Department of Immigration and the Mounted Police kept organizers in the area under close surveillance, and although neither union won enough recruits even to attempt collective bargaining, much less a strike, local farmers and threshers panicked at their appearance. A harvester who deliberately damaged a threshing machine by placing a stone in a wheat bundle raised the spectre of organized industrial sabotage. When assailants beat a harvester who boasted of his membership in a 'certain organization,' the Vulcan *Advocate*, mouthpiece for orderly conduct since its founding, condoned the attack 'as the most effective way to demonstrate the fact that the Vulcan district will not tolerate the antics of men of this particular ilk.' In subsequent years the local press continued to rail against the 'bellyachers' in the harvest crews: 'Very likely the OBU propagandists who were in evidence here in harvest time are now leading the movement for relief,' accused the Champion *Chronicle* on 13 January 1920.[2]

In spite of its sharpness, however, this particular class conflict did not rend the social fabric of local society. It involved itinerants rather than residents. This fact in itself sharpened local opinion against them. Lacking the opportunity to know them as ordinary people struggling for a living, local residents readily regarded them as dangerous riff-raff.[3] Not only did the conflict involve outsiders but it erupted only during the harvest season, and then only for a few years. Unionization of the harvest fields presented obstacles that could not be hurdled. Too migratory, too thinly scattered, and too indifferent to what they regarded as a temporary job at best, harvesters could not be reached, assembled, or persuaded to join a cause that they did not believe in and that might get them arrested or injured. In 1916 the AWO claimed eighteen thousand members in North America, but by 1920 the organization lay on its deathbed, and the OBU suffered a disastrous tailspin shortly after its founding. But the conflict also died for a more important reason: during the 1920s technology steadily eliminated the area's need for big harvest gangs.[4]

Conflicts between farmers and permanent hired hands also disappeared as bonanza farms failed and as fewer small farmers employed labour. But accurate generalizations about relations between farmers and their year-round employees are difficult to make. While a recent study suggests that Jake Trumper, W.O. Mitchell's fictional hired hand in *Jake and the Kid* (1961) – virtually a member of the family and trusted mentor and hero to farm children – has obscured the reality of bitter conflicts arising over wages, working hours, and bunkhouse conditions, some hired men none the less enjoyed cordial relations with their employers, even when they worked as members of large crews on seemingly impersonal bonanza farms. A former employee of the mammoth C.W. Carman farm recalled his boss with great fondness, and Maurice Lyman corresponded regularly with four of his hired men who went off to war.[5]

Aside from such concrete concerns as pay and living conditions, the social acceptance of the hired man varied considerably from farm to farm, for questions about his status and relationship with the farm family arose constantly. Letters sent to agricultural journals on the subject reflect ambivalent attitudes. While most noted that a hired man should sleep in a separate bunkhouse, they also agreed that he should take meals with the family to lessen the burden on the farm wife. And as one wife stated, '[if he] ... is not good enough to eat ... with the rest of the family, he is not good enough to work for you.' Wives agreed that they should also do his washing and mending. On the thorny question of familiarity, they thought he should be included in the evening family circle, 'but not for too long.' He might be included in some family celebrations, but not others. As to whether he should be invited to the sitting-room when company called, it depended on the company, the occasion, and the character of the hired man himself. Everyone agreed that hired men often fascinated farm children, the point that W.O. Mitchell successfully dramatized. But most farm parents insisted that some shackles be clamped on this relationship lest children hear language and advice of a dubious nature, to say nothing of the potential for sexual trouble.[6] It is not surprising that questions about the social role of hired men should concern women more than men, for they stood as guardians of morality and social conduct, especially where children were involved. In addition, a hired man meant more work for farm wives, even as it meant less for their husbands.

In general the social acceptability of the hired man depended on his skill and industry as a worker, on his character, on his length of service with the family, and on what employers believed his destiny to be. With homesteads still available, a young hand working to gain some experience and a grubstake before developing his own farm might win acceptance as a social equal, especially if he were a relative sent from the east to learn western farming. He often struck out on his own, with the financial and emotional support of his former employer. But an older bachelor, hired after homesteads disappeared or when the cost of land soared beyond his reach, rarely encountered such acceptance. Thus the status of hired men fell continually throughout the long period of their steady disappearance from prairie farms.[7]

But social acceptance did not erase certain realities. Almost always the hired hand worked long, hard hours and slept in a crude, uncomfortable bunkhouse. Yet even these conditions elicited few complaints if employers lived no better and the hired hand realized that his standard of living would not likely change even if he acquired his own farm. And since he ate with the family, he usually enjoyed plenty of good food. But the labour market determined wages. Since farmers received their cash income in lumps scattered unevenly through the year, they paid wages regularly and in full only with great difficulty, particularly in less prosperous years. An unscrupulous farmer might even goad a hired man into quitting before his agreed period of employment terminated, thus requiring the hand by law to forfeit his right to wages for work already completed. Regardless of the reason, the failure to pay wages on time always soured labour relations. Indeed, many hands resorted to legal action to collect pay. 'Wage cases seem to be rather plentiful,' reported the Vulcan *Advocate* in 1913, 'and for some time now this kind of dispute has engaged much of the attention of our worthy magistrate.'[8]

But beyond the lawsuits occasionally launched by individuals, year-round hired men voiced no formal protests. As with harvest gangs, transitory employment, isolation, and vast distances imposed logistical barriers to organization. Often too hopeful of moving to a better station in life, too close to their employers personally, and thus too apt to think in terms of good and bad employers, they did not even publicly question the nature of rural labour relations. The same can be said of non-agricultural workers. And the question of proper social relations with employers' families did not even arise in the towns, since employees assumed full responsibility for their own housing, meals, and transportation.

The lack of class consciousness among both town and year-round farm workers also revealed itself politically. The independent Socialist candidate running in the dominion election of 1911 polled only 12 votes in the entire area. Another Socialist fared better in the provincial election of 1913, winning over 7 per cent of the local vote, but he seems to have drawn more support from farmers than labourers, winning only 11 of his 66 votes in the three largest towns. An attempt to found a local Socialist party in Vulcan in 1915 failed utterly for lack of interest. As an ideology socialism subsequently enjoyed even less appeal until the formation of the Co-operative Commonwealth Federation during the Great Depression. Even then its popularity remained weak and only grew because farmers and merchants, rather than workers, provided the bulk of local supporters. And they believed that socialism should engulf only big corporations, not small businessmen like themselves.[9] Thus, in an area where geographic and social mobility thrust people out, drew them in, and teetered them up and down, a petite bourgeoisie that employed little labour presided over a dwindling labour force that faced too many difficulties for organized protest. These conditions all muted the classic Marxist conflict between social classes.

Another classic frontier conflict erupted briefly, not between social classes but between occupational groups of the same class, between ranchers and farmers, over frontier land use.[10] When settlers first arrived in the Vulcan area, range cattle still ran free, without regard to changes in lease laws, survey stakes, or pioneer shacks. Wild and dangerous, they not only damaged crops and other property but even attacked the settlers: No one dared to set anywhere on foot,' recalled one pioneer. Hans Lundgren concurred. As his son later recalled, 'One day a herd surrounded the shack and virtually kept him prisoner for several days, refusing to move away. They rubbed and scratched themselves on the corners of the shack, which shook crazily and gave my Dad some bad moments.'[11]

To protect their farmyards and crops, the pioneers strung barbed-wire fences. They grumbled about the cost. During the proving-up period the average homesteader in Township 17-25-4 spent $118 on fencing, compared to $166 for housing. Equally annoyed, ranchers argued that the fences injured cattle, interfered with round-ups and disrupted the free movement of the herds to water and shelter. They expressed open contempt for the settlers and accused them of rustling and of deliberately poisoning and shooting cattle. They claimed that farm-dominated local governments sued ranchers for back taxes, but not farmers. The settlers in turn accused the ranchers of poisoning dogs, pulling out survey stakes, cutting fences, and deliberately stampeding herds through farmyards. 'I remember the cowboys taking big herds of cattle through our place,' recalled one settler; 'they often came right past the house. We all had to run inside . . . when we saw them coming.' The local press blasted the ranchers at every opportunity and openly cheered the cancellation of every ranching lease. But strife between rancher and settler in the Vulcan area lasted less than three years. Most range cattle perished in the winter of 1906–7. The following spring the huge Circle ranch lost its contracts to supply beef to Indian reserves, and it moved the survivors of its herd from the area. Once ranching disappeared, no other resource industry arose to challenge wheat's monopoly on land use.[12]

Thus two sources of group conflict that ravaged some frontier communities surfaced only briefly in the Vulcan area. Other forms of group conflict reported elsewhere scarcely appeared at all. The celebrated occupational clashes between farmer and merchant, more commonly presented as town-country conflict, supposedly arose from differing economic interests and contrasting values.[13] Not unexpectedly, some Vulcan-area farmers regarded merchants as the last link in a chain of exploitation that stretched from manufacturers to retailers and shackled them with heavy living and production costs. Merchants also complained about farmers, especially when they let unpaid accounts accumulate, shopped in distant towns or through mail-order catalogues, or when they organized local co-operative stores.[14]

But disagreements over these matters remained subdued and polite and never burst into open conflict. Town and country quietly worked out understandings and compromises. The farmer-dominated Vulcan Co-operative Society carefully investigated local retailing practices before deciding on what goods to stock. Suppliers of some items, especially barbed wire, coal, and binder twine soon found themselves competing with the co-op, but regarding groceries and provisions the society discovered that the merchants in town 'had so reduced their prices as to give the farmer as good a deal as could be done, and for the present at any rate, it was decided to give the home merchant the benefit of all the trade possible.' But the co-operative movement in the area aimed its heaviest artillery at businesses that local merchants did not own: the grain elevators and the lumber yards. As a result, town and farm people alike insisted that relations remained cordial; they repeatedly issued statements to that effect at the time, and many interviews since confirm it.[15]

The Vulcan area simply lacked many of the ingredients that brewed trouble elsewhere. Town-country relations often deteriorated wherever one group, merchants or farmers, reaped larger financial rewards than the other. On the nineteenth-century American frontier farmers feared and resented the power and wealth of local bankers, railway entrepreneurs, and produce buyers. But advances in corporate consolidation soon stripped local businessmen of such functions, leaving them on a more equal footing with farmers. Battles on these grounds now assumed a regional rather than local character.[16]

And unlike so many North American towns that based at least part of their incomes on activities unrelated to agriculture, those of the Vulcan area bowed in absolute servitude to King Wheat. Merchants therefore supported whatever promised to enrich farmers. Often, they even shared identical economic interests. Many farmers speculated in town lots, and some bought or shared ownership in town businesses, just as many townsmen bought farmland. Such closely related economic activities also led to shared political aspirations. For all their talk of rural class consciousness, occupational representation, and group government (whereby farmers alone should represent farm interests), the United Farmers of Alberta and the Progressives captured almost as many votes in the towns as they did in the countryside. In every dominion and provincial election held during the area's first two decades, save one, townspeople voted for the same candidates as farmers, and usually by similar margins. In the 1930 provincial election UFA incumbent O.L. McPherson even captured the Little Bow riding by acclamation.[17]

Town-country conflict also erupted in communities where fundamental differences in outlook, style, and values developed. This divergence usually appeared when town-dwellers gravitated towards metropolitan fashions and standards while farmers clung tenaciously to traditional rural ideals. But as an earlier chapter explained, the progressive, metropolitan ethos influenced farmers in the area as much as it did townsmen. The flood of information with which modern communications networks saturated new settlements in the twentieth century robbed the frontier merchant of his once vital role as transmitter and interpreter of metropolitan ideas and attitudes.[18] Questions concerning social values often divided the area, but not along town-country lines. In the greatest debate of that nature, town-dwellers supported prohibition in the 1915 plebiscite by the same two-to-one margin as farmers.[19]

Ethnic conflict has been a strongly noted feature of many rural communities, but like town-country disputes, it rarely surfaced in the Vulcan area. Ethnic affiliations also reflected religious ones, but an earlier chapter on churches demonstrated that the pioneers fought no battles because of denominational differences, and thus one can concentrate solely on ethnicity here. Over-representation in positions of public leadership by those of British blood suggests an ongoing conflict between them and the ethnic minorities who comprised nearly one-third of the population. Furthermore, pioneers of British stock expressed the prevailing attitudes of Anglophiles everywhere regarding immigrant minorities. They upheld the Anglo-Celtic as the racial and cultural ideal, whose superiority clearly showed in the might of the British Empire and the vibrant energy of the emerging American giant. They graded other ethnic groups by how closely they corresponded to this racial-cultural ideal. Thus, northwest continental Europeans ranked as the most acceptable non-British groups, followed by central, southern, and eastern Europeans, and finally by the non-white races.[20]

But these prejudices ignited few ethnic fires in the area. Scandinavians, Germans, and Dutchmen, all members of acceptable northwest European stock, accounted for most of the area's non-British population. Secondly, many if not most of them arrived already anglicized to a considerable degree; a substantial number even claimed North American birth or upbringing. As his name suggests, British culture had already absorbed Wellington Tesky by the time he arrived in the area, and his east-European lineage did not prevent him from winning the hotly contested town elections of the 1910s. He served first as a councillor and then as mayor of Carmangay. Furthermore, ethnic minorities underwent rapid and relentless acculturation after arrival. Too small in number and too scattered throughout the area, they could not sustain traditional cultural institutions. Even the small contingent of French-Canadian families who migrated from western Massachusetts and settled together in the Brant district had trouble retaining whatever New England had left them of their heritage. Within a single generation the Gingras family pronounced its name 'Gin-grass,' and the popular blacksmith Tommy Lebeau counted more English than French among his many friends. By 1931, 96 per cent of the Vulcan-area population could speak no language except English.[21]

Acceptable racial origins, small numbers, scattered settlement, and rapid assimilation meant that Anglo-Celtic pioneers did not consider local ethnic minorities an economic, social, or cultural threat. Thus, they experienced little overt discrimination and faced no organized anti-immigrant crusades or mob violence. The English-speaking majority felt secure enough that the local press could dismiss the Ku Klux Klan as 'foolish' and its Saskatchewan organizers as 'morons.'[22]

Two exceptions to this placid scene should be noted. The Germans in the area, previously considered an acceptable group, came under verbal fire during the Great War, as they did throughout Canada, and the area shamelessly indulged in the same paranoia about them. In 1915 rumours circulated that alien enemies planned to set fire to crops and elevators in the area, and considerable excitement followed the arrest of Max Laurencz of Champion for sedition when he allegedly 'made some very strong statements.' Vulcan residents even lined up to see a travelling play entitled 'The Kaiser; the Beast of Berlin.' But while suspicion fell upon Germans as an entity, most individuals escaped harassment. Indeed, they often went to great lengths to nullify local concerns, usually by changing their names and staging great displays of loyalty to the Allied cause. Like other minorities in the area, they were too few in number, too dispersed, too assimilated, and too well known personally to invite organized discrimination or arose mob violence.[23]

Only one ethnic group faced persistent hostility: the Chinese. Just numerous enough (fifty lived in the area by 1931), concentrated enough (twenty-three lived in the town of Vulcan), and alien enough to be considered a threat, the Chinese confronted the same accusations hurled at them elsewhere in Canada. Whites portrayed them as dirty, cunningly dishonest, sexually depraved, and prone to opium and gambling addiction. Unlike any other group in the area, they could be openly ridiculed, bullied, and even beaten. Their tormentors risked little censure from the public at large, even though local authorities sometimes charged and punished them. The Chinese survived in the area only because of their virtual monopoly on restaurants and commercial laundries, two labour-intensive enterprises that yielded too little profit to satisfy most other businessmen. The Chinese offered extremely low prices to the many bachelors of the area who hated cooking and washing even more than they hated the Chinese. Except for these commercial relationships and their provision of facilities for illicit gambling, the community rebuked them at every opportunity.[24]

Perhaps because of the lack of enough minorities deemed worthy of special attention, the area concerned itself far more with relations among the different nationalities of the English-speaking majority itself, among those born in Canada, Britain, and the United States. Given the suspicion of the United States that Canadians have harboured since the American Revolution, it might be expected that Ontario settlers would have brought their animosity with them. But if they did, it evaporated upon arrival. Because they rapidly became free-trade advocates, if they were not already so before arriving, they could not share in the anti-American phobia implicit in the hated National Policy, and paraded openly during the 1911 reciprocity debate. More importantly, little distinguished Canadians and Americans in the Vulcan area anyway. Not only did they share the same language, social background, and values, but many had moved back and forth across the border several times. Canadian-born settlers often arrived from the United States with American-born children in tow, and many boasted of their dual citizenship.

As a result, Canadians and Americans got on famously. Local Canadians agreed with immigration officials who considered Americans the most desirable foreign settlers of all because of their wealth and their farming and pioneering experience. 'The majority of farmers are Americans of the very best class,' pronounced a newspaper stringer in the Brant district in 1906; 'they are thrifty, industrious, and intelligent, and know their business thoroughly.' Her comments echoed down through the years. Americans in turn expressed attitudes that sprang naturally from their enthusiasm for boosterism. They praised their new country for its hospitality and for the fine economic opportunities it presented.[25]

The celebration of both Dominion Day and the Fourth of July also exemplifies this mutual back-patting. Settlers of both nationalities readily joined in the festivities on both days. Americans insisted that observing the Fourth made them no less loyal to their adopted country, and few complaints about this practice arose. But the two holidays actually had little to do with nationality at all. Rather, they provided an opportunity to transform the beginning of July into the social highlight of summer. With agricultural activities at a low ebb, parades, band concerts, dances, fireworks, rodeos, baseball tournaments, horse races, and other sporting events filled both days and sometimes those in between. Towns in the area soon specialized. Carmangay, which held its major celebration on the First, asked Vulcan to switch to the Fourth in order to avoid conflicting bookings for band concerts and baseball tournaments. Vulcan declined, but the town between them, Champion, hosted its major celebration on the Fourth until the late 1920s, a practice that originated with the earliest settlement of that district.[26]

Canadians and Americans enjoyed such rapport that they often joined forces to lampoon their fellow English-speaking settlers, the British-born, and particularly the English-born. They considered Englishmen the most inexperienced, incompetent farmers of all, and they revelled in tales that illustrated the fact. Two enterprising settlers in the area even opened an agricultural school for English lads, and for a five-hundred-dollar fee promised to unveil the secrets of dryland farming. Such schools appeared elsewhere in the west, most of them designed to extract money and free labour from unsuspecting immigrants. Canadian and American settlers found it incredible that Englishmen fell for such scams. Besides naïveté, they also suspected Englishmen of laziness; after all, they did take tea in mid-afternoon. Many believed them 'soft' as well. The CPR actually built its ready-made farms in the area to 'attract the British farmer, who through long centuries of contact with settled conditions, was not disposed to leave his cozy place at home and take on . . . pioneer life.' In fact, the wealthier North Americans bought most of the farms. None the less, the myth of English farming ineptitude endured, even when some of the English settlers developed farms as large and profitable as those of their fellow North Americans.[27]

These views of the English settler sprang partly from reality. As a group the English actually were the most inexperienced farmers in the area, a fact many readily admitted and one that frequently concerned immigration officials. But Canadians and Americans also accused them of snobbishness, and this charge seems to have arisen more from preconceived notions than from direct observation. In the late nineteenth century Canada had attracted many Englishmen of the 'gentleman class.' Public-school-educated youths who could find no appropriate position at home came to the Alberta ranching frontier lusting for adventure. Some lived largely on remittances from home and, as a consequence of their upbringing and education, squandered inordinate amounts of time on sporting events and other leisurely pursuits. Magazines and newspapers frequently satirized this stereotypical remittance man.[28] English settlers of the Vulcan area sprang from less lofty origins; as small merchants and tradesmen they had lived a lower-middle-class existence of few pretensions. But North American settlers mistook their more reserved Old Country manner and their accents – so often parodied in popular publications – for snottiness itself.

If these derisive views do not seem to square with the glorification of Britain as the motherland of racial and cultural supremacy, they nevertheless sprang from the idealization itself. When the individual Englishman inevitably fell shy of the standard established for him, disenchantment followed. Ridicule served to remind British immigrants that while they might represent the ideal racial type, English-speaking North Americans stood as their equals in that respect and could teach them a thing or two besides. But any hostility directed towards Englishmen cannot be taken too seriously. North Americans never punished them socially. They welcomed them into all local organizations and awarded them positions of leadership disproportionate to their relatively small numbers. Thus, they could be made the butt of pranks and tall tales because North Americans knew they could withstand it without suffering social damage.

Disputes between employers and labourers, ranchers and settlers, farmers and merchants, and between ethnic and national groups either fizzled completely after an initial outburst, flared only at intervals, or else smouldered quietly. Group conflicts that burned more often, more steadily, and more passionately had even less to do with class, occupation, wealth, ethnicity, or nationality than any of the foregoing disputes. Frequent battles erupted over what might be described as social respectability.[29] While very real, disputes of this nature are extremely difficult to generalize about. In broad terms they consisted of the struggle by the 'respectable element' to establish and maintain decent, civilized communities against the brawling, drunken rowdies who threatened this vision. At first glance it might seem as though considerable differences in wealth and social class separated the two groups, for as the Mounted Police pointed out each autumn, 'Our chief offenders are ... the outsiders who are imported as harvesters.' After threshing they descended on the towns, got drunk, and fought. The resident ne'er-do-wells carried on the tradition between harvests.[30]

But the specific issues that bred conflicts over respectability did not neatly separate the haves from the have-nots. Farmers of every financial and social standing, for example, split over the question of Sunday threshing, although the vast majority supported it. Nearly everyone, however, condemned Carmangay justice of the peace J.W. Miller for illegally permitting bowling and billiards in his business establishment on the Sabbath. Some residents approved of stiff new provincial regulations imposed on pool halls in 1918, but the Vulcan *Advocate*, which appreciated their advertising, defended their honour against charges of indecency. A great row ensued when a pious group temporarily seized control of the Bowville school-board, prohibited dancing in the school, and fired the teacher for smoking at noon-hour. In the Reid Hill district, card playing won out over those who wished it banished from the community hall.[31]

In these disputes, and countless others like them, the social composition of the protagonists remained as nebulous as the outcome remained unpredictable. Sometimes young bachelors battled families, but citizens of every class, occupation, financial position, ethnicity, nationality, and religion lined up on both sides of every argument. Clearly, the 'respectable element' itself could not agree on what constituted proper behaviour. All but the most openly indecent, for example, agreed on the impropriety of playing poker in the back rooms of Chinese restaurants, but some thought a quiet, friendly game among gentlemen quite acceptable. Others considered poker playing disreputable under any circumstances but saw no harm in a small wager on baseball. A few even carried their condemnation of gambling to the commodity market, but nobody thought it immoral to gamble on real estate.[32]

The prohibition debate furnishes the most important and confusing example of this moral ambiguity. The 'wets' counted among their supporters substantial citizens and community leaders who granted that prohibition might be socially desirable but not at the expense of individual liberty, and some who simply opposed it as unenforceable. The 'drys' included a few intensely religious proponents who considered the consumption of alcohol sinful under any circumstances. Others regarded prohibition as a useful tool to help control and anglicize the immigrants thought responsible for moral and social degeneration throughout much of the west. But for many prohibitionists, morality scarcely mattered. Instead, many progressives thought drunkenness wasteful and inefficient; they pointed to new scientific and social evidence of its impact on the health of individuals and of society generally.

As with other issues involving respectability, people also changed their minds. Many wets became drys during the Great War when they agreed on the temporary need for greater efficiency both at home and abroad. Prohibition would also conserve grain for food and prevent the spread of venereal disease among the troops. (Only a drunk would visit a brothel.) Many of the drys, however, drank themselves and planned to continue doing so, but none the less supported prohibition as the only means of controlling the immoderate behaviour that threatened the social order of booster idealism. Perhaps the latter group even constituted a majority of the drys. Although many temperance and abstinence organizations cropped up in the area, their activities generated little active interest and they reported meagre turnouts at meetings. Too many prohibitionists found their moral fervour distasteful.[33]

Scores of documents also testify that prohibition failed to fulfil its promise. After reporting liquor offences almost weekly for two years, the Vulcan *Advocate* conceded that the ban on booze had scarcely slowed its flow. A surprised Ontario visitor reported that 'the liquor laws out there must be more elastic than ours for I saw one dray carrying several cases of Irish and Scotch and was informed it was for the Drug Store.' Those who supported prohibition merely to eliminate the conspicuous excesses of drink did not expect the law to be imposed on respectable imbibers like themselves. F.C. Alcock, police magistrate of Champion, curried local disfavour for his reported eagerness 'to nail people' on liquor charges. Declaring Alcock incapable of dispensing justice, the village reeve led a revolt that forced his resignation. Yet the hypocrisy that pervaded prohibition did not abate in the face of such incidents, for in the 1920 referendum the area voted more solidly in favour of its continuance than it had for its imposition in 1915.[34]

It is also a mistake to assume that fights over respectability pitted the religious against the hedonistic or the church-goers against the non-attenders, as others have concluded of some communities. Within the Vulcan Union Church opponents in the prohibition debate worshipped side by side. Among the reasons for his resignation as minister Rev. A.R. Schrag cited congregational opposition to his crusade against liquor and social vice. Within the Carmangay Anglican Church a debate raged over the behaviour of the new clergyman, A.W. Sale, who thought he could best win over non-attenders by joining them for a drink, a smoke, and a little religious conversation. The majority of the congregation disapproved and demanded his resignation, but the decision left 'many members . . . dissatisfied.'[35]

Various explanations have been advanced thus far to explain the relative absence of organized conflict along clearly established social lines in specific instances, but more pervasive forces also worked against such alignments on any and all issues. As it affected so much else in the new communities, low population density blunted organized conflict of any sort. When everyone knows everyone else, painful personal dilemmas arise – a theme eagerly exploited by novelists of small town life – but they most often afflicted those in positions of social responsibility: teachers, ministers, local politicians, and the officers of local institutions. As J.W. Miller explained when he resigned as Carmangay's justice of the peace in 1920: 'No matter how fair and impartial a man may try to be in handling cases brought before him, he is nearly bound to get in wrong with some person or persons in his community . . . I have found that the longer I continue to hold [my position], the greater effect it has on my private business. I cannot afford to lose good will in business any more than I want to lose private respect and support.'[36]

Aside from personal difficulties, Miller also stressed economic repercussions. Like other local businessmen, newspaper publishers fretted over these problems. Country weeklies led a precarious existence; they dared not cater to particular groups at the cost of offending others. The editor of the Vulcan *Advocate*, for example, felt compelled to support prohibition publicly because the majority of his readers favoured it. At the same time the proprietor of the Imperial Hotel advertised heavily and regularly, and actively supported the paper's booster campaigns. In addition, the editor surely knew him well in a variety of capacities and undoubtedly served with him in many local organizations. Perhaps personal friendship bound them. Such seems likely, for the editor agonized over his decision to support prohibition. In editorials he gushingly praised the Imperial for running a decent, respectable, and orderly saloon. He argued that if all bars in the west had maintained such impeccable standards, the question of prohibition would never have arisen. Alas, he concluded, the irresponsibility of others elsewhere led to the unfortunate victimization of an upstanding local businessman.[37]

Thus newspaper editors did everything possible to soothe disputes, especially between town and country, for if merchants provided most of the advertising, farmers bought most of the subscriptions. '[A newspaper man] hears a lot that common sense, common decency, and common prudence keep out of the paper,' confessed the editor of the *Advocate*. One historian has accused small-town newspapers of deliberately concealing community conflict even when it seethed relentlessly. But the emphasis is misplaced. Everyone, no less than editors, maintained an equally active interest in containing and subduing serious rifts. Nothing is more conspicuous by its absence in pioneer memoirs than references to social conflict.[38]

Aside from these personal and business considerations, low population density acted in other ways to smother the outbreak of trouble. When activities and organizations demand the participation of nearly everyone if they are to exist at all, great hazards to community stability arise if conflict along clearly defined social lines is permitted. A farmer might suspect hardware merchants of profit gouging, but his local dealer might be a fellow lodge member and a generous contributor to the agricultural society (and a pleasant chap besides). Urban society can tolerate social conflict without threatening the survival of its institutions, for one's enemies will not show up at church or baseball practice. In thinly populated rural areas, they will.

The consensus required for institutional survival helps to explain the relative lack of town-country conflict. Many historians have pointed to Hanna, Alberta, the subject of Jean Burnet's fine study *Next-Year Country*, as solid evidence of its existence, but at the same time they fail to note the harmony that she also reported between farmers and townspeople in the nearby Oyen district. Population differences accounted for this contrast. In 1951, the year Burnet published her book, Hanna boasted a population of 2,027, large enough for townspeople to sustain many formal organizations successfully without aid from the rural population, large enough for town and country to find friends and marriage partners within their own separate circles, and even large enough for them to patronize different restaurants. Under such circumstances town and country could vent their suspicions about each other, and they openly disagreed over co-operatives, mail-order catalogues, and retail profits and practises without risking personal involvement or threatening the tranquility of voluntary associations. Oyen, however, with a population of 433 in 1951, needed the co-operation of the surrounding farm population to accomplish anything, and the smaller population pool encouraged more ties of friendship and kinship.[39]

The point at which towns could afford open discord with their countrysides undoubtedly depended on more than size, but with 803 people by 1931, Vulcan had not yet reached that point. Virtually all its institutions included both farmers and townspeople, even those ostensibly concerned solely with the interests of one group. The number of town-dwellers who belonged to the Vulcan Agricultural Society, for example, never fell below 26 per cent of membership in the 1910s, and in 1915 they constituted a majority at 59 per cent. Merchants especially dependent on the goodwill of farmers predominated, but professionals, tradesmen, and general labourers also belonged. Some townsmen even served as officers.[40] These examples illustrate how institutions in areas of low population density encouraged harmony between town and country, but they exerted the same pressure on relations between employers and employees, rich and poor, and members of different ethnic and national groups. As a previous chapter demonstrated, churches could not even tolerate denominational squabbles if they hoped to survive.

If population pools as large as towns and their surrounding countrysides could not afford much organized conflict, rural neighbourhoods could scarcely tolerate it at all. Since they could not eradicate disputes altogether, however, they transmuted them into a form that did not threaten the well-being of the whole community. Conflict became intensely personal. When accused of favouritism in his decisions, rural councillor Peter McIntyre did not defend himself with any arguments that might split his municipal ward into opposing social camps. Instead he regarded the allegation as a personal challenge to his honour and integrity. He replied tersely: 'If he does not ... apologise for his insinuations, I shall certainly take other means of vindicating myself.' Public figures everywhere have often responded to criticism in a such a manner, but in an area where low population density could not tolerate wholesale disputes between sizeable groups, such responses became almost mandatory.[41]

In pinpointing the causes of personal disputes, it is important to ignore the drunken scraps common in the early years. Forgotten on the sober morrow, they seldom erupted from any motive beyond a desire for mere recreation. Specific incidents, however, could arouse personal animosities. Owing to the simplicity of the survey and land-title systems imposed on the west, arguments over farm boundaries did not arise, but disputes over homestead claims sometimes did. They began when someone informed the homestead inspector of cheating on the proving-up regulations. 'As land began to get scarce, settlers began to watch very closely the quarter sections lacking improvements or with absentee owners,' recalled Georgina Thomson. Almost always the informer intended to acquire the homestead for himself; when an investigation led to a cancellation, he inevitably filed the new claim.[42]

These early disputes often involved a stranger (the informer), but rifts between long-standing neighbours opened when they disobeyed the informal rules and regulations that governed neighbourly relations and soon hardened into an elaborate code of behaviour. Since everyone relied so heavily on machinery, tool, and labour exchanges, neighbours expected each other to participate in them cheerfully and energetically and to lend special aid whenever tragedy struck a local family. A series of commandments applied to the use of other people's property and included such courtesies as returning borrowed items in good condition and remembering to close gates after passing through a neighbour's property.[43]

Minor infractions of the rules led to grumbling, but more serious consequences flowed from two major violations: neglecting to cultivate weeds on fallow and failing to control livestock. 'There is nothing more disheartening than for a careful farmer who keeps his weeds under to have [a neighbour] who pays no attention to the matter,' lectured the local press; 'the seeds from the one travel into the other and the good work of the former is wasted.' By 1913 Alberta farmers could sue their neighbours for damages resulting from unchecked weed growth. Rural local governments hired weed inspectors, and if offenders ignored their warnings, they destroyed the weeds, billed the owner for costs, and fined him besides.[44]

More tiffs arose over livestock control. In settled parts of the continent the law usually required livestock owners to fence their animals, but on sparsely settled frontiers, logic dictated that farmers fence crops instead. The province disallowed early attempts by local governments to ban animals at large in the Vulcan area. Thus livestock conflicts plagued new communities more than settled ones; freed by official pardon, frontier farm animals enjoyed more opportunities to damage crops and property and to mate indiscriminately with neighbouring stock. Only when vacant lands disappeared in the Vulcan area did the province permit local authorities gradually to introduce restrictions and finally to outlaw roaming animals altogether.[45]

In spite of the new laws the more rebellious breeds often escaped captivity. 'His pigs and sheep number about 50,' complained one farmer of his neighbour; 'they come thru our fence breaking the lower wire and come to our buildings Destroying everything in their pathway ... Mrs. Moreash and I have been chasing them for two years.' Incensed by the persistent assaults of his neighbour's cattle, one farmer drove them from the area entirely. Another extracted promises of reform from his neighbour at gunpoint. In a fit of indignation the *Advocate* placed the crimes of marauding livestock above that of murder: 'Any man who allows his stock to make use of his neighbour's crop and pasture is guilty of the meanest offence that can be committed,' it intoned on 11 February 1920. Livestock owners complained too. They accused their neighbours of shooting, stealing, or impounding animals, of forgetting to close fence gates behind them, and of allowing dogs to run loose, harassing and killing livestock.[46] But in spite of these examples, most pioneers tried to uphold the code of good neighbourly relations, for persistent or flagrant violations could lead to painful social ostracization or costly expulsion from neighbourhood co-operative activities.

Livestock disputes reveal much about the nature of neighbourhood conflicts. Although reminiscent of the earlier group battles between ranchers and farmers, they led to individual squabbles rather than organized conflict between those who kept livestock and those who did not. Even so, personal quarrels posed problems for the whole community whenever shouting matches, fistfights, or lawsuits led to enduring feuds. While hauling grain, H. Parker found the road in bad repair and asked Steve Sallanbach if he could drive his wagon through his farm. Sallanbach refused permission. Parker drove through anyway, and a long and bloody fistfight ensued. Such intense encounters could not be forgotten easily when the combatants met at the UFA local or the church picnic. In the Hanna area during the 1940s, Jean Burnet noted, fights over stray cows and broken fences sometimes led to deadlocks over school business. In the Vulcan area an ongoing feud disrupted the business of one rural municipality for years. An unrecorded incident left two men bitter enemies. When one defeated the other in the municipal election, the vanquished launched a scathing vendetta. Describing his enemy as 'a dirty lying crook,' and a 'dirty yellow cur,' he unleashed a torrent of vindictive letters to several government departments, and even to the premier, in an attempt to have the man ousted from office for an astonishing array of alleged offences.[47]

Rural neighbourhoods could withstand personal feuds in a way that they could not survive group conflict, but they made community life so unpleasant and difficult that most pioneers took pains to avoid even arguments. Usually, the injured party complained gently and politely, or else held his tongue altogether. In connection with irregularities in the operation of the rural municipality of Marquis animal pound, a police report recorded a typical response: 'Owing to Mr. Hill being a neighbor of Marshall, he does not want his name mentioned in the matter.'[48] His dilemma explains why small communities prefer malicious gossip to open confrontation.

Because pioneering on the thinly populated wheat frontier demanded so much economic and social co-operation, the settlers found it socially useful to deny the existence of any conflict, just as they found it beneficial to believe that no differences of class or wealth separated them. Untainted by qualifications, glowing testimonies to the cordiality of neighbourly relations abound. Few memoirs fail to mention the generosity extended to sick or injured neighbours, or the unlocked doors that symbolized community trust. 'You couldn't beat the spirit of the people in those days,' remembered Harvey Beaubier; 'it was impossible.' 'We had wonderful neighbours at Champion,' recalled William Wigley; 'they were all so friendly.' In an apparent attempt to top all prior tributes, Tom Sletto remembered his neighbours as 'the finest people that God ever brought together in one area of this earth.' While such eulogies sprang from the reality imposed by necessity, they in turn suggest a need to reinforce good neighbourly relations constantly lest the vital co-operative spirit shatter.[49]

Further evidence of how low-density living muted conflict within communities may be seen in the battles that raged between them. Since the competition for railways, settlers, industries, and government institutions has already been discussed at length in connection with boosterism, only a few additional points require emphasis here. Such contests stand as the only examples of institutionalized group conflict in the area's history that openly persisted for decades. Since pioneers associated with few people at any great distance, no threat to local organizations and activities prevented open declarations of war against other communities. It is also important to note that these battles pitted each town and its surrounding countryside against other towns and their countrysides. Victories for the closest town meant ready access to more services for the surrounding countryside. A campaign for more settlers promised to raise the value of every farmer's land, just as it promised to swell the volume of town trade. And when farmers speculated directly in town lots, they usually did so in the nearest centre, just as merchants dabbled in nearby farmland. Because successful boosterism brought mutual benefits, merchants joined agricultural societies and farmers joined boards of trade. Local Improvement District 128, which bordered on the town of Champion, even formed a committee to work with the town on devising promotional campaigns for the district.[50]

The union of town and country against neighbouring town and country emerged clearly in the hospital debate of 1926. When the province approved a single hospital district to serve both Vulcan and Champion, a referendum determined which town won the new facility. The residents of Vulcan and Champion naturally voted overwhelmingly for their own towns. The rural polls closest to Champion voted 82 per cent in favour of a Champion location, while those closest to Vulcan voted 79 per cent in favour of a Vulcan location.

The two rural polls situated between the towns registered the closest splits.[51] Vulcan won the hospital by a narrow margin. Indeed, Vulcan's slow but steady emergence as the dominant town in the area, confirmed most strikingly in the 1950s, when it became the seat of the new county government and the home of the new consolidated vocational school, stirred such resentment in other towns and districts that it has not abated to this day.

But geographically based battles also raged within rural local governments. From the beginning of settlement the election of municipal councillors proceeded on the ward system. Each township in the local-improvement districts that formed the basis of rural government in Alberta before 1912 elected its own councillor, for a total of three to six councillors depending on the size of the LID. The first significant consolidation of these units came between 1912 and 1918 with the formation of rural municipal districts, which consisted of no less than nine townships each and five elected councillors. At first the province proposed elections at large, but rural protest soon permitted the option of election by wards. Ratepayers in Little Bow, the first MD formed in the Vulcan area, voted 90 per cent in favour of election by subdivisions so that 'each Councillor would have jurisdiction over the roads through his subdivision all the way to Town.'[52]

Rural local governments shouldered many responsibilities – for livestock, pest, weed, and fire control, for relief, sanitation, and ultimately for hospitals and hail insurance – but road building and maintenance remained their preeminent concern. Crucial to agricultural marketing and social activities alike, no other task consumed so much time and money or led to so much squabbling. Settlers demanded elections by ward because it gave them their own champion for better roads within a clearly prescribed and confined area. Each councillor screamed unceasingly for better service and cried that other wards always got preference. Municipal reeves struggled to divide road work and finances in an equitable manner. Even so, bickering persisted. Nearly all the complaints registered against councillors concerned road work in one way or another.[53]

In 1921 residents of the Queenstown district of the MD of Marquis asked the provincial Department of Municipal Affairs if they could break away from the municipality because 'the majority of [councillors] reside in the western half of the district and [get far more] in the matter of appropriations for road work.' The department refused the request, noting wearily how often such complaints reached its offices. LID 128 (later the MD of Harmony) tried to prevent such problems by making each ward responsible for buying and keeping its own road machinery and doing its own road work. Concern about the neglect of roads in particular districts constituted the chief opposition to further municipal consolidation right up to the inauguration of county government in 1952.[54]

While geographic units provided a basis for organized conflict in the area, in a more important sense they also acted as positive forces for solidarity and consensus. Boosterism and its closely related cousin, progressivism, bound frontier strangers together and ignited the co-operative flame required to forge new communities. Within each district they united rich and poor, townsman and farmer, newcomer and old-timer, immigrant and native son, and often even employer and employee, in common cause against the aspirations of other towns and districts. In large cities like Winnipeg boosterism could become a divisive wedge. It sucked up the financial resources of the city to benefit a minority, while huge numbers of slum-dwellers paid its price in shoddy and inadequate services.[55] But in rural frontier areas like Vulcan, where cheap, accessible land led to widespread property ownership and to the realistic hope of future ownership by the propertyless, boosterism promoted greater unity. Everyone shared its costs in some measure; everyone suffered for its failures, and almost everyone benefited from its rewards.

The booster ethos not only implied that individual success flowed from community success but assumed that only a finite number of rewards could be won. What one community gained in terms of services, neighbouring communities might lose, as the hospital contest of 1926 demonstrated. Thus boosterism demanded the concentrated effort of everyone to advance the claims of the community against those of rivals. 'Progress demands that there be no factions. Progress demands a unity of action,' pronounced the Vulcan *Advocate*. And just as formal institutions and organizations could not tolerate group conflicts that threatened their existence, so too did they act as positive forces that integrated people of different classes, occupations, wealth, and ethnicity. And because their survival demanded it, they actively encouraged temperate language and behaviour, and thereby promoted social order and control.[56]

If low population density, formal organizations, boosterism, and progressivism promoted consensus and social harmony among pioneers of diverse backgrounds and circumstances, so too did the shared experiences imposed by special events. The Great War provides a dramatic example. With the possible exception of a few German nationalists in the area who wisely kept their opinions to themselves, a floodtide of patriotism engulfed virtually everyone. It saturated countless speeches, newspaper stories, and casual conversations. At least ten new patriotic organizations of one sort or another appeared in the area. Some, like the Red Cross societies that cropped up in every town and rural district, served as local units of great international organizations, while others, like the Carmangay Patriotic Sewing Circle or Vulcan's Overseas Club, sprang from purely local inspiration.

These organizations enjoyed great success in raising money and goods for the war effort, especially the Red Cross Societies, which sponsored regular fund-raising dances. In one six-month period the Vulcan Red Cross collected 2,545 sheets and articles of clothing. The Ensign Society raised $1,100 in a single day. The forty-five-member Little Bow Red Cross held dances, operated booths at fairs, auctioned off donated livestock, knitted bandages and clothing, and collected money at picnics. In 1916 locals of the little Bow Patriotic Society surpassed the provincial association's request that they raise $3,500 four months before year's end.[57]

Many of the contributions to patriotic causes came from local governments. In addition to other gifts, Vulcan town council donated an eight-hundred-dollar gun. Town councils held banquets for recruits off to war and acted as returned-soldiers bureaus. The MD of Marquis asked the Department of Municipal Affairs if it could wipe out the back taxes of those who joined the service. The department replied that it could not, but suggested that enlistees be given a special grant under the relief provisions of the Rural Municipality Act. Following Canada's most impressive victory abroad, Local Improvement District 158 applied to the department to become a rural municipality named Vimy Ridge. Informed that another municipality in the province had already claimed the honour, the new MD contented itself with the name of Royal instead.[58]

Other institutions followed the lead of local governments in supporting the war. The Vulcan Co-operative Society erected a special grain bin where farmers could donate wheat. The congregation of Carmangay's Union Church acted in concert to buy Victory Bonds. War-bond drives canvassed each district with great success; by 1918 an area stretching from High River to Carmangay had subscribed over one million dollars, and the *Advocate* claimed that over two hundred thousand of it came from Vulcan and surrounding district alone. Many communities also launched special campaigns. The Queenstown area held a dance and basket social in October 1918 to raise 'Christmas money' for the boys at the front and collected $1,123. Following the great explosion in Halifax harbour, Vulcan residents quickly organized a Halifax Relief Fund. At Armistice the tide of patriotism still ran high. The towns organized parades, hung the Kaiser in effigy, and staged boisterous celebrations. They hastily erected war memorials, and Vulcan considered itself lucky to acquire some trench mortar for its display. Most local governments also followed the MD of Royal's lead in giving veterans preference for employment and contracts.[59]

At first glance, the explanation for these patriotic outbursts seems self-evident; pioneers carried the imperialist sentiment of Ontario to the frontier; schools and cultural organizations upheld it, and the metropolitan communications network reinforced it during the war itself. But that alone does not explain the intensity of patriotism, nor why the large contingent of Americans in the area enthusiastically embraced it, even before the United States entered the conflagration. Local circumstances also generated war patriotism. In one important commodity the region did not contribute much to the war effort: manpower. Although no comprehensive information on recruits in the area is available, random evidence suggests that employees, particularly those born in Britain, accounted for most of the volunteers. While this pattern is consistent with enlistments elsewhere in Canada, agricultural areas like Vulcan did not have a high proportion of wage-earners in their populations.

Armies the world over and throughout time have always experienced great difficulty recruiting farmers and merchants; unlike employees, they leave behind small enterprises that might well collapse in their absence, and often at a time when those enterprises earn substantial profits because of war. Thus the Vulcan area stoutly opposed conscription throughout the early years of the conflict; by 1916, when support for conscription swelled throughout much of English Canada, the Vulcan *Advocate* still resisted it. Many even opposed cadet training. At the outbreak of war Charles Murray, Carmangay school principal, tried to interest the older boys in an army cadet corps. When his efforts failed, he insisted that they sign up or face expulsion from school. Four boys refused to sign, and when Murray sent them home, angry complaints reached the school-board. It ruled that the boys need not join the cadets, but they had to participate in the military drill at school. The compromise did not satisfy parents, however, and in 1916 their pressure led to Murray's dismissal.[60]

By 1917, when so many English Canadians demanded conscription, local newspapers simply ignored the issue. In the end the area finally accepted it without complaint or debate when it realized that most local residents would win exemptions. Roy Burns went with twenty-five other men for physical examinations. Only six of them had to enlist, and a relieved Burns was not among them. He recalled the incident with a great pride: 'The man said to me "Son, we need some of you boys at home to raise wheat for the soldiers." '[61] Like Gander Stake, the fictional hero of Robert Stead's novel *Grain* (1926), local farmers clung to this rationale to excuse themselves from action. 'The farmer at work in the field is doing as much in this crisis as the man who goes to the front,' argued the *Advocate* on 28 April 1915, when it issued the first in a long series of soothing assurances.

Arising from their unwillingness to make the supreme sacrifice, collective guilt turned the population into fanatical patriots in other respects. They felt it all the more keenly, perhaps, because of the bushels of money reaped from the harvests of war. At the very outbreak of hostilities local residents could not hide their eager anticipation of the rewards that might follow. They subsequently enjoyed financial gains of such magnitude that they would not be witnessed again until the 1970s. In their excitement residents barely contained the view openly expressed by the fictional farmer in Edward McCourt's novel *Music at the Close* (1947) who confided to his neighbour, 'Matt, if them Huns can just hang on for about two more years we'll all be able to retire.' As Rev. Mr Schrag of the Vulcan Union Church noted, 'Too much indifference as to the outcome of the war is evidenced by many, the material gain to the individual by the continuance of it more considered than the cause we are fighting for.'[62]

To suppress nagging thoughts about 'war profiteering,' the settlers preferred to disregard any connection between the war and prosperity. Rev. J.T. Ferguson of the High River presbytery, whose own capacity for self-delusion knew few bounds, epitomized this tendency when he said, 'The nobility of self sacrifice rather than the allurement of material gain has impressed itself on the minds of young and old alike.' American settlers did not enjoy immunity from these concerns, even though their native country joined the war late. The justification given for the war reflected their integration into the patriotic campaign. Instead of stressing imperial glory and the survival of Britain and the Empire, the Vulcan area believed the war involved loftier, more ambiguous issues. Its purpose was to save 'civilization, freedom, and democracy,' or, as the clergymen of the High River presbytery put it, to uphold 'righteousness, truth, and human liberty.'[63]

The introduction of conscription forced Vulcan-area residents to reaffirm the nobility of their purpose in staying home and growing rich while others died. It is no coincidence that contributions to the war effort and other patriotic displays increased dramatically in 1918. By then patriots began badgering less demonstrative residents. Local newspapers published the names of all contributors to all war-related causes, as well as the amounts they contributed. They singled out the largest donors for special praise. Since they printed the names in lists by school district, anyone could ferret out the slackers. As John Love discovered, unpleasant consequences often followed: 'Six car loads of people motored out to the farm of Mr. John Love . . . with the idea of selling him some Victory Bonds . . . he said he could not afford any more than $50 . . . The visitors were of a different opinion, for they had assessed him at $2,000. The figure frightened him somewhat, for he still objected, but on it being pointed out to him that the crowd were in no cheerful mood, he took the pen and signed up for them.' Love not only faced the threat of violence, but received a humiliating rebuke in the local press as well.[64]

This incident reveals the darker side of community consensus, and the heavy toll it extracted. Boosterism, progressivism, formal organizations, low-density living, and special events like the war united almost everybody in common cause, but they also stifled freedom of expression for the few dissenters that remained. Thus E.M. Carruthers thought it wise to issue a public apology for his offhanded insult to the king, delivered while Carruthers had been drunk at a children's Christmas concert. Social crusaders effectively used war patriotism to silence local opponents of such reforms as prohibition and women's suffrage. Only those who already suffered economic and social ostracization – the ne'er-do-wells – dared openly ridicule such sacred cows as war patriotism or booster campaigns.[65]

The Great Depression represents another 'special event' that promoted social cohesion across lines of wealth, occupation, and ethnicity, but it is equally indicative of another unifying force in the community: commonly shared outside enemies. Blame for the Depression fell upon distant capitalists and the politicians who favoured them with high tariffs and other generous concessions. But these villains had shouldered responsibility for every economic setback since first settlement, and even in prosperous times they conspired to deny the west the realization of its full potential. Political historians have studied western grievances against large corporations and political machines in such detail that no purpose is served in repeating them all here, especially since the Vulcan area shared wholeheartedly in the complaints commonly expressed throughout the prairie region.

One point generally overlooked by historians of regional protest, however, is that some of the animosity towards distant institutions sprang from purely local circumstances. In the Vulcan area incidents of that sort involved the banks, the elevator companies, and the dominion post office in particular, but especially they were provoked by the CPR. Although universally despised throughout the rural west for its extraordinary success in extracting favours from government, for its freight-rate structure, and for its collusion with elevator companies and other nefarious corporations, it also earned much of its unsavoury reputation from many activities at the community level. Vulcan-area settlers resented its ownership of so much local land. Its refusal to run the Kipp-Aldersyde through existing hamlets enraged them. They grumbled for years about the poor sites upon which it had planted the towns of Champion and Vulcan. They resented the arbitrary naming of the towns. When the hamlet of Cleverville moved to its new townsite, the residents petitioned the CPR to retain the name of Cleverville. The CPR bluntly refused and named the town after H.T. Champion of the Winnipeg firm of Alloway and Champion. 'Many CPR men were close friends of my father,' recalled Champion's daughter.[66]

When the town of Vulcan wanted to buy a few acres of adjacent land from the CPR in 1913 for a nuisance ground, the railway refused to sell a lot any closer than three miles from the town. Seven years later the town asked the CPR to install a public telephone in the train station for the convenience of travellers. The CPR refused, but told the town it could install one itself at public expense. In spite of persistent complaints, the CPR neglected to repair its stockyards at Champion and Carmangay. Sometimes the company arbitrarily altered or reduced train service. Shortages of boxcars incensed farmers, particularly from 1911 to 1913 when the Kipp-Aldersyde line first began operating and acute shortages arose, forcing farmers to bribe the train crews to secure cars or secretly to steal boxcars allocated to other towns by hitching teams to them at night and hauling them away.[67]

Besides these episodic troubles, battles between the CPR and local governments over taxation erupted annually. When the CPR sold farmland in the area, purchasers immediately began paying local taxes. When they made their last land payments to the CPR, however, and applied for title, the railway informed them that it had been paying taxes on the land all along and insisted that the purchasers now owed it those sums. Rural governments denied that the CPR had paid the taxes, but the company insisted that it had met them in effect through a lump payment it made on tax arrears of the 'Calgary and Edmonton Railway Security Lands,' for the years 1910 to 1915. Farmers and local governments considered the claim nothing more than another CPR plot to plunder them. Confusion, legal chaos, and compromises that satisfied no one ensued.[68]

Further indignation arose over the payment of taxes on property still owned by the railway. When the towns and rural municipalities first attempted to levy assessments on CPR land, the company informed them that its charter exempted it from such taxation. The province informed the local governments that land originally granted to the Calgary and Edmonton but now under CPR control might be exempt from taxation as long as it remained unsold and unimproved, but added that CPR land sold prior to the building of the Kipp-Aldersyde line in the area and then repurchased for townsites and roadbed was most certainly subject to taxation. The CPR never conceded this point, but accepted it implicitly by subsequently objecting to the level of its assessments rather than to assessment itself. Indeed, scarcely a year passed that the CPR did not protest its assessments throughout the various jurisdictions of the area. Their ire raised, local courts of revision almost never lowered the assessments. The CPR responded by maintaining a hefty debt in back taxes, which goaded irate local governments into legal action for recovery.[69]

A second point that might be raised regarding regional protest is that the abuse hurled at outside agents clearly exceeded any realistic assessment of their responsibility for the area's woes, many legitimate complaints notwithstanding. An often-told anecdote tells of the prairie farmer who, upon inspecting his hail-damaged crop, shook his fist in the air and cried 'God damn the CPR.' But as with war patriotism, hatred for outside enemies served important social functions. It absolved local residents of blame for their own difficulties and diverted attention from individual differences in fortunes. Outside agents also acted as surrogate villains upon whom residents could vent frustrations that could not be directed against others in the community. Thus farmers need not blame local dealers for high machinery prices; as much as the farmer, they too fell victim to the machinations of big business and an unjust National Policy. The emergence of the giant corporation, then, stripped small communities of many economic decision-making powers that had once led to internal strife but now united the populations of local communities against an outside adversary.

The pioneers of the Vulcan area did not escape internal conflict entirely but they certainly avoided the more rigid battlelines drawn in cities, non-agricultural resource towns, and more densely populated agrarian communities. Confrontations between social classes, occupations, and ethnic and national groups seldom arose. The social demands of living in an area of low population density usually transformed such potentially damaging conflicts into socially benign personal rifts. And the most persistent and common group conflicts in the area – those between spatially based communities and those pertaining to standards of respectable behaviour – not only involved shifting alliances but united people of widely different origins and circumstances. By avoiding cleavages along any single social axis, those conflicts actually performed positive social functions.[70] Equally important, the common ethos provided by progressive boosterism, shared experiences like the Great War, and a set of common outside enemies transcended and smothered internal strife. If some experienced a stifling conformity as a result, the great majority welcomed the social order and the harmony it wrought.

New Societies and Models of Frontier Development

After a detailed look at attitudes, activities, institutions, and relationships in the Vulcan area, it should be possible to assess how well the traditional models of frontier development explain its early history. Clearly, one theory alone will not suffice. Evidence of the tremendous role that the heritage of southern Ontario and the American midwest played in shaping the new communities lies everywhere at hand. Even though that heritage sometimes arrived filtered through experiences in the Inland Empire or other localities, and even though some settlers originated from other places, southern Ontario and the American midwest supplied most of the bodies that populated the Vulcan area, as well as its dominant values and institutions.

But the settlers did not exactly replicate their home communities. Even before they arrived, metropolitan agents had imposed their will on future habitation. Through surveys and land policies, the dominion government and the CPR had predetermined much about the pattern of settlement and established the procedural rules. Concurrent with settlement, elaborate transportation and communication systems linked the new communities to the rest of the industrialized world, providing them with economic markets and bombarding them with outside goods, information, and values. Since these gifts of the metropolis included technologies and ideas that did not exist at first settlement, they intermingled with, and altered, the traditions brought west by the pioneers.

Two sorts of local conditions modified both the heritage of the settlers and the influence of the metropolis: the frontier and the environment. The cheap, unoccupied lands of the frontier not only affected the course of economic development but helped to determine the shape of the social structure and the nature of social relationships. Equally important, the settlers were not cross-sectional representatives of the societies they left. The frontier lured people of a particular social and demographic stripe, and these distinctive characteristics profoundly affected community life for over a decade.

Furthermore, the physical environment presented the settlers with unfamiliar problems that neither heritage nor metropolis could solve. Geographical determinism nearly received a death-blow when scholars realized that radically different cultures often survived side by side in the same environment.[1] The Vulcan area itself, for example, first sustained Blackfoot buffalo hunters, then ranchers, and finally farmers and merchants. Each group led a markedly different existence, implying that man could respond to the area in a tremendous variety of ways. None the less, the environment imposed severe restrictions on the activities of every cultural group that occupied it. In each case they could exist only by exploiting one of the area's few resources: the Indians lived off its animal life, the ranchers off its grass, and the farmers off its soil. The reasons that none of the three societies resembled lumber camps, fishing villages, or pineapple plantations had far more to do with environment than with culture. When man finally turned to its soil for sustenance, local topography, terrain, weather and climate, and the qualities of the soil itself all prescribed new patterns of behaviour.

Separately, then, heritage, metropolis, frontier, and environment cannot adequately account for the way of life that emerged on the Vulcan prairie. Only a consideration of the complex interplay among them will do. Low population density, for example, has been used repeatedly to help explain the nature of Vulcan-area society. But why did it develop at all? Low population density began with the vacant space that defines a frontier. The imported heritage of the settlers sustained it by favouring independent living on individual farms over a communal existence in centralized villages. Metropolitan land policy accommodated that cultural preference. An environment that demanded larger farms than either the pioneers had experienced or metropolitan land policy had anticipated ensured that population density would remain low. The metropolis further abetted the process by offering market values for wheat that required it be grown in vast quantities per farmer.

Can it be said of the interplay among heritage, metropolis, frontier, and environment that one or more of those forces predominated over the others? Their relative impact on frontier settlement has certainly changed over the course of history. Advances in transportation and communications technology since the advent of industrialization, for example, gave metropolitanism a role in shaping frontier development that scarcely existed in earlier times.[2] The first American settlers to cross the Appalachian Mountains established farming communities without benefit of much contact with older, established settlements. By 1914 the industrial world had become so interconnected that a war fought in the trenches of Europe profoundly affected virtually every aspect of life in the new communities of the Vulcan area nearly six thousand miles away.

Even so, people do not play out their lives on a world stage. They perform in the tiny theatres of specific localities, and those theatres each have their own unique dimensions and qualities, their own sets and props, that demand alterations to imported scripts never imagined by the original playwrights. Even today, when the impact of the metropolis on frontier development surpasses anything known in history, frontier and environment still exert themselves. In spite of instantaneous communications with the outside world, the modern resource towns of the far north must still grapple with frontier population structures and environments featuring rock, muskeg, permafrost, and long months of intense cold and darkness.[3]

If the relative impact of heritage, metropolis, frontier, and environment is difficult to measure in general terms, is it easier to determine if any of them worked harder than the others in shaping particular aspects of local society? While such often seems to be the case, closer investigation suggests that it is equally difficult to pinpoint their relative influence even in isolated instances. Frontier and environment, for example, appear to have won out over heritage and metropolis in determining the extent of agricultural diversification in the area. But the example is deceptive. While heritage and metropolis both urged mixed farming, both also inadvertently made it possible for a single-crop economy to prevail. The cultural baggage of the settlers included an acquisitive spirit that sprang from long experience with commercial agriculture, and that part of their heritage drew them to the most profitable crop regardless of their misgivings. And in spite of its boisterous advice, the metropolis quietly encouraged their choice by providing wheat with many transportation and marketing advantages.

In other particular instances, one or another influence seemed predominant at particular points in time. Continuing with examples drawn from agriculture, the imported traditions of midwestern tillage, reinforced by metropolitan advice, seemed to hold sway over a protesting environment for a long time. But the environment was not static. Indeed, changeability emerged as its most notable feature. The environment could tolerate imported agricultural practices for a time, but when it revealed its cyclical moodiness, it insisted on fundamental changes in tillage methods. Thus, no matter where attention is focused, the interplay of heritage, metropolis, frontier, and environment seems always present. As this study has attempted to demonstrate, it will no longer serve to repeat the trite observation that environment helped determine the frontier economy while transplanted heritage accounted for its social institutions.

Sorting out the relative impact of heritage, metropolis, frontier, and environment is rendered so difficult because the qualitative nature of their interaction is far more important than the quantities of each ingredient in the mix. The observation is hardly new; half a century ago Arthur Lower speculated that the frontier probably did advance democracy, but only when such a tendency also proved amenable to the cultural traditions of the group in question.[4] This qualitative exchange between heritage, metropolis, frontier, and environment can be demonstrated with brief examples drawn from other wheat frontiers. Consider how differences in the nature of metropolitanism affected developments in Australia and Argentina. The influence of the metropolis in South Australia seems overwhelming to the student of western Canada. Adelaide exerted tremendous control over its agricultural frontier in many ways, but most strikingly through government policies. The state not only laid out the survey pattern but acted as the sole agent for transferring raw lands to settlers. It decided where pioneers could settle and when. It determined all the railway routes and built and owned all the lines. It decided on the number, spacing, and location of townsites, and even planned their street patterns. It owned all the town lots and sold them off by auction.

Yet in spite of these and countless other contrasts with the western Canadian experience, one can envision Vulcan-area settlers adjusting to the South Australia frontier with no more difficulty than to the southern Alberta one. They could have purchased cheap government lands on credit and farmed them on a familiar scale using familiar technology. They could have listened to, and rejected, the same metropolitan advice to plough deeply and frequently and to practice mixed farming. They could have participated in social activities, joined in institutions, and experienced social relationships that would not have unduly strained their adaptive capabilities. They could have bought government town lots and joined with fellow British and Australian pioneers in booster campaigns to secure transportation advantages and lure settlers, industries, and government institutions. If successful, they could have sold out their holdings for a profit and rushed optimistically into the increasingly arid northern frontier in hopes of repeating the entire process. Thus, in spite of far more extensive metropolitan control, the pioneering experience in South Australia did not differ radically from that in the Vulcan area.[5]

By contrast, much about government activity on the pampas of Argentina superficially resembles Canadian frontier policy. Most raw lands quickly passed out of direct government control. The state did not determine railway routes nor own the railways. It did not plan towns or raise money by selling town lots. Yet one aspect of Argentine policy resulted in a way of life very alien to the experience of pioneers in both western Canada and South Australia.

When railways and other technological developments made wheat production feasible on isolated grasslands throughout the world, politically powerful business elites pressured their governments to devise land policies to encourage the new industry. Its capital and labour requirements opened up greater economic opportunities for them than did the continuation of livestock grazing. In Argentina, however, livestock had been the only major source of wealth for so long that the cattle barons retained an inordinate degree of political power. Land policy continued to reflect that power; the grazers retained ownership of the frontier, and little land became available for agricultural settlers.

When a European market opened for choice meats, Argentine ranchers discovered that pampas grass would not produce a suitable animal. Alfalfa would, but the expense and trouble of growing it irritated the ranchers, so they devised a means of convincing others to grow it for them. They rented portions of their holdings to Italian settlers for three-year terms and allowed them to grow wheat, providing they left the farms in alfalfa when their leases expired. The ranchers collected rent payments and got their alfalfa free of charge. The tenants then moved on to another district, another ranch, or another part of the same ranch, and repeated the whole process.

Rapid, compulsory mobility with no opportunity for capital gain stripped the settlers of any incentive to build up communities. They refused to construct anything more than hovels for houses. They built no other farm buildings at all, and no institutional facilities. No schools or churches appeared. Lacking even grain bins and elevators, they shipped wheat in sacks. Bizarre as this pioneering experience appears to western Canadian historians, it none the less proved highly effective in making Argentina a major wheat producer. Using modern technology and techniques common elsewhere, Argentina emerged as the world's third-largest wheat exporter by 1910.[6]

Settlers from the Vulcan area would have experienced far greater difficulties adjusting to the Argentine frontier, where metropolitan control differed in kind rather than degree, than they would have on the South Australian one, where it differed greatly in degree but not much in kind. Of course, it can readily be argued that differences in metropolitan control do not entirely account for the radically different ways of life on each frontier. Clearly, elements in the cultural heritage of Vulcan-area settlers would have permitted them to accept and work within the Australian system but not within the Argentine one.

The complicating factor of culture in the case of Australia and Argentina illustrates a more general difficulty in assessing the impact of any particular influence through comparative study. Testing by comparing requires keeping all elements constant save one. Western Canada looks like an ideal laboratory for examining the impact of imported heritage, for instance, because many diverse cultural groups all settled there at the same time. But the attempt to neutralize all influences save heritage will not work, for changing one element in the equation automatically changes all the others. The immigrants who understood English poorly, if at all, did not all listen to the same metropolitan voices, nor did they necessarily interpret messages in the same ways. Nor did the different cultural groups ever respond to identical environments. As we have seen, micro-environments within the Vulcan area itself led to numerous variations in basic agricultural techniques. In the immensity of the Canadian prairies even greater environmental diversity thwarts the attempt to isolate the impact of culture alone. And even when different groups settled within the same micro-environment, some found it more familiar to them than did others.

But the cultural groups themselves will introduce additional complications because they did not all arrive equally anxious to transplant heritage. Those bound tightly by some special purpose – especially communal religious groups like the Hutterites – preserved more of their traditions through sheer force of will. Such groups often moved to the frontier for reasons different from those of other settlers. Instead of searching for new opportunities, like so many Vulcan-area settlers, they often came to preserve a way of life under pressure back home. Some even came not to replicate what they had known but to conduct utopian social experiments that could not be launched in the home-land.[7]

It is hardly necessary to examine religious sects or ethnic minorities to detect such sweeping differences in attitude regarding transplanted heritage. They often appeared within the English-speaking majority itself. British settlers of the minor gentry, or with pretensions to that class, often clung stubbornly to certain traditions, oblivious of all else. In the most extreme cases they even tried to reproduce a way of life that had already disappeared (at least for them) back in England. In places like Cannington Manor, Saskatchewan, they struggled boldly to re-create the world of the landed aristocrat. While forced of necessity to make some concessions to the frontier, the environment, and Canadian metropolitan influences, they refused to make enough of them, and the settlement failed.[8]

Such experiments also reveal an important distinction between the desire to transplant culture and the ability to do so. Much more cultural heritage can be imported intact if a group is willing to subsidize it. So long as outside capital sustains a particular way of life, other considerations can be ignored more readily. Such a phenomenon helps to explain how English bureaucrats nurtured little bastions of genteel Victorian society throughout the diverse reaches of the British Empire. Indeed, the same phenomenon appeared on a much smaller scale in the Vulcan area itself. So long as the local environment and the metropolitan marketplace afforded settlers a satisfactory standard of living, the settlers in effect subsidized their midwestern agricultural practices. When both environment and metropolitan prices changed, they could no longer afford to do so and they altered their techniques.

But the ability of immigrants to replicate heritage also varied even when their desire and financial ability to do so did not. Immigrants separated from their fellows and thrown into communities dominated by other ethnic groups, such as the European settlers of the Vulcan area, not only lacked the human resources necessary to sustain many traditions but found themselves bombarded by the influence of the dominant culture. Numerous studies have pointed out that in such circumstances ethnic traits rapidly faded on the rural frontier. By contrast, ethnic groups that pioneered in great bloc settlements more successfully preserved their heritage. They commanded greater human resources and more easily avoided contaminating contacts with other ethnic groups.[9]

The appearance of a British aristocratic tradition in western Canada reveals another critical problem. Classification by ethnicity or nationality is simply too crude to employ in any assessment of how cultural variations shaped frontier communities. Some American studies have discovered surprisingly few differences among ethnic groups in their responses to similar environments on the same frontier within the same time-frame. Much more variation has emerged from studying communities populated by different social groups of the same ethnic minority, settlements distinguished by the particular class, occupational, religious, and regional origins of their populations.[10]

Historians of western Canadian ethnic groups have not served us well in unravelling these various problems. By eagerly focusing on the differences between their selected minorities and the dominant English-speaking society, they have piled up examples of transplanted heritage in enormous heaps. Yet they have failed to emphasize how each group's way of life differed from that in the homeland, and thus they have overlooked any important role that frontier, environment, and metropolis played in the new setting.[11]

The examples offered here suggest that the study of comparative frontiers does not promise to test the validity of any existing theory of development conclusively. When such attempts are extended to the study of different kinds of frontiers stretching over vast time periods, as in a comparison of the fur-trading, ranching, mining, and agricultural frontiers, these problems are compounded many times and new ones arise. For good reasons, perhaps, studies comparing the influence of the frontier are few in number, and good ones are scarcer still. The resulting lacunae periodically prompt historians to raise the old war cry for renewed efforts. Critics, however, rightly complain that too many other influences prevent the proper testing of the frontier thesis. Dismissing such projects as untenable, they instead urge frontier historians to test the more restricted and more rigorously defined hypotheses of modern demographers and other social scientists. But such a suggestion will not satisfy students who seek to know how new communities take shape and why they evolve differently from their parent societies. They must muddle on in spite of the obstacles.[12]

If compounding problems frustrates the testing of existing theories of frontier development, the assessing of their relative values, and the discovery of some mechanism that regulates the interplay among heritage, metropolis, frontier, and environment, these problems also thwart any attempt to devise a comprehensive new model that integrates existing ones and promises to serve all students of new societies. The complaint may seem like another shop-worn argument against the use of theories and models in historical inquiry, and a reaffirmation of the historian's duty to study the particular and the unique in human experience. But taken literally and carried to extremes, that goal serves no purpose. It leaves the historian wandering aimlessly through endless corridors of single instances. The human mind will not accept a vast collection of random oddities; it insists on comparing, classifying, and generalizing. And in fact, historians interpret and theorize all the time, as indeed they must if they hope to recover anything of value from the past.[13]

Ironically, even though they often shy away from hypotheses of social-scientific design, historians are quite susceptible to grand generalizations that employ woolly definitions and assumptions, and often rest for support on casual observations. Tossing out random illustrations as evidence, many have boldly asserted the legitimacy of a favoured notion, whether geographical determinism, cultural determinism, the frontier thesis, or the metropolitan thesis. A better course may be to refine historical models as much as possible, accept that they will remain crude tools at best, and use them delicately to make sense of past human experience.

A Note on Statistics

Although none of the sophisticated techniques of quantification have been employed here, statistical information represents an important aspect of this study. It has been gathered and compiled from many sources. The *Census of the Prairie Provinces* (1906, 1916, 1926, 1936) and the *Census of Canada* (1911, 1921, 1931, 1941) provided most of the aggregate data. In some cases new sets of statistics were created by using the information presented in two or more tables. But the census also posed several problems. One scholar warns that some United States census data may be in error as much as plus or minus 10 per cent, and many of his complaints may be valid for the Canadian census as well.[1] Changes in categories from one census year to the next presented some difficulties, but more serious ones emerged because of changes in geographical reporting units between 1906 and 1921. The most important units used in compiling statistics for the study area are portrayed on Map 13.

The earliest *Census of the Prairie Provinces* sometimes gave statistical breakdowns by townships for some categories, permitting me to match the data closely to the boundaries of the Vulcan area. Until 1916, however, the census lumped most data for the area in with the much larger Macleod census division. In 1916 it included the Vulcan area in the Bow River census division, another larger unit. My statistical profile of the area prior to 1921 was sometimes based on those two large divisions alone.

From 1921 to 1941 the census not only expanded the scope of its information greatly but reported it along consistent geographical lines. The Vulcan area now fell wholly within Census Division 4, another relatively large unit. While I was occasionally forced to rely on data presented for that unit alone, the census usually also presented statistics for rural municipal districts and incorporated towns and villages within Census Division 4. The Vulcan area embraced all of the MD of Royal 158 and almost all of the MD of Harmony

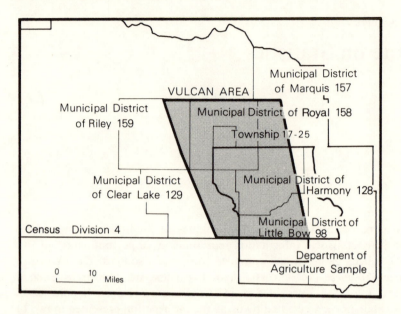

MAP 13
Statistical units employed in the study

128. These two units formed the basis for most of my statistics after 1916, although they were sometimes modified by the data for other municipal districts that invaded the study area's boundaries (see Map 13).

Another important source of statistical information often supplemented or modified census data. In 1935 the Prairie Farm Rehabilitation Administration funded a joint study by the Canadian and Alberta Departments of Agriculture of 232 farms. Most were located within the Vulcan area (see Map 13). The researchers assembled profiles of each farm's financial history based on information supplied by the farm operators. Although these original manuscripts were probably destroyed, the researchers produced dozens of statistical tables and presented them in a number of publications, as well as in an unpublished thesis.[2]

Homestead files, land titles, Canadian Pacific Railway land-sales records, tax rolls, directories, and biographical sketches published in community-written local histories were invaluable for compiling statistical profiles of rural neighbourhoods. Because of the immense quantity of this data, the cumbersome process needed to collect it, and the time required to sort out its errors, omissions, ambiguities, and contradictions, analysing this data for the entire

Vulcan area proved impossible. Township 17-25-4 received more intensive investigation than any other simply because it seemed to offer the most complete runs of all kinds of data (see Map 13). I also analysed the data for three other townships to produce some sets of statistics, and I often quickly surveyed the data for still other townships to assess the representativeness of 17-25-4. While it was ordinary enough in many respects, some other townships seemed subject to more land speculation, absentee ownership, and population turnover. I may, therefore, have understated my case in describing those matters. More manageable quantities of mass data permitted a more comprehensive statistical survey of the towns. R.G. Dun business ratings, tax rolls, Canadian Pacific Railway lot-sales records, directories, and biographical files provided the raw information.

The statistical information compiled for this study is presented in graphs instead of tables for several reasons. Whatever attempts I could have made to be as accurate as possible, tables would have demanded a degree of precision that is simply not warranted because of the problems discussed above. As a result, my analysis of statistical evidence is largely confined to major trends over time, and I hesitated to analyse any statistical trend in the absence of supporting literary information. More importantly, I used graphs because of their visual impact; the reader can readily grasp important changes without laboriously plodding through rows of figures. Graphs also permitted ready comparisons with Alberta at large (or sometimes with the prairie provinces) and with Ontario, the original home of many Vulcan-area settlers.

Bibliographical Note

An abundant, varied, and rich quantity of sources relating to the Vulcan area can be investigated by visiting many locations. Large collections exist in four places. The Glenbow-Alberta Institute in Calgary holds many pertinent manuscripts, land records, and rare publications. The Provincial Archives of Alberta in Edmonton contains homestead records and local government collections. The Alberta Legislative Library in Edmonton holds the largest number of local newspapers. As a hobby, M.D. Keenan of Pincher Creek, Alberta, has assembled a large private collection of materials relating to the Carmangay and Champion districts. Portions of this collection have now been photocopied by the Glenbow-Alberta Institute. Most of the remaining sources can only be examined by visiting many other individuals and institutions holding small collections. Most are located in the Vulcan area itself.

Many useful institutional records have survived. Those of special value in compiling statistics are discussed in the Appendix. While the records of local governments, churches, and the Mounted Police were intended to supply information about their own particular concerns, all of them contained important observations on many other aspects of local society. Corporations and other private businesses involved in the development of the area have either destroyed or misplaced their records; most also responded coolly to inquiries about them. Two large and important collections of business records were available, however: Dun and Bradstreet of Canada granted me access to credit-rating reports on businesses in the area, and Canadian Pacific Railway land records and correspondence files are open to researchers at the Glenbow-Alberta Institute.

Local newspapers constituted an invaluable source. Because they are rare, and no complete runs exist in any one place, I supplemented the holdings at the Alberta Legislative Library with many privately owned collections. The current offices of the Vulcan *Advocate* contain the largest supply. I also consulted many newspaper files and scrapbooks. Maps played an important role in reconstructing certain aspects of settlement, agricultural, and social history. Photographs proved surprisingly helpful in assessing the role of technology, and sometimes provided the only information available on certain matters.

A strong oral-history tradition has survived in the Vulcan area and may be tapped in a variety of ways. Although I conducted many interviews, the number of residents of adult age before 1920 had already dwindled significantly by the time I began my research. Indeed, nearly all the people I interviewed are now dead. None the less, many earlier interviews were conducted by others and preserved on tape in a variety of locations. A large quantity of unpublished memoirs is available. Reminiscences also appeared in local newspapers, and a great many others have been collected and published by local history-book committees. Regardless of the form they take, these oral sources provide abundant information on virtually every aspect of the area's history.

Notes

ABBREVIATIONS

ACC   Anglican Church of Canada, Diocese of Calgary Archives, University of Calgary Library
ALT   Southern Alberta Land Titles Office, Calgary
CDA   Calgary Diocesan Archives, Bishop's Office, Roman Catholic Church, Calgary
CVO   County of Vulcan No 2 Office, Vulcan, Alberta
DBC   Dun and Bradstreet Canada Ltd, Toronto
GAI   Glenbow-Alberta Institute, Calgary
MDK   M.D. Keenan, privately owned archival collection, Pincher Creek, Alberta
PAA   Provincial Archives of Alberta, Edmonton
PAC   Public Archives of Canada, Ottawa
TVO   Town of Vulcan Office, Vulcan, Alberta
UCA   United Church of Canada Archives, Toronto
VA   Vulcan Archives, Public Library, Vulcan, Alberta
VCAO Village of Carmangay Office, Carmangay, Alberta
VCHO Village of Champion Office, Champion, Alberta

INTRODUCTION: THE PROBLEM OF NEW COMMUNITIES

1 High River Pioneers' and Old Timers' Association, *Leaves from the Medicine Tree* (High River, Alta, 1960), 213–19; Carmangay and District History Book Committee, *Bridging the Years; Carmangay and District* (Carmangay, Alta, 1968), 1; Douglas Hardwick, taped interviewed by E.S. Bryant, 11 Sept. 1957, reel 2, side 1, counter no 199–209, PAA; Harvey Beaubier, taped interviewed by Barry Necyk and Sharilyn Ingram, 8 Mar. 1973, side 1, counter no 96–7, PAA
2 Carl Berger, *The Writing of Canadian History; Aspects of English-Canadian His-*

torical Writing: 1900 to 1970 (Toronto: Oxford University Press 1976), 137; Walter N. Sage, 'Some Aspects of the Frontier in Canadian History,' Canadian Historical Association Annual Reports (1928): 62–72; John L. McDougall, 'The Frontier School and Canadian History,' Canadian Historical Association Annual Reports (1929): 121–5; J.B. Brebner, 'Canadian and North American History,' Canadian Historical Association Annual Reports (1931): 37–48; George F.G. Stanley, 'Western Canada and the Frontier Thesis,' Canadian Historical Association Annual Reports (1940): 105–14; J.M.S. Careless, 'Frontierism, Metropolitanism, and Canadian History,' Canadian Historical Review 35, no 1 (Mar. 1954): 1–21; Michael S. Cross, ed., The Frontier Thesis and the Canadas: The Debate on the Impact of the Canadian Environment (Toronto: Copp Clark 1970); David H. Breen, 'The Turner Thesis and the Canadian West: A Closer Look at the Ranching Frontier,' in Lewis H. Thomas, ed., Essays on Western History in Honour of Lewis Gwynne Thomas (Edmonton: University of Alberta Press 1976), 147–58; Ray Allen Billington, America's Frontier Heritage (New York: Holt, Rinehart and Winston 1966), 15

3 Walter N. Sage, 'Geographical and Cultural Aspects of the Five Canadas,' Canadian Historical Association Annual Reports (1937): 28–34; Harold A. Innis, The Fur Trade in Canada: An Introduction to Canadian Economic History (Boston: Yale University Press 1930); Donald Creighton, The Empire of the St. Lawrence, 1760–1850 (Toronto: Ryerson Press 1937). Although the metropolitan thesis is often used to attack the frontier thesis, it is ironic that Turner himself did not oppose a metropolitan approach. Indeed, he was one of the first scholars to appreciate the important role that cities played in the development of the American west. See Ray Allen Billington, Frederick Jackson Turner: Historian, Scholar, Teacher (New York: Oxford University Press 1973), 492–3. On the lack of local studies focusing on these problems see Gilbert C. Fite, 'Expanded Frontiers in Agricultural History,' Agricultural History 35, no 4 (Oct. 1961): 177; W. Turrentine Jackson, 'A Brief Message for the Young and/or Ambitious: Comparative Frontiers as a Field for Investigation,' Western Historical Quarterly 9, no 1 (Jan. 1978): 5–18.

4 Careless, 'Frontierism.' See also idem, 'Metropolitanism and Nationalism,' in Nationalism in Canada, ed. Peter Russell (Toronto: McGraw-Hill 1966), 271–83; 'Somewhat Narrow Horizons,' Canadian Historical Association Annual Reports (1968): 1–10; ' "Limited Identities" in Canada,' Canadian Historical Review 50, no 1 (May 1969): 1–10; 'Metropolis and Region: The Interplay between City and Region in Canadian History Before 1914,' Urban History Review no 3 (1978): 99–119.

5 Robert F. Berkhofer Jr., 'Space, Time, Culture and the New Frontier,' Agricultural History 38, no 1 (Jan. 1964): 26–7

6 Frederick Jackson Turner, *The Frontier in American History* (New York: Henry Holt 1920)
7 Because of the exaggerated claims of its early advocates, geographic determinism has steadily declined in popularity in favour of cultural geography, yet no geographer would deny that environments shape human activity to a considerable extent. See Yi-Fu Tuan,' Humanistic Geography,' *Annals of the Association of American Geographers* 66, no 2 (June 1976): 266–76; J. Nicholas Entrikin, 'Contemporary Humanism in Geography,' *Annals of the Association of American Geographers* 66, no 4 (Dec. 1976): 615–32; Marvin W. Midesell, 'Tradition and Innovation in Cultural Geography,' *Annals of the Association of American Geographers* 68, no 1 (Mar. 1978): 1–16; Leonard Guelke, 'Regional Geography,' *Professional Geographer* 29, no 1 (Feb. 1977): 1–7.
8 Excepting the now antiquated 'germ theory,' a significant exception is Louis Hartz, *The Founding of New Societies: Studies in the History of the United States, Latin America, South Africa, Canada, and Australia* (New York: Harcourt, Brace and World 1964), which characterizes new societies as fragments of old ones that froze in time and failed to evolve with the parent societies.
9 Reynold M. Wik, 'Some Interpretations of the Mechanization of Agriculture in the Far West,' *Agricultural History* 49, no 1 (Jan. 1975): 73–83
10 Paul Voisey, 'Rural Local History and the Prairie West,' *Prairie Forum* 10, no 2 (Autumn 1985): 331

CHAPTER ONE: PIONEERS

1 Many studies have focused on rural mobility, but two classics include James C. Malin, 'The Turnover of Farm Population in Kansas,' *Kansas Historical Quarterly* 4, no 4 (Nov. 1935): 339–72; and Peter J. Coleman, 'Restless Grant County: Americans on the Move,' *Wisconsin Magazine of History* 46, no 1 (Autumn 1962): 16–20. For a good Canadian example see David Gagan, 'Geographical and Social Mobility in Nineteenth-Century Ontario: A Microstudy,' *Canadian Review of Sociology and Anthropology* 13, no 2 (June 1976): 152–64. The Vulcan-area example comes from Carmangay and District History Book Committee, *Bridging the Years: Carmangay and District* (Carmangay, Alta, 1968), 221.
2 Champion History Committee, *Cleverville-Champion, 1905 to 1970, A History of Champion and Area* (Champion, Alta, 1971), 576; Vulcan and District Historical Society, *Wheat Country: A History of Vulcan and District* (Vulcan, Alta, 1973), 686, 803; H.H. Thompson, 'The Thompsons in Alberta,' unpub. ms, nd, GAI; George B. Thompson, 'Memoirs of Charles H. Thompson and Dorcas L. Thompson: Their Ancestors, Their Family and Their Descendents,' unpub. ms, nd, GAI
3 D. Aidan McQuillan, 'The Mobility of Immigrants and Americans: A Compari-

son of Farmers on the Kansas Frontier,' *Agricultural History* 53, no 3 (July 1979): 576–96; Champion, *Cleverville-Champion*, 521–22; many interviews, especially Jack Dietz, interviewed near Milo, Alta, Apr. 1978

4 Karel Denis Bicha, *The American Farmer and the Canadian West, 1896–1914* (Lawrence, Kan.: Coronado Press 1968), 140–41, passim

5 Harold Martin Troper, *Only Farmers Need Apply: Official Canadian Government Encouragement of Immigration from the United States, 1896–1911* (Toronto: Griffin House 1972); Canada, *Sessional Papers*, no 25 (1905), pt 2, 42–3

6 Champion, *Cleverville-Champion*, 314, 582; Nanton *News*, 22 Feb. 1906; 'A Look into the Past, Vulcan Pioneer: D.O. Jantzie,' videotaped interview by County of Vulcan Education Television, 1975, CVO

7 Champion, *Cleverville-Champion*, 412–18; Vulcan, *Wheat*, 558

8 Allan G. Bogue, 'Social Theory and the Pioneer,' *Agricultural History* 34, no 1 (Jan. 1960): 30

9 Based on assembled biographical files

10 Carmangay, *Bridging*, 165–6

11 David J. Wisehart, 'Age and Sex Composition of the Population on the Nebraska Frontier, 1860–1880,' *Nebraska History* 54, no 1 (Spring 1973): 106–19; William L. Bowers, 'Crawford Township, 1850–1870: A Population Study of a Pioneer Community,' *Iowa Journal of History* 58, no 1 (Jan. 1960): 1–30

12 Calculated from Homestead Files, Township 17-25-4, PAA; John Proskie, 'Financial Progress of Settlers With Special Reference to the Vulcan-Lomond Area,' MA, Alberta 1937, 16

13 Irma Plunkett, untitled, unpub. ms, nd, privately held by Roy McIntyre, Vulcan, Alta; Elizabeth Akitt, taped interview by Barry Necyk and Sharilyn Ingram, Carmangay, 9 Mar. 1973, side 1, counter no 733–5, PAA; Carrie McIntyre, interviewed at Vulcan, June 1978

14 Blaine T. Williams, 'The Frontier Family: Demographic Fact and Historical Myth,' in Harold M. Hollingsworth and Sandra L. Myres, eds., *Essays on the American West* (Austin: University of Texas Press 1969), 63–5

15 For a summary of this change in American studies see Mary Young, 'The West and American Cultural Identity: Old Themes and New Variations,' *Western Historical Quarterly* 1, no 2 (1970): 137–60. For Canada, where the imitative view has nearly always prevailed, see Intro., n 2.

16 Robert Nisbet, *Social Change and History: Aspects of the Western Theory of Development* (New York: Oxford University Press 1969); Ray Allen Billington, *America's Frontier Heritage* (New York: Holt, Rinehart and Winston 1966), 159–79; L.L. Bernard, 'A Theory of Rural Attitudes,' *American Journal of Sociology* 22, no 5 (Mar. 1917): 630–49; William C. Smith, 'The Rural Mind: A Study in

Occupational Attitude,' *American Journal of Sociology* 32, no 5 (Mar. 1927): 771–86

17 Robert H. Wiebe, *The Search for Order, 1877–1920* (New York: Hill and Wang 1967); Samuel Haber, *Efficiency and Uplift: Scientific Management in the Progressive Era* (Chicago: University of Chicago Press 1964); Samuel P. Hays, *Conservation and the Gospel of Efficiency: The Progressive Conservation Movement, 1890–1920* (Cambridge: Harvard University Press 1959)

18 William L. Bowers, 'Country Life Reform, 1900–20: A Neglected Aspect of Progressive Era History,' *Agricultural History* 45, no 3 (July 1971): 211–22. See also Harry C. McDean, 'Professionalism in the Rural Social Sciences, 1896–1919,' *Agricultural History* 58, no 3 (July 1984): 373–92. In Canada a similar approach to rural reform can be seen in John MacDougall, *Rural Life in Canada, Its Trend and Tasks* (1913; Toronto: University of Toronto Press 1973).

19 David B. Danbom, 'The Industrialization of Agriculture, 1900–1930,' PH D, Stanford 1974. For the growing faith in science, technology, and efficiency among Ontario and American midwestern farmers see D.A. Lawr, 'The Development of Ontario Farming, 1870–1914: Patterns of Growth and Change,' *Ontario History* 64, no 4 (Dec. 1972): 241–2; Keach Johnson, 'Iowa Dairying at the Turn of the Century: The New Agriculture and Progressivism,' *Agricultural History* 45, no 2 (April 1970): 96; Philip H. Korth, 'The American Yeoman vs. Progress and the Non-partisan League,' *North Dakota History* 37, no 2 (Spring 1970): 137; Adam Ward Rome, 'American Farmers as Entrepreneurs, 1870–1900,' *Agricultural History* 56, no 1 (Jan. 1982): 37–49; Clifford B. Anderson, 'The Metamorphosis of American Agrarian Idealism in the 1920's and 1930's,' *Agricultural History* 35, no 4 (Oct. 1961): 182–8.

20 James H. Shideler, 'Flappers and Philosophers, and Farmers: Rural-Urban Tensions of the Twenties,' *Agricultural History* 47, no 4 (Oct. 1973): 289

21 Carmangay *Sun*, 17 Jan. 1913; Edward B. Swindlehurst, *Alberta's School of Agriculture, a Brief History* (Edmonton: Alberta Department of Agriculture 1966), 38; Champion *Chronicle*, 2 Dec. 1920

22 Ernest Davidge, 'Reminiscences,' unpub. ms, 197?, UCA

23 Carmangay *Sun*, 31 May 1911

24 Vulcan *Advocate*, 10 Nov. 1915; Carmangay *Sun*, 7 June 1916

25 Carmangay *Sun*, 10 Nov. 1911

26 Georgina Helen Thomson, *Crocus and Meadowlark Country; Recollections of a Happy Childhood and Youth on a Homestead in Southern Alberta* (Edmonton: Institute of Applied Art 1963), 83; Will E. Finley to Editor, Hastings [Michigan] *Journal-Herald*, May 1913, reprinted in Carmangay *Sun*, 30 May 1913. Based on questionnaires, Catherine Tulloch, 'Pioneer Reading,' *Saskatchewan History* 12,

no 3 (Autumn 1959): 97–9, suggests that one-third of Saskatchewan's pioneers were avid readers.

27 Thomson, *Crocus*, 84–7

28 For the importance of radio to farm communities in the United States see Reynold M. Wik, 'The Radio in Rural America During the 1920s,' *Agricultural History* 55, no 4 (Oct. 1981): 339–50.

29 For the social and cultural importance of the chautauqua see Donald Linton Graham, 'Circuit Chautauqua, a Middle Western Institution,' PH D, State University of Iowa 1953; Sheilagh Jameson, *Chautauqua in Canada* (Calgary: Glenbow-Alberta Institute 1979). For winter migration I relied on many interviews and newspaper announcements; for extended comment see Champion *Chronicle*, 7 Apr. 1921.

30 For this belief among Manitoba farmers in the 1920s see J.F. Newman, 'The Impact of Technology Upon Rural South-western Manitoba, 1920–1930, MA, Queen's 1971, 58–86.

31 'A Southern Alberta Town in the Making,' in *Why Go to Canada?* (Calgary: Calgary *Herald*, June 1910), GAI; see also Champion Board of Trade, *Grain Golden Champion* (Champion 1912), MDK.

32 Paul Voisey, 'The "Votes for Women" Movement,' *Alberta History* 23, no 3 (Summer 1975): 10–23

33 See by-law books for Carmangay, VCAO; Champion, VCHO; Vulcan, TVO; Vulcan *Review*, 26 Mar. 1913.

34 Nanton *News*, 26 May 1910; Calgary *Daily Herald*, 10 Feb. 1913, 14. Don Harrison Doyle, 'Social Theory and New Communities,' *Western Historical Quarterly* 8, no 2 (April 1977): 164, notes that during the settlement of the American midwest boosters linked the image of social order to town promotion in order to attract respectable families and state institutions.

35 Mrs Folk, 'A Eulogy of the Carmangay Ladies Aid From 1910 to 1935,' unpub. ms, 1935?, Carmangay Pastoral Charge Papers, United Church of Canada Records, PAA

36 Finley letter; Vulcan, *Wheat*, 39; Vulcan *Advocate*, 19 Nov. 1919

37 See for example records of the Berrywater Literary and Social Club, VA.

38 High River *Times*, 19 July 1906; Wilfred Eggleston, 'The Old Homestead: Romance and Reality,' in Howard Palmer, ed., *The Settlement of the West* (Calgary: University of Calgary and Comprint Publishing 1977), 117

39 Nicholas J. Karolides, *The Pioneer in the American Novel, 1900–1950* (Norman: University of Oklahoma Press 1967), 82–98; Linda Rasmussen and others, *A Harvest Yet to Reap: A History of Prairie Women* (Toronto: Women's Press 1976), passim, espec. 13

40 See Lewis Atherton, *Main Street on the Middle Border* (Bloomington: Indiana

University Press 1954), 122–3; and idem, 'The Midwestern Country Town – Myth and Reality,' *Agricultural History* 26, no 3 (July 1952): 80.

41 E.G. Luxton, 'Vulcan,' unpub. ms, 1958, Eleanor Luxton Papers, GAI; Lethbridge *Herald*, 15 July 1959; Vulcan, *Wheat*, 869–70. For the existence of settlers interested in culture in nearly all frontier communities see Billington, *America's Frontier*, 69–95; Louis B. Wright, *Culture on the Moving Frontier* (Bloomington: Indiana University Press 1955), passim.

42 Helen Ainslie, 'Why Do People Go West?' [Chicago] *North Shore Congregationalist*, May 1913, reprinted in Carmangay *Sun*, 6 June 1913

43 Vulcan *Advocate*, 2 Nov. 1921; Finley letter; Jantzie interview; Georgina 'Ina' Neilson, taped interview by Garry Necyk and Sharilyn Ingram, Carmangay, 6 Mar. 1973, side 1, counter no 598–601, PAA; Davidge, 'Reminiscences,' 9, 50–1; W.D. Reid in *Acts and Proceedings of the General Assembly of the Presbyterian Church in Canada* (1911), 22, UCA

44 Vulcan *Advocate*, 16 Feb. 1921, 17 April 1918; Champion *Chronicle*, 23, 30 Dec. 1920, 13 Jan. 1921; *Cleverville Pioneer Club, By-laws* (1949), 3–4, VA

45 Vulcan *Review*, 28 May 1912

46 Atherton, *Main Street*, 206–9; Norman Robertson, *The History of the County of Bruce* (Toronto: William Briggs 1906)

47 'Pioneer Days in a Prairie Setting,' unpub. ms, nd, book 13-U, MDK

48 Vulcan, *Wheat*, 347; Mary Boose, 'The Little Shack on the Prairie,' unpub. ms, nd, book 12-V, MDK

49 Vulcan, *Wheat*, 609; Dr Weston W. Upton to Margery Ramsay, 12 Apr. 1911, Margery Ramsay Papers, GAI

50 Gladys Lardlow to M.D. Keenan, 7 Nov. 1973, MDK; for a good analysis of western tall tales see Shirley Irene Paustian, 'Farm Life on the Great Plains as Represented in the Literature of Western America,' MA, Saskatchewan 1948, espec. 33–9.

51 Akitt interview, side 1, counter no 64, 72–4; Carmangay, *Bridging*, 47, 452; Margaret Hubka, interviewed at Carmangay, Feb. 1978. For similar attitudes across the west see Eliane Leslau Silverman, *The Last Best West: Women on the Alberta Frontier, 1880–1930* (Montreal: Eden Press 1984), 1–12.

52 See for example Vulcan *Advocate*, 29 Aug. 1923.

CHAPTER TWO: FARMS

1 High River *Times*, 2 Jan. 1913

2 Calculated from *Henderson's Alberta Gazetteer and Directory*, 1914; *Henderson's Province of Alberta Directory*, 1928–9; *Wrigley's Alberta Directory*, 1920, 1922

3 The statistics for Township 17-25-4 closely parallel those of a west Kansas county;

see Earl H. Bell, *The Culture of a Contemporary Rural Community: Sublette, Kansas* (Washington: u.s. Department of Agriculture, Bureau of Agricultural Economics, Rural Life Studies 2, 1942), 9. See also Don Harrison Doyle, 'Social Theory and New Communities,' *Western Historical Quarterly* 8, no 2 (April 1977): 155; James C. Malin, 'The Turnover of Farm Population in Kansas,' *Kansas Historical Quarterly* 4, no 4 (Nov. 1935). For similar patterns in a Saskatchewan community in the 1880s, see Lyle Dick, 'Factors Affecting Prairie Settlement: A Case Study of Abernathy, Saskatchewan in the 1880's,' *Canadian Historical Association Historical Papers* (1985): 23. Agreement is far from universal, however, as some scholars have found little change in mobility rates from decade to decade. See for example Richard G. Bremer, 'Patterns of Spatial Mobility: A Case Study of Nebraska Farmers, 1890–1970, *Agricultural History* 48, no 4 (Oct. 1974): 541.

4 Families of long residency were largely responsible for the organization, and much of the content, of community-written local histories. Generally, only their unpublished memoirs remain in a community, and usually only they or their descendants are available for interviews. Although scholars have always been aware of transient frontiersmen in western Canada, especially among Americans, they have generally regarded them as a small minority; see, for example, Paul F. Sharp, 'The American Farmer and the "Last Best West," ' *Agricultural History* 21, no 2 (Apr. 1947): 73.

5 C.H. 'Bud' Andrews, interviewed near Vulcan, Jan. 1978

6 G.H. Craig and J. Coke, *An Economic Study of Land Utilization in Southern Alberta* (Ottawa: Canadian Department of Agriculture, Economics Division, Marketing Service, Publication 610, Technical Bulletin 16, 1938), 17. Yasuo Okada, *Public Lands and Pioneer Farmers: Gage County, Nebraska, 1850–1900* (Tokyo: Keio Economic Society 1971), 91, discovered that only 60 per cent of the county's homesteaders held their land for more than ten years, and only 30 per cent for more than twenty years.

7 Otis Duncan, 'The Theory and Consequences of Mobility of Farm Population,' in Joseph J. Spengler and idem, eds., *Population Theory and Policy* (Glencoe, Ill.: Free Press 1956), espec. 418–19.

8 Many interviews and newspaper notices

9 Nanton *News*, 1 Sept. 1910

10 Will E. Finley to Editor, Hastings [Michigan] *Journal-Herald*, May 1913, repr. in Carmangay *Sun*, 30 May 1913

11 R.W. Murchie, *Agricultural Progress on the Prairie Frontier* (Toronto: Macmillan 1936), 73

12 Vulcan *Advocate*, 18 Jan., 23 Aug. 1922; most issues June to July 1914; most issues Apr. to June 1925; report of 1 June 1914 in monthly reports of D Division,

Macleod, Alta, RCMP Records, PAC; 'The History of Municipal Government of Vulcan by D.D. McQueen,' videotaped interview by County of Vulcan Educational Television 1975, CVO; J.T. Ferguson in *Acts and Proceedings of the General Assembly of the Presbyterian Church in Canada* (1914), 43, UCA; Vulcan and District Historical Society, *Wheat Country: A History of Vulcan and District* (Vulcan, Alta, 1973), 832

13 Mayor E. King to Deputy Minister of Municipal Affairs, 3 Dec. 1935, Town of Vulcan Correspondence, Municipality Correspondence Files, Alberta Department of Municipal Affairs Papers, PAA. The propensity for gambling is also confirmed by many newspapers articles, justice-of-the-peace files, and interviews.

14 Vulcan *Advocate*, 2 July 1919, 17 Oct. 1923; Alex Allan, 'Baseball Recollections,' magazine clipping, nd, book 21-M, MDK; Vulcan, *Wheat Country*, 791; Harvey Beaubier, interviewed at Champion, June 1978; Jack Dietz, interviewed near Milo, Apr. 1978

15 For American land values see John D. Hicks, 'The Western Middle West, 1900–1914,' *Agricultural History* 20, no 2 (Apr. 1946): 70; Marcus Lee Hansen, *The Mingling of the Canadian and American Peoples* (Toronto: Ryerson 1940), 219–35; Sharp, 'American Farmer,' 68. For the impact on Vulcan-area settlers see Carmangay *Sun, Dry Farming Congress Edition* (Carmangay, 21 Oct. 1912), MDK; Ken Miller, interviewed near Carmangay, May 1978.

16 See especially Sharp, 'American Farmer,' 68; and Hansen, *Mingling*, 219–35.

17 Rev. Evan Beechman, 'Script of Talk on the Early History of Milo,' unpub. ms, Mar. 1964, GAI; Mount Vernon [Iowa] *Hawkeye Record*, 22 May 1971, in book 15-D, MDK; Rena Burns, interviewed in Carmangay, Jan. 1978; Ken Miller interview. Statistics calculated from biographical files (see Appendix).

18 High River *Times*, 6 Dec. 1906; Vulcan *Advocate*, 17 Apr. 1918

19 This interpretation appears in many accounts but see Chester Martin, *'Dominion Lands' Policy*, part II of A.S. Morton, *History of Prairie Settlement* (Toronto: Macmillan 1938); and Donald M. Loveridge, 'The Settlement of the Rural Municipality of Sifton, 1881–1920,' MA, Manitoba 1977. Karel Denis Bicha, *The American Farmer and the Canadian West, 1896–1914* (Lawrence, Kan.: Coronado Press 1968), 140–1, even cites the high number of American settlers returning to the United States as evidence that they were poor settlers incapable of successfully competing for land.

20 Newspapers reported many gains of $3,000 to $6,000 per quarter-section between 1906 and 1913; see also Mounted Police reports, 10 Oct. 1912, 31 May 1913; Vulcan, *Wheat Country*, 747, 753; Champion History Committee, *Cleverville-Champion, 1905 to 1970, A History of Champion and Area* (Champion 1971?), 218.

21 High River *Times*, 4 Aug. 1910; Carmangay *Sun*, 23 Feb. 1911; Tom Sletto to Dale Keenan, 7 Dec. 1973, Correspondence file, MDK

22 Ray Allen Billington, *America's Frontier Heritage* (New York: Holt, Rinehart and Winston 1966), 29; Malin, 'Mobility,' 181

23 Carmangay and District History Book Committee, *Bridging the Years: Carmangay and District* (Carmangay 1968), 69; Municipal District of Royal 158 Minutes, 13 Nov. 1937, County of Vulcan No 2 Records, PAA

24 The literature is huge, but for a bibliographical overview see Robert P. Swierenga, 'Land Speculation and Its Impact on American Economic Growth and Welfare: A Historiographical Review,' *Western Historical Quarterly* 8, no 3 (July 1977): 283–302.

25 John L. Tyman, *By Section, Township and Range; Studies in Prairie Settlement* (Brandon: Assiniboine Historical Society 1972), argued that squatters' rights, reserves, bloc settlements, lands not fit for settlement, special colonization lands, and topography all interfered with the 'typical prairie township' to such a degree that a new visual image of dominion lands policy has to be drawn; see espec. 214.

26 Statistics calculated from homestead files, census reports, and other sources

27 Robert M. Finley, 'A Budgeting Approach to the Question of Homestead Size on the Plains,' *Agricultural History* 47, no 2 (Apr. 1968): 109–15

28 Thomas LeDuc, 'The Disposal of the Public Domain on the Trans-Mississippi Plains: Some Opportunities for Investigation,' *Agricultural History* 24, no 4 (Oct. 1950): 202; Martin, *Dominion Lands*, 507; Homer E. Socolofsky, 'Success and Failure in Nebraska Homesteading,' *Agricultural History* 47, no 2 (Apr. 1968): 106

29 Robin Barrie Mallett, 'Settlement Process and Land Use Change: Lethbridge-Medicine Hat Area,' MA, Alberta 1971, passim; R.R. Vogelesang, 'The Initial Agricultural Settlement of the Morinville-Westlock Area, Alberta,' MA, Alberta 1972, 48–73. Dick, 'Factors Affecting,' 11–28, has been more successful in isolating distance from a railway, land quality, and quick acquisition of additional land as ingredients for success, but admits that many other factors also played a role.

30 Vulcan, *Wheat Country*, 780; Champion, *Cleverville-Champion*, 210

31 Robert E. Ankli and Robert M. Litt, 'The Growth of Prairie Agriculture: Economic Considerations,' in Donald H. Akenson, ed., *Canadian Papers in Rural History*, vol. 1 (Gananoque, Ont.: Langdale Press 1978), 55; Lyle Dick, 'Estimates of Farm-Making Costs in Saskatchewan, 1882–1914,' *Prairie Forum* 6, no 2 (Fall 1981): 183–201; Irene M. Spry, 'The Cost of Making a Farm on the Prairies,' *Prairie Forum* 7, no 1 (Spring 1982): 95–100; Lyle Dick, 'A Reply to Professor Spry's Critique "The Cost of Making a Farm on the Prairies,"' *Prairie Forum* 7, no 1 (Spring 1982): 101

32 Jack Dietz interview; Harvey Beaubier interview; D.O. Jantzie, interviewed at Vulcan, May 1978; see also 'Sworn Statements,' in Homestead Files for Township 17-25-4, PAA.

33 Everett Dick, *The Lure of the Land: A Social History of the Public Lands from the Articles of Confederation to the New Deal* (Lincoln: University of Nebraska Press 1970), passim; Tyman, *By Section*, 141-3; Champion, *Cleverville-Champion*, 210, 216; Vulcan, *Wheat Country*, 746

34 Georgina H. Thomson, *Crocus and Meadowlark Country, Recollections of a Happy Childhood and Youth on a Homestead in Southern Alberta* (Edmonton: Institute of Applied Art 1963), 14; 'Declaration of Abandonment,' for NW 28-17-25-4, file 91565, Homestead Files, PAA. For the U.S. plains see Everett Dick, *The Sod House Frontier, 1854-1890: A Social History of the Northern Plains from the Creation of Kansas and Nebraska to the Admission of the Dakotas* (Lincoln, Neb.: Johnsen Publishing 1954), 128.

35 D.O. Jantzie interview; W. Wallace Miller, taped interview by Sharilyn Ingram and Barry Necyk near Carmangay, 5 Mar. 1973, side 2, counter no 388-90

36 For a list of twenty contractors of various specialties in the Vulcan area see Lethbridge *Herald*, 2 Apr. 1910, 53; architect plans of CPR farm buildings, 1913, GAI; Albert James Miller, 'The Trail to Alberta,' unpub. ms, 1957, book 9-K, MDK; Champion, *Cleverville-Champion*, 216; High River *Times*, 1 Mar. 1906.

37 Carmangay *Sun*, 25 Mar. 1910; Champion, *Cleverville-Champion*, 467. For statistics, consult the Appendix.

38 Rena Burns interview; Carrie McIntyre, interviewed at Vulcan, June 1978; Irma Plunkett, untitled, unpub. ms, nd, privately owned by Roy McIntyre, Vulcan; Nanton *News*, 16 Sept. 1909, 6 July 1905, 24 Mar. 1910; Vulcan, *Wheat Country*, 554, 850; Carmangay *Sun*, 26 Sept. 1913; W. Wallace Miller interview, side 1, counter no 784-5

39 Martin, *Dominion Lands*, 243

40 From its origin, the Calgary and Edmonton was closely associated with the CPR. The CPR leased the rail lines in 1892 and purchased the company outright in 1903, but the Calgary and Edmonton had already transferred its lands to a subsidiary, the Calgary and Edmonton Land Company, which employed Osler, Hammond, and Nanton Limited as its agent. Its land-sales policy differed somewhat from the CPR's: it advertised less, asked and received higher prices on terms less liberal, and sold more slowly. Technically, the CPR directly controlled only those Calgary and Edmonton lands selected after 1912, but by the time settlers arrived in the Vulcan area in 1904, it effectively controlled them all. It advertised them, recorded sales in its own ledgers, accepted the payments, and retained the profits. In addition the CPR enjoyed free access to those lands to construct 'ready-made' farms, the Kipp-Aldersyde rail line, and townsites in the Vulcan area. None the less, one complication arose. To escape property taxes, the Calgary and Edmonton had never taken title to their lands. Consequently, when a buyer delivered his final payment to the CPR and demanded title, the land office first had to issue a title in favour of the

Calgary and Edmonton Railway, cancel it, and then issue another in favour of the purchaser. For convenience, however, all railway lands in the Vulcan area may be regarded as CPR lands, subject to CPR selling policy. See Martin, *Dominion Lands*, 280, 288, 323, 330–1, 442; James B. Hedges, *The Federal Railway Land Subsidy Policy of Canada* (Cambridge: Harvard University Press 1934), 60, 105–6, 115–16, 122–3; idem, *Building the Canadian West: The Land Colonization Policies of the Canadian Pacific Railway* (New York: Macmillan 1939), 60, 106, 153–4; R.A. Christenson, 'The Calgary and Edmonton Railway and the Edmonton Bulletin,' MA, Alberta 1968, 226–7, 236–7, 240; CPR Land Sales Records, GAI; Land Titles, ALT.

41 Martin, *Dominion Lands*, 309–10; CPR Land Sales Records; Arthur Mitchell Company and A.J. Sayre correspondence, in Calgary Colonization Correspondence 1914–25, Land Sales Correspondence, CPR Papers, GAI

42 Canadian Pacific Railway Company, *Western Canada – Manitoba, Alberta, Saskatchewan – How to Reach It, How to Obtain Lands, How to Make a Home* (Winnipeg 1909 or 1910), 70–1; Martin, *Dominion Lands*, 314; Hedges, *Building*, 265–6

43 Loveridge, 'Settlement,' 69; Martin, *Dominion Lands*, 307; for Vulcan-area statistics see Appendix.

44 See Land Sales Correspondence, CPR Papers, GAI.

45 CPR Land Sales Records, esp. vol. 135, 56–7; Lethbridge *Herald*, 2 Apr. 1910, 57; *Alberta Farmer and Weekly Herald*, 1 May 1924; Ena Neilson newspaper-clipping scrapbooks, privately held by Ena Neilson, Carmangay; Carmangay, *Bridging*, 4, 27

46 Carmangay *Sun*, 21 Mar., 21 Nov. 1913; High River *Times*, 26 June 1913; Calgary *News Telegram*, 30 Apr. 1913; Nobleford-Monarch History Book Club, *Sons of Wind and Soil* (Nobleford, Alta, 1976), 296; Report of D Division, Macleod, Alberta, in Canada, *Sessional Papers* 28 (1914), 196

47 Champion, *Cleverville-Champion*, 520, 594; Carmangay *Sun*, 22 Dec. 1910; Vulcan *Advocate*, 2 Jan. 1918; Paul Frederick to Minister of Municipal Affairs, 17 Dec. 1917, and A.D. Fidler to John Perrie, 5 Jan. 1918, in Municipal District of Little Bow 98 Correspondence, Municipality Correspondence Files, Alberta Department of Municipal Affairs Papers, PAA; Washington School District 1431 Minutes, Jan. 1918, quoted in Carmangay, *Bridging*, 419

48 Vulcan *Review*, 28 May 1912; Nanton *News*, 10 Sept., 21 Nov. 1907; Vulcan *Advocate*, 1 Oct. 1913

49 See Appendix; also Carmangay *Sun*, 1 Dec. 1911; Albany [Oregon] *Register*, Jan. 1909, reprinted in Nanton *News*, 11 Feb. 1909.

50 Carmangay *Sun*, 17 Mar. 1911; Harvey Beaubier interview; William C. Wigley to M.D. Keenan, 17 Jan. 1974, book 15-E, MDK; Lloyd P. Jorgenson, 'Agricultural

Expansion into the Semi-arid Lands of the West North Central States During the
First World War,' *Agricultural History* 23, no 1 (Jan. 1949): 30–40; monthly
reports of D Division, 19 Mar. 1910, RCMP Records
51 Craig and Coke, *Economic Study*, 28; Ray Harrison Wellman, 'History, Ray and
Velma Wellman,' unpub. ms, 197–?, book 23-C, MDK; Carmangay, *Bridging*, 38

CHAPTER THREE: TOWNS

1 In somewhat altered form this chapter has been previously published as 'Boosting
the Small Prairie Town, 1904–1931: An Example from Southern Alberta,' in Alan
F.J. Artibise, ed., *Town and City: Aspects of Western Canadian Urban Development* (Regina: Canadian Plains Research Centre and the University of Regina
1981), 147–176.
2 Lewis Atherton, *Main Street on the Middle Border* (Bloomington, Ind.: Indiana
University Press 1954), 5–8; Donald W. Meinig, *The Great Columbia Plain: A
Historical Geography, 1805–1910* (Seattle: University of Washington Press 1968),
321–51
3 P.J. Haslam, 'History of Hearnleigh, Berrywater and Adjacent Districts,' unpub.
ms, nd, GAI; Lois Philpott Baebe, 'The Philpott Family – Early Days around
Champion,' unpub. ms, 197?, book 23-V, MDK.
4 Thompson carried $20,000 in stock and turned over $90,000 in business a year; see
High River *Times*, 1 Aug. 1906, 24 Oct. 1906, 2 July 1908. Between 1907 and
1911 the Brant Store maintained a net value of between $10,000 and $20,000; see
R.G. Dun and Co., *The Mercantile Agency Reference Book Containing Ratings*,
1907–11. Alberta Section, usually p 6, DBC. See also H.S. Parker, 'Brant, Alberta,'
unpub. ms, nd, GAI; H.H. Thompson, 'The Thompsons in Alberta,' unpub. ms,
nd, GAI; *Henderson's Manitoba and North West Territories Gazetteer and Directory*, 1905, 607; George B. Thompson, 'Memoirs of Charles H. Thompson and
Dorcas L. Thompson: Their Ancestors, Their Family and Their Descendants,'
unpub. ms, nd, GAI.
5 High River *Times*, 15 Mar., 22 Nov. 1906, 24 Oct. 1907, 30 July 1908; Nanton
News, 22 July 1909, 8 June 1905, 18 Jan. 1906; Claresholm *Review*, 11 Mar. 1909;
Carmangay and District History Book Committee, *Bridging the Years; Carmangay and District* (Carmangay 1968), 155
6 Carmangay *Sun, Dry Farming Congress Edition*, 21 Oct. 1912, MDK; Western
Canada Real Estate Company, *Some Truths of Carmangay, The Star Town of
Southern Alberta* (Toronto 1912), 15, MDK; CPR Land Sales records, vol. 135, 56–
7, GAI; *Henderson's*, 1905, 341; monthly reports of D Division, 7 Aug. 1907, RCMP
Records, PAC; *Farm and Ranch Review*, Jan. 1907, 37; Claresholm *Review*, 10
May, 11 Oct. 1907

7 Carmangay, *Bridging*, 6; Western Canada, *Some Truths*, 16; High River *Times*, 1 July 1909; CPR Land Sales Records, Carmangay, vol. 49, 62–79; Claresholm *Review*, 29 April, 6 May, 22 July 1909; monthly reports of D Division, 11 June 1909, 4; Nanton *News*, 13 May, 29 July 1909; Carmangay *Sun*, 24 May 1911

8 Champion History Committee, *Cleverville-Champion, 1905 to 1970: A History of Champion and Area* (Champion 1971?), 2; Harvey Beaubier, interviewed at Champion, June 1978; Nanton *News*, 3 Mar., 28 July 1910; Carmangay *Sun*, 15, 22 July 1910; Adrian A. Adams, untitled newspaper clipping, 1938, book 14-Y, MDK; photographs, book 14-L, MDK

9 Vulcan and District Historical Society, *Wheat Country: A History of Vulcan and District* (Vulcan 1973), 361; Nanton *News*, 15, 22 Sept. 1910; High River *Times*, 23 June 1910; Calgary *Herald*, 27 Apr. 1963; E.G. Luxton, 'Vulcan,' unpub. ms, 1958, Eleanor Luxton Papers, GAI; CPR Land Sales Records, Vulcan, vol. 49, 134–40

10 CPR Land Sales Records, Kirkcaldy, Brant, Ensign, vol. 49, 111–16, 145–8, 168–73; Parker, 'Brant'; High River *Times*, 10 June, 11 Aug., 6 Oct. 1910; 'Complaint of the Board of Trade of Ensign, Alberta,' Board of Railway Commissioners Transcripts of Hearings, 26 Nov. 1914, vol. 212, file 25119, 5881–5, PAC; Village of Champion Minutes, 8, 15 Jan. 1917, VChO. For poor railway-chosen townsites elsewhere in Alberta see Bodil J. Jensen, 'The County of Mountain View, 1890–1925,' MA, Alberta 1972, passim.

11 A typical description of the impact of the 1904 homestead rush appeared in the Nanton *News*, 7 April 1904: 'Last Saturday was a record breaker among the Nanton merchants for business, the streets being lined with teams from the country. Teams were lined up at the lumber yards awaiting their turns to get loaded up.' For quote see Vulcan, *Wheat Country*, 785.

12 J.W. Carson to C.R. Mitchell, 18 Oct. 1910, J.A. Lindsay File 886, Vulcan, Justices of the Peace Files, Attorney General of Alberta Records, PAA; newspaper clippings, book 2-L, MDK; Lethbridge *Herald*, 4 Jan. 1962; Carmangay *Sun*, 4, 21 Nov. 1913

13 Western Canada, *Some Truths*, 14; High River *Times*, 7 Sept. 1911; Champion Board of Trade, *Grain Golden Champion* (Champion 1912), 1, MDK

14 Carmangay Board of Trade to Deputy Minister of Public Works, June 1909, Village of Carmangay Correspondence; Vulcan Board of Trade to Deputy Minister of Public Works, 26 Nov. 1910, Deputy Minister of Public Works to A.A. Ballachey, 15 July 1912, Village of Vulcan Correspondence; all in Municipality Correspondence Files, Alberta Department of Municipal Affairs Papers, PAA; Village and Town Council of Carmangay Minutes, vol. 1, 26, VCaO; Claresholm *Review*, 24 June 1909; Carmangay *Sun*, 6 Aug. 1910; High River *Times*, 15 Mar. 1912; Vulcan *Review*, 19 Mar. 1912

15 Vulcan *Review*, 9 Mar. 1913; Champion *Chronicle*, 17 Mar. 1921; Village and Town Council of Carmangay Minutes, vol. 1, 177–8; Western Canada, *Some Truths*, 3

16 Vulcan *Advocate*, 11 June, 27 Aug. 1919

17 For promotional examples, see Calgary *Herald*, 'A Southern Alberta Town in the Making,' in *Why Go to Canada?* (Calgary, June 1910); Lethbridge *Herald*, 2 Apr. 1910, 57; Carmangay *Sun*, *Dry Farming Congress Edition*, 21 Oct. 1912, MDK. Original subscription lists have been lost; estimates of circulation are based on tax rolls, incidental sources, and information in Vulcan *Review*, 17 Dec. 1912; Calgary *Herald*, 10 Sept. 1936.

18 Canadian Pacific Railway Company, *Western Canada – Manitoba, Alberta, Saskatchewan – How to Reach it, How to Obtain Lands, How to Make a Home* (Winnipeg 1909 or 1910), 56; Western Canada, *Some Truths*; Carmangay *Sun*, 23 Feb. 1911; 13 Oct. 1916; Vulcan *Advocate*, 6 Sept. 1916; Harvey Beaubier interview. Efforts to locate this film and another made in 1925 have failed.

19 Vulcan *Advocate*, 10 Mar. 1915; Morton postcards, VA; Carmangay *Sun*, 24 Mar. 1911

20 Vulcan *Advocate*, 18 Aug. 1915, 7 July 1920, 22 June 1921; *Farm and Ranch Review*, 21 Oct. 1912, 882; Village and Town Council of Carmangay Minutes, vol. 1, 49, VCaO

21 Although local newspapers are loaded with information on semi-professional baseball, the best collection of materials were found in MDK, especially Alex Allan, 'Baseball Recollections,' book 21-M; John L. Edlund, 'Baseball in Claresholm as I Remember it From 1921–1928,' book 21-N; 'Early Years of the Champion Senior Baseball Teams in Summary,' book 22-L; Roy Orcutt, untitled, book 23-B. Also useful were Harvey Beaubier interview; John (Jack) D. Orr, taped interview by Sharilyn Ingram and Barry Necyk, at Suffield, Alta, 6 Apr. 1973, PAA. For a specific study of small-town professional baseball in the Great Plains see Gary Lucht, 'Scobey's Touring Pros: Wheat, Baseball, and Illicit Booze,' *Montana Magazine of Western History* 20, no 3 (Summer 1970): 88–93.

22 Vulcan *Advocate*, 20 Dec. 1922, 21, 28 Feb. 1923, 16 May 1923. More information and photographs appear in VA; Lethbridge *Herald*, *Fortieth Anniversary Progress and Development Edition*, 11 Dec. 1947, section 4, 9; Calgary *Herald*, 27 Apr. 1963; Vulcan, *Wheat Country*, 946–7

23 D.C. Jones interview, Calgary *Herald*, 27 Apr. 1963; see also 9 July 1927; A.B. Lowe and G.A. McKay, *The Tornadoes of Western Canada* (Ottawa: Canadian Department of Transport, Meteorological Branch 1962), 16. One of the Christmas cards is located in Adam Armey Papers, GAI.

24 Vulcan *Review*, 26 Mar. 1912; Carmangay *Sun*, *Dry Farming Congress Edition*, 21 Oct. 1912; Village and Town Council of Carmangay Minutes, vol. 1, 55–6

25 Western Canada, *Some Truths*, 9; Champion, *Grain Golden*, 15; Carmangay *Sun*, 18 Oct. 1912

26 Vulcan *Review*, 2 July 1912; Carmangay *Sun*, 1 Mar. 1912

27 Vulcan *Advocate*, 12 Feb., 21 May 1919; Municipal District of Royal 158 Minutes, County of Vulcan No. 2 Records, vol. 1, 93, PAA

28 Municipal District of Royal 158 Minutes, Apr. 1929; D.D. McQueen, 'The History of Municipal Government of Vulcan,' videotaped interview by Marg Weber (Vulcan: County of Vulcan Educational Television Production 1975), CVO; Vulcan, *Wheat Country*, 8

29 High River *Times*, 5 Sept. 1907; Nanton *News*, 22 Dec. 1910

30 Canada, *Sessional Papers*, 15 (1912), app. 1, 106; monthly reports of D Division, 24 Aug., 15 Nov. 1910, 15 June, 12 Dec. 1912; Thos. M. Melrose to Canon Hogbin, 14 Sept. 1911, Carmangay Anglican Church Papers, ACC; Thos. Little to Deputy Minister of Public Works, 20 Aug. 1909, Village of Carmangay Correspondence; Claresholm *Review*, 5, 26 Aug. 1909; Carmangay *Sun*, 18 Mar., 1 April, 29 Sept. 1910, 30 May 1913, 31 May 1912

31 Mrs Folk, 'A Eulogy of the Carmangay Ladies Aid From 1910 to 1935,' unpub. ms, 1935?, Carmangay Pastoral Charge Papers, United Church of Canada Records, PAA. Statistics calculated from 'accounting' data for all post offices in the Vulcan area in Canada, *Sessional Papers* 24, section C (1906–25); and from Mounted Police reports on grain shipments in *Sessional Papers* 28 (1914), 197

32 Directories list 99 businesses by 1914, but others opened that were not listed; see entries for Brant, Ensign, Vulcan, Kirkcaldy, Champion, and Carmangay in *Henderson's Alberta Gazetteer and Directory*, (1914); and R.G. Dun, *Mercantile Agency*, 1913, 1914; Carmangay *Sun*, 11 Aug. 1910. Those businesses not rated by R.G. Dun cannot be considered worthless. Sometimes a business with a high net value and credit rating disappeared from the listings only to return in a year or two with the same high net value and credit rating. Some businesses did not wish to be rated, and the company noted that the peculiar circumstances of many others precluded placing them in any specific category. Only locally owned businesses are considered here because the individual establishments of business chains were not rated independently of the parent companies that owned them.

33 Calculated from CPR Land Sales Records, vol. 49, 134–40; and High River *Times*, *Homeseekers Edition*, May 1912

34 Survey map, 11 Aug. 1910; A.V. Brown to Deputy Minister of Public Works, 23 Mar. 1911, both in Village of Champion Correspondence; see also Nanton *News*, 18 Aug. 1910; Carmangay *Sun*, 16 Feb., 1 May 1912; calculations based on Village of Champion Tax Rolls, 1914, VChO; and Village of Vulcan Tax Rolls, 1914, TVO

35 For the economic impact of railhead status on prairie towns generally see N.L. Whetten, 'The Social and Economic Structure of the Trade Centres in the Cana-

dian Prairie Provinces, With Special Reference to its Changes, 1910-1930,' PH D, Harvard 1932, 80. Many studies have noted that frontier towns often wielded a metropolitan influence far greater than their size would suggest; see Gilbert Stelter, 'The City and Westward Expansion: A Western Case Study,' *Western Historical Quarterly* 4, no 2 (April 1973): 190.

36 CPR Land Sales Records, vol. 49, 67; Carmangay *Sun*, 3 June 1910, 12 May 1911, 11 Oct. 1912; Village and Town Council of Carmangay Minutes, vol. 1, 134-5, 181; Village of Carmangay Assessment and Tax Rolls, 1912-14, VCAO; Carmangay Board of Trade to Minister of Public Works, 9 Nov. 1909, Village of Carmangay Correspondence

37 Canada, *Sessional Papers* 28 (1915), Report of D Division, 81; see also monthly reports of D Division, 31 July 1913, 1 Oct. 1914. The number of businesses in the Vulcan area listed by directories increased from 99 to only 111 between 1913 and 1920; see *Henderson's*, 1914; R.G. Dun, *Mercantile Agency*, 1914, 1920; *Wrigley's Alberta Directory*, 1920.

38 C. Rhodes to Deputy Minister of Municipal Affairs, 3 Apr., 9 Sept. 1936, Municipal District of Harmony 128 Correspondence, Municipality Correspondence Files, Alberta Department of Municipal Affairs Papers, PAA; Oldman River Regional Planning Commission, *Town of Vulcan, Alberta, Canada: General Plan, 1967; Revised Analysis of the Survey* (Lethbridge 1967), 25; Alberta Department of Public Works, *Annual Reports* (Edmonton 1916), 153-71

39 Carmangay *Sun*, many issues, 1911-23

40 Carmangay *Sun*, 1 Apr. 1910, 5 June 1914; 'Complaint of the Board of Trade of Ensign'; 'Restoration of Daily Day Service on CPR Lethbridge to Calgary via Aldersyde,' 10 July 1927, Board of Railway Commissioners Transcripts of Hearings, vol. 406; Village and Town Council of Carmangay Minutes, vol. 2, 257; MD of Royal 158 Minutes, 13 Jan. 1934; Vulcan *Advocate*, 20, 27 Dec. 1922

41 Although not particularly historical in approach, these problems are examined in detail by Peter Woroby, 'Functional Relationship Between Farm Population and Service Centres,' M SC, Manitoba 1957; Alan Roger Thirnbeck, 'An Analysis of a Group of Prairie Settlements North East of Calgary, Alberta,' MA, Calgary 1971; see also C.C. Zimmerman, *Farm Trade Centres in Minnesota, 1905-1920* (Minneapolis: University of Minnesota Agricultural Experimental Station, Bulletin 269) 10; C.A. Dawson and E.R. Young, *Pioneering in the Prairie Provinces; The Social Side of the Settlement Process* (Toronto: Macmillan 1940), 48-52; John C. Hudson, 'The Plains Country Town,' in Brian W. Blouet and Frederick C. Luebke, eds., *The Great Plains: Environment and Culture* (Lincoln: University of Nebraska Press 1979), 99-118.

42 Carle C. Zimmerman and Garry W. Moneo, *The Prairie Community System* (Ottawa: Agricultural Economics Research Council of Canada 1970), 7, notes that

prairie towns remained remarkably similar in function and even size between 1910
and 1940. Dawson, *Pioneering*, 293–7, shows that the proportion of various types
of businesses remained stable in towns under 1,000 population between 1910 and
1930, except for the rise of automotive businesses.

43 Calculated from R.G. Dun, *Mercantile Agency*, 1906–35; *Henderson's*, 1906–8,
1911, 1914, 1928–9; *Wrigley's*, 1920, 1922. Agricultural services would command a
slightly higher proportion of all businesses than indicated here if those farmers
who also provided them part time but were not listed in any directories could be
included in the total.

44 Whetten, 'Trade Centres,' 42–3, 93–6; Zimmerman, *Prairie Community*, 30. Nor
did general stores offer insignificant competition; by 1924 the Wengar General
Store at Eastway, northeast of Vulcan, operated with an 'estimated pecuniary
strength' of between $10,000 and $20,000. See R.G. Dun, *Mercantile Agency*,
Eastway entry, Sept. 1924.

45 Thorstein Veblen, 'The Country Town,' in *Absentee Ownership and Business
Enterprise in Recent Times: The Case of America* (1923; New York: Sentry Press
1964), 147–8; Dawson, *Pioneering*, 301–2; Whetten, 'Trade Centres,' 143–50. For
the impact of the automobile on a small Illinois town see Norman T. Molin,
Mobility and the Small Town 1900 to 1930 (Chicago: University of Chicago,
Department of Geography Research Paper 132, 1971). Vulcan *Advocate*, 3 Dec.
1913

46 Many issues of local newspapers; see also Canada, *Sessional Papers* 28 (1916), 71;
petition attached to By-law 11, and Revised By-law 11, Village of Champion By-
laws, VChO; By-law 53, Town of Vulcan By-laws, TVO; C.H. 'Bud' Andrews, interviewed near Vulcan, Jan. 1978

47 MD of Harmony 128 Minutes, 19 May 1927, County of Vulcan No. 2 Records,
PAA; Carmangay, *Bridging*, 351

48 Carmangay *Sun*, 1 Sept. 1910, 9 June 1911; Vulcan *Review*, 15 Oct. 1912, 25 Feb.
1913; Vulcan *Advocate*, 5 May 1920; Lethbridge *Herald*, *Alberta's Golden Jubilee
Edition*, 25 June 1955, section 3, 32; James Smart to A.G. Long, 27 Apr. 1917,
Calgary Fire Department Correspondence, GAI

49 For two examples see Jean Burnet, *Next-Year Country; A Study of Rural Social
Organization in Alberta* (Toronto: University of Toronto Press 1951), 55; Richard
G. Bremer, *Agricultural Change in an Urban Age: The Loup Country of
Nebraska, 1910–1970* (Lincoln: University of Nebraska Studies, New Series 51,
1976), 39. George Britnell, *The Wheat Economy* (Toronto: University of Toronto
Press 1939), 27–8, reports that Eaton's alone sold $22 million of goods in the prai-
rie provinces in 1930.

50 Village of Champion to Deputy Minister of Municipal Affairs, 29 Aug. 1913, 21
Apr. 1931, Village of Champion Correspondence; Town of Vulcan to Acting Min-

ister of Municipal Affairs, 1 June 1931, Town of Vulcan Correspondence; Carmangay *Sun*, 23 Mar. 1916; Nanton *News*, 10 Nov. 1915

51 Carmangay *Sun*, 23 Mar. 1916; Village and Town Council of Carmangay Minutes, vol. 2, 101, 199, 315; for a personal but interesting view of the aesthetic shortcomings of the prairie town see Ronald Rees, 'The Small Towns of Saskatchewan,' *Landscape* 18, no 3 (Fall 1969): 29–33.

52 Village and Town Council of Carmangay Minutes, vol. 1, 228; for other towns with the problem of undeveloped land see E.B. Mitchell, *In Western Canada before the War: A Study of Communities* (London: John Murray 1915), 13–14.

53 Eric J. Hanson, *Local Government in Alberta* (Toronto: McClelland and Stewart 1956), 40; for a general discussion of the single tax in prairie urban centres see Alan F.J. Artibise, 'Continuity and Change: Elites and Prairie Urban Development, 1914–1950,' in idem and Gilbert A. Stelter, eds., *The Usable Urban Past: Planning and Politics in the Modern Canadian City* (Toronto: Macmillan 1979), 130–54; Village and Town Council of Carmangay Minutes, vol. 1, 162, vol. 2, 38; Village and Town of Carmangay By-laws, 16A, 33, 37; Village and Town of Carmangay Tax Rolls, 1913; see also 'Statements of Unpaid Taxes,' in Village of Carmangay Correspondence, and Village of Champion Correspondence, 1911–13.

54 Hanson, *Local Government*, 39; Acting Deputy Minister of Municipal Affairs to Deputy Minister of Education, 24 July 1914; Town of Carmangay to Minister of Municipal Affairs, 22 Nov. 1913; W.L. McKinnon and Co. to Deputy Minister of Municipal Affairs, 7 June 1915; Town of Carmangay to Deputy Minister of Municipal Affairs, 14 Sept. 1921; all in Town of Carmangay Correspondence; Village and Town Council of Carmangay Minutes, vol. 1, 251–82, vol. 2, 83; Village of Champion Council Minutes, vol. 1, 60; Village of Vulcan Council Minutes, vol.1, 153; Village and Town of Carmangay Tax Rolls, 1914, 1923. For refusal to allow new subdivisions see Village and Town Council of Carmangay Minutes, vol. 1, 181, 216, 218; Carmangay *Sun*, 27 Mar. 1914. Through the Town Planning Act of 1913, the Department of Municipal Affairs could veto new subdivisions in any town; see David G. Bettison and others, *Urban Affairs in Alberta* (Edmonton: University of Alberta Press 1975), 18–23.

55 Village and Town of Carmangay Tax Rolls, Village of Champion Tax Rolls, Village and Town of Vulcan Tax Rolls, 1914–30; see also Vulcan *Advocate*, 31 Jan. 1923; many letters, 1931–3, Town of Vulcan Correspondence; Town of Carmangay to Deputy Minister of Municipal Affairs, 19 Sept. 1924; Secretary-Treasurer of Town of Carmangay to Deputy Minister of Municipal Affairs, 23 Mar. 1925, Town of Carmangay Correspondence; Village and Town Council of Carmangay Minutes, vol. 2, 329; Village of Champion to Deputy Minister of Municipal Affairs, 14 Mar. 1923; also 'Notice of Deputy Minister of Municipal Affairs,' 6 Apr. 1933, both in Village of Champion Correspondence; Village of Champion

Minutes, vol. 1, 219; MD of Royal 158 Minutes, vol. 2, 30 May 1925

56 C.A. Craig to Minister of Municipal Affairs, June 1937; Mayor E. King to Deputy Minister of Municipal Affairs, 11 Sept. 1934; Town of Vulcan to Supervisor of Tax Recovery, 20 Aug. 1937; all in Town of Vulcan Correspondence; Village of Champion to Deputy Minister of Municipal Affairs, 14 Sept. 1931, Village of Champion Correspondence; Village and Town of Carmangay By-laws, n, nos. 6 to 136; Village of Champion By-laws, nos. 29 to 73

57 Town of Carmangay to Deputy Minister of Municipal Affairs, 22 Mar. 1928; also 8 Dec. 1914; H.A. Kidney to Deputy Minister of Municipal Affairs, 21 Feb. 1933; all in Town of Carmangay Correspondence; Village of Champion Returning Officer to Deputy Minister of Municipal Affairs, Jan. 1917; Village of Champion to Minister of Municipal Affairs, 1 Jan. 1918; both in Village of Champion Correspondence; Town of Vulcan Returning Officer to Deputy Minister of Municipal Affairs, 10 Feb. 1923, Town of Vulcan Correspondence; inspectors' reports for Carmangay, 7 July 1927, 3 June 1931, 14 Dec. 1935, Alberta Department of Municipal Affairs Papers, PAA; Carmangay *Sun*, 2 Dec. 1916; Vulcan *Advocate*, 16 Sept. 1914, 29 June 1921; Champion *Chronicle*, 10 Dec. 1925

58 E.B. Nowers to Alex Cameron, 19 Nov. 1931; J.A. Kidney to Acting Deputy Minister of Municipal Affairs, 8 Apr. 1931; and dozens of other letters, 1929–32, all in Town of Vulcan Correspondence; see also much correspondence and many inspectors' reports for Vulcan and for the MD of Royal 158, 1929–33.

CHAPTER FOUR: CROP SELECTION

1 In slightly altered form this chapter has been previously published as 'A Mix-Up Over Mixed Farming: The Curious History of the Agricultural Diversification Movement in a Single Crop Area of Southern Alberta,' in David C. Jones and Ian MacPherson, eds., *Building Beyond the Homestead: Rural History on the Prairies* (Calgary: University of Calgary Press 1985), 179–206.

2 For the latest and most forceful example see John H. Thompson, ' "Permanently Wasteful but Immediately Profitable": Prairie Agriculture and the Great War,' *Canadian Historical Association Historical Papers* (1976): 193–206. James C. Malin, *Winter Wheat in the Golden Belt of Kansas: A Study in Adaptation to Sub-Humid Geographical Environment* (Lawrence: University of Kansas Press 1944), remains one of the few detailed studies of crop selection in the Great Plains.

3 Vulcan *Advocate*, 10 Aug. 1921; Carmangay *Sun*, 8 Nov. 1912; *Farm and Ranch Review*, 20 Oct. 1911, 667

4 Carmangay *Sun*, 29 Mar. 1912; Champion Board of Trade, *Grain Golden Champion* (Champion 1912), 6–8, MDK; Vulcan *Advocate*, 14 Dec. 1921; John Glambeck, 'Fruit on Alberta's Prairie,' nd, John Glambeck Papers, GAI. See also Can-

ada, *Sessional Papers* 28 (1915), 81; annual reports of D Division, 1 Oct. 1914, RCMP Records, PAC.

5 Saskatchewan, *Report of the Royal Commission of Inquiry into Farming Conditions* (1921), 55–65; 'Report of Agricultural Institute Meeting,' 1913, Carmangay Agricultural Society Papers, GAI; Vulcan *Advocate*, 25 April 1923, 1 Feb. 1922; High River *Times*, 1 April 1909; Carmangay *Sun*, 19 Jan. 1912

6 Carmangay *Sun*, 9 Feb. 1911, 31 Jan. 1913, 17 April 1915; Vulcan *Advocate*, 25 May 1921, 17 May 1922; Vulcan *Review*, 19 Nov. 1912; W.T. Easterbrook, *Farm Credit in Canada* (Toronto: University of Toronto Press 1938), 58, 110; E.B. Swindlehurst, *Alberta's Schools of Agriculture: A Brief History* (Edmonton: Alberta Department of Agriculture 1964?), 7

7 P.R. Talbot to Jas. McNaughton, 6 June 1924; also P.R. Talbot to C.H. Messenger, 22 Apr. 1924, both in Carmangay Agricultural Society Papers. For the number of competition categories and prizes see 'Returns: Re Exhibition Forms,' Carmangay Agricultural Society Papers, and Vulcan Agricultural Society Papers, GAI. For the role of fairs in promoting mixed farming generally see Grant MacEwan, *Agriculture on Parade* (Toronto: Thomas Nelson and Sons 1950); David C. Jones, *Midways, Judges, and Smooth-Tongued Fakirs: The Illustrated Story of Country Fairs in the Prairie West* (Saskatoon: Western Producer Prairie Books 1983). For further details of provincial encouragement of mixed farming see A.S. Morton, *History of Prairie Settlement* (Toronto: Macmillan 1938), 159–68; G.C. Church, 'Government Assistance to the Dairy Industry in Saskatchewan, 1906–1917,' *Saskatchewan History* 31, no 3 (Autumn 1978): 97–110.

8 For CPR support for mixed farming see monthly reports of D Division, 12 Dec. 1912, RCMP Records; High River *Times*, 21 Aug. 1913; Vulcan *Review*, 2 July 1912; Vulcan *Advocate*, 20 Aug. 1913, 18 Jan. 1922; Carmangay *Sun*, 22 July 1910.

9 Vulcan *Advocate*, 7 Apr. 1915; 20 Aug., 3 Sept. 1913; 21 Sept. 1921; 1 Aug. 1923; Carmangay *Sun*, many issues, 1913

10 Monthly reports of D Division, 12 Dec. 1912, RCMP Records; Alberta Department of Agriculture, *Annual Report*, 1912; Vulcan *Advocate*, 7 July 1915, 1 Feb. 1922; reports of Agricultural Institute meetings, 1913, 1915, Carmangay Agricultural Society Papers; Carmangay *Sun*, 9 Feb. 1923

11 For local farm organizations devoted to mixed farming see many letters, 1918, Vulcan Agricultural Society Papers; 'Returns: Re Exhibition Forms,' Carmangay Agricultural Society Papers; MD of Royal 158 Minutes, 30 July 1921, 5 Mar. 1923, County of Vulcan No. 2 Papers, PAA; Vulcan and District Historical Society, *Wheat Country: A History of Vulcan and District* (Vulcan 1973), 208; and many issues of local newspapers.

12 Carmangay *Sun*, 5 May 1911, and *Dry Farming Congress Edition*, 21 Oct. 1912,

MDK; J.W.G. Hathaway to S. Houlton, 17 June 1918, Anglican Church of Carmangay Correspondence, ACC; MD of Royal 158 Minutes, 22 Sept. 1936

13 John Proskie, 'Financial Progress of Settlers With Special Reference to the Vulcan-Lomond Area,' MA, Alberta 1937, 105; G.H. Craig and J. Coke, *An Economic Study of Land Utilization in Southern Alberta* (Ottawa: Canada, Department of Agriculture, Economics Division, Marketing Service, Publication 610, Technical Bulletin 16, 1938) 8; Varge Gilchrist, 'Changing Conditions on Specialized Wheat Farms in Southern Alberta,' *Economic Annalist* 25, no 1 (Feb. 1955): 16

14 *Farm and Ranch Review*, 5 Dec. 1911, 789; for a discussion of the complexities involved see 5 June 1915, 332. Although I discovered many of these problems through my own examination of farm records, inadequate bookkeeping is also discussed in the Vulcan *Advocate*, 19 May, 13 Oct. 1915; see also R.W. Murchie, *Agricultural Progress on the Prairie Frontier* (Toronto: Macmillan 1936), 74. As late as 1966 an economic study of the Vulcan area noted that few farmers kept records sufficiently detailed to permit close analysis of their business operations; see Hedline Menzies and Associates Ltd, *The County of Vulcan Agricultural Survey* (Vulcan: County of Vulcan No. 2, 1969), 5. In some years the dominion census reported some but not all farm expenses.

15 Thompson, 'Permanently Wasteful,' 200; *Farm and Ranch Review*, 5 Apr. 1915, 206

16 *Farm and Ranch Review*, 20 Dec. 1915, 727; see also 5 Apr. 1915; Ernest Boyce Ingles, 'Some Aspects of Dry Land Agriculture in the Canadian Prairies to 1925,' MA, Calgary 1973, 28.

17 *Farm and Ranch Review*, 5 Nov. 1915, 620; also 5 Apr. 1915, 192

18 J.N. Scobbie to editor, Vulcan *Advocate*, 8 Dec. 1920. Michael Bliss, *A Canadian Millionaire: The Life and Times of Sir Joseph Flavelle, Bart. 1858–1939* (Toronto: Macmillan 1978), 38–9, explains how highly specialized markets for pork products developed in the 1890s.

19 W.A. Mackintosh, *Agricultural Co-operation in Western Canada* (Kingston: Queen's University Press 1924), 3. The classical staple theory of Canadian economic development seems especially applicable to frontiers with good transportation systems to outside markets. On many land-locked, pre-railway frontiers, however, pioneers necessarily developed a more self-sufficient, if less prosperous, economy.

20 Magazine clipping, 24 Mar. 1926, in Ena Neilson newspaper-clipping scrapbooks, privately held by Ena Neilson, Carmangay; many interviews, especially Ena Neilson, interviewed at Carmangay, May 1978; Vulcan *Advocate*, 7 Apr. 1915

21 David H. Breen, *The Canadian Prairie West and the Ranching Frontier, 1874–1924* (Toronto: University of Toronto Press 1983), discusses these problems in many places.

22 Vulcan, *Wheat Country*, 575; Ethel Diemert to M.D. Keenan, 5 Feb. 1974, M.D. Keenan Correspondence Files, MDK; Carmangay *Sun*, 19 Jan. 1912. For many other problems concerning water supply see Nanton *News*, 4 May 1911; W. Wallace Miller, taped interview by Sharilyn Ingram and Barry Necyk, near Carmangay, 5 Mar. 1973, counter no 756, PAA; Carmangay and District History Book Committee, *Bridging the Years; Carmangay and District* (Carmangay 1968), 232; H.S. Parker to E.H. Farewell, 13 July 1926, Carmangay Colonization Board Correspondence, CPR Papers, GAI; John Stuart Marsh, 'The Chinook and its Geographic Significance in Southern Alberta,' M SC, Calgary 1965.

23 A classic study by Walter Prescott Webb, *The Great Plains* (New York: Ginn and Co. 1931), 348–65, 431–52, demonstrates how large-scale irrigation and traditional riparian law proved impractical in the region. For the problems in launching irrigation schemes in the Vulcan area see Carmangay *Sun*, 25 Mar. 1910; 12, 19 Nov. 1920; many issues of Lethbridge *Herald*, Feb., Mar. 1938; 24 Aug. 1938; 28 Feb. 1950; Village and Town Council of Carmangay Minutes, 7 Mar. 1919, VCaO.

24 For descriptions see monthly reports of D Division, 6 Feb., 6 Mar. 1907, RCMP Records; Jeanette (Norem) Godser to M.D. Keenan, nd, M.D. Keenan Correspondence Files, MDK; Rena Burns, interviewed at Carmangay, Jan. 1978; Harvey Beaubier, taped interview by Barry Necyk and Sharilyn Ingram at Champion, 8 Mar. 1973, side 1, counter no 342–5, PAA; Calgary *Herald*, 27 Apr. 1963. Breen, *Ranching Frontier*, 147, claims 50 per cent of all western range cattle died that winter. For huge losses in other years, see in particular Vulcan *Advocate*, 14 May 1919.

25 Many newspaper articles; many interviews, especially Ken Miller, interviewed near Carmangay, May 1978

26 For example, Vulcan *Review*, 19 Nov. 1912; Vulcan *Advocate*, 17 Dec. 1913, 28 Oct. 1914; Champion *Chronicle*, 13 Jan. 1920

27 'Daniel Evelyn McNiven,' unpub. notes of interview by Donald A. McNiven, 26 Jan. 1960, privately held by Donald A. McNiven, Vulcan; Nanton *News*, 15 June 1911; Mary Ann Carter, interviewed at Calgary, Mar. 1978

28 Vulcan *Advocate*, 13 Aug. 1913. For a discussion of this problem in Kansas see Earl H. Bell, *The Culture of a Contemporary Rural Community: Sublette, Kansas* (U.S. Department of Agriculture, Bureau of Agricultural Economics, Rural Life Studies 2, 1942), 43.

29 Ken Miller interview; lists of farm machinery in newspaper auction-sale notices seldom included manure spreaders; Alex Johnston, *To Serve Agriculture: The Lethbridge Research Station 1906–1976* (Ottawa: Canadian Department of Agriculture, Research Branch, Historical Series 9, 1977), 9. The experimental farm gradually introduced the bacteria to southern Alberta soils.

30 K.A. Gilles, 'Wheat as Human Food,' and Carle C. Zimmerman, 'The North American Plains to the Emergence of the Wheat Empire,' both in Carle C. Zim-

merman and Seth Russell, eds., *Symposium on the Great Plains of North America* (Fargo: North Dakota State University 1967), 82–3, 27; Henry George Latimer Strange, *A Short History of Prairie Agriculture* (Winnipeg: Searle Grain Company 1954), 36; James E. Shepherd, 'The Development of Wheat Production in the Pacific Northwest,' *Agricultural History* 49, no 1 (Jan. 1975): 265; Edward B. Swindlehurst, *Alberta Agriculture, A Short History* (Edmonton: Alberta Department of Agriculture 1967), 22; Roy L. Fowler, 'Chronology of Farming in the Okotoks-High River Area (1879–1930),' *Alberta Historical Review* 2, no 2 (1954): 25; Carmangay *Sun*, 13 Oct. 1910

31 Grant MacEwen, *Between the Red and the Rockies* (Toronto: University of Toronto Press 1952), 108–9, 194–7; idem, *Illustrated History of Western Canadian Agriculture* (Saskatoon: Western Producer Prairie Books 1980), 100–4; Bruce Proudfoot, 'Agriculture,' in P.J. Smith, ed., *Studies in Canadian Geography: The Prairie Provinces* (Toronto: University of Toronto Press 1972), 52; Strange, *Short History*, 33; Carmangay *Sun*, 16 Aug. 1912, 4 Apr. 1913; calculations from 'Cereal Map of Alberta; Showing Acreage Under Crop in Each Township in Wheat, Oats, Barley and Flax' (Canada, Department of the Interior, Railway Lands Branch, 2nd edn 1910)

32 Strange, *Short History*, 34; MacEwan, *Between*, 275–6; L.H. Newman, 'New Wheat Creations and Their Significance to Canada,' *Canadian Geographical Journal* 18, no 4 (Apr. 1939): 213–15; G.N. Irvine and J.A. Anderson, 'Some Technical Factors in the Production and Marketing of Canadian Wheat,' *Canadian Journal of Economics and Political Science* 25, no 4 (Nov. 1959): 441; A.W. Platt, 'Breeding Wheats for Sawfly Resistance,' *Canadian Geographical Journal* 33, no 3 (Sept. 1946): 141; Vulcan, *Wheat Country*, 945

33 In 1897 the CPR reduced freight rates in return for a government subsidy to build a line through the Crow's Nest Pass. By fixing rates on certain commodities, suspending them in 1919, and restoring them in 1922 only for grain and flour, the government increased the advantage to wheat growers. See W.L. Morton, *The Progressive Party in Canada* (Toronto: University of Toronto Press 1950), 156–7.

34 Ethel Diemert to M.D. Keenan, 5 Feb. 1974, M.D. Keenan Correspondence Files, MDK

35 Robert E. Ankli, 'Farm Income in the Great Plains and Canadian Prairies, 1920–1940,' *Agricultural History* 51, no 1 (Feb. 1977): 97; Vernon Ernest Nelson, 'An Analysis of the Effectiveness of Diversification as a Means of Overcoming the Instability Characteristic of Farm Income in Manitoba,' M SC, Manitoba 1959, argues that mixed farming did not stabilize incomes, largely because the prices of all farm commodities tended to rise and fall together.

36 James H. Gray, *Men against the Desert* (Saskatoon: Prairie Books, Modern Press 1967), 107, 144–5, notes that in many districts the cost of shipping in relief feed

and shipping cattle out exceeded the market value of the animals; George Spence, 'Soil and Water Conservation on the Prairies,' *Canadian Geographical Journal* 33 (Sept. 1946): 233; J.H. Rhodes to George Coote, 6 Feb. 1932, George Gibson Coote Papers, file 7, GAI; Vulcan, *Wheat Country*, 456; Ken Miller interview; Craig, *Economic Study*, 50.

37 Murchie, *Agricultural Progress*, 27, 45

38 These and other examples of farmers who raised unusually large quantities of secondary products were frequently recorded in local newspapers.

39 Edith Rowles, 'Bannock, Beans and Bacon: An Investigation of Pioneer Diets,' *Saskatchewan History* 5, no 1 (Winter 1952): 11; Carrie McIntyre, interviewed at Vulcan, June 1978

40 Jack Dietz, interviewed near Milo, Alta, Apr. 1978

41 Many memoirs and interviews; for a discussion of these issues see Vulcan *Advocate*, 25 Jan. 1922; for the west generally see Mary W.M. Hargreaves, 'Women in the Agricultural Settlement of the Northern Plains,' *Agricultural History* 50, no 1 (Jan. 1976): 184; and on North American farms generally see Newell L. Sims, *Elements of Rural Sociology*, 3rd edn (New York: Thomas Y. Crowell 1940), 431–3.

42 Greg Thomas and Ian Clarke, 'The Garrison Mentality and the Canadian West; the British-Canadian Response to Two Landscapes: The Fur Trade Post and the Ontarian Prairie Homestead,' *Prairie Forum* 4, no 1 (Spring 1979): 83–104; Ronald Rees, 'Nostalgic Reaction and the Canadian Prairie Landscape,' *Great Plains Quarterly* 2, no 3 (Summer 1982): 157–67

43 Vulcan *Advocate*, 19 July 1922; Glambeck, 'Fruit'

44 Canada, *Sessional Papers* 28 (1909), Report of D Division, Macleod, Alta, 60; examples of local landscaping projects and of institutional support for them are drawn from Carmangay, *Bridging*, 42; Canada, Department of the Interior, *Successful Tree Planters; Letters from All Over Prairie Provinces Tell of Benefits Derived from Plantations* (Ottawa 1910), 8; report of Agricultural Institute meeting, 1912, Carmangay Agricultural Society Papers; and many newspaper articles.

45 Canada, *Successful Tree Planters*, 7, 37; Carmangay, *Bridging*, 64–5; Carmangay *Sun*, 20 Dec. 1912

46 Vulcan *Advocate*, 16 Feb. 1921, 17 May 1922, 18 Mar. 1925. This pattern of migration is described in countless memoirs, but it may best be appreciated through the reading of western novels, particularly Wallace Stegner, *Angle of Repose* (New York: Doubleday 1971), where the hero precedes his wife to each of their many frontier homes. To appease what he considers her refined eastern tastes, he builds a huge frame house on an arid plane in Idaho, plants hundreds of trees and eastern rosebushes, and labours long hours to keep them alive.

47 In North Dakota, sod huts never represented as much as 50 per cent of the houses on the frontier, and by 1910 they virtually disappeared; see John Hudson, 'Fron-

tier Housing in North Dakota,' *North Dakota History* 42, no 4 (Fall 1975); 4–16. Lumber shacks also accounted for nearly all early housing in western Canada; see Thomas, 'Garrison,' 93; Kathleen M. Taggart, 'The First Shelter of Early Pioneers,' *Saskatchewan History* 11, no 3 (Autumn 1958): 81–3. Vulcan Catholic Church Minutes, 28 May 1917, Vulcan File, CDA. Other examples are taken from Carmangay, *Bridging*, 362; W. Wallace Miller interview, side 2, counter no 75–6; CPR, Department of Natural Resources, Development Branch, architect's plans of farm buildings, Calgary, 1913, GAI. See also photographs of Vulcan, Champion and Carmangay districts in MDK, GAI, and VA. For discussions of how little architectural styles changed as they moved across the west, see Ray Allen Billington, *America's Frontier Heritage* (New York: Holt, Rinehart and Winston 1966), 51; Fred B. Kniffen, 'Folk Housing: Key to Diffusion,' *Annals of the Association of American Geographers* 55, no 4 (Fall 1965): 549–77.

48 *Farm and Ranch Review*, 20 Nov. 1913, 971; Grant MacEwan, *Charles Noble: Guardian of the Soil* (Saskatoon: Western Producer Prairie Books 1983), 130; many interviews

49 Carmangay *Sun*, 3 Oct. 1913; 'Just a Farmer' to editor, *Farm and Ranch Review*, 5 Apr. 1915, 206; letter to editor, 20 Jan. 1913, 53

CHAPTER FIVE: TECHNIQUE

1 Elizabeth Akitt, taped interview by Sharilyn Ingram and Barry Necyk, at Carmangay, 9 Mar. 1973, side one, counter no 110–13, 144, PAA; D.H. Galbraith, 'Interview re the Political Nature of Alberta From 1917 to 1935,' taped interview by Una MacLean, at Calgary, 4 June 1962, GAI. For the virtues of American farmers see Robert W. Sloan, 'The Canadian West; Americanization or Canadianization,' *Alberta Historical Review* 16, no 1 (Winter 1968): 3–4; Paul F. Sharp, 'The American Farmer and the "Last Best West," ' *Agricultural History* 21, no 2 (Apr. 1947): 72; A.S. Morton, *History of Prairie Settlement* (Toronto: Macmillan 1938), 113; Harold Martin Troper, *Only Farmers Need Apply: Official Canadian Government Encouragement of Immigration from the United States, 1896–1911* (Toronto: Griffin House 1972), passim.

2 Mary W.M. Hargreaves, 'Dry Farming Alias Scientific Farming,' *Agricultural History* 22, no 1 (Jan. 1948): 30–40; idem, *Dry Farming in the Northern Great Plains, 1900–1925* (Cambridge: Harvard University Press 1957), 126–33; James F. Shepherd, 'The Development of Wheat Production in the Pacific Northwest,' *Agricultural History* 49, no 1 (Jan. 1975): 259–60

3 A. Galbraith to A.E. Quayle, 30 Apr. 1917, Carmangay Agricultural Society Papers, GAI

4 *Times* quoted in Carmangay *Sun*, 8 Apr. 1910; see also 13 Oct. 1916.

5 Herbert F. Lionberger, *Adoption of New Ideas and Practices: A Summary of the Research Dealing with the Acceptance of Technological Change in Agriculture, with Implications for Action in Facilitating Such Change* (Ames: Iowa State University Press 1960); Roy V. Scott, *The Reluctant Farmer: The Rise of Agricultural Extension to 1914* (Urbana: University of Illinois Press 1970); Allan G. Bogue, 'Pioneer Farmers and Innovation,' *Iowa Journal of History* 56 (Jan. 1958): 1–36

6 Monthly reports of D Division, 8 Feb. 1912, 7 Feb. 1913, RCMP Records, PAC; reports of Agricultural Institute meetings, 1911, 1914, in Carmangay Agricultural Society Papers; and 19 Dec. 1914, 1 Dec. 1916, in Vulcan Agricultural Society Papers, GAI; Alberta Department of Agriculture, annual reports, 1913–1925, usually 37–8

7 Carl Stettner, interviewed at Carmangay, Feb. 1978; also Ken Miller, interviewed near Carmangay, May 1978

8 C.H. 'Budd' Andrews, interviewed near Vulcan, Jan. 1978; report of Agricultural Institute meeting, 12 Dec. 1914, Vulcan Agricultural Society Papers; Vulcan *Advocate*, 9 Feb. 1916

9 Jack Dietz, interviewed near Milo, Apr. 1978

10 Ibid.; Canada, *Sessional Papers* 28 (1914), Report of D Division, Macleod, Alta, 195

11 A good description of ploughing techniques can be found in Saskatchewan, *Report of the Royal Commission of Inquiry Into Farming Conditions* (1921), 35.

12 W.E. Finley to editor, Hastings [Michigan] *Journal*, reprinted in Carmangay *Sun*, 3 Oct. 1913; also 9 May; see also *Farm and Ranch Review*, 5 April 1915, 202.

13 *Farm and Ranch Review*, 5 June 1915, 334; Carmangay *Sun*, 19 Jan. 1912, 16 Feb. 1911

14 Hargreaves, *Dry Farming*, passim. Important sections of this long book are condensed in 'Dry Farming Alias,' and 'The Dry Farming Movement in Retrospect,' *Agricultural History* 51, no 1 (Jan. 1977): 149–65.

15 Hargreaves, *Dry Farming*, 83–125; Donald W. Meinig, *The Great Columbia Plain: A Historical Geography, 1805–1910* (Seattle: University of Washington Press 1968), 411–13

16 Seager Wheeler, *Seager Wheeler's Book on Profitable Grain Growing* (Winnipeg: Grain Growers' Guide Ltd 1919); John Bracken, *Crop Production in Western Canada* (Winnipeg: Grain Growers' Guide Ltd 1920); idem, *Dry Farming in Western Canada* (Winnipeg: Grain Growers' Guide Ltd 1921); Allan R. Turner, 'W.R. Motherwell and Agricultural Education, 1905–1918,' *Saskatchewan History* 12, no 3 (Autumn 1959): 88–90; James McCaig, *Alberta: A Survey of the Topography, Climate, Resources, Industries, Transportation and Communication, and Institutional Services of the Province of Alberta* (Edmonton: Alberta Department

of Agriculture 1919), 26–7; *Grain Growers' Guide*, 20 Sept. 1910; Alex Johnson, *To Serve Agriculture: The Lethbridge Research Station 1906–1976* (Ottawa: Canadian Department of Agriculture, Research Branch, Historical Series 9, 1977), 19

17 Claresholm *Review*, 28 June 1907; Carmangay *Sun*, 16 Feb. 1911; 23 Aug., 1 Nov. 1912; Johnston, *To Serve Agriculture*, 19; Vulcan and District Historical Society, *Wheat Country: A History of Vulcan and District* (Vulcan 1973), 365. For variations associated with Campbell's name see Hargreaves, 'Dry Farming Alias,' 45.

18 Scott, *The Reluctant Farmer*, passim; Frederick C. Fliegel and Joseph E. Kirlin, 'Attributes of Innovations as Factors in Diffusion,' *American Journal of Sociology* 72, no 3 (Nov. 1966): 235–48; Vulcan *Review*, 2 Apr. 1912

19 W. Wallace Miller, taped interview by Sharilyn Ingram and Barry Necyk, near Carmangay, 5 Mar. 1973, side one, counter no 756, PAA; Carmangay *Sun*, 24 Nov. 1910; D.O. Jantzie, interviewed at Vulcan, May 1978; *Alberta Farmer and Weekly Herald*, 1 May 1924; Vulcan *Advocate*, 22 Oct. 1913, 24 Apr. 1918; see also 12 Jan. 1921, 3 May 1922.

20 Hargreaves, 'Dry Farming Alias,' 52; James H. Gray, *Men against the Desert* (Saskatoon: Prairie Books, Modern Press 1967), 71; Saskatchewan, *Farming Conditions*, 61–4; *Farm and Ranch Review*, 5 May 1911, 281; Johnston, *To Serve Agriculture*, 22; Asael E. Palmer, *When the Winds Came: How the Battle Against Soil Drifting Was Won on the Canadian Prairies* (Lethbridge 1968?), 15

21 Gray, *Men Against*, 110–16, 232; Palmer, *When the Winds Came*, 15, 35; George Spence, 'Soil and Water Conservation on the Prairies,' *Canadian Geographical Journal* 35, no 5 (Nov. 1947): 232; Vulcan *Advocate*, 4 Oct. 1922

22 Meinig, *The Great Columbia*, 394; *Farm and Ranch Review*, 20 Mar. 1914, 206; Anton Hansen to Glenbow Foundation, 6 May, 9 June 1974, Anton Hansen Papers, GAI; Champion *Chronicle*, 3 Feb. 1921; Carmangay and District History Book Committee, *Bridging the Years; Carmangay and District* (Carmangay 1968), 397; Edward B. Swindlehurst, *Alberta Agriculture, A Short History* (Edmonton: Alberta Department of Agriculture 1967), 68; R. Barry Rogers and D. Tracy Anderson, 'The History, Development and Use of Tillage and Cultivation Implements in Alberta Agriculture, 1870–1955,' unpub. ms, 1985, 122–73, Reynolds-Alberta Museum, Wetaskiwin, Alta

23 H.H. Ingram to M.D. Keenan, 12 June 1975, Correspondence Files, MDK; Gray, *Men against*, 39; Vulcan *Advocate*, 10, 24 May, 26 July 1922; MD of Royal 158 Minutes, County of Vulcan No 2 Records, vol. 2, 13 June 1938; H.G. Crawford, 'Insects As a Factor in Wheat Production On the Canadian Prairies,' *Canadian Geographical Journal* 18, no 4 (Apr. 1939): 223–4. The Dutch at Monarch are usually given credit for the introduction of strip farming to western Canada; see

Grant MacEwan, *Between the Red and the Rockies* (Toronto: University of Toronto Press 1952), 271–2; Swindlehurst, *Alberta Agriculture*, 67–8; Johnston, *To Serve Agriculture*, 22; Palmer, *When the Winds Came*, 12–13; Ken Miller interview; Jack Dietz interview; Lethbridge *Herald*, 16 Apr. 1938.

24 Johnston, *To Serve Agriculture*, 22; Lethbridge *Herald*, *Alberta's Golden Jubilee Edition*, 25 June 1955, 2nd section, 10; Gray, *Men against*, 72–81; Alberta Department of Agriculture, *A Report on the Rehabilitation of the Dry Areas of Alberta and Crop Insurance 1935–36* (Edmonton 1936), 28–30, demonstrates the provincial government's conversion to the new techniques. Palmer, *When the Winds Came*, 36

25 R.A. Stutt, 'Changes in Extent and Effect of Mechanization on Saskatchewan Farms,' *Economic Annalist* 14 (Aug. 1944): 59–60

26 Vulcan *Review*, 4 June 1912

27 The *Census of Canada* and the *Census of the Prairie Provinces* report certain farm expenses for some years but provide no comprehensive data. For prosperity see monthly reports of D Division, 1 Nov., 31 Aug. 1913; 1 Dec. 1916; and Annual Report 1911, 64; all in RCMP Records; Canada *Sessional Papers* 28, Report of D Division, Macleod, Alta (1909), 60; (1912), 64; (1914), 196; (1916), 73; D.O. Jantzie interview; Vulcan *Advocate*, 3 Nov. 1915; 10 Oct. 1923; Carmangay *Sun*, 13 Oct. 1916; Lethbridge *Herald*, 14 Apr. 1917; Vulcan, *Wheat Country*, 719; Champion History Committee, *Cleverville-Champion, 1905 to 1970, A History of Champion and Area* (Champion 1971), 598.

28 George Geddes to editor, St. Thomas [Ontario] *Times-Journal*, reprinted in Vulcan *Advocate*, 27 Sept. 1922; W.A. Mackintosh, *Economic Problems of the Prairie Provinces* (Toronto: Macmillan 1936), 6

29 G.H. Craig and J. Coke, *An Economic Study of Land Utilization in Southern Alberta* (Canada, Department of Agriculture, Marketing Service, Economics Division, Publication 610, Technical Bulletin 16, 1938), 54

30 Palmer, *When the Winds Came*, 30–1; Lethbridge *Herald*, *Fortieth Anniversary Progress and Development Edition*, 2nd edition, 37; Gray, *Men Against*, 10

31 John Proskie, 'Financial Progress of Settlers with Special Reference to the Vulcan-Lomond Area,' MA, Alberta 1937, 105–7; Lethbridge *Herald*, 25 May 1938; H.H. Bennett, 'Emergency and Permanent Control of Wind Erosion in the Great Plains,' *Scientific Monthly* 47 (Nov. 1938): 391; J. Fergus Grant, 'Implementing Agriculture,' *Canadian Geographical Journal* 18, no 4 (Apr. 1939): 173–5; Vulcan *Advocate*, 9 Oct. 1918

32 Palmer, *When the Winds Came*, 11; Canada, Department of Agriculture, Division of Field Husbandry, Soils, and Agricultural Engineering, Experimental Farms Service, Soil Research Laboratory, *Soil Moisture, Wind Erosion and Fertility of Some Canadian Prairie Soils* (Swift Current, Sask.: Publication 819, Technical

Bulletin 71, 1949), 39–66; Alberta, *Report on Rehabilitation*, 31

33 Roy Potter, formerly of the Western Development Museum, Saskatoon, interviewed at Calgary, June 1979

34 Many interviews confirmed these complaints for the Vulcan area; for complaints about these implements in western Canada generally see Palmer, *When the Winds Came*, 15; Gray, *Men against*, 75–76, 229.

35 Many interviews; most of these techniques are still used today.

36 Canada, Department of Marine and Fisheries, Meteorological Service of Canada (later Meteorological Division of Air Services), annual meteorological summaries, Calgary and Lethbridge

37 Ibid. Although rainfall is the most important determinant of yield, it is not the only one; the extent of crop damage caused by an enormous number of other hazards also affects it.

38 J.G. Nelson, 'Some Reflections on Man's Impact on the Landscape of the Canadian Prairies and Nearby Areas,' in P.J. Smith, ed., *Studies in Canadian Geography: The Prairie Provinces* (Toronto: University of Toronto Press 1972), 45; Vulcan *Advocate*, 24 Mar., 28 July 1920

39 Roy Jackson Fletcher, 'The Climate of Southern Alberta,' in Frank J. Jankunis, ed., *Southern Alberta: A Regional Perspective* (Lethbridge: University of Lethbridge 1972), 29–30; Rena Burns, taped interview by Barry Necyk and Sharilyn Ingram at Carmangay, 7 Mar. 1973, side one, counter no 492–3, PAA; Harvey Beaubier, taped interview by Barry Necyk and Sharilyn Ingram, at Champion, 8 Mar. 1973, side one, counter no 49–50, PAA

40 Vulcan *Advocate*, 17 Dec. 1913, 25 June 1919, 4 Oct. 1922; W. Wallace Miller interview, side one, counter no 303–5; Nanton *News*, 16 Nov. 1908; High River *Times*, 23 April 1908; Champion, *Cleverville-Champion*, 306

41 Nanton *News*, 8 Feb. 1906; Vulcan *Advocate*, 11 June 1919; Mr and Mrs Otto Mueller, untitled, unpub. ms, 197?, book 23-D, MDK; Carmangay, *Bridging*, 54

42 Fletcher, 'The Climate,' 33; Alberta, Department of Economic Affairs, *Economic Survey of Vulcan, Alberta* (Edmonton 1958), 2; Carmangay *Sun*, 12 Jan. 1911; Vulcan *Advocate*, 28 Feb. 1923

43 Based on weather reports in local newspapers and Mounted Police observations in monthly reports of D Division, 1910, 1915

44 Carmangay *Sun*, 29 July 1915; Vulcan *Advocate*, 3 Nov. 1915; 11 July, 10 Oct. 1923. From 1905 to 1911 the Alberta government offered hail insurance under an old territorial plan, and in 1912 private companies began offering it. From 1914 to 1918 many municipal districts ran compulsory insurance programs; from 1918 to 1936 many ran voluntary schemes. Meanwhile, the Alberta government launched its Hail Insurance Board in 1919. See A. Paul, 'The Development of Investigations into Hail Occurrence,' *Alberta Geographer* 3 (1966–7): 7; Alberta Hail Insurance

Board, *A Short History of the Development of Hail Insurance in Alberta* (Calgary 1945), 3–6.

45 *Alberta Farmer and Weekly Herald*, 1 May 1924

46 Arleigh H. Laycock, 'The Diversity of the Physical Landscape,' in Smith, *Prairie Provinces*, 1–32. Map 9 suggests lower long-term yields for the area generally than does Figure 16 because it is based on the years from 1925 to 1950, a period lower in productivity than the 1905–35 period portrayed in Figure 16. Carmangay *Sun*, 3 Sept. 1914

47 Because of the lack of weather stations within the Vulcan area consistently in use over long periods of time, climatic differences within the area are difficult to document. None the less, they are very real, as any long-time resident of the area knows. An attempt has been made here, however, to document them from more general environmental studies. For rainfall differences within the area see L.J. Chapman and D.M. Brown, *The Climates of Canada for Agriculture* (Ottawa: Canadian Department of Forestry and Rural Development, Canada Land Inventory Report No 3, 1966), figs. 4, 9, 15; Richmond W. Longley, *Climatic Maps for Alberta by the Alberta Climatological Committee* (Edmonton: University of Alberta, Department of Geography 1968), map 13. See also W.A. Mackintosh, *Prairie Settlement: The Geographic Setting* (Toronto: Macmillan 1934), 172. For variability across the prairies generally see A.K. Chakravarti, 'Precipitation Deficiency Patterns in the Canadian Prairies, 1921 to 1970,' *Prairie Forum* 1, no 2 (Nov. 1976): 95–110; Fletcher, 'The Climate,' 28–9, 32; Alberta, 'Alberta Resource Maps,' 1971–2; R.W. Longley, 'The Frequency of Chinooks in Alberta,' *Alberta Geographer* no 3 (1966–7), 20–3; John Stuart Marsh, 'The Chinook and Its Geographic Significance in Southern Alberta,' MS, Calgary 1965, 49–53.

48 C.B. Beatty, 'Geomorphology, Geology, and Non-Agricultural Resources,' in Jankunis, *Southern Alberta*, 11–12; James A. Robertson, 'The Soils of the Interior Plains of Western Canada,' *Prairie Forum* 9, no 2 (Fall 1984): 217–30

49 The inventory considers many topographical features, including slope, stoniness, and drainage, as well as soil depth, permeability, chemical fertility, moisture-holding capacity, water-table depth, seepage, salinity, rainfall, erosion damage, and other special adverse soil conditions. It considers the productive potential of the soil under adequate management practices, mechanized cultivation, and assumes that all feasible improvements have or can be made by individual farmers. It does not, however, depict the overall profitability of different soil types, for it does not consider distance from market, quality of roads, location, farm size, type of ownership, cultural patterns, the skill or resources of the farmer, market price, or crop damage from storms, diseases, insects, or animals. See D.F. Symington, 'Land Use in Canada: The Canada Land Inventory,' *Canadian Geographical Journal* 76, no 2 (Feb. 1968): 44–56; and the lengthy 'Descriptive Legend' on Canada,

Department of Agriculture, Research Branch, Soil Research Institute, Canada Land Inventory Map Sheet, 'Soil Capability for Agriculture,' Gleichen Sheet 82 I, 1969.

50 Proskie, 'Financial Progress,' 199; for the relationship between soil type and farm prosperity in the area generally see Craig, *Economic Study*, 53, 68. Neil MacDougal Campbell, 'A Case Study in Economic Development: The Bonnyville and Red Deer Farming Communities,' MS, Alberta 1966, demonstrates that soil quality was the most important factor in explaining differences in prosperity between the two communities.

51 Terry G. Jordan, 'Between the Forest and the Prairie,' *Agricultural History* 38, no 4 (Oct. 1964): 205–16; T.R. Weir, 'Pioneer Settlement of Southwest Manitoba, 1879–1901,' *Canadian Geographer* 8, no 2 (1964): 68

52 Mackintosh, *Prairie Settlement*, 55; Donald M. Loveridge, 'The Settlement of the Rural Municipality of Sifton, 1881–1920, MA, Manitoba 1977, 204–5, argues that settlers in Sifton, Manitoba, picked the best lands rather than those close to the railway, but given the state of soil knowledge, they must have done so inadvertently. Harvey Beaubier interview; Carl Stettner interview; Carmangay, *Bridging*, 223; Vulcan *Review*, 19 Nov. 1912; Vulcan *Advocate*, 29 Oct. 1913; High River *Times*, 7 Jan. 1909. P.L. McCormick, 'Transportation and Settlement: Problems in the Expansion of the Frontier of Saskatchewan and Assiniboia in 1904,' *Prairie Forum* 5, no 1 (Spring 1980), espec. 5; and Lyle Dick, 'Factors Affecting Prairie Settlement: A Case Study of Abernathy, Saskatchewan in the 1880's,' *Canadian Historical Association Historical Papers* (1985): 18–19, strongly argue for the necessity of being close to a railway, but important exceptions existed, as the following paragraph demonstrates.

53 Wilfred Eggleston, 'The Old Homestead: Romance and Reality,' in Howard Palmer, ed., *The Settlement of the West* (Calgary: University of Calgary and Comprint Publishing 1977), 115

54 Carmangay *Sun*, 29 Dec. 1911; Carmangay, *Bridging*, 396; Albert James Miller, 'The Trail to Alberta,' unpub. ms, 1957, book 9-K, MDK; Champion, *Cleverville-Champion*, 216; for homestead locators in Saskatchewan see Allan R. Turner, 'Pioneering Farming Experiences,' *Saskatchewan History* 8, no 2 (Spring 1955): 43; B.B. Peel, 'R.M. 45: The Social History of a Rural Municipality,' MA, Saskatchewan 1946, 146.

55 F.A. Wyatt and J.D. Newton, 'Social Survey of McLeod Sheet' (map), University of Alberta Extension Bulletin No 11, Sept. 1925; Oldman River Regional Planning Commission, *Town of Vulcan, Alberta, Canada: General Plan, 1967; Revised Analysis of the Survey* (Lethbridge 1967), 19; Carrie McIntyre, interviewed at Vulcan, June 1978; see also Carmangay, *Bridging*, 337.

56 Craig, *Economic Study*, 13; Alberta, *Report on the Rehabilitation*, 28; E.S.

Archibald and William Dickson, 'Research in Prairie Farm Rehabilitation,' *Canadian Geographical Journal* 28, no 2 (Feb. 1944): 58; Sami Ahmad Sobhi Ibrahim, 'An Assessment of Wind Erosion Damage to Alberta Soils,' M SC, Alberta 1961, 4–6. Mixtures of clay and sand form and hold clods much better under drought conditions than either soil will do on its own. See also Bennett, 'Emergency,' 397–8; Canada, *Soil Moisture*, 39–63.

57 R.E. English, 'Early Explorations and the Reports of the Surveyor General of Canada, with Reference to Agricultural Possibilities in Alberta's Dry Area,' unpub. ms 1937, O.S. Longman Papers, 5, 6, GAI; John L. Tyman, 'Subjective Surveyors: The Appraisal of Farm Lands in Western Canada, 1870–1930,' in Brian W. Blouet and Merlin P. Lawson, eds., *Images of the Plains: The Role of Human Nature in Settlement* (Lincoln: University of Nebraska Press 1975), 75–100. See also Dominion Lands Office, 'Township Plans of the Canadian West' (maps), vols. 138–45, 1884–1920, PAC; Calgary *Herald*, 10 Feb. 1913, 15; Carmangay *Sun*, 4 Mar. 1910; Archibald, 'Research in,' 54; Wyatt, 'Social Survey.' The long, tedious process of accurately assessing soil quality can be followed in J.A. McKeague and P.C. Stobbe, *History of Soil Survey in Canada, 1914–1975* (Ottawa: Canadian Department of Agriculture, Research Branch, Soil Research Institute, Historical Series No 11, 1978).

58 Craig, *Economic Study*, 16, 20, 72–3

59 Proskie, 'Financial Progress,' 110; Hedlin Menzies and Associates Ltd, *The County of Vulcan Agricultural Survey* (Calgary 1969), 48; Craig, *Economic Study*, 53–4; Paul, 'The Development of Investigations,' 5; idem, 'An Analysis of Surface Hailfall Reports in Southern Alberta,' *Alberta Geographer* 5 (1968–9): 45; 'Descriptive Legend,' Gleichen Sheet

60 Champion, *Cleverville-Champion*, 320; Grace Lillian Powell, 'The Relationship of Physiography to the Hail Distribution Pattern in Central and Southern Alberta,' MS, Alberta 1961, 14, 18–19, 51–4, and app. 14

61 Fred A. Shannon, *The Farmer's Last Frontier: Agriculture, 1860–1897* (New York: Harper and Row 1945), 9. The role of luck in selecting good land on the southern Alberta frontier is stressed by Proskie, 'Financial Progress,' 79; and by Robin Barrie Mallett, 'Settlement Process and Land Use Change: Lethbridge-Medicine Hat Area,' MA, Alberta 1971, 22. One geographer even claims that luck guided the purchase of good land throughout most of Canada before 1950; see Symington, 'Land Use,' 48.

62 'Descriptive Legend,' Gleichen Sheet

63 Carl Stettner interview; Ken Miller interview; Grant MacEwan, *Charles Noble: Guardian of the Soil* (Saskatoon: Western Producer Prairie Books 1983), 160–71; Rogers, 'The History,' 163–6; Proskie, 'Financial Progress,' 105–7; Lethbridge *Herald*, Jan. 1938, 15 May 1939

64 Jack Dietz interview; Ken Miller interview; Paul W. Riegert, 'Insects on the Canadian Plains,' *Prairie Forum* 9, no 2 (Fall 1984): 331; Alberta, *Report on the Rehabilitation*, 31; Johnston, *To Serve Agriculture*, 27; Gray, *Men against*, 46–7; Palmer, *When the Winds Came*, 39

65 Vulcan *Advocate*, 23 Apr. 1919; Alberta Department of Agriculture, *Annual Reports* (1920), 129; F.E. Hawkins to Alex Galbraith, 9 July 1919, Vulcan Agricultural Society Papers; 'Liquidation Files,' Vulcan Agricultural Society Papers, 1931, and Carmangay Agricultural Society Papers, 1936

66 The Lethbridge Experimental Farm and other agencies placed demonstration plots in places like the Vulcan area to overcome that fear and take their findings closer to farmers; see Johnston, *To Serve Agriculture*, 17.

67 W. Wallace Miller interview, side one, counter no 286

CHAPTER SIX: FARM SIZE

1 This view springs largely from Chester Martin, *'Dominion Lands' Policy*, pt II of A.S. Morton, *History of Prairie Settlements* (Toronto: Macmillan 1938), 415, 506, passim, and may be found, with minor variations, in most general descriptions of western settlement and agriculture.

2 David Gagan, *Hopeful Travellers: Families, Land, and Social Change in Mid-Victorian Peel County, Canada West* (Toronto: University of Toronto Press 1981), 48–9; John W. Bennett, *Northern Plainsmen: Adaptive Strategy and Agrarian Life* (Chicago: Aldine Publishing 1969), 228–31; idem and Seena B. Kohl, 'Characterological, Strategic, and Institutional Interpretations of Prairie Settlement,' in Anthony W. Rasporich, ed., *Western Canada Past and Present* (Calgary: McClelland and Stewart West 1975), 21

3 Morton Rothstein, 'The Big Farm: Abundance and Scale in American Agriculture,' *Agricultural History* 49, no 4 (Oct. 1975): 585; Paul Wallace Gates, 'Large-Scale Farming in Illinois, 1850 to 1870,' *Agricultural History* 6, no 1 (Jan. 1932): 14–25; Harold E. Briggs, 'Early Bonanza Farming in the Red River Valley of the North,' *Agricultural History* 6, no 1 (Jan. 1932): 26–37; Stanley Norman Murray, *The Valley Comes of Age: A History of Agriculture in the Valley of the Red River of the North, 1812–1920* (Fargo: North Dakota Institute for Regional Studies 1967), 131–8; Hiram M. Drache, *The Day of the Bonanza, A History of Bonanza Farming in the Red River Valley of the North* (Fargo: North Dakota Institute for Regional Studies 1964); idem, 'Bonanza Farming in the Red River Valley,' *Historical and Scientific Society of Manitoba Transactions*, III, no 24 (1967–8): 53–64; E.C. Morgan, 'The Bell Farm,' *Saskatchewan History* 19, no 2 (Spring 1966): 41–60; Don G. McGowan, *Grasslands Settlers: The Swift Current Region during the Era of the Ranching Frontier* (Regina: Canadian Plains Research Centre 1976),

57–79; Grant MacEwan, *Illustrated History of Western Canadian Agriculture* (Saskatoon: Western Producer Prairie Books 1980), 66–71

4 Carmangay *Sun, Dry Farming Congress Edition*, 21 Oct. 1912, MDK; Carmangay *Sun*, 4 Mar. 1910; Lethbridge *Herald*, 2 Apr. 1910, 57; *Alberta Farmer and Weekly Herald*, 1 May 1924; Carmangay and District History Book Committee, *Bridging the Years; Carmangay and District* (Lethbridge 1968), 4, 27

5 Lethbridge *News*, 14 Aug. 1905; High River *Times*, 1 Aug. 1906, 2 July 1908; *Farm and Ranch Review*, July 1907, 5; *Henderson's Manitoba and North West Territories Gazetteer and Directory* (1905), 607; Roy L. Fowler, 'Chronology of Farming in the Okotoks–High River Area (1879–1930),' *Alberta Historical Review* 2, no 2 (Spring 1954): 25

6 Vulcan and District Historical Society, *Wheat Country: A History of Vulcan and District* (Vulcan 1973), 399–400; Champion History Committee, *Cleverville-Champion, 1905 to 1970, A History of Champion and Area* (Champion 1971), 199–200; Nanton and District Historical Society, *Mosquito Creek Roundup, Nanton-Parkland* (Nanton 1975), 184–5

7 Carmangay *Sun, Dry Farming Congress Edition*, 21 Oct. 1912

8 G.H. Craig and J. Coke, *An Economic Study of Land Utilization in Southern Alberta* (Ottawa: Canadian Department of Agriculture, Economics Division, Marketing Service, Publication 610, Technical Bulletin 16, 1938), 66; Carmangay *Sun*, 16 Feb., 30 June 1911, 4 May 1917, *Dry Farming Congress Edition*, 21 Oct. 1912; Vulcan *Advocate*, 29 Aug. 1923; Ken Miller, interviewed near Carmangay, May 1978; W. Wallace Miller, taped interview by Sharilyn Ingram and Barry Necyk, near Carmangay, 5 Mar. 1973, side 2, counter no 10–20, PAA; Carmangay, *Bridging*, 447; Champion, *Cleverville-Champion*, 285; Vulcan, *Wheat Country*, 856–7

9 Reports of big farm ambitions echoed from every district in the area; see Nanton *News*, 18 May 1905; Carmangay *Sun*, 5 May 1911; Alvin Baker to editor, Continental [Ohio] *News-Review*, 10 May 1928, book 14-Y, MDK; Jack Dietz, interviewed near Milo, Apr. 1978; Vulcan, *Wheat Country*, 431, 637; Cummins Map Company, *Cummins Rural Directory Maps* (Winnipeg 1923), no 50.

10 Martin, *Dominion Lands*, 417–21; John Proskie, 'Financial Progress of Settlers, with Special Reference to the Vulcan-Lomond Area,' MA, Alberta 1937, 418

11 Calculated from assessment rolls and registers for Local Improvement District 9-T-4, 1907, and MD of Royal 158, 1914, in County of Vulcan No 2 Records, PAA; many interviews; Carmangay *Sun*, 17 Mar. 1911

12 D.O. Jantzie, interviewed at Vulcan, May 1978. The aggressive campaign by mortgage companies ended during the First World War, when financial institutions invested more money into high-yielding war bonds, but the demand for farm mortgage money fell anyway because of high farm incomes; see W.T. Easter-

brook, *Farm Credit in Canada* (Toronto: University of Toronto Press 1938), 48–51. Statistics based on a survey of 232 Vulcan-area farmers; see Craig, *Economic Study*, 65. These proportions may approximate those for the prairies generally; a survey of 161 Saskatchewan pioneers also revealed that about one-third had never mortgaged their farms; see Allan R. Turner, 'Pioneer Farming Experiences,' *Saskatchewan History* 8, no 2 (Spring 1955): 44.

13 These terms applied only to purchasers of 640 acres or less who actually settled in the area; purchases of more than one section by absentee landlords called for one-sixth down and the balance over five years at 6 per cent; see CPR, *Western Canada, Manitoba, Alberta, Saskatchewan. How to Reach it, How to Obtain Lands, How to Make a Home* (Winnipeg 1906), 45; (1921), 69. For the influence of these terms on other sellers, see Nanton *News*, 4 Mar. 1909. See also Martin, *Dominion Lands*, 314; James B. Hedges, *Building the Canadian West: The Land and Colonization Policies of the Canadian Pacific Railway* (New York: Macmillan 1939), 265–6.

14 This seems evident when we match the names of buyers listed in CPR Land Sales Records, GAI, with randomly collected biographical information, including addresses listed in local tax rolls. Unfortunately, however, it is difficult to determine the proportion of buyers who defaulted because the sales records are very unclear. Of 68 purchases in the Vulcan area in 1910 and 1911 recorded in vol. 170, for example, 30 were subsequently transferred to other persons before all the payments had been made. Many of those changed hands several times. It is often impossible to distinguish repossessions and CPR resales from sales by the first buyers to second owners who simply took over the payments. Land-title records do not solve the problem, since titles were never issued until all land payments had been made. Successive sales of CPR lands involving missed payments commonly resulted in tangled disputes among not only the company and the original purchasers but subsequent purchasers, tenants, financial institutions, lawyers, and tax collectors, who generated mountains of angry letters; see Land Sales Correspondence, in CPR Papers, GAI. For success generally in meeting land payments in the Vulcan area before 1920 see Craig, *Economic Study*, 70; Proskie, 'Financial Progress,' 101.

15 *Canadian Annual Review* (1914), 670; Canada, *Sessional Papers* 25 (1911), xxix; R.W. Murchie, *Agricultural Progress on the Prairie Frontier* (Toronto: Macmillan 1936), 72, 76. Thirty per cent of the settlers arrived with more than $4,000, and 15 per cent with more than $7,000 (based on a sample of 231 Vulcan-area farmers in Craig, *Economic Study*, 66–7); see also a sample of 282 land transactions in Proskie, 'Financial Progress,' 100.

16 Easterbrook, *Farm Credit*, 150; Proskie, 'Financial Progress,' 95–6, 100,113–4; D. McGinnis, 'Farm Labour in Transition: Occupational Structure and Economic

Dependence in Alberta, 1921–1951,' in Howard Palmer, ed., *The Settlement of the West* (Calgary: University of Calgary and Comprint Publishing 1977), 176; Craig, *Economic Study*, 56, 70

17 H.S. Parker to James Colley, 17 Feb. 1926, Carmangay Colonization Board Correspondence, and various 'Farm Cards,' both in CPR Papers, GAI; Craig, *Economic Study*, 22

18 Everett G. Smith Jr., 'Fragmented Farms in the United States,' *Annals, Association of American Geographers* 65, no 1 (Mar. 1975): 58–70; Vulcan, *Wheat Country*, 371

19 Many interviews, especially C.H. 'Budd' Andrews, interviewed near Vulcan, Jan. 1978

20 Proskie, 'Financial Progress,' 151; Vulcan *Advocate*, 29 Aug. 1923; see Appendix concerning statistics.

21 Robert P. Swierenga, 'Land Speculation and its Impact on American Economic Growth and Welfare: A Historiographical Review,' *Western Historical Quarterly* 8, no 3 (July 1977): 283–302; Murchie, *Agricultural Progress*, 92–3, 129; Donald L. Winters, 'Tenant Farming in Iowa, 1860–1900: A Study of the Terms of Rental Leases,' *Agricultural History* 48, no 1 (Jan. 1974): 130–50; idem, *Farmers without Farms: Agricultural Tenancy in Nineteenth-Century Iowa* (Westport, Conn.: Greenwood Press 1978); Seddie Cogswell Jr., *Tenure, Nativity and Age as Factors in Iowa Agriculture, 1850–1880* (Ames: Iowa State University Press 1975); Robert Diller, *Farm Ownership, Tenancy, and Land Use in a Nebraska Community* (Chicago: University of Chicago Press 1941)

22 Budd Andrews interview; Roy Burns, interviewed at Carmangay, Jan. 1978; Vulcan *Advocate*, 7 Apr. 1920; Craig, *Economic Study*, 47. Many American studies have also discovered an inverse relationship between speculation and tenancy; see Cogswell, *Tenure*, 25–7; Winters, *Farmers without Farms*, passim; Edward O. Moe and Carl C. Taylor, *Culture of a Contemporary Rural Community – Irwin, Iowa* (U.S. Department of Agriculture, Bureau of Agricultural Economics, Rural Life Studies 5, 1942), 30; Swierenga, 'Land Speculation,' 283–302, traces the historiographical changes on this point.

23 Harvey Beaubier, interviewed at Champion, June 1978; Craig, *Economic Study*, 55, 69. For one of the first studies to note the advantages of combining ownership and tenancy, see James C. Malin, 'Mobility and History: Reflections on the Agricultural Policies of the United States in Relation to a Mechanized World,' *Agricultural History* 17, no 4 (Oct. 1943): 183; see also William Strojich, 'Land Tenure in Western Canada with Particular Reference to the Special Areas of Alberta,' MA, Alberta 1940, 28, 77–9. On the terms of leases see H.S. Parker to E.D. Bennett, 13 July 1926, Carmangay Colonization Board Correspondence; for leases of similar duration in Saskatchewan see George Britnell, *The Wheat Economy*

(Toronto: University of Toronto Press 1939), 46; Murchie, *Agricultural Progress*, 95, argued that short-term leases only encouraged farmers to overtax the soil, but landlords in the Vulcan area voiced no complaints on that account. Their tenants were usually large farmers with some land of their own who were interested in long-range development, and in any event, owners could always protect their land with a compulsory summerfallowing clause.

24 Murchie, *Agricultural Progress*, 94–8, argued that cash renting made farmers more efficient than did sharecropping because it placed pressure on the tenant to meet his commitments in poor years, but no evidence from the Vulcan area supports this assertion, and given the state of tillage knowledge until the 1930s, it is doubtful that any great differences in efficiency emerged between cash renters and sharecroppers. See also Kenneth Norrie, 'Dry Farming and the Economics of Risk Bearing: The Canadian Prairies, 1870–1930,' *Agricultural History* 51, no 1 (Jan. 1977): 146; Parker to Bennett, Parker to E.L. Miller, 6 Aug. 1926, Carmangay Colonization Board Correspondence; Craig, *Economic Study*, 48; Britnell, *Wheat Economy*, 46. For the American south see C. Vann Woodward, *Origins of the New South, 1877–1913*, 2nd edn (Baton Rouge: Louisiana State University Press 1971), 175–210. For the lack of any strong relationship between social class or status and tenancy in the midwest see Moe, *Culture*, 27–9; Winters, *Farmers without Farms*, passim; Earl H. Bell, *The Culture of a Contemporary Rural Community: Sublette, Kansas* (U.S. Department of Agriculture, Bureau of Agricultural Economics, Rural Life Studies 2, 1942), 36–7; Lowry Nelson, *The Minnesota Community: Country and Town in Transition* (Minneapolis: University of Minnesota Press 1960), 10–12.

25 Murchie, *Agricultural Progress*, 119, 125; Karel Denis Bicha, *The American Frontier and the Canadian West, 1896–1914* (Lawrence, Kan.: Coronado Press 1968), espec. 88, 140; idem, 'The American Frontier and the Canadian West, 1896–1914; A Revised View,' *Agricultural History* 38, no 1 (Jan. 1964): 46; Craig, *Economic Study*, 47

26 Parker to Bennett

27 W. Wallace Miller interview, side 2, counter no 10–20; H.H. Thompson, 'The Thompsons in Alberta,' unpub. ms, nd, GAI; Carmangay *Sun*, 26 Sept. 1913, 4, 25 May 1917; Lethbridge *Herald*, 9 Mar. 1938; Carmangay, *Bridging*, 27; Champion, *Cleverville-Champion*, 299–300; Vulcan, *Wheat Country*, 400; Nanton, *Mosquito Creek*, 184–5

28 W. Wallace Miller interview, side 2, counter no 10–20; Ken Miller interview; Lethbridge *Herald*, 9 Mar. 1938, 28 Dec. 1967; By-law 68, 14 May 1921, By-Law Register, Town of Carmangay, VCO; Carmangay *Sun*, 9 Feb. 1923; Noble Foundation Ltd, *The Noble Foundation Limited; Owners and Operators of 30,619 Acres of Farm Land* (Nobleford, Alta, 1919?); Grant MacEwan, *Charles Noble: Guardian*

of the Soil (Saskatoon: Western Producer Prairie Books 1983), 125–34; Vulcan *Advocate*, 7 Sept. 1921; *Census of Canada*, vol. 12 (1931), 126; see also A.W. Mahaffy, 'The Machine Process in Agriculture, with Special Reference to Western Canada,' MA, Saskatchewan 1923, 26.

29 Drache, *Day of the Bonanza*, 204–17; Briggs, 'Early Bonanza,' 26–37; Fred A. Shannon, *The Farmer's Last Frontier: Agriculture, 1860–1897* (New York: Harper and Row 1945), 160; Drache, 'Bonanza Farming,' 61–2; MacEwan, *Charles Noble*, 125–34; W.J. Anderson, 'The Place of the Small Farm in the Agricultural Economy of Saskatchewan,' M SC, Saskatchewan 1944, 84–5; Helen C. Abell, 'Some Reasons for the Persistence of Small Farms,' *Economic Annalist* 26, no 5 (Oct. 1956): 115–20; Harriet Friedmann, 'World Market, State, and Family Farm: Social Bases of Household Production in the Era of Wage Labor,' *Comparative Studies in Society and History* 20 (1978): 567–81

30 Craig, *Economic Study*, 52; Rudolf Susko,'Economies of Size on Alberta Grain Farms,' M SC, Alberta 1971, espec. 91, 112–13. Susko's conclusion applied both before and after taxation, and he seems to have taken great care to neutralize all other factors except size. *Farm and Ranch Review*, 20 Jan. 1912, 55; James C. Malin, *The Grasslands of North America, Prolegomena to Its History* (Gloucester, Mass.: Peter Smith 1947), 296–9; Friedmann, 'World Market,' 545–86; Joseph Schafter, 'Some Enduring Factors in Rural Polity,' *Agricultural History* 6, no 4 (Oct. 1932): 168–9; Howard W. Ottoson and others, *Land and People in the Northern Plains Transition Area* (Lincoln: University of Nebraska Press 1966), 152–3; D. Aidan McQuillan, 'Farm Size and Work Ethic: Measuring the Success of Immigrant Farmers on the American Grasslands, 1875–1925,' *Journal of Historical Geography* 4, no 1 (Jan. 1978): 57–76; Philip M. Raup, 'Corporate Farming in the United States,' *Journal of Economic History* 33, no 1 (Mar. 1973): 282

31 For a basic introduction to most of these changes see Stewart H. Holbrook, *Machines of Plenty; Pioneering in American Agriculture* (New York: Macmillan 1955); Wayne D. Rasmussen, 'The Impact of Technological Change on American Agriculture, 1862–1962,' *Journal of Economic History* 22, no 4 (Dec. 1962); 578–91.

32 *Farm and Ranch Review*, 20 Sept. 1911, 599; also W.E. Finley to Editor, Hastings [Michigan] *Journal*, reprinted in Carmangay *Sun*, 3 Oct. 1913; for the Great Plains generally see Howard F. Gregor, 'The Industrial Farm as a Western Institution,' *Journal of the West* 9, no 1 (Jan. 1970): 78–92.

33 Quoted in R.E. English, 'Early Explorations and the Reports of the Surveyor General of Canada, with Reference to Agricultural Possibilities in Alberta's Dry Area,' unpub. ms, 1937, 22, O.S. Longman Papers, GAI

34 Earle D. Ross, 'Retardation in Farm Technology Before the Power Age,' *Agricultural History* 30, no 1 (Jan. 1956): 11–17; report of the Agricultural Institute

meeting, 1912, Carmangay Agricultural Society Papers, GAI; Carmangay *Sun*, 8 Mar. 1912. For problems with steam tractors see John Stahl, 'Prairie Agriculture: A Prognosis,' in David P. Gagan, ed., *Prairie Perspectives* (Toronto: Holt, Rinehart, and Winston 1970), 68; Mahaffy, 'The Machine Process,' 23–5, 62; Ernest Boyce Ingles, 'Some Aspects of Dry-Land Agriculture in the Canadian Prairies to 1925,' MA, Calgary 1973, 56–7; J.W.G. MacEwan, *Power for Prairie Plows* (Saskatoon: Western Producer Prairie Books 1971), 43–5.

35 Ingles, 'Some Aspects,' 53, 60, 79–80; Robert E. Ankli, H. Dan Helsberg, and John Herd Thompson, 'The Adoption of the Gasoline Tractor in Western Canada,' in Donald H. Akenson, ed., *Canadian Papers in Rural History*, vol. 3 (Gananoque, Ont.: Langdale Press 1980), 12–15; Carmangay *Sun*, 1, 15 Apr. 1910, 10 Mar. 1911; monthly reports of D Division, 30 Apr. 1913, RCMP Records, PAC; MacEwan, *Power*, 55; James H. Gray, *The Roar of the Twenties* (Toronto: Macmillan 1975), 46–50; David Spector, 'Field Agriculture in the Canadian Prairie West 1870–1940 with Emphasis on the Period 1870–1920,' unpub. ms, Canadian Department of Indian and Northern Affairs, Parks Canada, National Historic Parks and Sites Branch, Manuscript Report 205, 1977, pp 61–83

36 Levi Hummon to Editor, Leipsic [Ohio] *Free Press*, reprinted in Carmangay *Sun*, 10 Nov. 1911; Grant MacEwan, *Between the Red and the Rockies* (Toronto: University of Toronto Press 1952), 224; photographs, book 9-S, MDK; *Farm and Ranch Review*, 5 July 1913, 618; Mahaffy, 'The Machine Process,' 66–75; E.G. Grest, *An Economic Analysis of Farm Power in Alberta and Saskatchewan* (Ottawa: Canadian Department of Agriculture, Division of Farm Management, Agricultural Economics Branch 1936), 67

37 Roy Burns interview; Champion, *Cleverville-Champion*, 455; Jack Dietz interview; Carl Stettner, interviewed at Carmangay, Feb. 1978

38 Ankli, 'The Adoption,' 15–18, 33; Mahaffy, 'The Machine Process,' 25; Grest, *Economic Analysis*, 51, 60; Ross, 'Retardation,' 16; Ingles, 'Some Aspects,' 69; J. Fergus Grant, 'Implementing Agriculture,' *Canadian Geographical Journal* 18, no 4 (Apr. 1939): 175; Massey-Harris Company, *100 Years of Progress in Farm Implements, 1847–1947* (Toronto 1947), 45

39 *Henderson's Manitoba and North West Territories Gazetteer and Directory* (1905), 341; *Farm and Ranch Review*, Jan. 1907, 37; Claresholm *Review*, 10 May 1907; Carmangay *Sun*, 3 Oct. 1913

40 Many sources revealed these difficulties, but especially Harvey Beaubier interview; Father McLaughlin to J.T. Kidd, nd, Champion Parish File, CDA; for the prairies generally see Mahaffy, 'Machine Process,' 69; Ankli, 'The Adoption,' 16.

41 Mahaffy, 'Machine Process,' 17; Grest, *Economic Analysis*, 52; many photos, book 32-W, MDK; '1915 Binding Wheat West of Vulcan,' Vulcan and District Historical Society Photograph Collection, VA; Vulcan *Advocate*, 25 Aug. 1915; Vul-

can, *Wheat Country*, 609; *Farm and Ranch Review*, July 1907, 5

42 Many photos, books 19-L, 9-S, 26-Y, MDK; High River *Times*, 12 Sept. 1907; for a good description of the specialized labour requirements of a threshing crew see MacEwan, *Between*, 211-13.

43 John Herd Thompson, 'Bringing in the Sheaves: The Harvest Excursionists, 1890-1929,' *Canadian Historical Review* 59, no 4 (Dec. 1978): 469, 474-7; Vulcan *Advocate*, 4 Feb. 1920; Champion *Chronicle*, 20 Aug. 1925; Carmangay *Sun*, 7 Sept. 1917, 22 Aug. 1918. For similar problems on the U.S. plains see Allen Gale Applen, 'Migratory Harvest Labor in the Midwestern Wheat Belt, 1870-1940,' PH D, Kansas State 1974, 109, 116-44.

44 Vulcan *Advocate*, 22 Dec. 1920

45 Allen G. Applen, 'Labour Casualization in Great Plains Wheat Production: 1865-1902,' *Journal of the West* 16, no 1 (Jan. 1977): 5-9. Farm accidents filled the local newspapers every summer; while some involved horses and others the lack of safety equipment, a great many resulted from simple carelessness and the unfamiliarity of workers with the dangers of various machines.

46 Vulcan *Advocate*, 29 Aug. 1923; Carmangay, *Bridging*, 170. For the general ineptitude of farm workers from England and the largely unsuccessful attempts to train them see W.J.C. Cherwinski, 'Wooden Horses and Rubber Cows: Training British Agricultural Labour for the Canadian Prairies, 1890-1930,' *Canadian Historical Association Historical Papers* (1980): 133-54; Lloyd G. Reynolds, *The British Immigrant: His Social and Economic Adjustment in Canada* (Toronto: Oxford University Press 1935), 269-72.

47 *Farm and Ranch Review*, 20 Jan. 1912, 55; 5 Aug. 1913, 699; Mahaffy, 'Machine Process,' 37-8; Anderson, 'Place of the Small Farm,' 1-2; John D. Hicks, 'The Western Middle West, 1900-1914,' *Agricultural History* 20, no 2 (Apr. 1946): 74-5; Report of D Division, Fort Macleod, Canada, *Sessional Papers* 28 (1910), 65; Vulcan *Advocate*, 5 Mar. 1919; MacEwan, *Charles Noble*, 66-7; Nobleford-Monarch History Book Club, *Sons of Wind and Soil* (Nobleford, Monarch, Alta, 1976), 299

48 Lethbridge *Herald*, 2 Apr. 1910, 53; Vulcan *Advocate*, 27 Sept. 1922; for contract work involving steam power in the west generally see Ingles, 'Some Aspects,' 92, 131.

49 Harvey Beaubier interview

50 Statistics based largely on biographical sketches in Carmangay, *Bridging*; quote from p 69. D.O. Jantzie interview; Carrie McIntyre, interviewed at Vulcan, June 1978. This system functioned much the same way elsewhere in North America; see Bennett, *Northern Plainsmen*, 285-6; Solon T. Kimball, 'Rural Social Organization and Co-operative Labor,' *American Journal of Sociology* 55, no 1 (July 1949): 38-49.

51 Monthly report of D Division, 12 Mar. 1912, 3; see also High River *Times*, 23 Dec. 1911; Carmangay *Sun*, 24 Nov. 1911

52 Vulcan *Advocate*, 26 Nov. 1913. Although Figure 24 provides statistics on the absolute cost of labour per farm in the area, it is very difficult to illustrate consistently what proportion of total costs those figures represented. McGinnis, 'Farm Labour,' 181–2, maintains that labour constituted the greatest single operating expense of Alberta farmers during the 1920s. He suggests that expenditures on hired help ranged from 8 per cent of the total net value of agricultural production in 1925 to 19 per cent in 1930, even though absolute labour costs had fallen. See also Mahaffy, 'Machine Process,' 55.

53 Vulcan *Advocate*, 20 Apr., 16 May 1921; for previous attempts to fix wages see 21, 28 July 1915; Carmangay *Sun*, 23 Aug. 1912. For the failure of this tactic in the west generally see Thompson, 'Bringing In,' 484.

54 Vulcan *Advocate*, 5 Sept. 1923; H.S. Parker to Mr Colley, 29 Mar. 1926, and CPR Department of Colonization and Development to H.S. Parker, 10 Apr. 1926, both in Carmangay Colonization Board Correspondence; see also H.S. Kent correspondence, espec. file 751, CPR Papers.

55 The role of mechanization in eliminating labour is discussed in John Lier, 'Farm Mechanization in Saskatchewan,' *Tijdschrift Voor Economishce en Sociale Geografie* 62, no 3 (1971): 187; Richard E. Duwors, 'Prevailing Life Perspectives and Population Shifts in the Canadian Prairie Provinces,' in Carle C. Zimmerman and Seth Russell, eds., *Symposium on the Great Plains of North America* (Fargo: North Dakota State University 1967), 77; C. Horace Hamilton, 'The Social Effects of Recent Trends in the Mechanization of Agriculture,' *Rural Sociology* 4, no 1 (Mar. 1939): 3–25; Mahaffy, 'Machine Process,' 55; Applen, 'Labor Casualization,' 9; Vulcan *Advocate*, 2 May 1921; Duncan Marshall, *Farm Management* (Calgary: Imperial Oil 1931), 69; *Facts, Figures and Fortunes of the Vulcan District* (Vulcan 1920?), VA.

56 *Farm and Ranch Review*, 5 July 1913, 618; Carmangay, *Bridging*, 30–1; Vulcan, *Wheat Country*, 269

57 Ingles, 'Some Aspects,' 128; Ankli, 'The Adoption,' 19; *Census of Canada*, vol. 8 (1931), 696; Massey-Harris, *100 Years*, 43 50

58 Carmangay, *Bridging*, 258; Opal V. Orcutt, 'Orcutt History,' unpub. ms, 1975, book 29-E; photo '1916,' book 14-G; both in MDK; Ken Miller interview; Carmangay *Sun*, 19 Sept. 1913; Vulcan *Advocate*, 3 Oct. 1923; Ingles, 'Some Aspects,' 130; Lewis H. Thomas, 'Early Combines in Saskatchewan,' *Saskatchewan History* 8, no 1 (Winter 1955): 1–5; see also Robert Higgs, 'Tractors or Horses? Some Basic Economics in the Pacific Northwest and Elsewhere,' *Agricultural History* 49, no 1 (Jan. 1975): 281–3; Thomas B. Keith, *The Horse Interlude: A Pictorial His-*

tory of Horse and Man in the Inland Northwest (Moscow: University Press of Idaho 1976), passim.

59 Photos, book 14-G, 23-F, MDK. The disadvantages of combines in the 1920s are discussed in J.K. MacKenzie, *The Combine-Reaper-Thresher in Western Canada* (Ottawa: Canadian Department of Agriculture, Pamphlet, ns no 83, 1927), 11–12; J.G. Taggart and J.K. MacKenzie, *Seven Years' Experience with the Combined Reaper-Thresher, 1922–28* (Ottawa: Canadian Department of Agriculture, Bulletin, ns no 118, 1929) 6–16; Oliver L. Symes, 'Agricultural Technology and Changing Life on the Prairies,' in *Development of Agriculture on the Prairies: Proceedings of Seminar* (Regina: University of Regina 1975), 39–40.

60 Massey-Harris, *100 Years*, 38–9; Grest, *Economic Analysis*, 45; Thomas, 'Early Combines,' 5; Taggart, *Seven Years*, 6; many interviews, espec. Ken Miller

61 Helmer H. Hanson, *The History of Swathing and Swath Threshing* (Saskatoon: Western Producer 1967); Symes, 'Agricultural Technology,' 39–40

62 Carmangay *Sun*, 19 Sept. 1913

63 Mahaffy, 'Machine Process,' 9

64 Taggart, *Seven Years*, 6, 9–10; MacKenzie, *The Combine-Reaper-Thresher*, 5, 9–10; Massey-Harris, *100 Years*, 43–50

65 Proskie, 'Financial Progress,' 107; Lethbridge *Herald*, 1 Sept. 1938; Carmangay, *Bridging*, 169; Craig, *Economic Study*, 44

CHAPTER SEVEN: ACTIVITIES AND INSTITUTIONS

1 Examples abound, but a particularly forceful interpretation is found in Robert F. Berkhofer Jr., 'Space, Time, Culture and the New Frontier,' *Agricultural History* 38, no 1 (Jan. 1964): 21–31. Berkhofer argues that instead of demanding innovation in institutions, the frontier afforded the opportunity for existing ones to expand and proliferate.

2 Vulcan and District Historical Society, *Wheat Country: A History of Vulcan and District* (Vulcan 1973), 259

3 Vulcan, *Wheat Country*, 346

4 Carrie McIntyre, interviewed at Vulcan, June 1978

5 Albert James Miller, 'The Trail to Alberta,' unpub. ms, 1957, book 9-K, MDK; Elizabeth Akitt, taped interview by Sharilyn Ingram and Barry Necyk at Carmangay, 9 Mar. 1973, side 1, counter no 733–735, PAA; Vulcan, *Wheat Country*, 525; Carrie McIntyre interview

6 Four letters from Alva Baker in Continental [Ohio] *News-Review*, 10 May 1928, book 14-Y, MDK; Carmangay *Sun*, 9 Feb. 1911; Lethbridge *Herald*, 15 June 1939; Joe McNaughton to M.D. Keenan, 11 Feb. 1974, book 15-C, MDK

7 D.O. Jantzie, 'Writings,' unpub. ms, 1965, 7, privately owned by D.O. Jantzie, Vulcan; Champion History Committee, *Cleverville-Champion 1905 to 1970, A History of Champion and Area* (Champion, 1971?), 639, reports that seven men lived together one winter and played cards 'day and night'; Oscar Hagg, interviewed at Carmangay, June 1978.

8 John Warkentin, 'Manitoba Settlement Patterns,' *Historical and Scientific Society of Manitoba Transactions* III, no 16 (1961): 69–71; Carl O. Sauer, 'Homestead and Community on the Middle Border,' *Landscape* 12, no 1 (Autumn 1962): 5

9 A study of Biggar, Saskatchewan, found that by 1961, 62 per cent of all formal organizations were affiliates, 28 per cent international; see Richard Laskin, *Organizations in a Saskatchewan Town* (Saskatoon: Research Division, Centre for Community Studies, University of Saskatchewan 1961), 25.

10 Vulcan *Advocate*, 28 Feb. 1923; for the introduction of baseball to the U.S. Great Plains generally see Duane A. Smith, 'A Strike Did Not Always Mean Gold,' *Montana Magazine of Western History* 20, no 3 (Summer 1970): 76–81; High River *Times*, 18 Aug. 1910; David H. Breen, *The Canadian Prairie West and the Ranching Frontier, 1874–1924* (Toronto: University of Toronto Press 1983), passim; Patrick A. Dunae, *Gentlemen Emigrants; From the British Public Schools to the Canadian Frontier* (Vancouver: Douglas and McIntyre 1981), 91–139.

11 Although presented in a great many places, the reasons are perhaps best explained by S.M. Lipset, *Agrarian Socialism: The Cooperative Commonwealth Federation in Saskatchewan: A Study in Political Sociology* (Los Angeles: University of California Press 1950), passim.

12 James H. Gray, *Red Lights on the Prairies* (Toronto: Macmillan 1971); idem, *Booze: the Impact of Whiskey on the Prairie West* (Toronto: Macmillan 1972); Jean Burnet, *Next-Year Country: A Study of Rural Social Organization in Alberta* (Toronto: University of Toronto Press 1951), 53–4, 117–18, noted the tendency of these social activities to persist in prairie communities as late as the 1940s.

13 For the relationship between sports, games, and gambling on the U.S. plains see Everett Dick, *The Sod House Frontier, 1854–1890: A Social History of the Northern Plains from the Creation of Kansas and Nebraska to the Admission of the Dakotas* (Lincoln, Neb.: Johnsen Publishing 1954), 277.

14 Mr and Mrs Oscar Hagg, taped interview by Barry Necyk and Sharilyn Ingram at Champion, 8 Mar. 1973, side 1, counter no 151–3, PAA; Mrs J. Smith, 'My Recollections of Ridgeway District, Carmangay,' unpub. ms, nd, book 32-J, MDK; High River *Times*, 18 Apr. 1907; J.W. Miller Reports, Carmangay, 1910–1920, Justices of the Peace Files, Attorney General of Alberta Records, PAA; see also monthly reports of D Division, Macleod, Alta, 1904–18, RCMP Records, PAC.

15 Miller reports, 15 Aug. 1913; J.E. Charters reports, 25 Oct. 1924, 31 May 1925,

all in Justices of the Peace Files; Minutes of the Village and Town Councils of Carmangay, Dec. 1917, VCAO; Vulcan *Advocate*, 16 Feb. 1916; minutes of the High River Presbytery, 11 Feb. 1919, United Church of Canada Records, PAA

16 The best study of prairie sports is Morris K. Mott, 'Manly Sports and Manitobans; Settlement Days to World War One,' PH D, Queen's University 1980; see also idem, 'One Solution to the Urban Crisis: Manly Sports and Winnipegers, 1900–1914,' *Urban History Review* 12, no 2 (Oct. 1983): 57–70, although the concept of 'manly' sports does not seem particularly applicable in the Vulcan area. Carmangay *Sun*, 3, 17 June 1910; George Geddes letter to St Thomas [Ontario] *Times-Journal*, reprinted in Vulcan *Advocate*, 27 Sept. 1922; interview with Bessie Siler, wife of a professional pitcher, in Lethbridge *Herald*, 17 May 1975

17 Alex Allan, 'Baseball Recollections,' magazine clipping, nd, book 21-M, MDK; 'Early Years of the Champion Senior Baseball Teams in Summary,' unpub. ms, nd, book 22-L, MDK; Calgary *Daily Herald*, 24–30 Aug. 1917; John (Jack) D. Orr, taped interview by Sharilyn Ingram and Barry Necyk at Suffield, 6 Apr. 1973, side 1, counter no 167; Champion, *Cleverville-Champion*, 532; Harvey Beaubier interviewed at Champion, June 1978

18 Carmangay *Sun*, 1 Sept. 1911, 3 June 1910; Vulcan *Advocate*, 29 May 1918

19 Vulcan, *Wheat Country*, 948; Town of Vulcan Returning Officer to Deputy Minister of Municipal Affairs, 11 July 1923, in Town of Vulcan Correspondence, Municipality Correspondence Files, Alberta Department of Municipal Affairs Papers, PAA; Vulcan *Advocate*, 7 Feb. 1923

20 High River *Times*, 2 May 1907, 26 Nov. 1908; records of the Berrywater Literary and Social Club, VA

21 *Census of Canada* (1931), vol. 1, 371

22 Georgina H. Thomson, *Crocus and Meadowlark Country, Recollections of a Happy Childhood and Youth on a Homestead in Southern Alberta* (Edmonton: Institute of Applied Art 1963), 99. For extensive informal socializing in the midwest see Jane Marie Pederson, 'The Country Visitor: Patterns of Hospitality in Rural Wisconsin, 1880–1925,' *Agricultural History* 58, no 3 (July 1984): 347–64.

23 Horace Miner, *Culture and Agriculture: An Anthropological Study of a Corn-Belt County* (Ann Arbor: University of Michigan Press 1949), 70–1; Vulcan *Advocate*, 30 Aug. 1922; Georgina 'Ina' Neilson, taped interview by Barry Necyk and Sharilyn Ingram at Carmangay, 6 Mar. 1973, PAA

24 Carmangay *Sun*, 16 May 1913, 3 Aug. 1917. The number of organizations that the average person joined seems impossible to determine with any accuracy. Documents on particular individuals tend to mention membership in organizations only when the individual belonged to a great many, and especially if he or she served often as an officer. A 1961 study that marvelled at the highly institutionalized social life in and around Biggar, Saskatchewan, found that nearly every rural

man and three-quarters of the rural women belonged to at least one formal voluntary organization; the average farm man belonged to 4.4 organizations in 1961 and the average farm woman to half as many. The authors suggest that such levels may be valid historically as well. See Donald E. Willmott, 'The Formal Organizations of Saskatchewan Farmers, 1900–1965,' in A.W. Rasporich, ed., *Western Canada Past and Present* (Calgary: McClelland and Stewart West 1975), 29–30. Scattered evidence from the Vulcan area suggests that these levels have been much higher, for the institutionation of frontier social life sprang largely from a combination of low population densities and crude transportation systems.

25 Thomas Bender, *Community and Social Change in America* (New Brunswick, NJ: Rutgers University Press 1978), 5–6, points out that not all communities are based on territory, nor is the size of a territory necessarily important. For 'rurban communities' see Charles J. Galpin, *The Social Anatomy of an Agricultural Community* (Madison: University of Wisconsin, Agricultural Experimental Station, Research Bulletin 34, 1915); see also D.G. Marshall, 'Hamlets and Villages in the United States: Their Places in the American Way of Life,' *American Sociology Review* 11, no 2 (Apr. 1946): 164–5; Carle C. Zimmerman and Garry W. Moneo, *The Prairie Community System* (Ottawa: Agricultural Economics Research Council of Canada 1970).

26 Burnet, *Next-Year*, 68–9. I have relied on an important essay by Wilmott, 'Formal Organizations,' 28–44, for much of my analysis, although I have altered, rearranged, and detailed certain aspects of it.

27 Champion, *Cleverville-Champion*, 189; for the unreliability of autos in the prairie environment generally see James Gray, *The Roar of the Twenties* (Toronto: Macmillan 1975), 46–50.

28 Monthly reports of D Division, 17 July 1912, 7 Feb. 1913, RCMP Records; Vulcan *Advocate*, 26 Nov. 1919; Vulcan, *Wheat Country*, 90; Champion, *Cleverville-Champion*, 78–9; records of the Ensign Mutual Telephone Company, VA. With a population of 2,662 in 1961, Biggar headquartered 140 formal organizations; Laskin, *Organizations*, 6.

29 For the supposed ill effects of mobility see Newell L. Sims, *Elements of Rural Sociology*, 3rd edn (New York: Thomas Y. Crowell 1940), 247–58; R.W. Murchie, *Agricultural Progress on the Prairie Fronter* (Toronto: Macmillan 1935), 118. For an opposing view see Don H. Doyle, 'The Social Functions of Voluntary Associations in a Nineteenth-Century American Town,' *Social Science History* 1, no 3 (Spring 1977), 346. Carmangay *Sun*, 22 Dec. 1910. For 'limited liability' see Bender, *Community*, 9–10.

30 *Farm and Ranch Review*, 20 Sept. 1916, 705–6; Carmangay and District History Book Committee, *Bridging the Years; Carmangay and District* (Carmangay 1968), 306; many newspaper articles

31 Records of the Berrywater Literary and Social Club
32 A.H. Anderson, 'Space as a Social Cost: An Approach Toward Community
Design in the Sparsely Populated Areas of the Great Plains,' *Journal of Farm
Economics* 32, no 3 (Aug. 1950): 411–31; for the best use of this concept see Carl
Kraenzel, *Great Plains in Transition* (Norman: University of Oklahoma Press
1955); see also Mary W.M. Hargreaves, 'Space: Its Institutional Impact in the
Development of the Great Plains,' in Brian W. Blouet and Frederick C. Luebke,
eds., *The Great Plains: Environment and Culture* (Lincoln: University of
Nebraska Press 1979), 205–23. For statistics on roads see *Census of Canada*
(1931), vol. 8, 696.
33 Vulcan, *Wheat Country*, 45–7; Mary Boose, 'Vulcan's First Hospital,' unpub. ms,
nd, Mary Boose Papers, GAI; Champion, *Cleverville-Champion*, 213; A.S. Abell,
'Rural Municipal Government in Alberta: Taxation and Finance,' MA, Toronto
1940, 29; Eric J. Hanson, *Local Government in Alberta* (Toronto: McClelland
and Stewart 1956), 38–9; Champion *Chronicle*, 17 Sept. 1925; High River *Times*,
5 Sept. 1907; Carmangay *Sun*, 7 Mar., 31 Oct. 1913
34 Elizabeth Akitt interview, side 1, counter no 600–2
35 Vulcan *Advocate*, 27 Mar. 1918

CHAPTER EIGHT: SCHOOLS AND CHURCHES

1 High River *Times*, 19 July 1906; Wilfred Eggleston, 'The Old Homestead:
Romance and Reality,' in Howard Palmer, ed., *The Settlement of the West* (Calgary: University of Calgary and Comprint Publishing 1977), 117; Vulcan and District Historical Society, *Wheat Country: A History of Vulcan and District* (Vulcan 1973), 449; Elizabeth Akitt, taped interview by Barry Necyk and Sharilyn
Ingram, at Carmangay, 9 Mar. 1973, side 1, counter no 330–1, PAA; Thomas Little
to Deputy Minister of Public Works, 20 Aug. 1909, Village of Carmangay Correspondence, and Donald Sinclair to Minister of Municipal Affairs, 21 Feb. 1930,
MD of Marquis 157 Correspondence, both in Municipality Correspondence Files,
Alberta Department of Municipal Affairs Papers, PAA; Champion History Committee, *Cleverville-Champion, 1905 to 1970, A History of Champion and Area*
(Champion 1971), 247; Carrie McIntyre, interviewed at Vulcan, June 1978; Car-
mangay *Sun*, 15 Sept. 1910
2 John C. Charyk, *The Little White Schoolhouse* (Saskatoon: Western Producer
Prairie Books 1968), 2; C.A. Dawson and E.R. Young, *Pioneering in the Prairie
Provinces: The Social Side of the Settlement Process* (Toronto: Macmillan 1940),
173, 186–7; John W. Chalmers, *Schools of the Foothills Province: The Story of
Public Education in Alberta* (Toronto: University of Toronto Press 1967), 187–8;
Bernal E. Walker, 'The High School Program in Alberta During the Territorial

Period, 1889–1905,' in David C. Jones and others, eds., *Shaping the Schools of the Canadian West* (Calgary: Detselig Enterprises 1979), 211–21; Nancy M. Sheehan, 'Education, the Society and the Curriculum in Alberta 1905–1980: An Overview,' in idem, J. Donald Wilson, David C. Jones, eds., *Schools in the West: Essays in Canadian Educational History* (Calgary: Detselig 1986), 38–40; Louis B. Wright, *Culture on the Moving Frontier* (Bloomington: Indiana University Press 1955), passim

3 Harry Theodore Sparby, 'A History of the Alberta School System to 1925,' PH D, Stanford University 1958, 38–9; Charyk, *White Schoolhouse*, 3–7, 10–11; Vulcan, *Wheat Country*, 449; Elizabeth Akitt interview, side 1, counter no 330–1

4 Charyk, *White Schoolhouse*, 3–5, 11; Chalmers, *Schools*, 26; Vulcan, *Wheat Country*, 152; minutes of Fireguard School District No 3679, p 111, VA

5 Sparby, 'A History,' 64–6; minutes of the Boyne School District No 1778, 24 Dec. 1912, in Willow Creek School Division Records, PAA; Vulcan *Advocate*, 28 Jan. 1914. For the west generally see Charyk, *White Schoolhouse*, 42; Chalmers, *Schools*, 26; David C. Jones, 'Schools and Social Disintegration in the Alberta Dry Belt of the Twenties,' *Prairie Forum* 3, no 1 (Spring 1978): 1–20.

6 Carmangay *Sun*, 11 Dec. 1915, 20 Apr. 1917; Chalmers, *Schools*, 26; minutes of Fireguard School District No 3679, p 38. Statistics calculated from minutes and cashbooks of eleven school districts in Willow Creek School Division Records; annual financial statement and auditor's report of Buffalo School District No 1700, 10 Jan. 1938, Bow Valley School Division Papers, GAA.

7 Mary Boose, untitled, unpub. ms, nd, Mary Boose Papers, GAA; most of the physical problems of one-room prairie schools are discussed in Irene A. Poelzer, 'Local Problems of Early Saskatchewan Education,' *Saskatchewan History* 32, no 1 (Winter 1979): 1–15.

8 Cashbook, Boyne School District No 1778, 1910–20, Willow Creek School Division Records; report of Inspector of High Schools, E.L. Fuller, to Department of Education, 1 Dec. 1932, and H.G. Newland, 28 Nov. 1933, both in Carmangay School District No 2087 Correspondence Files, Alberta Department of Education Records, PAA

9 Minutes of Bow Valley School Division No 1409, 8 Jan. 1927, 29 Dec. 1938, Willow Creek School Division Records; Chalmers, *Schools*, 31–2, 48

10 Chalmers, *Schools*, 37; Poelzer, 'Local Problems,' 1–15; Rena Burns, taped interview by Barry Necyk and Sharilyn Ingram at Carmangay, 7 Mar. 1973, side 1, counter no 195–6, PAA; monthly attendance returns, Sanderson School District No 2210, Sept. 1915, School Attendance Files, Attorney-General of Alberta Records, PAA. For many of the problems facing teachers, see Robert S. Patterson, 'Voices From the Past: The Personal and Professional Struggle of Rural School Teachers,' in Sheehan, *Schools in the West*, espec. 107–10.

11 Carmangay and District History Book Committee, *Bridging the Years; Carmangay and District* (Lethbridge 1968), 152, 355–6, 389; Mrs Roy Burns, interviewed at Carmangay, June 1978; John C. Charyk, *The Little White Schoolhouse*, vol. 2, *Pulse of the Community* (Saskatoon: Western Producer Prairie Books 1970), 29–58; Alston School Reunion Committee, *Alston Echoes, 1906–1949* (Champion 1981), 51; D.O. Jantzie, 'Writings,' unpub. ms, 1965, privately owned by D.O. Jantzie, Vulcan; Champion, *Cleverville-Champion*, 201

12 Minutes of Fireguard School District No 3679, 14 Sept. 1922; Mrs J. Smith, 'My Recollections of Ridgeway District, Carmangay,' unpub. ms, nd, book 32-J, MDK; Alston Trustees to Department of Education, 14 Jan. 1935, Alston School District No 1538 Correspondence, Alberta Department of Education Correspondence Files

13 Mary Boose, untitled; Carmangay *Sun*, 4 July 1913

14 Irene Parlby as quoted in L.J. Wilson, 'Educational Role of the United Farm Women of Alberta,' *Alberta History* 25, no 2 (Spring 1977): 30; Vulcan *Review*, 11 June 1912; see also Jones, 'Schools,' 10–14. Robert M. Stamp, *The Schools of Ontario, 1876–1976* (Toronto: University of Toronto Press 1982), 65–6, notes that the school garden program in rural Ontario not only proved impractical but was rarely combined with any real agricultural training.

15 Dawson, *Pioneering*, 186–7; Sheehan, 'Education,' 44–8

16 Champion, *Cleverville-Champion*, 8–9; Chalmers, *Schools*, 40; Carmangay *Sun*, 9 Mar. 1917; Vulcan *Advocate*, 28 July 1915, 9 Feb. 1916

17 Champion *Chronicle*, 21 Oct. 1920; Vulcan *Advocate*, 28 July 1915; see also Dawson, *Pioneering*, 184.

18 Vulcan *Advocate*, 1 Apr. 1925; Calgary *Herald* , 6 Oct. 1939; Vulcan, *Wheat Country*, 171

19 Stamp, *Schools*, 14–15, 76–8; Wayne F. Fuller, *The Old Country School: The Story of Rural Education in the Middle West* (Chicago and London: The University of Chicago Press 1982), argues that schools performed well in spite of some of the same problems. *Census of Canada* (1921, 1931); *Census of the Prairie Provinces* (1926); see also Dawson, *Pioneering*, 188–92.

20 Rev. David J. Carter, 'A History of the Anglican Diocese of Calgary,' Bachelor of Sacred Theology Thesis, Anglican Theological College of British Columbia 1968, 49–50; 'Minutes of the Alberta Conference,' in *Minutes of Annual Conferences of the Methodist Church* (1906), 9; Champion United Church, 'The Background and History of the United Church in Champion,' unpub. ms, 196?, book 9-Z, MDK; minutebook of the Board of Managers of Vulcan Presbyterian Church, 9 July 1912, Vulcan Pastoral Charge Papers, United Church of Canada Records, PAA

21 Minutes of Carmangay Methodist Church Quarterly Official Board, 11 Oct. 1929, 13 Aug. 1921, Carmangay Pastoral Charge Papers, United Church of Canada

Records, PAA; Vulcan *Advocate*, 15 Apr. 1914; Presbyterian Church in Canada, *Acts and Proceedings of the General Assembly of the Presbyterian Church in Canada* (1919), 39; minutes of the High River Presbytery, 20 Nov. 1917, 10 Feb. 1919, 15 Mar. 1927, United Church of Canada Records, PAA; Rev. D.F. Kemp to Mr Adam, 19 Nov. 1931, Vulcan Anglican Church Papers, ACC; Father Cunningham? to Father Ritter, 6 Feb. 1938, Vulcan Roman Catholic Church File, CDA; Carmangay, *Bridging*, 132

22 *Census of Canada* (1901–41)

23 P.J. Haslam, 'History of Hearnleigh, Berrywater and Adjacent Districts,' unpub. ms, nd, 3, GAI; Vulcan, *Wheat Country*, 130; Carmangay, *Bridging*, 131; Champion, *Cleverville-Champion*, 391; Georgina H. Thomson, *Crocus and Meadowlark Country, Recollections of a Happy Childhood and Youth on a Homestead in Southern Alberta* (Edmonton: Institute of Applied Art 1963), 134

24 Murray Wenstob, 'The Work of the Methodist Church among Settlers in Alberta up to 1914, with Special Reference to the Formation of New Congregations and Work among the Ukranian People,' BD, St Stephen's College, Edmonton, 1959, 53–4; John S. Moir, *Enduring Witness: A History of the Presbyterian Church in Canada* (Toronto: Presbyterian Publications 1974), 161; E.G. Luxton, 'Vulcan,' unpub. ms, 1958, 5, Eleanor Luxton Papers, GAI; Nanton *News*, 9 Mar. 1911; Carmangay *Sun*, 2 Mar. 1911; Vulcan *Review*, 19, 26 Mar., 17, 24 Sept. 1912

25 Minutes of Carmangay Methodist Church Quarterly Official Board, 18 Mar. 1912, 29 Jan. 1913; Nanton *News*, 1 Dec. 1915; minutes of the High River Presbytery, 26 Aug. 1915; minutes of annual district meetings of High River, vol. 2, 29, Methodist Church District Records, United Church of Canada Records, PAA

26 Dawson, *Pioneering*, 239. For early mergers in Saskatchewan see Christine Macdonald, 'Pioneer Church Life in Saskatchewan,' *Saskatchewan History* 13, no 1 (Winter 1960): 12–15; Edmund H. Oliver, *His Dominion of Canada: A Study in the Background, Development, and Challenge of the Missions of the United Church of Canada* (Toronto: Board of Home Missions and the Woman's Missionary Society of the United Church of Canada 1932), 138. For a weakening of denominational ties on the mid-nineteenth century midwestern frontier see Don Doyle Harrison, *The Social Order of a Frontier Community: Jacksonville, Illinois, 1825–70* (Chicago: University of Illinois Press 1978), 47–8, 159.

27 Letter of D.K. Allan in *Acts and Proceedings* (1914), 379, (1913), 49–50; Luxton, 'Vulcan,' 5; Vulcan *Advocate*, 11 Oct. 1916; David Smith, 'Instilling British Values in the Prairie Provinces,' *Prairie Forum* 6, no 2 (Fall 1981): 133; Vulcan, *Wheat Country*, 124

28 Many newspapers. See Michael Gauvreau, 'The Taming of History: Reflections on the Canadian Methodist Encounter with Biblical Criticism, 1830–1900,' *Canadian*

Historical Review 65, no 3 (Sept. 1984): 315–46, for the movement of Methodism from scriptural literalism to modernism.

29 See especially such influential books as William E. Mann, *Sect, Cult and Church in Alberta* (Toronto: University of Toronto Press 1955); John A. Irving, *The Social Credit Movement in Alberta* (Toronto: University of Toronto Press 1959); C.B. Macpherson, *Democracy in Alberta: The Theory and Practice of a Quasi-Party System* (Toronto: University of Toronto Press 1953); Richard Allen, *The Social Passion: Religion and Social Reform in Canada 1914–1928* (Toronto: University of Toronto Press 1973).

30 *Census of Canada* (1901–41)

31 Thos M. Melrose to Canon Hogbin, 5 Sept. 1911, Carmangay Anglican Church Papers, ACC. For scholarly studies that agree on the general failure of fundamentalism on the prairies see Wenstob, 'Methodist Church,' 60; William H. Brooks, 'The Uniqueness of Western Canadian Methodism, 1840–1925,' *Journal of Canadian Church Historical Society* 19, no 1–2 (Mar.–June 1977), 58; Gerald M. Hutchinson, 'The Rural Church in Alberta,' BD, St Stephen's College, Edmonton 1943, 7.

32 Richard Allen, 'The Social Gospel as the Religion on the Agrarian Revolt,' in Carl Berger and Ramsay Cook, eds., *The West and the Nation: Essays in Honour of W.L. Morton* (Toronto: McClelland and Stewart 1976), 174–86; *Vulcan Advocate*, 28 June 1916, 24 May 1922; minutes of the High River Presbytery, 4 May 1932

33 R.A. Mowat to Archdeacon Hogbin, 29 Aug. 1913, Carmangay Anglican Church Papers

34 J.T. Ferguson in *Acts and Proceedings* (1913), 2, (1915), 47; see also W.D. Reid in 1911, 22.

35 Minutes of the Alberta Conference of the Methodist Church (1906), 18–19; *Acts and Proceedings* (1908–13); minute book of the Armada Circuit of the Alberta Conference of the Free Methodist Church, 1916–40, GAI; Thos Melrose to Canon Hogbin, 5 Dec. 1911, Carmangay Anglican Church Papers

36 United Church of Canada, *Year Book and Record of Proceedings* (1926–40), UCA; Trustee Board of the Methodist Church minutes, 2 Aug. 1917, Champion-Carmangay Pastoral Charge, United Church Records, PAA.

37 Financial statements, Carmangay Methodist Church, Carmangay Pastoral Charge Records, 1916; R.A. Mowat to Rev. Canon Hogbin, 9 Oct. 1911; Thos M. Melrose to Archdeacon Hogbin, 10 Feb. 1913, both in Correspondence, Carmangay Anglican Church Papers; minutes of the High River Presbytery, 4 May 1927; Father Ritter to Bishop, 27 July 1938, 11 Jan. 1940, Vulcan Roman Catholic File.

38 *Nanton News*, 19 Jan. 1911; W.S. Hinchey to Rev. Canon Hogbin, 28 Nov. 1910, Carmangay Anglican Church Papers; *Acts and Proceedings* (1913), 51; minute

book of Vestry and Congregation, Emmanuel Church Carmangay, 5 Jan. 1919,
Anglican Church, Carmangay; High River *Times*, 15 Mar. 1906; minutebook of
the Board of Managers, Vulcan Presbyterian Church, 15 Jan. 1914, Vulcan Pastoral Charge Papers, United Church of Canada Records, PAA; minutes of the
Alberta Conference of the Methodist Church, 69; High River Parish Files, CDA;
M.B. Venini Byrne, *From the Buffalo to the Cross: A History of the Roman
Catholic Diocese of Calgary* (Calgary: Calgary Archives and Historical Publishers
1973), 323–4. Dawson, *Pioneering*, 219–23, claimed that of 929 rural prairie families surveyed in the 1930s, 27 per cent did not attend services at all and another
quarter rarely attended; Jean Burnet, *Next-Year Country: A Study of Rural
Social Organization in Alberta* (Toronto: University of Toronto Press 1951), 67,
estimated that non-church-goers in the Oyen, Alberta, area outnumbered any single congregation in the 1940s.
39 Vulcan *Advocate*, 22 Aug. 1923, 20 Jan. 1915; Dr Weston W. Upton to Margery
Ramsay, 12 Apr. 1911, Margery Ramsay Papers, GAI; Carmangay *Sun*, 8 July
1910
40 R.A. Mowat to Archdeacon Hogbin, 29 Aug. 1913, Carmangay Anglican Church
Papers; Alfred Lee to Secretary, Diocese of Calgary, 9 Dec. 1914, Vulcan Anglican Church Papers; copy of letter, J.W. Oliver to Champion United Church, 17
Oct. 1956; Mansfield Newton to Rev. Huston, 1956, both in Champion United
Church, 'The Background'
41 Upton to Ramsay; A. Beausoliel to Bishop of Calgary, 9 June 1914, High River
Parish File; Father Ritter to Bishop of Calgary, 3 Nov. 1938, Vulcan Roman
Catholic Church File
42 Harvey Beaubier, interviewed at Champion, June 1978; Quarterly Official Board
of Carmangay Methodist Church to Mr and Mrs J.F. Synder, nd, Correspondence Files, Carmangay Pastoral Charge Papers; minutes of Carmangay Methodist Church Quarterly Official board, 10 May 1915; minutes of Annual District
Meetings of High River, p. 29, Methodist Church District Records, United
Church of Canada Records, PAA; Vulcan *Advocate*, 1 Feb. 1922
43 Quoted in Byrne, *From the Buffalo*, 323; see minutes of annual district meetings
of High River, Methodist Church District Records; T.C.B. Boon, *The Anglican
Church from the Bay to the Rockies* (Toronto: Ryerson Press 1962), 335; High
River Parish Files
44 Quoted in Byrne, *From the Buffalo*, 323; Carmangay, *Bridging*, 129; see also
J.W.G. Hathaway to S. Houlton, 17 June 1918, Correspondence, Carmangay
Anglican Church Papers.
45 Minutes of the Alberta Conference (1927), 17; Ernest Davidge, 'Reminiscences,'
unpub. ms, 197?, UCA
46 Minutes of the High River Presbytery, 1907–25; Wenstob, 'The Work of the

Methodist,' 119-20; United Church of Canada, Vulcan, 'Church Anniversary and Dedication Services, 1911-1953,' unpub. ms, 1953, in Vulcan Pastoral Charge Papers; Carmangay, *Bridging*, 135-6; 'The Carmangay United Church 1910-1952,' unpub. ms, nd, Carmangay Pastoral Charge Papers; minutes of the Alberta Conference of the Methodist Church (1909-22); Champion United Church, 'The Background,' 2-10. For similar problems throughout rural Alberta, western Canada, and the United States see Mann, *Sect*, 96-7; Brooks, 'The Uniqueness,' 67; Myles W. Rodehaver, 'Ministers on the Move: A Study of Mobility in Church Leadership,' *Rural Sociology* 13, no 4 (1948): 400-10.

47 Wenstob, 'The Work of the Methodist,' 60; Brooks, 'The Uniqueness,' 57-74; Burnet, *Next-Year*, 146; Dawson, *Pioneering*, 67, 203, 214-27; George N. Emery, 'Ontario Denied: The Methodist Church on the Prairies, 1896-1914,' in F.H. Armstrong and others, eds., *Aspects of Nineteenth-Century Ontario* (Toronto: University of Toronto Press 1974), 312-26; L.M. Wenham, 'The Baptist Home Mission Problem in Western Canada,' BD, McMaster University 1947. For rural North America generally see G.T. Nesmith, 'The Problem of the Rural Community, with Special Reference to the Rural Church,' *American Journal of Sociology* 8, no 6 (May 1903): 812-37; Kenyon L. Butterfield, 'The Social Problems of American Farmers,' *American Journal of Sociology* 10, no 5 (Mar. 1905): 619-21; Warren H. Wilson, 'The Church and the Rural Community,' *American Journal of Sociology* 16, no 5 (Mar. 1911): 668-93; Clayton S. Ellsworth, 'Theodore Roosevelt's Country Life Commission,' *Agricultural History* 34, no 4 (Oct. 1960): 168; J.H. Riddell, *Methodism in the Middle West* (Toronto: Ryerson Press 1946), 231-4; A.B. Hollingshead, 'The Life Cycle of Nebraska Rural Churches,' *Rural Sociology* 2, no 2 (June 1937): 180-91.

48 George Thomas Daily, *Catholic Problems in Western Canada*(Toronto: Macmillan 1921), 33; minutes of the Alberta Conference of the Methodist Church, 27; *Acts and Proceedings* (1913), 50

49 Annual reports of High River Presbytery, *Acts and Proceedings* (1905-11); Daly, *Catholic*, 36; Thos M. Melrose to Canon Hogbin, 5 Dec. 1911, Carmangay Anglican Church Papers

50 Calculations based on minutes of annual district meetings of High River, 1913-18, Methodist Church District Records; minutebook of the Board of Managers, Vulcan Presbyterian Church, 5 Jan. 1915; Vulcan *Advocate*, 13 Jan. 1915; Cleverville Union Sunday School attendance records, 1908, book 9-z, MDK. Minutes of the Alberta Conference (1919), 19, (1923), 15, estimated that in all Alberta the attendance of Protestant children at Sunday School ran no more than 50 per cent.

51 Davidge, 'Reminiscences,' 135; N. Heaston to M.D. Keenan, 23 Apr. 1975, Correspondence Files, MDK; Methodist Church Carmangay, 'Memorial Album,' unpub. ms, 1920?, Carmangay Pastoral Charge Papers

52 Thomson, *Crocus*, 134; see also Macdonald, 'Pioneer Church,' 16; Brooks, 'The Uniqueness,' 64; report of visit by Dr Dorey, in 'Report of the Rural Commission of the Western Conferences,' unpub. ms, Mar. 1947, in Board of Home Missions Records, box 18, file 514, UCA

53 Hutchinson, 'Rural Church,' 56; H.R. Leaves to Bishop of Calgary, 6 May 1912, Carmangay Anglican Church Papers; Vulcan *Advocate*, 1 Nov. 1916

54 'Report of Rev. R.J. McDonald on Southern Alberta and Southern Saskatchewan,' *United Church of Canada Year Book* (1938), 123; for membership see 1925–40; Father Ritter to Bishop, 11 Jan. 1940, Vulcan Roman Catholic Church File; *Census of Canada* (1931), vol. 2, 672–5, (1941), vol. 2, 546–7.

55 Vulcan *Advocate*, 21 Feb., 11 July, 19 Sept. 1935; Irving, *Social Credit*, 85, 313–14 (the sole piece of evidence I have found linking religion with Social Credit in the Vulcan area is on p 281). Vulcan, *Wheat Country*, 130. Mann, *Sect*, 22, notes that province-wide membership in the Prophetic Bible Institute never surpassed 3,000. Rena Burns interview; Champion *Chronicle*, 22 Aug., 10 Oct. 1935

56 Based on seven interviews; see also many newspaper clippings, book 19-S, MDK; many items in George Gibson Coote Papers, GAI.

57 I have been unable to local many primary documents relating to the nominations, but see Champion *Chronicle*, 16 May 1935; Vulcan *Advocate*, 19 Sept. 1935; John Irving's interview with Ernest G. Hansell, 28 Oct. 1957, John A. Irving Papers, Thomas Fisher Rare Book Room, University of Toronto Library; E.G. Hansell Information File, PAA.

58 Copy of letter from Hidegarde C. Dawson to Champion United Church, nd, Champion United Church, 'The Background'; David R. Elliott, 'Antithetical Elements in William Aberhart's Theology and Political Ideology,' *Canadian Historical Review* 59, no 1 (Mar. 1978): 38–58; idem, 'The Dispensational Theology and Political Ideology of William Aberhart,' MA, Calgary 1975; Owen A. Anderson, 'The Alberta Social Credit Party: An Empirical Analysis of Membership, Characteristics, Participation and Opinions,' PH D, Alberta 1972, espec. 215–19

CHAPTER NINE: SOCIAL STRUCTURE

1 Frederick Jackson Turner, *The Frontier in American History* (New York: Henry Holt 1920); Daniel J. Boorstin, *The Americans: The National Experience* (New York: Random House 1965), passim; Joseph Schafer, *Social History of American Agriculture* (New York: Macmillan 1936), 199–208; Stanley Elkins and Eric McKitrick, 'A Meaning for Turner's Frontier,' 1: 'Democracy in the Old Northwest,' *Policial Science Quarterly* 69, no 3 (Sept. 1954): 321–53; Merle Curti, *The Making of an American Community: A Case Study of Democracy in a Frontier County* (Stanford: Stanford University Press 1959); Lewis Atherton, *Main Street*

on the Middle Border (Bloomington: Indiana University Press 1954), passim; Earl
H. Bell, *The Culture of a Contemporary Rural Community: Sublette, Kansas*
(Washington: U.S. Department of Agriculture, Bureau of Agricultural Economics,
Rural Life Studies 2, 1942), espec. 97–8; Elvin Hatch, 'Stratification in a Rural
California Community,' *Agricultural History* 49, no 1 (Jan. 1975): espec. 27; C.A.
Dawson and E.R. Young, *Pioneering in the Prairie Provinces; The Social Side of
the Settlement Process* (Toronto: Macmillan 1940), espec. 71; C.B. McPherson,
Democracy in Alberta: The Theory and Practice of a Quasi-Party System
(Toronto: University of Toronto Press 1953)

2 August B. Hollingshead, 'Class and Kinship in a Middle Western Community,'
American Sociological Review 14, no 4 (Aug. 1949): 469–75; John Useem, Pierre
Tangent, Ruth Useem, 'Stratification in a Prairie Town,' *American Sociological
Review* 7, no 3 (June 1942): 331–42; Robert R. Dykstra, *The Cattle Towns* (New
York: Alfred A. Knopf 1968); Evon Z. Vogt, Jr, 'Social Stratification in the Rural
Middlewest: A Structural Analysis,' *Rural Sociology* 12, no 4 (1947): 364–75;
Lewis G. Thomas, 'Okotoks: From Trading Post to Suburb,' *Urban History
Review* 8, no 2 (Oct. 1979), espec. 15; Robert V. Hine, *Community on the Ameri-
can Frontier: Separate but not Alone* (Norman: University of Oklahoma Press
1980), 148–52; James West, *Plainville, U.S.A.* (New York: Columbia University
Press 1945, Columbia paperback 1961), 115–41

3 For emphasis on a great variety of social distinction see West, *Plainville*, 115–41;
Useem, 'Stratification,' 331–42; Vogt, 'Social Stratification,' 364–75; Jean Burnet,
Next-Year Country: A Study of Rural Social Organization in Alberta (Toronto:
University of Toronto Press 1951), 69–71, 96–111; Carl Kraenzel, *Great Plains in
Transition* (Norman: University of Oklahoma Press 1955), 227–83.

4 'Census of Carmangay,' unpub. ms, 1912, PAA; other calculations from *Wrigley's
Alberta Directory* (1920), 669–71, (1922), 231, 238–9, 669–71; *Henderson's Province of Alberta Directory* (1928–9), 186–7, 610–11; and *Census of Canada*
(1931)

5 Calculated from Homestead Files, 17-25-4, PAA; *Census of Canada* (1941). A
higher percentage of farmers in Alberta at large and in Ontario earned outside
income; in the Vulcan area some of it undoubtedly came from contracting or non-
farm investment. The importance of earning outside income is stressed by Dawson, *Pioneering*, 16; and David McGinnis, 'Farm Labour in Transition: Occupational Structure and Economic Dependency in Alberta, 1921–1951,' in Howard
Palmer, ed., *The Settlement of the West* (Calgary: University of Calgary and
Comprint Publishing 1977), 174–186.

6 H.S. Parker to CPR Dept of Colonization and Development, 26 Apr. 1926, Carmangay Colonization Board Correspondence, CPR Papers, GAI. See also E.B. Mitchell, *In Western Canada before the War: A Study of Communities* (London:

John Murray 1915), 49, on shortages of servants and labourers in western Canada generally.

7 Figures 27 and 28 are based on listings in R.G. Dun and Co., *The Mercantile Agency Reference Book Containing Ratings ...* (1909–35), DBC. The figures exclude those businesses that were not locally owned (banks, grain elevators, most lumber yards) and those that were never rated (insurance and real-estate agents, and most professions). Because so many service businesses were not rated, agricultural and consumer services have been grouped together on Figure 28 to provide a wider sample.

8 G.H. Craig and J. Coke, *An Economic Study of Land Utilization in Southern Alberta* (Ottawa: Canadian Dept. of Agriculture, Economics Division, Marketing Service, Publication 610, Technical Bulletin 16, 1938), 66

9 Calculated from Homestead Files, 17-25-4

10 Craig, *Economic Study*, 71; John Proskie, 'Financial Progress of Settlers with Special Reference to the Vulcan-Lomond Area,' MA, Alberta 1937, 35

11 Based on many documents relating to E.G. Hansell, Peter Dawson, O.L. MacPherson, James McNaughton, and D.H. Galbraith

12 Village of Carmangay Returning Officer to Department of Public Works, 10 Feb. 1910, Village of Carmangay Correspondence; Village of Champion Returning Officer to Deputy Minister of Public Works, 2 June 1911, 22 Jan. 1912, Village of Champion Correspondence; Village of Vulcan Returning Officer to Deputy Minister of Municipal Affairs, 28 Jan. 1913, Village of Vulcan Correspondence, all in Municipality Correspondence Files, Department of Municipal Affairs Papers, PAA. Also Carmangay *Sun*, 21 Apr. 1911; Calgary *Albertan*, 18 Apr. 1911; High River *Times*, 23 Jan. 1913; Vulcan *Advocate*, 17 Dec. 1913. This evidence seems to support the thesis advanced by Elkins and McKitrick, 'A Meaning,' 321–53, who argued that the immense task of community-building forced pioneers to make many decisions, resulting in widespread interest and participation in local government, especially in the American midwest, where town promotion promised to enrich everyone.

13 Based on biographical files assembled from many sources

14 Based on returning officer reports, 1911–19, in village and town correspondence for Carmangay, Champion, and Vulcan

15 Champion History Committee, *Cleverville-Champion, 1905 to 1970, A History of Champion and Area* (Champion 1971?), 19; Dun, *Mercantile Agency* (1921–30); James McNaughton to Deputy Minister of Education, 28 Mar. 1936, Carmangay School District 2087 Correspondence, Correspondence with School Districts, Alberta Dept. of Education Correspondence Files, PAA

16 'The History of Municipal Government of Vulcan by D.D. McQueen,' videotaped interview by Marg Weber, County of Vulcan Educational Television Production, 1975, CVO

17 J.M.S. Careless, 'Aspects of Urban Life in the West, 1870–1914,' in Anthony W. Rasporich and Henry C. Klassen, eds., *Prairie Perspectives 2* (Toronto: Holt, Rinehart and Winston 1973), 34

18 Village and Town Council of Carmangay Minutes (1910), 19, 179; Carmangay *Sun*, 3 June 1910, 19 May 1911; Carl Stettner, interviewed at Carmangay, May 1978

19 Vulcan Curling Club Minutes, 1915–33, VA; Dun, *Mercantile Agency* (1915–33). Morris Mott, 'One Solution to the Urban Crisis: Manly Sports and Winnipeggers, 1900–1914,' *Urban History Review* 12, no 2 (Oct. 1983): 66, notes how both curling and tennis lost their upper- and middle-class distinctiveness after 1900, even in the largest western city.

20 Rev. Evan Beechman, 'Script of Talk on the Early History of Milo,' unpub. ms, Mar. 1964, GAI; Carrie McIntyre, interviewed at Vulcan, June 1978

21 Little Bow Branch (Alston) of the Canadian Red Cross Society Minutes, 1918–19, 1–5, VA; Bell, *Culture*, 99–101; Burnet, *Next-Year*, 69

22 Newspapers often made brief references to this group, but for the best descriptions see justices-of-the-peace files for Carmangay, Champion, and Vulcan, Attorney General of Alberta Records, PAA. The best characterization, however, is the fictional 'Old Ben' in W.O. Mitchell's *Who Has Seen the Wind* (1947). For the presence of such people in the American midwest see Atherton, *Main Street*, 65–108, where he discusses community standards and the difficulty of upholding and enforcing them.

23 For a social and economic examination of the Chinese that includes information on Vulcan see Paul Voisey, 'Chinatown on the Prairies: The Emergence of an Ethnic Community,' in Christina Cameron and Martin Segger, eds., *Selected Papers from the Society for the Study of Architecture in Canada* (Ottawa: Society for the Study of Architecture in Canada 1981), 33–52.

24 A study of a low population density, dryland grain-farming community in California from 1900 to 1920 also noted that while wealth was stratified, it did not lead to major social cleavages; see Hatch, 'Stratification,' 27. For a similar community in Kansas see Bell, *Culture*, 98.

25 See Bell, *Culture*, 97, for a similar situation in a Kansas farming community.

26 S. Ching Lee, 'The Theory of the Agricultural Ladder,' *Agricultural History* 21, no 1 (Jan. 1947): 53–60; Erven J. Long, 'The Agricultural Ladder – Its Adequacy as a Model for Farm Tenure Research,' *Land Economics* 26, no 3 (Aug. 1950): 268–73. For a careful study tracing its validity and that of frontier social mobility in general see Curti, *The Making*, passim. A variation on this theme for post-frontier conditions describes a movement from birth and training on a father's farm to a partnership with the father to full ownership and control after the father's retirement or death; see Marshall Harris, 'A New Agricultural Ladder,' *Land Economics*, 26, no 3 (Aug. 1950): 258–67.

27 Many letters, 1933-5, George Gibson Coote Papers, espec. file 9, GAI; and in Town of Vulcan Correspondence

28 Newspaper clippings, 1942, book 7-X, MDK; Calgary *Herald*, 30 May 1942; many interviews

29 David Gagan, *Hopeful Travellers: Families, Land, and Social Change in Mid-Victorian Peel County, Canada West* (Toronto: University of Toronto Press 1981), 51-52; Horace Miner, *Culture and Agriculture: An Anthropological Study of a Corn-Belt County* (Ann Arbor: University of Michigan Press 1949), 58-9

30 D.O. Jantzie, 'Writings,' unpub. ms, 1965, privately held by D.O. Jantzie, Vulcan; 'A Look Into the Past, Vulcan Pioneer: D.O. Jantzie,' videotaped interview by Don Jantzie, County of Vulcan Educational Television, 1975, CVO; D.O. Jantzie, interviewed at Vulcan, May 1978

31 Vulcan and District Historical Society, *Wheat Country: A History of Vulcan and District* (Vulcan 1973), 782-3. John C. Hudson, 'Migration to an American Frontier,' *Annals of the Association of American Geographers* 66, no 2 (June 1976): 258-9, also argues that continuous shifts in occupations, class, wealth, and residency in rural North Dakota render the question of frontier social mobility almost meaningless.

32 Vulcan *Advocate*, 18 June 1919

33 Annual report, 19 Dec. 1914, Vulcan Agricultural Society Papers, GAI; Annual District of High River Minutes, 32-4, Methodist Church District Records, United Church of Canada Records, PAA; Vulcan Ladies Community Society Minutes, 1924, VA; Carmangay *Sun*, 9 Mar. 1913

34 Lethbridge *Herald*, 12 Oct. 1937; Harvey Beaubier, interviewed at Champion, June 1978. John C. Charyk, *The Little White Schoolhouse*, vol. 2: *Pulse of the Community* (Saskatoon: Western Producer, Prairie Books 1970), 249, noted that those first elected to school boards were usually totally inexperienced in public administration but that good members tended to be re-elected again and again. The experience of the Vulcan area confirms much about the democratic tendencies of frontiers first noted by Turner but argued in more sophisticated fashion in Elkins and McKitrick, 'A Meaning,' espec. 321-40, and extensively documented in Curti, *The Making*.

35 See espec. Gagan, *Hopeful Travellers*, 139-40; West, *Plainville*, 115-41; Cole Harris, 'Of Poverty and Helplessness in Petite-Nation,' *Canadian Historical Review* 52, no 1 (Mar. 1971): 44-5.

36 The pioneers often used the word 'class' but gave it a variety of debased meanings. Sometimes it referred to ethnicity ('Scotsmen are a good class of people'), sometimes to morality ('They don't drink and fight; they are not of that class'), and sometimes to behaviour ('The farmers here are a hard-working class'), but rarely did the word refer to differences in occupation or wealth.

37 Carmangay and District History Book Committee, *Bridging the Years; Carmangay and District* (Lethbridge 1968), 37; Elizabeth Akitt, taped interview by Sharilyn Ingram and Barry Necyk, at Carmangay, 9 Mar. 1973, side 1, counter no 210–12. Thus the area no longer shared the levels of status attached to various occupations in the late nineteenth-century midwest; see Atherton, *Main Street*, 148–80.

CHAPTER TEN: SOCIAL RELATIONS

1 Carmangay *Sun*, 24 Aug. 1917; Champion *Chronicle*, 13 Jan. 1920; Vulcan *Advocate*, 19 Sept. 1923; Cecilia Danysk, ' "Showing These Slaves Their Class Position": Barriers to Organizing Prairie Farm Workers,' in David C. Jones and Ian MacPherson, eds., *Building Beyond the Homestead: Rural History on the Prairies* (Calgary: University of Calgary Press 1985), 171–2; John Herd Thompson, 'Bringing in the Sheaves: The Harvest Excursionists, 1890–1929,' *Canadian Historical Review* 59, no 4 (Dec. 1978): 486; Allen Gale Applen, 'Migratory Harvest Labor in the Midwestern Wheat Belt, 1870–1940,' PH D, Kansas State 1974, 151–65; David G. Wagaman, 'The Industrial Workers of the World in Nebraska, 1914–1920,' *Nebraska History* 56, no 3 (Fall 1975): 295–337
2 Danysk, 'Showing These Slaves,' 171–2; Vulcan *Advocate*, 19, 26 Sept. 1923; Applen, 'Migratory Harvest,' 151–65
3 For these views of itinerant harvesters in the U.S. see Applen, 'Migratory Harvest,' 103–12.
4 Thompson, 'Bringing in,' 486; Wagaman, 'Industrial Workers,' 295–337; Danysk, 'Showing These Slaves,' 164–7
5 W.J.C. Cherwinski, 'In Search of Jake Trumper: The Farm Hand and the Prairie Farm Family,' in Jones and MacPherson, *Building beyond*, 111–34; Carl Stettner, interviewed at Carmangay, May 1978; Vulcan and District Historical Society, *Wheat Country: A History of Vulcan and District* (Vulcan 1973), 609
6 These matters are all raised in *Farm and Ranch Review*, 20 Aug. 1913; see also Newell L. Sims, *Elements of Rural Society*, 3rd edn (New York: Thomas Y. Crowell 1940), 441–4; Applen, 'Migratory Harvest,' 52–5, 101; Cherwinski, 'In Search,' 111–34.
7 This interpretation is suggested by Paul H. Johnstone, 'Old Ideals Versus New Ideas in Farm Life,' in *Farmers in a Changing World; The Yearbook of Agriculture* (Washington: U.S. Department of Agriculture 1940), 149–51; and in Cherwinski, 'In Search,' 111–34. For an explanation of declining social status in terms of the increasingly unskilled nature of farm labour see Allen G. Applen, 'Labor Casualization in Great Plains Wheat Production: 1865–1902,' *Journal of the West* 16, no 1 (Jan. 1977): 5–9. For the impact of the decline of year-round help on the status of hired men see Newell, *Elements*, 441–4.

8 Farm-hands in Alberta could lose wages for work already performed because unlike non-agricultural labour, their legal status was prescribed by the stringent and grossly obsolete Masters and Servants Act; see Danysk, 'Showing These Slaves,' 168; Vulcan *Advocate*, 26 Nov. 1913. See also monthly reports of D Division, 1914–16, RCMP Records, PAC; justices-of-the-peace files for Carmangay, Champion, and Vulcan, 1910–18, Attorney General of Alberta Records, PAA.

9 Carmangay *Sun*, 13 Oct. 1911, 22 Sept. 1913; Vulcan *Advocate*, 7 Apr. 1915. For farmers as socialists in the area see John Glambeck Papers, GAI.

10 Long recognized as a major conflict on the western American frontier, it has been largely ignored in western Canada, but see David H. Breen, 'Plain Talk From Plain Western Men,' *Alberta Historical Review* 18, no 3 (Summer 1970): 8–13; idem, 'The Canadian Prairie West and the "Harmonious" Settlement Interpretation,' *Agricultural History* 47, no 1 (Jan. 1973): 63–75.

11 Champion History Committee, *Cleverville-Champion, 1905 to 1970, A History of Champion and Area* (Champion 1971?), 633, also 198; Carmangay and District History Book Committee, *Bridging the Years; Carmangay and District* (Carmangay 1968), 391; Harvey Beaubier, interviewed at Champion, June 1978; Vulcan, *Wheat Country*, 696

12 Homestead Files, Township 17-25-4, PAA; monthly reports of K Division, 24 July, 18 Sept. 1906, RCMP Records, PAC; Canada, *Sessional Papers* 25 (1904), pt 3, 114; Harvey Beaubier interview; Georgina Neilson, taped interview by Barry Necyk and Sharilyn Ingram at Carmangay, 6 Mar. 1973, side 1, counter no 268–75, PAA; Douglas Hardwick, taped interview by E.S. Bryant, 11 Sept. 1957, reel 2, side 1, counter no 216, PAA; Roy Burns, interviewed at Carmangay, Feb. 1978; Vulcan *Advocate*, 14 June, 18 Oct. 1916; Carmangay *Sun*, 19 Jan. 1912; Calgary *Herald*, 29 June 1962; N. Heaston to Dale Keenan, 23 Apr. 1975, M.D. Keenan Correspondence Files, MDK; Vulcan, *Wheat Country*, 746; Carmangay, *Bridging*, 436; Champion, *Cleverville-Champion*, 216, 647; High River Pioneers' and Old Timers' Association, *Leaves from the Medicine Tree* (High River, Alta, 1960), 2–13

13 Sims, *Elements*, 119–24; Stanley B. Parsons, *The Populist Context: Rural versus Urban Power on a Great Plains Frontier* (Westport, Conn.: Greenwood Press 1973); Roy W. Meyer, *The Middle Western Farm Novel in the Twentieth Century* (Lincoln: University of Nebraska Press 1965), 11–12; Richard G. Bremer, *Agricultural Change in an Urban Age: The Loup Country of Nebraska, 1910–1970* (Lincoln: University of Nebraska Studies, no 51, 1976), espec. 37; William Robbins, 'Community Conflict in Roseburg, Oregon, 1870–1885,' *Journal of the West* 12, no 4 (Oct. 1973): 618–32; Jean Burnet, *Next-Year Country: A Study of Rural Social Organization in Alberta* (Toronto: University of Toronto Press 1951), 54, 75–84; idem, 'Town-Country Relations and the Problem of Rural Leadership,' *Canadian Journal of Economics and Political Science* 13, no 3 (Aug. 1947): 395–410

14 See Chap. 3; also Vulcan *Advocate*, 24 Dec. 1913.

15 Vulcan *Advocate*, 6 Aug., 24 Dec. 1913, 21, 28 June 1922; Carmangay *Sun*, 2 Mar. 1911, 29 June 1912; Harvey Beaubier interview; Roy Burns interview; Jack Dietz, interviewed near Milo, Apr. 1978; Ken Miller, interviewed near Carmangay, May 1978

16 Sims, *Elements*, 121; Earl H. Bell, *The Culture of a Contemporary Rural Community: Sublette, Kansas* (Washington: u.s. Dept. of Agriculture, Bureau of Agricultural Economics, Rural Life Studies 2, 1942), 96–7, argues that the absence of wealth and class divisions between town and country resulted in peaceful relations between the two groups. The loss of independent economic decision-making in small American towns was first noted by Thorstein Veblen, 'The Country Town,' in *Absentee Ownership and Business Enterprise in Recent Times: The Case of America* (1923; New York: Sentry Press 1964), 151–6.

17 Based on individual poll returns published in Carmangay *Sun*, 13 Oct. 1911, 18 Apr. 1913, 8 June 1917; Vulcan *Advocate*, 20 July 1921. The one exception was the 1921 provincial election, and it resulted from overwhelming personal support in Carmangay for local businessmen and Liberal James McNaughton, who lost. See also *A Report on Alberta Elections, 1905–1982* (Edmonton: Office of the Chief Electoral Officer 1983), 46.

18 For conflicts based on values see Sims, *Elements*, 123; Bremer, *Agricultural Change*, 43–5; Burnet, *Next-Year*, 94; Burnet, 'Town-Country,' 395–410; Don S. Kirschner, *City and Country: Rural Responses to Urbanization in the 1920's* (Westport, Conn.: Greenwood Press 1970), passim. For the changing role of pioneer merchants see Lewis E. Atherton, *The Frontier Merchant in Mid-America* (Columbia: University of Missouri Press 1971).

19 Based on individual polling-station results reported in Carmangay *Sun*, 29 July 1915. Erhard Pinno, 'Temperance and Prohibition in Saskatchewan,' MA, Saskatchewan at Regina 1971, argues that prohibition was not basically anti-urban, nor did it deal with issues particularly amenable to rural-urban splits.

20 These attitudes are more fully described in Howard Palmer, *Patterns of Prejudice: A History of Nativism in Alberta* (Toronto: McClelland and Stewart 1982), 22–37.

21 Carmangay, *Bridging*, 52–3; D.A. McNiven, interviewed near Vulcan, June 1978

22 Vulcan *Advocate*, 5 Oct. 1921, 6 May 1925. According to local opinion, Russian Doukhobors who settled just beyond the northeastern fringe of the Vulcan area, and Blackfoot Indians situated on the Gleichen reserve to the north, did constitute a threat, but as they lived far from most of the area's population and took their trade to other towns, the occasional verbal barbs slung at them did not constitute part of local conflict patterns within the area itself. Fewer still bothered to launch any direct action against them, but when the boundaries of the MD of Marquis encompassed the Doukhobor colony, the municipality begged the province to

administer it separately as a Special Area; see J.K. McLean to Minister of Municipal Affairs, 6 July 1937, in MD of Marquis 157 Correspondence, Municipality Correspondence Files, Alberta Department of Municipal Affairs Papers, PAA. The province declined the request, since Special Areas were only established for municipalities that suffered financial collapse.

23 Carmangay *Sun*, 18 Sept., 20 Jan. 1915, 1 June 1917; Vulcan *Advocate*, 5 June 1918

24 Vulcan *Advocate*, 14 July 1915, 13 Sept. 1922, May 1923. For discrimination against the Chinese, and their economic and social position in Vulcan, see Paul Voisey, 'Chinatown on the Prairies: The Emergence of an Ethnic Community,' in Christina Cameron and Martin Segger, eds., *Selected Papers From the Society for the Study of Architecture in Canada* (Ottawa: Society for the Study of Architecture in Canada 1981), 33–52.

25 J.D. Hall, 'Clifford Sifton: Immigration and Settlement Policy, 1896–1905,' in Howard Palmer, ed., *The Settlement of the West* (Calgary: University of Calgary and Comprint Publishing 1977), 70; Harold Martin Troper, *Only Farmers Need Apply: Official Canadian Government Encouragement of Immigration from the United States, 1896–1911* (Toronto: Griffin House 1972), espec. 12–13; High River *Times*, 19 July, 22 Nov. 1906. For similar congeniality throughout western Canada generally and southern Alberta in particular see Robert W. Sloan, 'The Canadian West: Americanization or Canadianization,' *Alberta Historical Review* 16, no 1 (Winter 1968), espec. 4; Paul F. Sharp, 'The American Farmer and the "Last Best West," ' *Agricultural History* 21, no 2 (Apr. 1947): 74.

26 Carmangay *Sun*, 30 June, 7 July 1911; Vulcan *Advocate*, 10 June 1914; High River *Times*, 7 July 1910; Harry J. Higgins, untitled, unpub. ms, 1955, book 15-Z, MDK

27 For the local school see 'An Interview with Clifford N. Clarke and C. Elmer Dovey about the Majorville Area,' taped interview by Fran Fraser at Calgary, 9 Feb. 1961, side 1, counter no 58–64, GAI. For similar schools elsewhere see Patrick A. Dunae, *Gentlemen Emigrants: From the British Public Schools to the Canadian Frontier* (Vancouver: Douglas and McIntyre 1981), 171–91. For CPR farms see Calgary *Herald*, 16 Sept. 1914. For local views of Englishmen I have relied heavily on seven interviews, two with English immigrants; also William C. Wigley to M.D. Keenan, 17 Jan. 1974, book 15-E, MDK.

28 Elizabeth Akitt, taped interview by Sharilyn Ingram and Barry Necyk at Carmangay, 9 Mar. 1973, side 1, counter no 110–13; Mrs Roy Burns, interviewed at Carmangay, Jan. 1978; Sloan, 'Canadian West,' 3–4; Dunae, *Gentlemen Emigrants*, passim

29 For similar disputes in the rural midwest see Edward O. Moe, *The Culture of a Contemporary Rural Community – Irwin, Iowa* (Washington: U.S. Dept. of Agri-

culture, Bureau of Agricultural Economics, Rural Life Studies 5, 1942), 53-4;
Horace Miner, *Culture and Agriculture: An Anthropological Study of a Corn-Belt County* (Ann Arbor: University of Michigan Press 1949), 22-3.

30 Annual Reports of the RNWMP, D Division, MacLeod, Alberta, in Canada, *Sessional Papers* 28 (1913), 200; Carmangay *Sun*, 27 Aug. 1914; Harvey Beaubier interview

31 Vulcan *Advocate*, 27 Oct. 1915, 22 May 1918; four letters, Feb. 1912, in J.W. Miller File, Carmangay justices-of-the-peace files; Carmangay, *Bridging*, 152-3; Carrie McIntyre, interviewed at Vulcan, June 1978

32 Harvey Beaubier interview; Jack Dietz interview; Ken Miller interview

33 Carmangay *Sun*, 12 June 1914, 15 May 1915. Although many studies have examined the justifications for prohibition, few emphasize that many prohibition supporters did not agree with all the arguments. See John H. Thompson, ' "The Beginning of Our Regeneration": The Great War and Western Canadian Reform Movements,' *Canadian Historical Association Historical Papers* (1972): 227-46; James H. Gray, *Booze: The Impact of Whiskey on the Prairie West* (Toronto: Macmillan 1972); idem, *Bacchanalia Revisited: Western Canada's Boozy Skid to Social Disaster* (Saskatoon: Western Producer Prairie Books 1982); Robert Irwin McLean, 'A Most Effectual Remedy: Temperance and Prohibition in Alberta, 1875-1915,' MA, Calgary 1969; Dianne Kathryn Stretch, 'From Prohibition to Government Control: The Liquor Question in Alberta, 1909-1929, MA, Alberta 1979; J.P. Bates, 'Prohibition and the U.F.A.,' *Alberta Historical Review* 18, no 4 (Autumn 1970): 3-4.

34 George Geddes in St Thomas [Ontario] *Times-Journal*, repr. Vulcan *Advocate*, 27 Sept. 1922; see also 14 Aug. 1918, 27 Oct., 3 Nov. 1920; Carmangay *Sun*, 29 July 1915; many letters in F.C. Alcock File, 1918-21, espec. Charles McLean to Deputy Attorney General, 18 Apr. 1921, Champion justices-of-the-peace files.

35 Vulcan *Advocate*, 12 Feb. 1919; High River Presbytery Minutes, 10 Feb. 1919, United Church of Canada Records, PAA. In the end Schrag withdrew his resignation. Vestry and Congregation Minutes, 25 Jan. 1912, Emmanuel Church, Carmangay; Ena Neilson, interviewed at Carmangay, May 1978

36 J.W. Miller to Deputy Attorney General, 28 May 1920, J.W. Miller File

37 Vulcan *Advocate*, 28 July 1915

38 Vulcan *Advocate*, 17 Aug. 1921; Robert R. Dykstra, 'Town-Country Conflict: A Hidden Dimension in American Social History,' *Agricultural History* 38, no 4 (Oct. 1964): 196; see also Lewis Atherton, *Main Street on the Middle Border* (Bloomington: Indiana University Press 1954), 63, 160-8; Robbins, 'Community Conflict,' 618-20.

39 Burnet, *Next-Year*, 54, 75-94, 154; idem, 'Town-Country,' 395-410

40 Calculated from annual reports, 1914-19, Vulcan Agricultural Society Papers,

GAI; see also annual reports and lists of members in Carmangay Agricultural Society Papers, GAI.

41 High River *Times*, 20 Mar. 1913. Carl Kraenzel, *Great Plains in Transition* (Norman: University of Oklahoma Press 1955), espec. 234, noted that conflict tended to be highly personal and bitter on the U.S. plains. Don Harrison Doyle, 'Social Theory and New Communities,' *Western Historical Quarterly* 8, no 2 (Apr. 1977): 157-8, argues that conflict in frontier communities progressed through various stages of maturity. It began with interpersonal violence and family feuds, gradually progressed to occupational and neighbourhood disputes, and finally emerged as sophisticated social conflict played out through formal organizations. But all three types of dispute could be found simultaneously in the Vulcan area from early settlement onwards, and low population density always awarded precedence to the primitive, personal variety.

42 Georgina H. Thomson, *Crocus and Meadowlark Country, Recollections of a Happy Childhood and Youth on a Homestead in Southern Alberta* (Edmonton: Institute of Applied Art 1963), 170; see for example Homestead Files 1156826, 944591, 120874A, 1252974, all in Homestead Records, PAA; also J.W. Stafford to Alexander McIntyre, 3 Dec. 1909, Alex McIntyre Papers, privately held by Roy McIntyre, Vulcan; Harvey Beaubier interview; Carmangay, *Bridging*, 224. For similar conflicts in Manitoba and Saskatchewan see John L. Tyman, *By Section, Township and Range: Studies in Prairie Settlement* (Brandon: Assiniboine Historical Society 1972), 147; Lloyd Rodwell, 'Saskatchewan Homestead Records,' *Saskatchewan History* 18, no 1 (Winter 1965): 141.

43 Many of the rules and taboos had also been common in the American midwest; see Gary Koerselman, 'The Quest for Community in Rural Iowa: Neighborhood Life in Early Middleburg History,' *Annals of Iowa*, 3rd s, vol. 41, no 5 (Summer 1972): 1006-19.

44 See for example, Carmangay *Sun*, 9 May 1913; Vulcan *Advocate*, 27 Aug. 1913; 24 Feb., 28 July 1915; 27 Mar. 1918; 27 Apr. 1921; Local Improvement District 128 (later MD of Harmony 128) Minutes, 12 Feb. 1916, 3 Sept. 1920, County of Vulcan No 2 Records, PAA.

45 R.E. House to Deputy Minister of Municipal Affairs, 15 Apr. 1916, 10 Mar. 1919, and reply, 25 Apr. 1916, MD of Marquis 157 Correspondence; MD of Harmony 128 Minutes, 2 Mar. 1919, 13 Mar. 1929; MD of Royal 158 Minutes, June 1923, County of Vulcan No 2 Records, PAA. For similar developments on the American frontier see Earl W. Hayter, 'Livestock-Fencing Conflicts in Rural America,' *Agricultural History* 37, no 1 (Jan. 1963): 10-21.

46 P.C. Moreash to Livestock Branch, Department of Agriculture, 30 Dec. 1933, MD of Marquis 157 Correspondence; C.J. Bradley to Attorney General's Office, 28 July 1913, C.J. Bradley File, Carmangay justices-of-the-peace files; Harvey Beau-

CONCLUSION: NEW SOCIETIES AND MODELS OF FRONTIER DEVELOPMENT

1 Frederick C. Luebke, 'Regionalism and the Great Plains: Problems of Concept and Method,' *Western Historical Quarterly* 55, no 1 (Jan. 1984): 19–38. For a contemporary study that focuses on how four different groups each responded differently to the environment of southwestern Saskatchewan see John W. Bennett, *Northern Plainsmen: Adaptive Strategy and Agrarian Life* (Chicago: Aldine Publishing 1969).

2 The importance of this point has been stressed by Robert F. Berkhofer Jr., 'Space, Time, Culture and the New Frontier,' *Agricultural History* 38, no 1 (Jan. 1964): 25, 29; see also David H. Breen, 'The Turner Thesis and the Canadian West: A Closer Look at the Ranching Frontier,' in Lewis H. Thomas, ed., *Essays on Western History* (Edmonton: University of Alberta Press 1976), 147.

3 See in particular Norman E.P. Pressman and Kathleen Lauder, 'Resource Towns as New Towns,' *Urban History Review*, no 1 (June 1978): 84–8.

4 A.R.M. Lower, 'The Origins of Democracy in Canada,' *Canadian Historical Association Annual Reports* (1930): 65–70

5 Donald W. Meinig, *On the Margins of the Good Earth: The South Australian Wheat Frontier, 1869–1884* (Chicago: Association of American Geographers 1962)

6 James R. Scobie, *Revolution on the Pampas: A Social History of Argentine Wheat, 1860–1910* (Austin: Institute of Latin American Studies and University of Texas Press 1964)

7 See A.W. Rasporich, 'Utopian Ideals and Community Settlements in Western Canada, 1880–1914,' in Henry C. Klassen, ed., *The Canadian West, Social Change and Economic Development* (Calgary: University of Calgary and Comprint Publishing 1977), 37–62.

8 Patrick A. Dunae, *Gentlemen Emigrants: From the British Public Schools to the Canadian Frontier* (Vancouver: Douglas and McIntyre 1981), 151–227

9 This point is still demonstrated best in C.A. Dawson, *Group Settlement: Ethnic Communities in Western Canada* (Toronto: Macmillan 1936). A survey of recent American literature on this theme is presented in Robert P. Swierenga, 'The New Rural History: Defining the Parameters,' *Great Plains Quarterly* 1, no 4 (Fall 1981): 217–18.

10 Swierenga, 'New Rural,' 218–19; John G. Rice, 'The Role of Culture and Community in Frontier Prairie Farming,' *Journal of Historical Geography* 3, no 2 (Apr. 1977): 155–75

11 Although not concerned specifically with these questions, a model study that few have emulated is George Woodcock and Ivan Avakumovic, *The Doukhobors* (Toronto: Oxford University Press 1968). By devoting half the book to the sect's

bier interview; Carmangay *Sun*, 7 July 1911; Vulcan *Advocate*, 8 Mar. 1916, 14 May 1919; Vulcan, *Wheat Country*, 614

47 Vulcan *Advocate*, 9 June 1920; Burnet, *Next-Year*, 135; many letters from A.I. Somerville to various government officials, espec. three letters to Minister of Municipal Affairs, Mar. 1936, and to W. Aberhart, 23 Mar. 1937; see also Chief Municipal Inspector to Mr Reashaw and Mr Ritchie, 22 Aug., 26 Sept. 1938, all in MD of Harmony 128 Correspondence, Municipality Correspondence Files, Alberta Department of Municipal Affairs Papers, PAA.

48 Cst J. Valk, 'Alberta Provincial Police Report; Re M.P. Marshall, Poundkeeper, Eastway,' 25 Apr. 1928, in MD of Marquis 157 Correspondence

49 Harvey Beaubier, taped interview by Barry Necyk and Sharilyn Ingram, at Champion, 8 Mar. 1973, side 1, counter no 57–60, PAA; William C. Wigley to M.D. Keenan, 17 Jan. 1974, book 15-E, MDK; Tom Sletto to M.D. Keenan, 7 Dec. 1973, M.D. Keenan Correspondence Files, MDK. Donald E. Willmott, 'The Formal Organizations of Saskatchewan Farmers, 1900–65, in A.W. Rasporich, ed., *Western Canada Past and Present* (Calgary: McClelland and Stewart West 1975), 37, argues that the community support system 'involved an ideology which grew out of, and in turn reinforced, the loyalty and solidarity which the early farmers developed among themselves.'

50 MD of Harmony 128 Minutes, 10 Mar. 1914

51 Calculated from poll results reported in Champion *Chronicle*, 18 Mar. 1926

52 Carmangay *Sun*, 24 Oct. 1913; Fred J. Rowley, 'Returning Officer's Statement,' 27 Oct. 1913, A.F. Wilson to J. Perrie, 13 Nov. 1913, both in MD of Little Bow 98 Correspondence, Municipality Correspondence Files, Alberta Department of Municipal Affairs Papers, PAA. For rural local government development, see Eric J. Hanson, *Local Government in Alberta* (Toronto: McClelland and Stewart 1956), 22–6; A.S. Abell, 'Rural Municipal Government in Alberta: Taxation and Finance,' MA, Toronto 1940, 15–26; idem, 'Rural Municipal Difficulties in Alberta,' *Canadian Journal of Economics and Political Science* 6, no 4 (Nov. 1940): 555–6; 'The History of Municipal Government of Vulcan by D.D. McQueen,' videotaped interview by Marg Weber, County of Vulcan Educational Television Production, 1975, CVO.

53 F.C.C. Andrews to Deputy Minister of Municipal Affairs, 6 May 1932; J.N. Brown to Deputy Minister of Municipal Affairs, 8 July 1919, G.W. Parker to Minister of Municipalities, 27 May 1931, all in MD of Royal 158 Correspondence; C.L. Purcell to E.C. Manning, 10 Oct. 1938, MD of Harmony 128 Correspondence

54 H.F. Harvey to Minister of Municipal Affairs, 3 May 1921; Deputy Minister of Municipal Affairs to Hon. C.R. Mitchell, 6 May 1921, both in MD of Marquis 157 Correspondence; MD of Harmony 128 Minutes, 9 Nov. 1932; Annual Meetings of Ratepayers Minutes, 1942, MD of Harmony 128, County of Vulcan No 2 Records,

PAA. Bodil J. Jensen, *Alberta's County of Mountain View . . . A History* (Didsbury, Alta: Mountain View County No 17, 1983), 122, also notes that most municipal conflicts concerned roads.

55 Alan F.J. Artibise, *Winnipeg: A Social History of Urban Growth, 1874–1914* (Montreal: McGill-Queen's University Press 1975)

56 Vulcan *Advocate*, 24 Mar. 1920. For the unifying effect of boosterism in small communities elsewhere see Stanley Elkins and Eric McKitrick, 'A Meaning for Turner's Frontier,' I: 'Democracy in the Old Northwest,' *Policial Science Quarterly* 69, no 3 (Sept. 1954), espec. 321–40; Don Harrison Doyle, *The Social Order of a Frontier Community: Jacksonville, Illinois, 1825–1870* (Chicago: University of Illinois Press 1978), 62–91; Elvin Hatch, *Biography of a Small Town* (New York: Columbia University Press 1979), passim. The promotion of social order by formal organizations has been studied in particular detail by Don H. Doyle, 'The Social Functions of Voluntary Associations in a Nineteenth-Century American Town,' *Social Science History* I, no 3 (Spring 1977): 341–5.

57 Vulcan *Advocate*, 2 Jan., 3 Apr., 30 Oct. 1918; Little Bow Branch (Alston) of the Canadian Red Cross Society Minutes, nd, 15, VA; Carmangay *Sun*, 15 Sept. 1916

58 Village of Vulcan Minutes, 12 July 1915, TVO; Vulcan *Advocate*, 21 July 1915; Village and Town Councils of Carmangay Minutes, Feb. 1916, VCAO; Carmangay *Sun*, 9 Mar. 1916; R.E. House to Deputy Minister of Municipal Affairs, 18 Dec. 1915, 1 June 1916, and reply, 6 June 1916, MD of Marquis 157 Correspondence; MD of Royal 158 Minutes, 14 May 1917, 14 Jan. 1916; Deputy Minister of Municipal Affairs to A.J. Flood, 27 Sept. 1917, MD of Royal 158 Correspondence

59 'Memorial Album, Methodist Church Carmangay,' unpub. ms, 1920, Carmangay Pastoral Charge Papers, United Church of Canada Records, PAA; Vulcan *Advocate*, 16 Jan., 13 Mar., 23 Oct., 13 Nov. 1918, 5 Jan. 1921; Gleichen *Call*, 10 Oct. 1918; E. Roy Orcutt to M.D. Keenan, 7 Aug. 1975, M.D. Keenan Correspondence File, MDK; MD of Royal 158 Minutes, 29 Mar. 1919

60 Vulcan *Advocate*, 3 May 1916. Somewhat conflicting accounts of the Murray episode are presented in Carmangay, *Bridging*, 87; Carmangay *Sun*, 9 Jan. 1915, 7 July 1916. School-board records could not be located.

61 D.H. Galbraith, 'Interview re the Political Nature of Alberta from 1917 to 1935,' taped interview by Una MacLean at Bowness, Alta, 4 June 1962, side 1, counter no 749, GAI; Roy Burns interview

62 See any issue of Carmangay *Sun*, Aug., Sept. 1914; Vulcan *Advocate*, 2 Sept. 1914, Shragg quote, 27 Mar. 1918; Edward McCourt, *Music at the Close* (Toronto: McClelland and Stewart, New Canadian Library 1966), 18.

63 J.T. Ferguson in *Acts and Proceedings of the General Assembly of the Presbyterian Church in Canada* (1915), 47; High River Presbytery Minutes, 9 July 1917.

John Herd Thompson, *The Harvests of War: The Prairie West, 1914–1918* (Toronto: McClelland and Stewart 1978), 83, also notes that appeals based on such reasons were more successful among western Canadian Americans than were appeals to Empire.

64 Vulcan *Advocate*, 13 Nov. 1918

65 Vulcan *Advocate*, 7 Jan. 1914. For the impact of the war on social reforms see Thompson, 'The Beginning,' 227–46; Paul Voisey, 'The "Votes for Women" Movement,' *Alberta History* 23, no 3 (Summer 1975): 10–23.

66 Carmangay *Sun*, 13 May 1910; Harvey Beaubier interview, side 1, counter no 714–16; Calgary *Herald*, 18 June 1970; Helen Waugh to M.D. Keenan, 13 July 1973, M.D. Keenan Correspondence File, MDK

67 Village of Vulcan to Deputy Minister of Municipal Affairs, 8 May 1913, Village of Vulcan Correspondence; Vulcan *Advocate*, 11 Feb., 10 Mar. 1920; 'Complaint of Mr. W.F. Stevens,' 15 June 1916; 'Complaint of Board of Trade of Ensign,' 26 Nov. 1914, both in Board of Railway Commissioners Transcript of Hearings, vol. 250, file 8234.9, and vol. 212, file 25119, PAC; Nanton *News*, 8 Feb. 1912; monthly reports of D Division, 8 Feb., 12 Dec. 1912, 7 Feb. 1913; Vulcan, *Wheat Country*, 416, 747; Carmangay *Sun*, 26 Jan. 1912, 3 Jan. 1913

68 Bell and Wilson to Department of Municipal Affairs, 30 Mar. 1917, and reply, 4 Apr. 1917; A.J. Flood to Deputy Minister of Municipal Affairs, 25 Sept. 1916, and reply, 30 Sept. 1916, all in Local Improvement District 158 (later MD of Royal 158) Correspondence; see also many letters, 1916, espec. Deputy Minister of Municipal Affairs to J.A. Gow, 16 May 1916, MD of Little Bow 98 Correspondence. Neither documents relating to the Vulcan area nor the secondary literature on the CPR and the Calgary and Edmonton Railways shed much light on the validity of the claims of either the company or the farmers.

69 Copies of many letters between CPR and Department of Public Works, and Alberta Tax Commissioner to Village of Champion, 20 June 1911, all in Village of Champion Correspondence; Village and Town Councils of Carmangay Minutes, 1910, espec. 20–1; see also Aug. 1914, July 1916, Aug. 1917, May 1924, for example of CPR protests of assessments. For legal action see Village of Vulcan Minutes, 12 Dec. 1913; Vulcan *Advocate*, 17 Dec. 1913. Once again, neither documents relating to the area nor secondary literature on railways have helped to untangle the legalities of this conflict. The important point, however, is that they stirred considerable local resentment. For local conflicts elsewhere that generated hostility towards the CPR see Bodil, *Alberta's County*, 40, 75–6.

70 For the positive benefits of certain kinds of conflict see Lewis Coser, *The Social Functions of Conflict* (London: Routledge and Kegan Paul 1956); Doyle, 'Social Theory,' 158.

history in Europe, the authors are better able to reveal the extent and nature of the changes that Doukhobor society underwent after emigrating to western Canada. Many of the issues raised here concerning the study of ethnic minorities also appear in Frederick C. Luebke, 'Ethnic Minority Groups in the American West,' in Michael P. Malone, ed., *Historians and the American West* (Lincoln: University of Nebraska Press 1983), espec. 393–6.

12 See W. Turrentine Jackson, 'A Brief Message for the Young and/or Ambitious: Comparative Frontiers as a Field for Investigation,' *Western Historical Quarterly* 9, no 1 (Jan. 1978): 5–18. For criticism of this approach see John C. Hudson, 'Theory and Methodology in Comparative Frontier Studies,' in David Harry Miller and Jerome O. Steffen, eds., *The Frontier: Comparative Studies* (Norman: University of Oklahoma Press 1977), 11–31; Marvin W. Mikesell, 'Comparative Studies in Frontier History,' *Annals, Association of American Geographers* 50, no 1 (Mar. 1960): 64–74. While important insights often emerge from comparative frontier studies, they rarely text existing theory adequately or contribute much to the development of more refined models. A recent example by Jerome O. Steffen, *Comparative Frontiers: A Proposal for Studying the American West* (Norman: University of Oklahoma Press 1980), attempts to compare agricultural settlement between the Appalachians and the Mississippi with trans-Mississippi fur trading, ranching, mining, and farming activities in the hope of evaluating the impact of the frontier experience on each activity respectively. He notes that all of the frontier subcultures differed from their parents societies, but by drawing a seemingly arbitrary and debatable distinction between 'fundamental change' and 'non-fundamental change,' he concludes that only the Appalachian-Mississippi agricultural frontier produced a new way of life. The trans-Mississippi frontiers did not, because in each case their populations enjoyed a greater contact with their parents societies thanks to the superior communications technology that had since evolved. Thus, instead of concentrating on the influence of the frontier, as he purports to do, he reveals much more about changes in metropolitan influence.

13 David Hackett Fischer, *Historians' Fallacies: Toward a Logic of Historical Thought* (New York: Harper and Row, Torchbooks 1970), 3–5

APPENDIX: A NOTE ON STATISTICS

1 Sam B. Warner Jr, 'Writing Local History: The Use of Social Statistics,' Technical Leaflet 7, *History News* 25, no 10 (Oct. 1970): 216
2 John Proskie, 'Financial Progress of Settlers With Special Reference to the Vulcan-Lomond Area,' MA, Alberta 1937; G.H. Craig and J. Coke, *An Economic Study of Land Utilization in Southern Alberta* (Ottawa: Canadian Department of Agriculture, Economics Division, Marketing Service, Publication 610, Technical

Bulletin 16, 1938). Portions of the latter study and closely related articles also appeared in the following issues of the *Economic Annalist*: G.H. Craig, 'Agricultural and Land Organization in Southern Alberta, Part I,' 8, no 1 (Feb. 1938): 3–9; idem, 'Part II,' 8, no 2 (Apr. 1938): 21–24; idem, 'Land Settlement and Tenancy in the Lomond and Vulcan Districts, Alberta,' 7, no 2 (Apr. 1937): 22–3; idem, 'Objectives in the Alberta Land Utilization Survey,' 6, no 5 (Oct. 1936): 70–1; idem and J. Proskie, 'The Acquisition of Land in the Vulcan-Lomond Area of Alberta,' 7, no 5 (Oct. 1937): 68–74; W.N. Watson, 'A Study of 126 Abandoned Farms in the Lomond Area of Southern Alberta,' 6, no 3 (June 1936): 38–44. See also W.J. Hansen and J. Proskie, 'Life Insurance Carried by Farmers in the Lomond and Vulcan Districts, Alberta,' *Scientific Agriculture* 17, no 2 (1936): 100–3.

Index